Computer Science Signal Processing Applications in Higher Learning

Carlo Ciulla

Computer Science Signal Processing Applications
in Higher Learning

ISBN-10: 1-477-56752-6
ISBN-13: 978-1-477-56752-4

The contents of this book is of university-academic nature thus the natural way of utilizing productively the contents is through referencing this book in your own works.

Part I: ObjNet

Part II: ANN98

Part I: ImageViewer 2009

Part II: ImageTool 2009

PREFACE

This book is written for undergraduate and graduate students of signal-image processing within the context of scientific computing disciplines. Also, instructors can take advantage of the materials contained here, given the specificity of the software coding and the ease of implementation in courses' projects and homework assignments.

The book presents a set of science problems customarily addressed in academic context within courses in computing in the computer science and computer engineering curriculum, also in intersections between mathematics and computing and/or physics and computing. The science problems are solved through a combination of three programming environments: ANSI C ®, Visual C++ ® and OpenGL ®. The C language is employed to address the specific task and solve the computing problem, thus making possible for the student to devise routines which perform tasks of various nature and that relates to topics like for instance the Fourier transformation (direct and inverse), the Whittaker-Shannon interpolation formula [1], k-Space sampling, Booth algorithm for binary multiplication [2], rotation translation of 3D volumes, Artificial Neural Network for pattern recognition, data randomization and also creation of artificial data sets. The routines written in C language are embedded inside methods of a wider Visual C++ project having a Graphical User Interface (GUI) and making use of the data visualization counterpart written with the OpenGL ® programming language.

The primary course for which there is best fit for this book is scientific computing Master's project in non Computer Science (CS), Computer Engineering (CE) majors, and scientific computing intermediate courses in Computer Science and Computer Engineering majors. Due to the level of details, CS and CE majors will find that this book provides the basis for further development, whereas non majors in CS and CE will find that this book will provide them with higher level of understanding of concepts of theoretical nature which require applications provided in the manuscript in terms of source code.

In teaching a science course, the instructor may encounter problems related to the high level of specificity of the theoretical concepts, with specific concern with the students which are requested to pay lots of attention. Similarly, the students may encounter problems in understanding the concepts and the course materials unless these are within their interests. The book takes an alternative approach to teaching while initiating students' capability in developing programming in computing disciplines in research settings, thus the level of commitment is expected to be adequate but to the extent of providing students the immediate application of the theoretical concepts.

The aforementioned courses are expected to educate the student to discover interest in their professional life. To tailor a programming course to standard guideline is a framework that might not be sufficient for the students to find their spiritual wisdom. To serve society at their best, students need to know what they really want to do.

Students might encounter in this book a topic of their interest with a level of details that might arouse the interest in pursuing further and thus such interest might be of usefulness in career development settings. The future development in the courses mentioned above is therefore that of being a horizon to explore actively instead of being passively received for the sake of curricular demands. In this respect the last chapter of the book explores the chance for students to build their career on the basis of what they really want to do in life and this is possible once they find in themselves the consciousness of their spiritual wisdom.

The average class size for the course is twenty students and the course might be taught every semester in schools with Computer Science and/or Computer Engineering majors as primary audience and also Mathematics-Computer Science intersections or Mathematics/Physics-Computer Science intersections as secondary audience. In such settings the book might be adopted as good complementary resource to build upon and to expand the students' horizon for example with the customization of the course project to the students' intellectual interest.

The *rationale* of the book is that of presenting the solution to a scientific problem in computing. The goal of the book is that of letting students find a topic of interest which is understood in theory. And through the use of the book's materials, understand the practical implications and also further their interest while researching on the chosen topic.

The nature of the book is educational in that provides the students with a wide array of science problems with a level of depth which goes beyond the theory, into the real application, and the teacher with the possibility to instruct the classmates with semi-advanced programming techniques while addressing computing in science applications. The benefits to the students are that of deepening their interest into the real life problem in computing. Initiate students to research-like classroom settings and thus provide them with the means to develop further a topic of their interest during the course and eventually beyond the course. It is thus possible to open the door to prospects of the students' extra curricular activities in academic context. The benefits to the teacher are those of making possible to device customized course assignments and/or projects which are tailored to the students' interest and also to the teacher's knowledge.

The approach of the book is research-like because initiates the students' process of understanding of the science problem in computing disciplines with a focused practical approach which is driven through the implementation in source code of the theoretical concepts. The combination of structured programming techniques with Graphical User Interfaces and routines employed for data visualization make also possible the discovery of new concepts, which are related to the practicality of the science problem being addressed, and that broaden the array of capabilities and skills acquired by the students while taking the course. The approach followed in the writings of the book is also useful to understand the issues in the system development counterpart of the computing project and this is made possible because each problem in the book is presented with the relevant GUI. Combining computing in science settings with system development broaden the array of knowledge provided through the lecture.

The treatment of the programming details is expansive and corroborated with explanations of the coding along with pictures of the Graphical User Interfaces at work with the OpenGL ® windows for data visualization.

It is practical in its extent and cutting edge in the teaching/learning approach. Within such approach the teaching strategy sees the teacher becoming the leader in research while teaching and the students follow thereafter. The prospect is to improve the outcome in classroom settings. The topics are multivariate and even if available in similar books, they might have been not readily available in such level of programming details.

Usually, the major teaching and learning challenges have to be dealt when the teacher encounters a passive classroom setting. This might frequently happen when the student is taking the course because of curricular demands and not specifically for personal interests.

This book is dedicated to students who know why they are taking the course and they want the best outcome since it is in their understanding that they will benefit from these materials in terms of career and future prospects. Thus, the keywords of the book as connected to teaching (instructor) and learning (student) are *research for the instructor* and *impact for the student*.

The conceptual and organizational approaches in this book are those of letting the student be active under the prompt lead of the teacher. Active means that the student is willing to expand his/her horizon through the book materials in one specific topic of interest to set the basis for future development in his/her career life. The book is wide in covering many computing problems and thus is the array of topics the student can chose from.

The instructor does not need to have any special teaching devices other than conventional Visual C++ ® compilers with OpenGL ® libraries and possibly the Matlab ® programming environment. The competitive edge of the book is that of being a practical guide to the solution of problems in computing.

The main components of the book to augment the textual discussion are: (i) source code, (ii) pictures of Graphical User Interfaces which relates to the source code in high level of match, (iii) PowerPoint ® Slides (PPTs) to express concepts.

The function of the source code is that of providing the practicality of the solution to a theoretical problem of scientific nature and this is a benefit to the teacher because the code is already provided, and a benefit to the student because the source code can be a start to an higher level of understanding.

The pictures of the GUIs provide the benefit to the student because of their perfect degree of match with the source code and therefore the reproduction of the GUIs during classroom activity can be a challenging opportunity for learning. Additionally, the PPTs are to the benefit of both instructor and students because they deep the theoretical aspect of the problem addressed and solved in software coding.

Figures and graphics of the Graphical User Interfaces are extracted from the actual programs at work. Pictures of the flow charts of a given GUI explain the top-down approach customarily used in software engineering settings. PPTs slides are provided as complement. There are 7 figures in the first chapter and from 1 to 10 figures in each remaining chapter for a total of 10 chapters.

This book is not meant to compete with existing books, it has instead distinctive features which makes it in the view of the author, a good complement to books on the topic of scientific computing in higher education [3-21]. The point in buying this book for instructors and students is to have a higher outcome in terms of more effective and efficient teaching and also deeper understanding by the students of the topics treated in the manuscript. It might be an alternative in that provides level of details and specificity to selected topics and also an alternative because of the conceptual framework under which is written. The teacher has a good database to use to expand the students' horizons.

References

[1] Whittaker, E. T. (1915). *On the functions which are represented by the expansions of interpolation theory.* Proceedings of the Royal Society Edinburgh, UK, Sec. A(35), 181-194.

[2] Booth, A.D. (1951). *A Signed Binary Multiplication Algorithm.* Quarterly Journal of Mechanics and Applied Mathematics. Clarendon Press; Oxford University Press. England.

[3] Evens, M. & Michael, J. (2005). *One-on-One Tutoring by Humans and Computers.* Lawrence Erlbaum Associates.

[4] Morris, S. (2003). *Teaching and Learning Online: A Step-by-Step Guide for Designing an Online K-12 School Program.* Scarecrow Education.

[5] Orvis, K.L. & Lassiter, A. L. R. (2008). *Computer-Supported Collaborative Learning: Best Practices and Principles for Instructors.* Information Science Reference.

[6] Howard, S., Hope, G. & Carolee, G. (1989). *Evaluating Educational Software: A Guide for Teachers.* Prentice Hall College Div.

[7] Pflaum, W. D. (2004). *The Technology Fix: The Promise and Reality of Computers in Our Schools.* Association for Supervision and Curriculum Development.

[8] Mendes, A., J., Pereira, I. & Costa, R. (2010). *Computers and Education: Towards Educational Change and Innovation.* Springer.

[9] Pride, B. & Pride, M. (1992). *Prides' Guide to Educational Software.* Crossway Books.

[10] Lajoie, S. P. & Derry, S. J. (1993). *Computers As Cognitive Tools (Technology and Education Series).* 2nd Edition. Routledge.

[11] Schofield, J. W. (1995). *Computers and Classroom Culture.* Cambridge University Press.

[12] Bitter, G. G. & Gore, K. (1984). *The Best of Educational Software for Apple II Computers.* Sybex Inc., U.S.

[13] Self, J. (1985). *Microcomputers in Education: A Critical Evaluation of Educational Software.* Salem House Academic Division.

[14] Williams, F. & Williams, V. (1985). *Success with Educational Software.* Praeger Publishers.

[15] Murray, T., Blessing, S. & Ainsworth, S. (2010). *Authoring Tools for Advanced Technology Learning Environments: Toward Cost-Effective Adaptive, Interactive and Intelligent Educational Software.* Springer.

[16] Miller, S. K. (1987). *Selecting and Implementing Educational Software.* Allyn & Bacon.

[17] Berg, G. A. (2002). *The Knowledge Medium: Designing Effective Computer-Based Educational Learning Environments.* IGI Global.

[18] VanHuss, S. H., Forde, C. M. & Woo, D. L. (2011). *Integrated Computer Applications.* 6th Edition. South-Western Educational Pub.

[19] Kirschner, P. A., Buckingham-Shum, S. J. & Carr, C. S. (2003). *Visualizing Argumentation: Software Tools for Collaborative and Educational Sense-Making (Computer Supported Cooperative Work).* Springer.

[20] Squires, D. & McDougall, A. (1994). *Choosing And Using Educational Software: A Teachers' Guide.* Routledge.

[21] Davidson, C. N., Goldberg, D. T. & Jones, Z. M. (2009). *The Future of Learning Institutions in a Digital Age (The John D. and Catherine T. MacArthur Foundation Reports on Digital Media and Learning).* The MIT Press.

CHAPTER 1

Overview

Introduction

These works are intended to present Computer Science (CS) signal processing applications useful in higher learning. They provide hands on approach to students and might be viewed as educational material that the teacher develops while teaching in colleges at undergraduate and graduate levels. The CS applications herein presented belongs to sampling and Fourier theory, image interpolation, computer architecture, image rotation, creation of artificial data, and artificial intelligence in pattern recognition. Higher learning necessitates of hands on approach in developing computer science applications. Specifically, these works are focused on the signal processing aspect of the curriculum in computer science academia and they can be useful resources to undergraduate and graduate students. The release of such educational material poses a demand on the teacher as much a possibility to practice the profession with schemes that are customized to his/her own background, also to grow along with the students' curricular interests.

The Rationale and the Scope

Many text books in computing and programming disciplines do report on examples of source code tailored to the problem being solved. In the specifics, computing may require full explanations on how to solve the scientific problem which is being explained in class. As far as programming books are concerned, it is rare to find the combination ANSI C/Visual C++ ®/OpenGL ® as much as it is rare to encounter a book which gives explanation beyond the programming issue being explained.

The *rationale* which inspired the writings of this book is that of introducing to the audience a novel framework to teaching computing in college/university settings. The framework steams from a well accepted view point, tangible in academic environment, which sees teaching as a science because structured through well defined methods. In this book, the methods underling teaching, redefine the roles of both teacher and students in the classroom. *The teacher is seen as main researcher* whom develops instructional materials prior to the deliverance of the lecture. The instructional material comprises of theoretical concepts corroborated through practical applications consisting of the solution to the science problem being addressed. The solution is presented through semi-advanced programming techniques. This entails that the teacher leads the students to the full understanding of the science problem in computing, avoiding to disregarding the practical application of the concepts, thus managing to set the students in such a condition to deliver a concrete and real outcome at the end of the course. The students' outcome goes beyond the comprehension of the theory and is such to reach the form of a programming tool which is the witness of the understanding of the theory underlying the science being explained. Under this framework, *the students' role in classroom settings is redefined as that of the research apprentice* whom benefits from the teacher approach because of his/her level of activity. The student takes an active role which goes beyond that of the passive role maintained while absorbing theory and lacking the practical application of the concepts. The level of activity of the student is thus manifest through the deliverance of a real outcome which is that of the programming project which incorporates the concepts object of study.

Therefore *the scope of this book is that of providing the complement to computing books* through the coding of the science being explained *and the complement to programming books* through the level of details in the source code. In this regard, the book is needed because the source code goes beyond what many books have as target, which is that of the explanation of the basics in programming, providing the opportunity to students and instructors to produce a final outcome comprehensive of all the features of a project assignment. Along this line of thought it is deduced that the book is complementary to existing resources and provides with the basis for further development for the main researcher (the instructor) and the students following the explanations. *In summary the audience of the book is among but not only limited to students and instructors* but also to professional whose task is to educate the public to think and which would be interested in seeing an alternative approach in teaching computer science in academic environment.

Further on these concepts, the author expresses a view point which is that College/University curriculums should be designed in order for the students to reach their spiritual wisdom. Spiritual wisdom springs from the conscious awareness of the self and can be attained by students when they are at the level of understanding of what they can do to serve society within the good and at the best of their potentiality. Within this framework, the book provides examples which may capture the attention of the students, involve them into something they feel will be useful in their life and at the same time appreciate the level of details that the manuscript provides.

Computer Science Applications
Description of the Graphical User Interfaces

Fig. 1 shows the project named *pointSource2010* written in Visual C++ ®. Wave of lights elliptical and Gaussian like are sampled with the Whittaker-Shannon interpolation formula [1]. Fourier Transforms both direct and inverse are implemented to make the connection possible between k-Space and image space. The light source is set to be either circular or elliptical (see Fig. 1.b), and the sampling surface is defined through the object size thus resulting in a rectangle that can have uniform or non uniform illumination.

At each processing step, a '.log' file is created and displayed on the screen and so it is possible to retrieve the image name obtained from the routines. Visualization is included through OpenGL ® graphics which display plane images, after sampling and/or after Fourier transforms, in both image space and k-Space. *pointSource 2010* among other learning tools allows students to understand the basics of Fourier Transformations, the basics of sampling theory and the Nyquist Theorem [2]. In Fig. 1 the user is requested to set a square image size with number of pixels along X and Y in between 17 and 129, and the image sizes both along X and Y must be odd numbers. The user is also requested to set the *'Object Size'* with number of pixels in between 4 and 32 pixels (object half size) for both X and Y directions. For what concerns the simulation of Gaussian, circular and elliptical like front waves of light and the calculation of the sampled signal, the light rate and the sampling rate have to be such to determine ratio greater than 1:2 to fulfill the Nyquist Theorem. For example, possible values are: light rate 0.00017 and sampling rate 0.0017. For what concerns the calculation of the direct and inverse Fourier transforms, the user makes sure that the input file in the edit box is *'sampledSignal.img'* as this is necessary to insure direct Fourier transformation of the object sampled with the push button *'Calculate Signal'*.

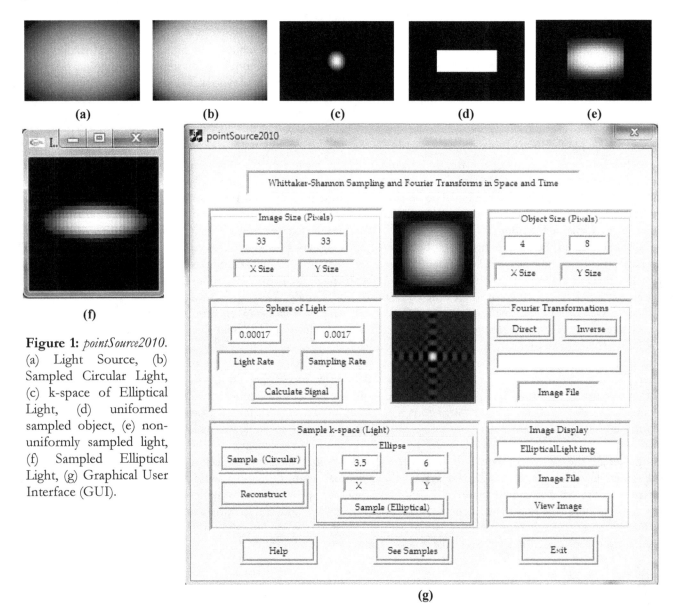

Figure 1: *pointSource2010.* (a) Light Source, (b) Sampled Circular Light, (c) k-space of Elliptical Light, (d) uniformed sampled object, (e) non-uniformly sampled light, (f) Sampled Elliptical Light, (g) Graphical User Interface (GUI).

The reconstruction is calculated through the inverse Fourier transform of the object sampled with the push button *'Calculate Signal'*. Image I/O happens in the local directory and the data type is *'DOUBLE'* (64-bits Real). The program displays image data through the use of OpenGL ® routines with a single 2D window.

Fig. 2 shows the Graphical User Interface (written in Matlab ®) of the *Sub-pixel Efficacy Region (SRE)* validation programs utilized in [3], and OpenGL ® is employed through *Image Viewer* which is connected to the GUI. To give control to the window, the user moves the mouse arrow and hits *'U'* and *'D'* keys to see the image or hits the *'Esc'* key to Exit the program. Alternatively, the user will perform the following steps to quit the program: 1. close the display window where the image data is seen; 2. click on the *'Exit'* button.

It is possible to run mono-dimensional interpolation paradigms like quadratic, cubic and Sinc, also two-dimensional and three-dimensional linear paradigms. Each button except the trivariate cubic Lagrange provides the user with the functionality to obtain results using both classic and SRE-based interpolation. With this learning tool the student can understand the basics in image interpolation and also learn the SRE-based methodology for the improvement of the interpolation error. Also, the student can learn how to create a Graphical User Interface in Matlab ® and to connect Visual C++ ® and OpenGL ® to it.

Fig. 3 presents a direct example of the educational value of the book. The problem is the Booth algorithm [4-5] for binary multiplication. The approach followed in the manuscript to illustrate the solution to the problem is here detailed. (i) A set of PowerPoint slides (PPTs) is presented at the aim to solve the problem and an example is given in the PPTs. (ii) The Booth algorithm is then transformed in a set of logical gates making use of concepts of Computer Organization and Architecture. (iii) The Booth algorithm is then implemented in code (see chapter 4) and included inside a method of the Visual C++ ® project which can serve as homework assignment or even as semester project.

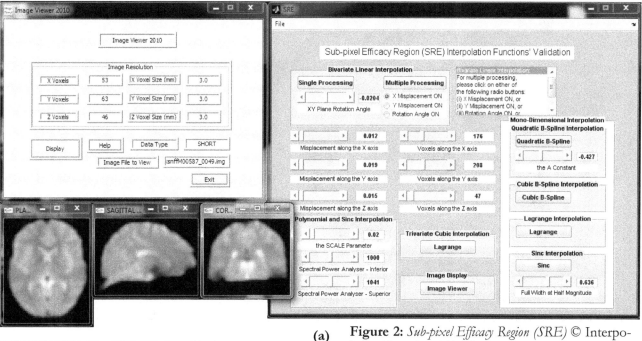

Figure 2: *Sub-pixel Efficacy Region (SRE)* © Interpolation Functions' Validation: (a) GUI, fMRI data is courtesy of www.fil.ion.ucl.ac.uk [6], (b) MRI data belongs to the OASIS database: www.oasis-brains.org [7-12] and it is courtesy of Dr. Daniel Marcus, (c) and (d): Novel Re-sampling Locations (intra-pixel wise sampling location able to make the SRE-based interpolation error lower than the classic interpolation error); cubic (c) and Sinc (d) (misplacement x = 0.014).

Following is the description of the functionality offered through the Graphical User Interface (GUI) of *ROTRA 2008* seen in Fig. 4. In order to input the edge's size of the isotropic volume (the number of voxels along the X, Y and Z directions are the same) and the edge's size of the isotropic cube, the GUI provides the user with two edit boxes lo-

Computer Science Applications

cated in the panel named '*Create Artificial Image Cube*'. The push button named '*Create Cube*' creates the image volume with the cube inside it. Both, size of the volume and size of the cube need to be integer numbers powers of 2.

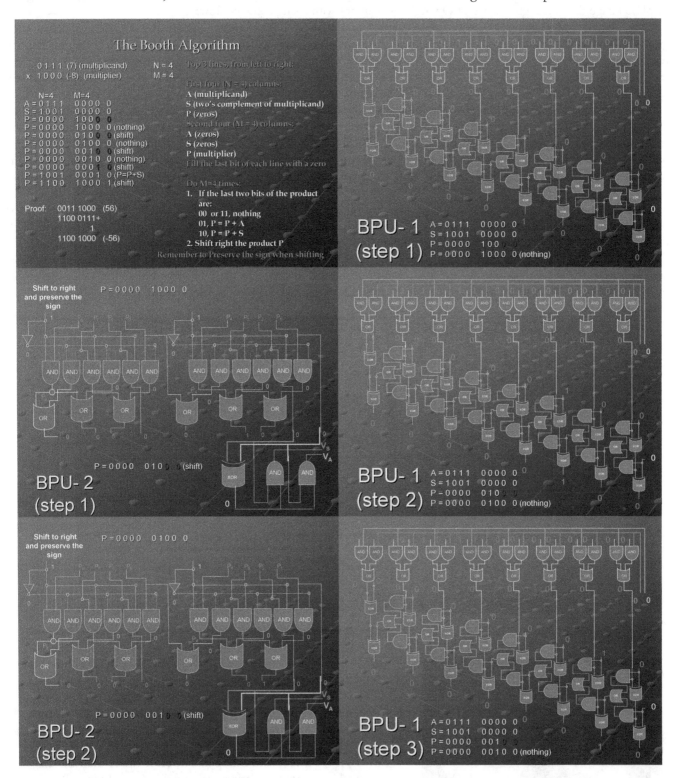

In the panel named '*Input the Rigid Body Transformation*' the user inputs the six parameters defining the six degrees of freedom of the rigid object in 3D. These parameters are: (i) pitch angle (rotation about the X-axis), (ii) roll angle (rotation about the Y-axis), (iii) yaw angle (rotation about the Z-axis) and (iv) the shift along the X, Y and Z axis. In the same panel is located another push button which is named '*Calculate Rigid Body Transformation*', and which purpose is to generate the rotation translation corresponding to the parameters defining the rigid body transformation. The parameters to enter in the edit boxes are the three rotational angles and the three shifts of the center of mass of the rigid body. The rigid body transformation will be saved in the text file named '*RTMATRIX.txt*'.

In the panel named '*Image Volume Parameters*' the user input the following entries: '*X Voxels*', '*Y Voxels*', '*Z Voxels*' (the number of voxels of the Image Volume along X, Y and Z axis), '*X Resolution (mm)*', '*Y Resolution (mm)*', '*Z Resolution (mm)*' (the voxel's size along the three principal directions), and the '*Threshold*', which is used in order to calculate the Center of Mass (COM).

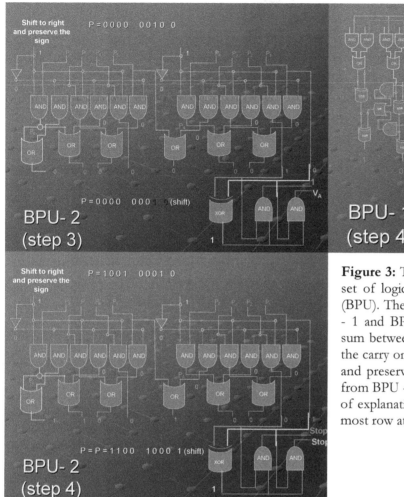

Figure 3: The Booth algorithm [4-5] implemented in a set of logical gates called the Booth Processing Unit (BPU). The BPU is composed of two parts called BPU - 1 and BPU - 2 respectively. BPU - 1 performs the sum between two binary numbers while taking care of the carry on bit. BPU - 2 performs the shift to the right and preserves the sign of the binary number resulting from BPU - 1. The implementation follows the scheme of explanation seen in the first slide located at the top most row at the left (see page 4).

Additional inputs from the GUI's panel named '*Image Volume Parameters*' are: (i) the '*SCALE*' parameter, used in order to scale the convolution of the trivariate cubic interpolation function, and (ii) the '*DataType*', which can be set as: '*CHAR*' or '*SHORT*' or '*INT*' or '*FLOAT*'. The push button named '*Add Slices to the Image Volume*', located in the panel named '*Image Volumes Processing*', has the function to add an even number of empty slices to the image volume. The result is a new digitized object which has a total number of slices given by sum of the entries given through the edit boxes located in the panels '*Image Volume Parameters*' ('*Z Voxels*') and '*Image Volumes Processing*' ('*Add Slices*'). The sum of the aforementioned two entries needs to be given as input to the edit box labeled as '*Number of Slices*' which is located in the panel '*Image Volume Processing*'.

For what pertains to the file name of the image volume to process, the GUI provides the user with the edit box just below the caption named '*Image Volume*' (inside the panel named '*Image Volumes Processing*') and the entry in this edit box will serve as input to the two push buttons: '*Add Slices to the Image Volume*' and '*Apply Rotation Translation*'. Before using either of the two push buttons named '*Add Slices to the Image Volume*' and '*Apply Transformation*', the user needs to make sure that the edit boxes located in the panels named '*Image Volumes Processing*' and '*Image Volumes Parameters*' are filled with the entries that are consistent with the image volume being processed. For what relates to the data type, '*FLOAT*' (32 bits Real) is the only acceptable by the push button named '*Apply Rotation Translation*'. When using the push button '*Apply Rotation Translation*', ROTRA 2008 creates two new digitized volumes. One is re-sliced with the trivariate cubic interpolation paradigm (the file name of the new volume ends with the suffix '*INT*'), and the other is not processed with any interpolation algorithm (the file name of the new volume ends with the suffix '*RAW*'). For every push button of the GUI is also written code which saves in the local directory a '*log*' file accessible to the user view and where is stored information relevant to processing. To view an image volume the user can utilize the push button named '*Run Image Viewer*' which sends in execution the program called *Image Viewer 2009*.

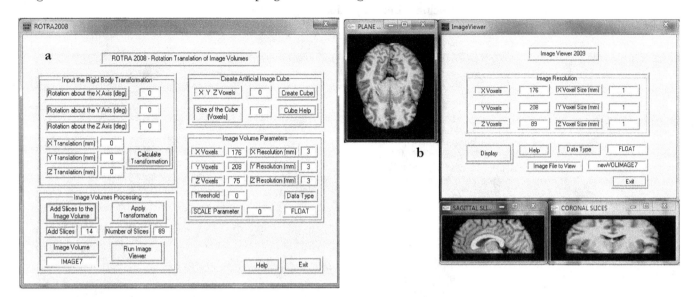

Figure 4: *ROTRA 2008* © (shown in (a)) is the application package used to rotate image volumes and/or shift the center of gravity of a given number of pixels, also to create artificial data consisting of a uniform cube inside a volume, and to add slices to existing volumes. *Image Viewer 2009* (shown in (b)) is the package connected to the GUI employed to visualize 2D and 3D images. The T1 MRI was kindly provided by the Open Access Series of Imaging Studies (OASIS), www.oasis-brains.org [7-12], courtesy of Dr. Daniel Marcus.

ANN98, shown in Fig. 5, allows running three different programs through the use of the push buttons of the GUI. The programs are (i) *NET98*, (ii) *NEWNET* and (iii) *TESTNET*. Both of *NET98* and *NEWNET* are executables capable to generate an artificial neural network. Additionally, *NET98* has the capability to adapt the hidden layer architecture to the given patter recognition problem [3], thus allowing user interaction during the learning process such to add neurons and/or re-train a given number of neurons. Also, *NET98* does not restrict the user to a maximum number of output neurons. Because of compatibility with *TESTNET*, it is suggested though, that *NET98* terminates the learning process with 2, 3 or 4 output neurons. On the other hand, *NEWNET* is an executable capable to generate an artificial neural network with a fixed architecture for the hidden layer. The number of neurons in the hidden layer (which can be either 2, 3 or 4) is given as input before the beginning of the learning process (training), and does not change till the end of the training. Consequentially, *NET98* and *NEWNET* are capable to determine completely different neural network architectures even if the number of hidden and output neurons is the same for both programs. Practically, the numerical value of the weighting connections of *NET98* and *NEWNET* (in both hidden and output layers) might be different. This is consequential to the feature added to *NET98* which consists in re-training neurons of the hidden layer during the learning process. At the end of the learning process, each of *NET98* and *NEWNET* saves four text files in the local directory where the programs run. The maximum value and the minimum value of each parameter included in the pattern to classify is calculated across the full training set (all of the patterns taking part to the learning process) and these parameters' values are saved in the files named '*BIGGEST.A1*' and '*SMALLEST.A1*' respectively. The weighting connections between the input layer and the output layer are saved in the text file called '*WEIGHT.A1*', whereas, the weighting connections between the hidden layer and the output layer are saved in the text file called '*WEIGHT.A2*'.

TESTNET is an executable capable to load in the weighting connections of either *NET98* or *NEWNET* and to generate a response in order to classify a given pattern or a set of patterns. To function properly, *TESTNET* requires the number of neurons for the input, the hidden and the output layers to be exactly the same as that number of neurons obtained from the learning process of either *NEWNET* or *NET98*. *TESTNET* can be used to validate the non linear separation capability achieved through *NEWNET* or *NET98* across the patterns of the training set, or can be used to classify a pattern not belonging to the training set. When the learning process of the artificial neural network is successfully brought to convergence, and the number of patterns of the training set (for each class type) is large and comprehensive enough, the outcome of *TESTNET* is likely to be a correct classification.

NEWNET, *NET98* and *TESTNET* run from the system command window and necessitate that the system has available a drive by the name of '*C*'. Input is given upon prompt request of the programs. Another requirement relating to the learning process is that of storing into text files the numerical values of the patterns to be employed for the learning process. Naming the patterns for each class type requires that the files' extension (e.g. '.A1', '.A2', etc...) identifies a different class of the pattern recognition problem.

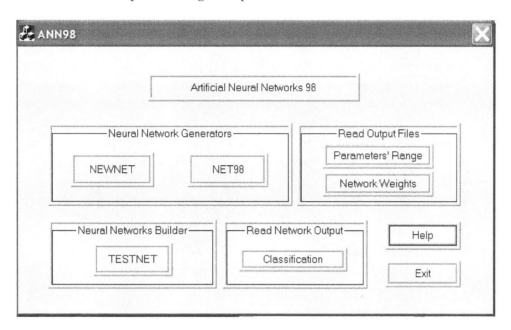

Figure 5: *ANN98* © is the application GUI written in Visual C++ ® to interface the artificial neural network weights' calculators: *NEWNET* © and *NET98* ©; and the neural network builder called *TESTNET* ©. The main feature of this GUI is that of being the interface to executables files running under Windows ® Systems. The GUI also allows reading the text files containing the parameters' range, the network weights and the classification performed through *TESTNET* ©.

In Fig. 6 is shown the GUI of the application named *ImageTool 2009* which is employed to produce random image data in standardized and not standardized form and also to display the data through OpenGL ® subroutines in 2D or 3D. The push button named '*Cube and Slice*' creates chaotic image data through randomization. In order to display the image data, the user can employ the push buttons named '*Display Image 2D*' and '*Display Image 3D*' located in the panel named '*OpenGL Display*'. *ImageTool 2009* is written in such a way that image data contained in binary files having header information conforming to program's requirements can also be imported and visualized.

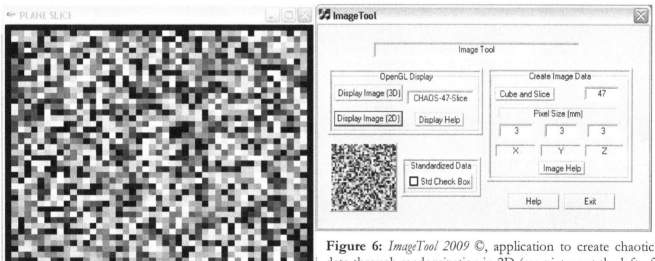

Figure 6: *ImageTool 2009* ©, application to create chaotic data through randomization in 2D (see picture at the left of the GUI), in 3D, and with the option to standardize the image data.

To create image data in standardized form, the '*Std Check Box*' needs to be checked, and consistently, it is necessary to keep the '*Std Check Box*' checked when importing image data stored elsewhere in standardized form. The push buttons '*Clear Memory 2D*' and '*Clear Memory 3D*' located in the panel named '*OpenGL Display*' allow the user to erase the memory employed by OpenGL ® to visualize the image data. Help to the user is provided through the push button '*Image Help*' located in the panel '*Create Image Data*', and also through the push button '*Help*'. When exiting the program the user can either close all of the display windows and then push the button named '*Exit*', or simply use the push button '*Exit*'.

Computer Science Applications

In Fig. 7 is shown the GUI of *SPACE 2010* which is an application grouping under the same interface several executables among which *Invert Image 2010* and *Image Viewer 2010* are two applications made combining Visual C++ ® and OpenGL ® to calculate the inverse of an image volume and to view it after processing. The button *'Intensity Curvature Functional'* was implemented using the math explained in [3] in 2D and it runs after proper insertion of the file name of the image to process, and the intra-pixel misplacement along X and Y axis. Help *'.log'* files are provided for each of the programs.

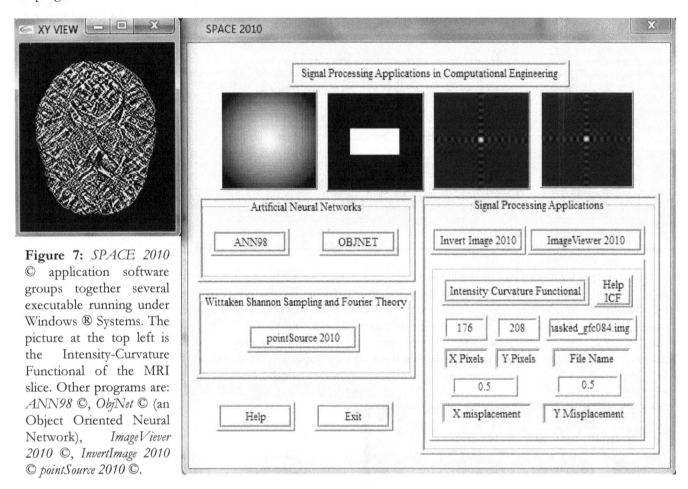

Figure 7: *SPACE 2010* © application software groups together several executable running under Windows ® Systems. The picture at the top left is the Intensity-Curvature Functional of the MRI slice. Other programs are: *ANN98* ©, *ObjNet* © (an Object Oriented Neural Network), *ImageViever 2010* ©, *InvertImage 2010* © *pointSource 2010* ©.

Summary

This chapter provides the reader with a list of the functionalities of each of most the projects' GUI presented in the book. Specifically, the chapter grants the students with the description of the outcome of the GUI components while running the programs. It is also presented a set of educational slides which illustrates how the Booth algorithm for binary multiplication [4-5] works and can be implemented in a processing unit made of logical gates.

The book is a presentation of programming concepts written in ANSI C ® embedded in Visual C++ ® projects having Graphical User Interfaces (GUIs) connected to OpenGL ® for interactive graphics visualization of data. The field is scientific computing at graduate and undergraduate levels of college and university. And given the approach, the book serves as educational resource for those students who are willing to expand their horizons in programming as well as those instructors who are willing to use the book materials as data base for the development of course projects, homework assignments and syllabi. Given the specificity of the materials and the topics, the book serves as complement of existing text books in programming, and also proposes one conceptual framework under which teaching can be structured and customized to the students' need such to have an outstanding outcome in the classroom settings. In other words, the teacher becomes the leading researcher in class, tailoring projects and course work for students in such a way that concepts are understood in their practical implications.

Generally, programming books present concepts using the framework of explaining case studies tailored to the concepts being addressed. Under the same framework, this manuscripts addresses higher learning problems like Whittaker-Shannon anterpolation [1], k-Space sampling, software flow chart presentation, Booth [4] algorithm for binary multiplication, creation of an artificial neural network for pattern recognition and its testing, rotation and translation of 3D digitized volumes, creation of random data and its visualization through OpenGL ®, the connection of OpenGL ® with Visual C++ ® for data visualization, Fourier Transformation (direct and inverse). Such problems are solved in the book while devising the solution to real case programming studies and provide the students and the instructor with a high level of details.

Because of the *alternative and complementary rationale* followed in the writings of this book, it is not easy to find a similar learning resource that presents the full solutions to scientific problems in computing. Usually, text books in science give the theory and this might not be sufficient to the students to absorb and understand the practicality involved in the implementation of the concepts. On the other hand, programming books do not go beyond the conceptual framework adopted in explaining the issues in programming and do not address the specificity of some science problems. This book combines the lack of specificity in the two aforementioned categories, thus providing practical implications in details and semi-advanced programming approaches that are not necessarily found elsewhere.

References

[1] Whittaker, E. T. (1915). *On the functions which are represented by the expansions of interpolation theory.* Proceedings of the Royal Society Edinburgh, UK, Sec. A(35), 181-194.

[2] Nyquist, H. (2002). *Certain topics in telegraph transmission theory.* Proceedings of the IEEE. *90*(2), 280-305.

[3] Ciulla, C. (2009). *Improved Signal and Image Interpolation in Biomedical Applications: The Case of Magnetic Resonance Imaging (MRI)* - Medical Information Science Reference - IGI Global Publisher, Hershey, PA, U.S.A.

[4] Booth, A.D. (1951). *A Signed Binary Multiplication Algorithm.* Quarterly Journal of Mechanics and Applied Mathematics. Clarendon Press; Oxford University Press. England.

[5] Null, L. & Lobur J. (2007). *The Essentials of Computer Organization and Architecture.* Second Edition. Jones and Bartlett Publishers. Sudbury, MA, U.S.A.

[6] Buchel, C., & Friston, K. (1997). *Modulation of connectivity in visual pathways by attention: Cortical interactions evaluated with structural equation modelling and fMRI.* Cerebral Cortex, 7, 768-778.

[7] Buckner, R. L., Head, D., Parker, J., Fotenos, A. F., Marcus, D., Morris, J. C., & Snyder, A. Z. (2004). *A unified approach for morphometric and functional data analysis in young, old, and demented adults using automated atlas-based head size normalization: Reliability and validation against manual measurement of total intracranial volume.* Neuroimage, 23(2), 724-738.

[8] Fotenos, A. F., Snyder, A. Z., Girton, L. E., Morris, J. C., & Buckner, R. L. (2005). *Normative estimates of cross-sectional and longitudinal brain volume decline in aging and AD.* Neurology, 64, 1032-1039.

[9] Marcus, D. S., Wang, T. H., Parker, J., Csernansky, J. G., Morris, J. C., & Buckner, R. L. (2007). *Open Access Series of Imaging Studies (OASIS): Cross-sectional MRI data in young, middle aged, nondemented, and demented older adults.* Journal of Cognitive Neuroscience, 19(9), 1498-1507.

[10] Morris, J. C. (1993). *The clinical dementia rating (CDR): current version and scoring rules.* Neurology, 43(11), 2412b-2414b.

[11] Rubin, E. H., Storandt, M., Miller, J. P., Kinscherf, D. A., Grant, E. A., Morris, J. C., & Berg, L. A. (1998). *A prospective study of cognitive function and onset of dementia in cognitively healthy elders.* Archives of Neurology, 55(3), 395-401.

[12] Zhang, Y., Brady, M., & Smith, S. (2001). *Segmentation of brain MR images through a hidden markov random field model and the expectation maximization algorithm.* IEEE Transactions on Medical Imaging, *20*(1), 45-57.

CHAPTER 2

The Source Code of pointSource2010

Introduction

As note to the reader is worth to mention that all variable having the suffix '*m_*' as initial to their name are those variables which are input from the Graphical User Interface shown in Fig. 1.

In the panel named '*Image Size*' there are two edit boxes named '*X*' and '*Y*' respectively. The variables that the user input from the GUI are named '*m_Xpixels*' and '*m_Ypixels*' respectively. In the panel named '*Object Size (pixels)*' there are two edit boxes named '*X*' and '*Y*'. The variables that the user input from the GUI are named '*m_ ObjectYSize*' and '*m_ObjectYSize*' respectively.

In the panel named '*Sphere of Light*' there are two variables assigned to the '*Light Rate*' and the '*Sample Rate*' and they are named '*m_lightRate*' and '*m_TheSamplingRate*' respectively. In the same panel the push button named '*Calculate Signal*' calls in the method *void CPointSource2010Dlg::OnCalculateSignal()*.

In the panel named '*Fourier Transformations*' there is a single variable assigned to the edit box and its name is '*m_ImageFile*'. And also two push buttons named '*Direct*' and '*Inverse*', which call in the two methods *void CPointSource2010Dlg::OnFourierTransform()* and *void CPointSource2010Dlg::OnInverseFourierTransform()* respectively.

Whereas the name of the variable assigned to the edit box of the panel named '*Image Display*' is '*m_VolumeFileName*' and the push button named '*View Image*' calls in the method *void CPointSource2010Dlg::OnDisplayON()*.

In the panel named '*Sample k-Space (Light)*' there are three push buttons called '*Sample Circular*', '*Sample Elliptical*' and '*Reconstruct*' and they call in the three methods *void CPointSource2010Dlg::OnSamplekspace()*, *void CPointSource2010Dlg::OnSampleEllipticalLight()*, *void CPointSource2010Dlg::OnReconstructObject()* respectively. The two edit boxes in the sub-panel called '*Ellipse*' are assigned to the two variables named '*m_ex*' and '*m_ey*' respectively in '*X*' and '*Y*'.

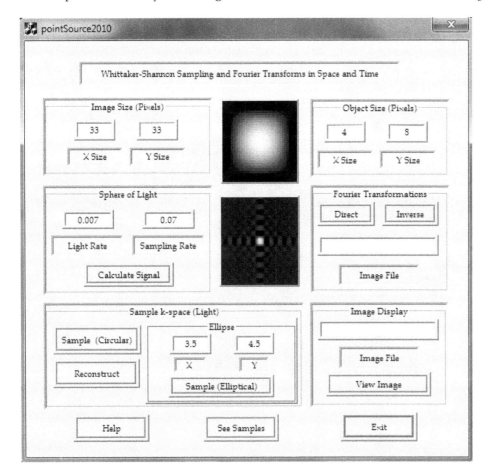

Figure 1: The Graphical User Interface of *pointSource2010*.

The Source Code

The function *void CPointSource2010Dlg::init()* initializes the OpenGL ® 2D window to display data [1]. This function is useful to the OpenGL ® main loop located in *void CPointSource2010Dlg::LaunchOpenGL()*.

The initialization is provided through the instruction '*glutGetWindow() == pw*' which allows the code to identify the window. The indentification is carried over in the the '*glut*' main loop through the integer variable '*pw*' which represents the plane window.

All of the functions and project's methods located in this chapter are part of the implementation file. The functions are distinct from the methods because they are not objects of any class, while the methods are part of the major class container called *CPointSource2010Dlg*.

Worth noting that in the projects reported in this manuscript it is engineered to import the projects' variable into those functions that are not part of the main class. As an immediate example, to import projects' variable inside a function which is not member of *CPointSource2010Dlg*, is performed through an I/O file which is called *'imageDisplay.log'* as visible in the function *void keyboard(unsigned char key, int x, int y)*. The function *void keyboard(unsigned char key, int x, int y)* requires the user to push either of the *'U'* or *'D'* keys to display the 2D image.

```
double Xsize = 4.0, Ysize = 4.0;
float *ImageData = NULL;

int pw,
float PSPX, PSPY;

GLfloat  * pimage = NULL;

//2010
double *lightSource = 0, *sampledSignal = 0;
double *kSpaceR = 0, *kSpaceI = 0, *Signal = 0, *reconSignal=0;
double *xCoord = 0, *yCoord = 0;
int pEraseMemoryFlag = 0;
int imEraseMemoryFlag = 0;
//2010
```

The method *void CPointSource2010Dlg:init()* serves the purpose to initialize the windows employed in 2D visualization. The assignment *'glutGetWindow() == pw'* is in place for such purpose. The reader is referred to chapter 8, for a detailed explanation about the purpose of the instructions [1]: *'glClearColor(0.0, 0.0, 0.0, 0.0)'*, *'glShadeModel(GL_FLAT)'*, *'glViewport(0, 0, (GLsizei)winx, (GLsizei)winy)'*, *'glLoadIdentity()'* and *'gluOrtho2D(0.0, (GLdouble)winx, 0.0, (GLdouble)winy)'*

void CPointSource2010Dlg::init()
```
{

    UpdateData(true);

    static int rcxres = m_Xpixels;
    static int rcyres = m_Ypixels;
    PSPY=Ysize;
    PSPX=Xsize;
    int winx = ((int) rcxres * PSPX);
    int winy = ((int) rcyres * PSPY);

    glClearColor(0.0, 0.0, 0.0, 0.0);
    glShadeModel(GL_FLAT);

    if(glutGetWindow() == pw)
    {
        glViewport(0, 0, (GLsizei)winx, (GLsizei)winy);
        glLoadIdentity();
        gluOrtho2D(0.0, (GLdouble)winx, 0.0, (GLdouble)winy);
    }

}
```

The functions *void display(void)*, *void keyboard(unsigned char key, int x, int y)* and *void reshape(int w, int h)* are not part of the main project class container named *CPointSource2010Dlg*. The reason to this is that these three functions are input to other OpenGL ® functions. Particularly, *'glutDisplayFunc(display)'*, *'glutKeyboardFunc(keyboard)'* and *'glutReshapeFunc(reshape)'* are the instructions found in the method *void CPointSource2010Dlg::LaunchOpenGL()* which make use of *void display(void)*, *void keyboard(unsigned char key, int x, int y)* and *void reshape(int w, int h)*.

Computer Science Applications

While *void display(void)* is employed to clear the OpenGL ® window which is being displayed, *void keyboard(unsigned char key, int x, int y)* is employed for interactive graphics. This is manifest through the user interaction happening when the keys 'U' and 'D' are selected from the keyboard at the purpose of showing the planar image. These two keys connect with the instruction '*(pimage + k2) = (GLfloat) *(ImageData+k2)/255*' which assigns the global pointer '*(ImageData)*' to the pointer '*(pimage)*'. Worth noting that the value assigned to '*(ImageData)*' is inside the range [0, 1] as required by the instruction *glDrawPixels((GLsizei)rcxres, (GLsizei)rcyres, GL_LUMINANCE, GL_FLOAT, pimage)* and this is made possible because data contained in '*(ImageData)*' is inside the range [0, 255] and each pixel intensity value is divided by 255 before is used into '*glDrawPixels*'.

void display(void)

```
{
        glClear(GL_COLOR_BUFFER_BIT);
}
```

Further, the image display happens inside *void keyboard(unsigned char key, int x, int y)* with the additional instructions [1]: '*glDrawBuffer(GL_FRONT)*', '*glRasterPos2i(0, 0)*', '*glPixelZoom((GLfloat) PSPX, (GLfloat) PSPY)*', '*glDrawPixels((GLsizei)rcxres, (GLsizei)rcyres, GL_LUMINANCE, GL_FLOAT, pimage)*' and '*glFlush()*'. These instructions are relevant to the window display and they perform the action of (i) drawing the buffer, (ii) setting the raster position, (iii) zooming the pixel, (iv) drawing the pixel and (v) flushing the display.

void keyboard(unsigned char key, int x, int y)

```
{

        int j, i, k2;
        static int rcxres;
        static int rcyres;

        /// read the keaboard matrix resolution///
        FILE * pointToKeaboardFile;
        char keaboard[128]="imageDisplay.log";

        if ((pointToKeaboardFile = fopen(keaboard,"r"))==NULL)
        {
        CString ExitMessage;
        ExitMessage.Format("%s\n" , "Cannot Open File: imageDisplay.log; Exit" );
        AfxMessageBox(ExitMessage);
        exit(0);
        }
        else{
        fscanf(pointToKeaboardFile,"%d\n", &rcxres);
        fscanf(pointToKeaboardFile,"%d\n", &rcyres);
        fclose(pointToKeaboardFile);
        }

        key=toupper(key);
        if(glutGetWindow() == pw)
        {
            switch(key){

            case 'U':

                for(j=0;j<rcyres;j++){
                    for(i=0;i<rcxres;i++){

                        k2=(j*rcxres+i);
                        *(pimage + k2)   = (GLfloat) *(ImageData+k2)/255;
                        *(pimage + k2*2) = (GLfloat) *(ImageData+k2)/255;
```

12

```
                              *(pimage + k2*3) = (GLfloat) *(ImageData+k2)/255;

                                         }
                                }

        glDrawBuffer(GL_FRONT);
        glRasterPos2i(0,0);
        glPixelZoom((GLfloat) PSPX, (GLfloat) PSPY);
        glDrawPixels((GLsizei)rcxres, (GLsizei)rcyres, GL_LUMINANCE, GL_FLOAT, pimage);
        glFlush();
        break;

        case 'D':

            for(j=0;j<rcyres;j++){
                for(i=0;i<rcxres;i++){

                k2=(j*rcxres+i);

                *(pimage + k2)   = (GLfloat) *(ImageData+k2)/255;
                *(pimage + k2*2) = (GLfloat) *(ImageData+k2)/255;
                *(pimage + k2*3) = (GLfloat) *(ImageData+k2)/255;

                                }
                        }

        glDrawBuffer(GL_FRONT);
        glRasterPos2i(0,0);
        glPixelZoom((GLfloat) PSPX, (GLfloat) PSPY);
        glDrawPixels((GLsizei)rcxres, (GLsizei)rcyres, GL_LUMINANCE, GL_FLOAT, pimage);
        glFlush();
        break;

        //2010
        case 27:

            free(ImageData);
            exit(0);
            break;
        // 2010

        default:

        break;

    }///switch

  }///if

}
```

The method *void CPointSource2010Dlg::AllocateMemoryforOpenGLGraphics()* has the functionality to allocate the memory for visual display and its core is in the use of dynamic allocation of memory through the pointer *'pimage'* and the function *'malloc'*. This is visible in the instruction *'pimage = (float *) malloc(m_Xpixels * m_Ypixels * 3 * sizeof(float))'*.

```
void CPointSource2010Dlg::AllocateMemoryforOpenGLGraphics()
{
    UpdateData(true);

        //2010
        CString HelpMessage;
        // 2010
        //// memory allocation for Image Data Display ///
        if ( pimage == NULL )
        { // if (2)
            pimage = (float *) malloc( m_Xpixels * m_Ypixels * 3 * sizeof(float) );
            pEraseMemoryFlag = 0;
            if ( pimage == NULL )
            { // if (1)

                CString ExitMessage;
                ExitMessage.Format("%s\n" , "Cannot Allocate Data for Display: Exit");
                AfxMessageBox(ExitMessage);
                free(ImageData);
                exit(0);

            } // if (1)

        } // if (2)
        //// memory allocation for Image Data Display ///
}
```

The function *void reshape(int w, int h)* also makes use of the I/O from the file *'imageDisplay.log'* in order to reshape the 2D window employed for data display [1]. This happens through the assignments *'PSPX=((float)w/rcxres)'* and *'PSPY=((float)h/rcyres)'* where the size of the window becomes a ratio of the two variables *'rcxres'* and *'rcyres'* and is assigned to *'PSPX'* and *'PSPY'* to be used inside the *'glut'* main loop by the instruction *'glPixelZoom((GLfloat) PSPX, (GLfloat) PSPY)'*.

```
void reshape(int w, int h)
{
        static int rcxres;
        static int rcyres;

        /// read the keaboard matrix resolution///
        FILE * pointToKeaboardFile;
        char keaboard[128]="imageDisplay.log";
        if ((pointToKeaboardFile = fopen(keaboard,"r"))==NULL)
        {
        CString ExitMessage;
        ExitMessage.Format("%s\n" , "Cannot Open File: imageDisplay.log. Exit" );
        AfxMessageBox(ExitMessage);
        exit(0);
        }else{
        fscanf(pointToKeaboardFile,"%d\n", &rcxres);
        fscanf(pointToKeaboardFile,"%d\n", &rcyres);
        fclose(pointToKeaboardFile);
        }
        glViewport(0, 0, (GLsizei)w, (GLsizei)h);
        glLoadIdentity();
        gluOrtho2D(0.0, (GLdouble)w, 0.0, (GLdouble)h);

        if(glutGetWindow() == pw)
```

```
    {
        PSPX=((float)w/rcxres);
        PSPY=((float)h/rcyres);
    }
}
```

The method *float * CPointSource2010Dlg::data(char filename[], int rcyres, int rcxres, char datatype[], FILE * logfile)* is an input function which reads in the data in '*DOUBLE (64 bits)*' format and returns a pointer readily accessible inside the other methods of the project. The file containing data is binary and is accessed thorough the instruction '*pf = fopen(filename,"rb+")*'. The pointer is released from the function '*calloc*' through the assignment '*pointer = (double *) calloc(rcyres*rcxres, sizeof(double))*' which makes available a matrix with '*rcyres*rcxres*' memory cells each having 64 bits of data. Data is read in with the instructions:

- ✓ *for(j=0; j<rcyres; j++){*
- ✓ *for(i=0; i<rcxres; i++){*

- ✓ *fread(&number, sizeof(double), 1, pf);*

- ✓ *k2=(j*rcxres+i);*

- ✓ **(pointer+k2) = (double)number;*

- ✓ *}*
- ✓ *}*

Where each of the single piece of data consisting of 64 bits (Real) is read in through the instruction '*fread(&number, sizeof(double), 1, pf)*' and is localized inside the '*rcyres*rcxres*' matrix through the index '*k2=(j*rcxres+i)*', then placed inside the memory cells through the instruction '**(pointer+k2) = (double)number*'. Data is scaled inside the range [0, 255] before is released to the rest of the program. In order to do so, the maximum and minimum of the data set is searched and found through the instructions:

- ✓ *max = (float)-500000;*
- ✓ *min = (float) 500000;*

- ✓ *for(i=0; i<rcxres*rcyres; i++){*

- ✓ *if(*(pointer+i) > max){*

- ✓ *max=*(pointer+i);*

- ✓ *}*

- ✓ *if(*(pointer+i) < min){*
- ✓ *min=*(pointer+i);*
- ✓ *}*

- ✓ *}*

Then, the instruction '**(bdata+k2) = (float)(((float)*(pointer+k2)-min)/ ((float)max-min))*255*', with '*k2*' spanning across the matrix of memory cells, converts data inside the range [0, 255]. The pointer '**(bdata)*' is allocated through the instruction '*bdata = (float *) calloc(rcyres*rcxres, sizeof(float))*'. Worth noting that the program saves into a text log file the result of processing as it progresses. The following instructions are employed inside the method *float * CPoint-Source2010Dlg::data(char filename[], int rcyres, int rcxres, char datatype[], FILE * logfile)* to save data: '*fprintf(logfile,"%s%s\n", "Cannot open file: ", filename)*' (if the input file cannot be open), '*fprintf(logfile,"%s\n", "Not enough memory to allocate Image data")*' (if data cannot be allocated), '*fprintf(logfile,"%s\n", "IMAGE DATA LOADED AND CONVERTED")*' and '*fprintf(logfile,"%s%s\n", "DataType not DOUBLE" , "Now Exit")*' (if data is not conforming to the specifications).

```
float * CPointSource2010Dlg::data(char filename[], int rcyres, int rcxres, char datatype[], FILE * logfile)
{

            FILE *pf;
            int j,i,k2;
            double number = 0;
            double *pointer = 0;
            float * bdata = 0;
            double max, min;
             // 2010
             CString HelpMessage;

            // clear memory here not necessary here
            // because this function allocates memory
            // to be used in succeding OpenGL ® related
            // routines.

            if ((pf = fopen(filename,"rb+"))==NULL)
            {

                fprintf(logfile,"%s%s\n", "Cannot open file: " , filename );
                // clear memory here not necessary here
                // because this if statement takes place
                // after blocks of memory have not been allocated.
                exit(0);
            } else { // else (1)

            if(strcmp(datatype,"DOUBLE")==0)
            { // if
                if ((pointer = (double *) calloc( rcyres*rcxres, sizeof(double)) ) == NULL)
                {
                    fprintf(logfile,"%s\n", "Not enough memory to allocate Image data");
                    exit(0);
                }
                for(j=0;j<rcyres;j++){
                    for(i=0;i<rcxres;i++){
                        fread(&number,sizeof(double),1,pf);
                        k2=(j*rcxres+i);
                        *(pointer+k2) = (double)number;

                                }
                            }
                fclose (pf);

                if ((bdata = (float *) calloc( rcyres*rcxres, sizeof(float)) ) == NULL)
                {
                    fprintf(logfile,"%s\n", "Not enough memory to allocate Image Data");
                    // FIFO memory deallocation method
                    free(pointer);
                    exit(0);
                }

                /*scale to 0-255 float type*/
                max = (float)-500000;
                min = (float) 500000;
```

```
        for(i=0; i<rcxres*rcyres; i++){ // for
            if( *(pointer+i) > max ){

                max=*(pointer+i);

                            }

            if( *(pointer+i) < min ){

                min=*(pointer+i);

                            }

                    } // for
    /*convert data and store into bdata*/

        for(j=0;j<rcyres;j++){
            for(i=0;i<rcxres;i++){

            k2=(j*rcxres+i);
            *(bdata+k2)=(float)(((float)*(pointer+k2)-min)/((float)max-min))*255;

                    }
                }

        fprintf(logfile,"%s\n", "IMAGE DATA LOADED AND CONVERTED");
        // FIFO memory deallocation method
        free(pointer);
    } // if
else {
    fprintf(logfile,"%s%s\n", "DataType not DOUBLE" , "Now Exit" );
    // FIFO memory deallocation method
    free(bdata);
    exit(0);
    }

}// else (1)
    // clear memory here not necessary here
    // because this function allocates memory
    // to be used in succeeding OpenGL ® related
    // routines.
return bdata;

}
```

The method *void CPointSource2010Dlg::LaunchOpenGL()* creates the OpenGL ® routines and initializes the *glutMainLoop()* [1]. Along with *float * data(char filename[], int rcyres, int rcxres, char datatype[], FILE * logfile), void AllocateMemoryforOpenGL-Graphics()* and *void init(), void CPointSource2010Dlg::LaunchOpenGL()* is declared inside the main class *CPointSource2010Dlg*. The following set of instructions [1]: '*glutInitDisplayMode(GLUT_ALPHA)*', '*glutInitWindowSize(((int)winx), ((int)winy))*', '*glutInitWindowPosition(100, 100)*', '*pw = glutCreateWindow("XY VIEW")*' (plane window), '*init()*', '*glutDisplayFunc(display)*', '*glutReshapeFunc(reshape)*', '*glutMainLoop()*' perform the following tasks: (i) initialize the display mode, (ii) set the window size, (iii) set the window position, (iv) create the window, (v) initialize, (vi) manage the display, (vii) manage the window reshape, (viii) initialize the '*glut MainLoop*'.

Computer Science Applications
void CPointSource2010Dlg::LaunchOpenGL()
{

       UpdateData(true);
       static int rcxres = m_Xpixels;
       static int rcyres = m_Ypixels;
       PSPY=Ysize;
       PSPX=Xsize;
       int winx = ((int) rcxres * PSPX);
       int winy = ((int) rcyres * PSPY);

       AllocateMemoryforOpenGLGraphics();
       glutInitDisplayMode(GLUT_ALPHA);

       //create window
       glutInitWindowSize(((int)winx), ((int)winy));
       glutInitWindowPosition(100,100);

       pw = glutCreateWindow("IMAGE VIEW");
       init();
       glutDisplayFunc(display);
       glutKeyboardFunc(keyboard);
       glutReshapeFunc(reshape);
       glutMainLoop();

}

The method *void CPointSource2010Dlg::OnCalculateSignal()* calculates a circular signal called *lightSource* (see Fig. 2.a) and samples the light with the Whittaker-Shannon interpolation formula [2-4] such to obtain a uniform sampled signal as shown in Fig. 2.b. The first task of the method is that of making sure that the user inputs the sampling rate at least more than two times bigger than the sampling rate as requested by the Nyquist theorem. This happens through the following set of instructions:

- ✓ *if ((m_TheSamplingRate > 2.0*m_lightRate))*
- ✓ *{*

- ✓ *if ((logfile = fopen(logfilename,"w+"))==NULL)*
- ✓ *{*

- ✓ *HelpMessage.Format("%os\n %os\n" , "Unable to open log File", "Now Exit");*
- ✓ *MessageBox(HelpMessage);*
- ✓ *exit(0);*

- ✓ *}*

The second task of this method is to make sure that the user input a square image size which is in between 17 and 129 pixels, also that the image width and lengh is powers of two (2) plus one (1). This requirement is necessary to the direct and inverse Fourier transformations such to center the spectrum. The third task of the method is that of making sure that the user sets the object half size between 4 and 32 pixels. If any of these two tasks is not fullfilled by the user input through the Graphical User Inteface, then the program provides a safe exit to the user. The following instructions are employed:

- ✓ *if (NofXpixels != NofYpixels || NofXpixels < 17 || NofXpixels > 129 || NofYpixels < 17 || NofYpixels > 129)*
- ✓ *{*

✓ *HelpMessage.Format("%os\n %os\n %os\n %os\n %os\n" , "Please set a Square Image Size", "Between 17 and 129 Pixels", "The Image Width and Lengh", "must be both powers of 2, plus 1:", "Now Exit");*

✓ *MessageBox(HelpMessage);*

✓ *exit(0);*

✓ *}*

✓ *if (m_objectXSize < 4 || m_objectXSize > 32 || m_objectYSize < 4 || m_objectYSize > 32)*

✓ *{*

✓ *HelpMessage.Format("%os\n %os\n %os\n" , "Please set the Object Half Size", "Between 4 and 32 Pixels", "Now Exit");*

✓ *MessageBox(HelpMessage);*

✓ *exit(0);*

✓ *}*

✓ *else { // test condition object size (power of 2)*

✓ *a = ((int)m_objectXSize % 2);*

✓ *b = ((int)m_objectYSize % 2);*

✓ *if (a != 0 || b != 0)*

✓ *{// test condition object size even number of pixels*

✓ *HelpMessage.Format("%os\n %os\n %os\n %os\n" , "Please set a Square or Rectangular", "Object Size with Width and Lengh", " which must be both powers of 2", "Now Exit");*

✓ *MessageBox(HelpMessage);*

✓ *exit(0);*

✓ *}// test condition object size even number of pixels*

✓ *} // test condition object size (power of 2)*

✓ *a = ((int)NofXpixels % 2);*

✓ *b = ((int)NofYpixels % 2);*

✓ *if (a == 0 || b == 0)*

✓ *{// test condition image size odd number of pixels: powers of 2, plus 1*

✓ *HelpMessage.Format("%os\n %os\n %os\n %os\n" , "Please set a Square Image Size", "The Image Width and Lengh", "must be both powers of 2, plus 1", "Now Exit");*

✓ *MessageBox(HelpMessage);*

✓ *exit(0);*

✓ *}// test condition image size odd number of pixels: powers of 2, plus 1*

Thereafter, the method proposes two main steps: (i) generate the light source, (ii) sample the light source with the Whittaker-Shannon interpolation formula.

To generate the light source, the instruction '**(lightSource+index) = (double) K * exp(-((double) 2.0 * pi * lightFrequency * gridPoint))*' is employed where '**(lightSource)*' is the pointer recipient of the pixel intensity value and the distance: '*((double) 2.0 * pi * gridPoint)*' defines the circle of sampling located in the 2D plane. The value of the radius of the circle of sampling is given as: '*gridPoint = (double) sqrt (((double) (dx * dx) + (dy * dy)))*', with '*dx*' and '*dy*' calculated as function of the

Computer Science Applications

sampling interval at each pixel 2D location, specifically: '*dx = (double)SamplingInterval * ((double) (NofXpixels/2) - i)*' and '*dy = (double)SamplingInterval * ((double) (NofYpixels/2) - j)*'. The following two '*for*' loops generate the light source:

- ✓ *for (i=0; i<NofXpixels; i++) {*
- ✓ *for (j=0; j<NofYpixels; j++) {*

- ✓ *index = ((j*NofXpixels)+i);*

- ✓ *dx = (double)SamplingInterval * ((double) (NofXpixels/2) - i);*
- ✓ *dy = (double)SamplingInterval * ((double) (NofYpixels/2) - j);*

- ✓ *gridPoint = (double) sqrt (((double) (dx * dx) + (dy * dy)));*

- ✓ **(lightSource+index) = (double) K * exp(-((double) 2.0 * pi * lightFrequency * gridPoint)) ;*

- ✓ *}*
- ✓ *}*

To sample the light source inside the spatial extent of the object size is possible through the two instructions:

- ✓ '*i<=((int)(NofXpixels/2)+objectXSize) && i>=((int)(NofXpixels/2)-objectXSize)*'

- ✓ '*j<=((int)(NofYpixels/2)+objectYSize) && j>=((int)(NofYpixels/2)-objectYSize)*'.

The Whittaker-Shannon interpolation formula further requires: '*dx = (double) pi * (2.0 * bandwidth * di - dtx)*' and '*dy = (double) pi * (2.0 * bandwidth * dj - dty)*' with '*dtx = ((double)((int) i - NofXpixels/2) * m_TheSamplingRate*' and '*dty = ((double)((int) j - NofYpixels/2) * m_TheSamplingRate*' to calculate the Sinc functions '*sincx*' and '*sincy*'. The following instructions sample the light source with the Whittaker-Shannon interpolation formula:

- ✓ *for (i=0; i<NofXpixels; i++) {*
- ✓ *for (j=0; j<NofYpixels; j++) {*
- ✓ *di = ((int) i - NofXpixels/2);*
- ✓ *dj = ((int) j - NofYpixels/2);*

- ✓ *dtx = ((double)((int) i - NofXpixels/2) * m_TheSamplingRate); // space (pixel) * frequency (1/sec)*
- ✓ *dty = ((double)((int) j - NofYpixels/2) * m_TheSamplingRate); // space (pixel) * frequency (1/sec)*

- ✓ *index = ((j*NofXpixels)+i);*
- ✓ **(sampledSignal+index) = (double)0.0;*

- ✓ *if (i<=((int)(NofXpixels/2)+objectXSize) && i>=((int)(NofXpixels/2)-objectXSize) &&*
- ✓ *j<=((int)(NofYpixels/2)+objectYSize) && j>=((int)(NofYpixels/2)-objectYSize))*
- ✓ *{*
- ✓ *dx = (double) pi * (2.0 * bandwidth * di - dtx);*
- ✓ *dy = (double) pi * (2.0 * bandwidth * dj - dty);*

- ✓ *if ((double)fabs((double) dx) > toll)*

- ✓ *sincx = (double) sin((double) dx) / ((double) dx);*

- ✓ *else sincx = (double)1.0;*

- ✓ *if ((double)fabs((double) dy) > toll)*

- ✓ *sincy = (double) sin((double) dy) / ((double) dy);*

- ✓ *else sincy = (double)1.0;*

- ✓ **(sampledSignal+index) = ((double) *(lightSource + ((j*NofXpixels)+i)) * sincx * sincy);*

- ✓ *}*
- ✓ *}*
- ✓ *}*

Finally the method *void CPointSource2010Dlg::OnCalculateSignal()* saves the data with the following instructions:

- ✓ *for (i=0; i<NofXpixels; i++) {*
- ✓ *for (j=0; j<NofYpixels; j++) {*

- ✓ *index = ((j*NofXpixels)+i);*

- ✓ *savedata = (double)*(lightSource+index);*
- ✓ *fwrite(&savedata,sizeof(double),1,pf1);*

- ✓ *savedata = (double)*(sampledSignal+index);*
- ✓ *fwrite(&savedata,sizeof(double),1,pf2);*

- ✓ *}*
- ✓ *}*

void CPointSource2010Dlg::OnCalculateSignal()
{

```
        UpdateData(true);
        double *lightSource = 0, *sampledSignal = 0;
        int NofXpixels = m_Xpixels, NofYpixels = m_Ypixels;
        int i, j, index;
        double TheSamplingRate = m_TheSamplingRate;

        // 2010
        double SamplingInterval = ((double)1.0);
        // to see sampled signal with non uniform illumination
        // find suitable TheSamplingRate and LightRate.

        //2010
        /// What is the relationship needed between the light rate and the sampling rate? 1:2 ///
        /// Such to see a uniformly calculated signal with the (2) Whittaker-Shannon interpolation formula below ///
        double lightRate = m_lightRate; // frequency (1/sec)

        double lightFrequency = ((double)lightRate); // frequency (1/sec)

        double bandwidth = ((double)m_lightRate); // frequency (1/sec)
        /// What is the relationship needed between the light rate and the sampling rate? 1:2 ///
        /// Such to see a uniformly calculated signal with the (2) Whittaker-Shannon interpolation formula below ///

        // the emitting source 'K' is emitting
        // constantly at the rate of m_lightRate per sec.
        double K = 1000.0;
        int a, b;

        FILE * logfile;
```

```
        char logfilename[128]="pointSource.log";
        CString HelpMessage;
        if ( (m_TheSamplingRate > 2.0*m_lightRate) )
        { // 2010

        if ((logfile = fopen(logfilename,"w+"))==NULL)
        {

            HelpMessage.Format("%s\n %s\n" , "Unable to open log File", "Now Exit");
            MessageBox(HelpMessage);

          // clear memory here not necessary here
          // because this if statement takes place
          // after blocks of memory have not been allocated.
          exit(0);

        } else { // allocate data and test condition
        //2010
        if ( NofXpixels != NofYpixels || NofXpixels < 17 || NofXpixels > 129 ||
            NofYpixels < 17 || NofYpixels > 129 )
        {// test condition image size

        HelpMessage.Format("%s\n %s\n %s\n %s\n %s\n" , "Please set a Square Image Size", "Between 17 and
        129 Pixels", "The Image Width and Lengh", "must be both powers of 2, plus 1:", "Now Exit");

        MessageBox(HelpMessage);
        // clear memory here not necessary here
        // because this if statement takes place
        // after blocks of memory have not been allocated.
        exit(0);

        }// test condition image size

        if ( m_objectXSize < 4 || m_objectXSize > 32 || m_objectYSize < 4 || m_objectYSize > 32 )
        {// test condition object size

        HelpMessage.Format("%s\n %s\n %s\n" , "Please set the Object Half Size", "Between 4 and 32 Pixels",
        "Now Exit");
        MessageBox(HelpMessage);
        // clear memory here not necessary here
        // because this if statement takes place
         // after blocks of memory have not been allocated.
            exit(0);

        }// test condition object size

        else { // test condition object size (power of 2)

        a = ((int)m_objectXSize % 2);
        b = ((int)m_objectYSize % 2);

        if ( a != 0  || b != 0 )
        {// test condition object size even number of pixels

        HelpMessage.Format("%s\n %s\n %s\n %s\n" , "Please set a Square or Rectangular", "Object Size with
        Width and Lengh", " which must be both powers of 2", "Now Exit");
        MessageBox(HelpMessage);
```

```
        // clear memory here not necessary here
        // because this if statement takes place
        // after blocks of memory have not been allocated.
            exit(0);

    }// test condition object size even number of pixels
    } // test condition object size (power of 2)

        a = ((int)NofXpixels % 2);
        b = ((int)NofYpixels % 2);

if ( a == 0  || b == 0 )
{// test condition image size odd number of pixels: powers of 2, plus 1

HelpMessage.Format("%s\n %s\n %s\n %s\n" , "Please set a Square Image Size", "The Image Width and
Lengh", "must be both powers of 2, plus 1", "Now Exit");
MessageBox(HelpMessage);

// clear memory here not necessary here
// because this if statement takes place
// after blocks of memory have not been allocated.

exit(0);
}// test condition image size odd number of pixels: powers of 2, plus 1
if ((lightSource = (double *) calloc( NofXpixels*NofYpixels, sizeof(double)) ) == NULL)
{
    fprintf(logfile,"%s\n", "Not enough memory to allocate Real Image data: Exit");
    exit(0);
}

if ((sampledSignal = (double *) calloc( NofXpixels*NofYpixels, sizeof(double)) ) == NULL)
{
    fprintf(logfile,"%s\n", "Not enough memory to allocate Imaginary Image data: Exit");
    free(lightSource);
    exit(0);
}
}// allocate data and test condition
// 2010
        // Note to the reader:
        // In this program, memory deallocation is performed with the
        // method FIFO (first in, first out). In this specific
        // case of the routine OnCalculateSignal(), the two
        // pointers 'lightSource' and 'sampledSignal' are erased
        // from memory in the order they were allocated.

        // Suggestion: since the controller of the CPU manages
        // the RAM and additional memory like casche memory for
        // instance, please consider that the architecture of the
        // controller might be eventually set to manage the RAM with FIFO
        // or LIFO methods. If LIFO method is implemented, then
        // is possible that the memory should to be erased as:
        // 1. free(sampledSignal); 2. free(lightSource);
        // since RAM and additional memory like casche memory
        // are volatile, it is practice in this program to erase
        // the pointers not necessarily preceeding an 'exit( )'
        // fuction call. Such in the case of a mesage Box
```

```
            // announcing that the program will quit.
            // Unless two or more 'exit( )' function calls follow
            // each another and each 'exit( )' is preceeded of memory
            // allocation instruction (such as 'calloc' or 'malloc',
            // for instance) in which case deallocation takes place with
            // FIFO method.
            // OR Unless the 'exit( )' function call operates
            // when file I/O takes place and after blocks of memory
            // have been allocated.
            // Generally, when exiting the program, the volatile memory
            // is automatically erased from the memory blocks.
            // 2010


    double dx, dy, gridPoint, sincx, sincy;
    double toll = 0.000001;
    double pi = 3.141592;
    // 2010
    int objectXSize = ((int)m_objectXSize/2);
    int objectYSize = ((int)m_objectYSize/2);
    // 2010


    for (i=0; i<NofXpixels; i++)
    { ///calculate Light Source
        for (j=0; j<NofYpixels; j++)
        {

            index = ((j*NofXpixels)+i);

            dx = (double)SamplingInterval * ((double) (NofXpixels/2) - i);
            dy = (double)SamplingInterval * ((double) (NofYpixels/2) - j);

            gridPoint = (double) sqrt ( ((double) (dx * dx) + (dy * dy)) );

            // 2010
            // Exponential front wave (simulating the projection
            // of a Gaussian like front wave onto the 2D space
            // imaging plane). Where the distance:
            // 'd' =((double) 2.0 * pi * gridPoint)
            // is the circle of sampling located in the 2D plane.
            // The value of the radius of the circle of sampling
            // is given as: 'gridPoint' =
            //(double) sqrt ( ((double) (dx * dx) + (dy * dy)) );

            *(lightSource+index) = (double) K * exp( -((double) 2.0 * pi * lightFrequency * gridPoint) ) ;
            // 2010
        }
    } ///calculate Light Source
        //2010

    int di ,dj;
    double dtx, dty;
    for (i=0; i<NofXpixels; i++)
    { ////Sample Signal
        for (j=0; j<NofYpixels; j++)
        {
        di = ((int) i - NofXpixels/2);
        dj = ((int) j - NofYpixels/2);
```

```
        dtx = ((double)((int) i - NofXpixels/2) * m_TheSamplingRate); //space (pixel) * frequency (1/sec)
        dty = ((double)((int) j - NofYpixels/2) * m_TheSamplingRate); //space (pixel) * frequency (1/sec)

        index = ((j*NofXpixels)+i);

        *(sampledSignal+index) = (double)0.0;

        if ( i<=((int)(NofXpixels/2)+objectXSize) && i>=((int)(NofXpixels/2)-objectXSize) &&
            j<=((int)(NofYpixels/2)+objectYSize) && j>=((int)(NofYpixels/2)-objectYSize) )
        { /// set the object position

            /// (2) Whittaker-Shannon interpolation formula
            dx = (double) pi * (2.0 * bandwidth * di - dtx);
            dy = (double) pi * (2.0 * bandwidth * dj - dty);
            // Where 2.0 * bandwidth * di is: frequency (1/sec) * space (pixel)
            // 2.0 * bandwidth * dj is: frequency (1/sec) * space (pixel)

            if ( (double)fabs( (double) dx ) > toll )
            sincx = (double) sin( (double) dx ) /  ((double) dx);

            else sincx = (double)1.0;

            if ( (double)fabs( (double) dy ) > toll )

            sincy = (double) sin( (double) dy ) /  ((double) dy);

            else sincy = (double)1.0;

            // *(sampledSignal+index) =
            // ((double) *(lightSource + ((j*NofXpixels)+i) ) * sincx * sincy );
            // The front wave (lightSource) is Exponential (Gaussian like).
            // Regardless to the position of the surface (which is
            // a 2D plane in the space dimension), there is one front
            // wave which intersects the surface in 4 points. These 4 points
            // could be one single point in case the front wave is tangential
            // to the surface).

            *(sampledSignal+index) = ((double) *(lightSource + ((j*NofXpixels)+i) ) * sincx * sincy );
            /// (2) Whittaker-Shannon interpolation formula

                }
            }
} ///Sample Signal
        //2010
double savedata = 0.0;
FILE *pf1, *pf2;
char filename1[128];
char filename2[128];
sprintf(filename1, "%s", "lightSource.img");
sprintf(filename2, "%s", "sampledSignal.img");
fprintf(logfile, "%s\t%s\t%s\n", "Now Saving: ", filename1, filename2);

if ((pf1 = fopen(filename1,"wb+"))==NULL)
{
    fprintf(logfile, "%s%s\n", "Cannot open file to save: ", filename1);
    //2010
```

Computer Science Applications

```c
        // FIFO memory deallocation methodd
        free(lightSource);
        free(sampledSignal);
        //2010
        exit(0);
    }

    if ((pf2 = fopen(filename2,"wb+"))==NULL)
    {
        fprintf(logfile, "%s%s\n", "Cannot open file to save: ", filename2);
        //2010
        // FIFO memory deallocation method
        free(lightSource);
        free(sampledSignal);
        //2010
        exit(0);
    }
    for (i=0; i<NofXpixels; i++)
    { ///save image data
        for (j=0; j<NofYpixels; j++)
        {
            index = ((j*NofXpixels)+i);
            savedata = (double)*(lightSource+index);
            fwrite(&savedata,sizeof(double),1,pf1);
            savedata = (double)*(sampledSignal+index);
            fwrite(&savedata,sizeof(double),1,pf2);
        }
    } ///save image data
    fprintf(logfile,"%s\n", "Image Data Saved");
    fclose (pf1);
    fclose (pf2);
    fprintf(logfile,"%s\n", "Processing Completed");
    fclose(logfile);

    system( logfilename );

    // FIFO memory deallocation method
    free(lightSource);
    free(sampledSignal);

    // clear memory here not necessary here
    // because this function allocates memory
    // to be used in succeding OpenGL ® related
    // routines.
    }
    else{

    HelpMessage.Format("%s\n %s\n %s\n %s\n" , "Please make sure that" , "lightRate and The SamplingRate",
    "fulfill the Nyquist Theorem.", "Rerun before proceeding to FT");
    MessageBox(HelpMessage);

        }

}
```

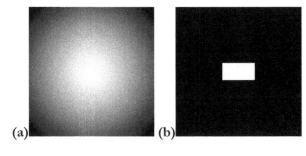

(a)   **(b)**

Figure 2: The image size is 129x129 pixels, the half of the object size is 16x32 pixels, the light rate is 0.00017 and the sampling rate is 0.0017. The lightSource is shown in (a) and the sampled signal is shown in (b).

The calculation of the direct Fourier transformation of the image data is made through the method called *void CPoint-Source2010Dlg::OnFourierTransform()* and this happens when the user pushes the button *'Direct'* of the GUI located inside the panel *'Fourier Transformations'* (see Fig. 3). This processing was made possible thorugh the knowledge provided in www.wikipedia.org.

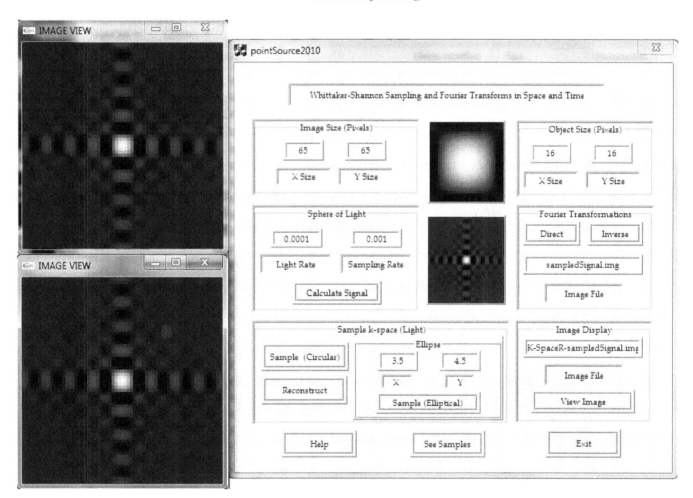

Figure 3: A sample case of calculation of direct Fourier Transformation through the use of *pointSource 2010*. The half of object size was set to a square of 16 pixels' edge, the size of the image is 66x66 pixels, the light rate is 0.0001 and the sampling rate is 0.001.

The method calculates the phase at each pixel location with the formula: '*phase = ((double) 2.0 * pi * k2 * k3 / (NofXpixels*NofYpixels))*'. Also, the real and imaginary parts of the k-Space with the formulas: '*complexR = (double) cos((double) phase)*' and '*complexI = - (double) sin((double) phase)*'. Noteworthy is the calculation of the values: '*dx = ((int) i - NofXpixels/2)*' and '*dy = ((int) j - NofYpixels/2)*' to calculate '*k2 = ((int)(dx*NofYpixels)+dy)*'. And, the calculation of the values: '*ds = ((int) s - NofXpixels/2)*' and '*dp = ((int) p - NofYpixels/2)*' to calculate '*k3 = ((int)(dp*NofXpixels)+ds)*'. k-Space data is stored in its real '*(*(kSpaceR+w))*' and imaginary counterpart '*(*(kSpaceI+w))*' and is localized in memory through pointers which are responsible of dynamic memory allocation and management. The instructions employed to compute the direct Fourier Transformation are:

Computer Science Applications

- ✓ *for (i=0; i<NofXpixels; i++) {*
- ✓ *for (j=0; j<NofYpixels; j++) {*

- ✓ *dx = ((int) i - NofXpixels/2);*
- ✓ *dy = ((int) j - NofYpixels/2);*

- ✓ *k2 = ((int)(dx*NofYpixels)+dy);*

- ✓ *w = ((j*NofXpixels)+i);*

- ✓ *for (int s=0; s<NofXpixels; s++) {*
- ✓ *for (int p=0; p<NofYpixels; p++) {*

- ✓ *ds = ((int) s - NofXpixels/2);*
- ✓ *dp = ((int) p - NofYpixels/2);*

- ✓ *k3 = ((int)(dp*NofXpixels)+ds);*

- ✓ *t = ((p*NofXpixels)+s);*

- ✓ *phase = ((double) 2.0 * pi * k2 * k3 / (NofXpixels*NofYpixels));*

- ✓ *complexR = (double) cos((double) phase);*
- ✓ *complexI = - (double) sin((double) phase);*

- ✓ **(kSpaceR+w) += (double) *(Signal+t) * (double) complexR;*
- ✓ **(kSpaceI+w) += (double) *(Signal+t) * (double) complexI;*

- ✓ *}*

- ✓ *}*
- ✓ *}*

- ✓ *}*

k-Space data is subsequently saved into binary files and is promptly accessible for display with the part of the GUI dedicated to image display with OpenGL ® routines. The instructions comprise of the following lines:

- ✓ *for (i=0; i<NofXpixels; i++) {*
- ✓ *for (j=0; j<NofYpixels; j++) {*

- ✓ *index = ((j*NofXpixels)+i);*
- ✓ *savedata = (double)*(kSpaceR+index);*
- ✓ *fwrite(&savedata,sizeof(double),1,pf);*

- ✓ *}*
- ✓ *}*

- ✓ *for (i=0; i<NofXpixels; i++) {*
- ✓ *for (j=0; j<NofYpixels; j++) {*

- ✓ *index = ((j*NofXpixels)+i);*
- ✓ *savedata = (double)*(kSpaceI+index);*
- ✓ *fwrite(&savedata,sizeof(double),1,pf);*
- ✓ *}*
- ✓ *}*

```
void CPointSource2010Dlg::OnFourierTransform()
{

        UpdateData(true);
        int NofXpixels = m_Xpixels, NofYpixels = m_Ypixels;
        int i, j, index;
        int dx, dy;
        int ds, dp;
        int k2, k3, w, t;
        double pi = 3.141592;
        FILE * logfile;
        char logfilename[128]="Fourier-T.log";

        CString HelpMessage;
        if ((logfile = fopen(logfilename,"w+"))==NULL)
        {
            HelpMessage.Format("%s\n %s\n" , "Unable to open log File", "Now Exit");
            MessageBox(HelpMessage);
          // clear memory here not necessary here
          // because this if statement takes place
          // after blocks of memory have not been allocated.
        exit(0);
        } else { // allocate memory

        if ((kSpaceR = (double *) calloc( NofXpixels*NofYpixels, sizeof(double)) ) == NULL)
        {
            fprintf(logfile,"%s\n", "Not enough memory to allocate Real Image data: Exit");
            exit(0);
        }

        if ((kSpaceI = (double *) calloc( NofXpixels*NofYpixels, sizeof(double)) ) == NULL)
        {
            fprintf(logfile,"%s\n", "Not enough memory to allocate Real Image data: Exit");
            // FIFO memory deallocation method
            free(kSpaceR);
            exit(0);
        }

        if ((Signal = (double *) calloc( NofXpixels*NofYpixels, sizeof(double)) ) == NULL)
        {
            fprintf(logfile,"%s\n", "Not enough memory to allocate Imaginary Image data: Exit");
            // FIFO memory deallocation method
            free(kSpaceR);
            free(kSpaceI);
            exit(0);
        }

        } // allocate memory

        //// read image data and initialize pointers
        FILE *image;
        char imageFilename[128];
        sprintf(imageFilename, "%s" , m_ImageFile);

        if ((image = fopen(imageFilename,"rb+"))==NULL)
        {
```

```
        fprintf(logfile, "%s%s\n", "Cannot open Image File: ", imageFilename);
        // FIFO memory deallocation method
        free(kSpaceR);
        free(kSpaceI);
        free(Signal);
        exit(0);
    } else { // read data and initialize pointers
        double number = 0.0;

        for (i=0; i<NofXpixels; i++)
        {
            for (j=0; j<NofYpixels; j++)
            {
                index = ((j*NofXpixels)+i);
                fread(&number,sizeof(double),1,image);
                *(Signal+index)= (double)number;
                *(kSpaceR+index) = (double) 0.0;
                *(kSpaceI+index) = (double) 0.0;
            }
        }
        fclose(image);

    }// read data and initialize pointers

    double phase, complexR, complexI;

    ///// Fourier Transform //////
    for (i=0; i<NofXpixels; i++)
    { ///calculate k-space data
        for (j=0; j<NofYpixels; j++)
        {
            dx = ((int) i - NofXpixels/2);
            dy = ((int) j - NofYpixels/2);

            k2 = ((int)(dx*NofYpixels)+dy);
            w = ((j*NofXpixels)+i);

            for (int s=0; s<NofXpixels; s++)
            { ///calculate k-space data
                for (int p=0; p<NofYpixels; p++)
                {
                    ds = ((int) s - NofXpixels/2);
                    dp = ((int) p - NofYpixels/2);

                    k3 = ((int)(dp*NofXpixels)+ds);
                    t = ((p*NofXpixels)+s);

                    phase = ((double) 2.0 * pi * k2 * k3 / (NofXpixels*NofYpixels) );

                    complexR = (double) cos( (double) phase );
                    complexI = - (double) sin( (double) phase );

                    *(kSpaceR+w) += (double) *(Signal+t) * (double) complexR;
                    *(kSpaceI+w) += (double) *(Signal+t) * (double) complexI;
                }

            }///calculate k-space data
```

```
        }
} ///calculate k-space data
///// Fourier Transform //////
double savedata = 0.0;
FILE * pf;
char filename[128];

sprintf(filename, "%s%s", "K-SpaceR-", m_ImageFile);

fprintf(logfile, "%s\t%s\n", "Now Saving K-Space Signal (Real) in File. ", filename);

if ((pf = fopen(filename,"wb+"))==NULL)
{

fprintf(logfile, "%s\n", "Cannot open file to save K-Space Signal");
// FIFO memory deallocation method
free(kSpaceR);
free(kSpaceI);
free(Signal);
exit(0);
} else { // save data

for (i=0; i<NofXpixels; i++)
{ ///save k-space data
    for (j=0; j<NofYpixels; j++)
    {
        index = ((j*NofXpixels)+i);
        savedata = (double)*(kSpaceR+index);
        fwrite(&savedata,sizeof(double),1,pf);
    }
} ///save k-space data
fprintf(logfile,"%s\n", "K-Space Signal (Real) Saved");
fclose (pf);
} // save data

sprintf(filename, "%s%s", "K-SpaceI-", m_ImageFile);
fprintf(logfile, "%s\t%s\n", "Now Saving K-Space Signal (Imaginary) in File: ", filename);

if ((pf = fopen(filename,"wb+"))==NULL)
{
fprintf(logfile, "%s\n", "Cannot open file to save K-Space Signal");
// FIFO memory deallocation method
free(kSpaceR);
free(kSpaceI);
free(Signal);
exit(0);
} else { // save data

for (i=0; i<NofXpixels; i++)
{ ///save k-space data
    for (j=0; j<NofYpixels; j++)
    {

        index = ((j*NofXpixels)+i);
        savedata = (double)*(kSpaceI+index);
        fwrite(&savedata,sizeof(double),1,pf);
```

```
            }
    } ///save k-space data
    fprintf(logfile,"%s\n", "K-Space Signal (Imaginary) Saved");
    fclose (pf);
    } // save data

    fprintf(logfile,"%s\n", "Processing Completed");
    fclose(logfile);
    system( logfilename );
    // FIFO memory deallocation method
    free(kSpaceR);
    free(kSpaceI);
    free(Signal);


}
```

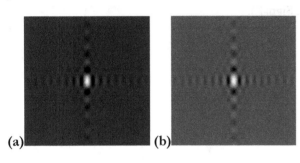

(a) **(b)**

Figure 4: Fourier transformation of the rectangular object of size 16x32 that was seen in Fig. 2.b; (a) real component, (b) imaginary component.

The method *void CPointSource2010Dlg::OnInverseFourierTransform()* calculates the inverse of the Fourie transform. These materials were written using the knowledge provided in www.wikipedia.org.

This method requires that the data input is constistent with the data employed to calculate the direct Fourier transform. Both real and imaginary counterparts of the signal are imported into the method and they serve to the calculation of the reconstructed object as shown in Fig. 5. The instructions to import k-Space data are:

- ✓ *for (i=0; i<NofXpixels; i++) {*
- ✓ *for (j=0; j<NofYpixels; j++) {*

- ✓ *index = ((j*NofXpixels)+i);*
- ✓ *fread(&number,sizeof(double),1,image);*
- ✓ **(kSpaceR+index) = (double) number;*

- ✓ *}*
- ✓ *}*

- ✓ *for (i=0; i<NofXpixels; i++) {*
- ✓ *for (j=0; j<NofYpixels; j++) {*

- ✓ *index = ((j*NofXpixels)+i);*
- ✓ *fread(&number,sizeof(double),1,image);*
- ✓ **(kSpaceI+index) = (double) number;*

- ✓ *}*
- ✓ *}*

The core of the method is in the calculation of the real and imaginary parts of the reconstructed k-Space and this is done through the instructions:

- ✓ *'real += (double) *(kSpaceR+t) * cos((double) phase)'*
- ✓ *'imaginary -= (double) *(kSpaceI+t) * sin((double) phase)'*

where '*phase = ((double) 2.0 * pi * k2 * k3 / (NofXpixels*NofYpixels))*'. Real and imaginary parts are summed up and reconstructed thorugh the formula: '**(reconSignal+w) = ((double) sqrt(((double)real*real + (double)imaginary*imaginary)))*'. Noteworthy are the values '*k2 = ((int)(dx*NofYpixels)+dy)*' and '*k3 = ((int)(dp*NofXpixels)+ds)*', which are involved in the calculation of the phase and are the same as those seen in the calulation of the direct Fourier transformation. At the end of the reconstruction process the signal is divided by the factor '*scale = ((double)m_Xpixels*m_Ypixels*emittingSource)*' to scale back the pixel intensity. The full set of instruction that calculates the inverse Fourier transformation comprise of:

- ✓ *for (i=0; i<NofXpixels; i++)*   {
- ✓ *for (j=0; j<NofYpixels; j++)*   {

- ✓ *dx = ((int) i - NofXpixels/2);*
- ✓ *dy = ((int) j - NofYpixels/2);*

- ✓ *k2 = ((int)(dx*NofYpixels)+dy);*
- ✓ *w = ((j*NofXpixels)+i);*

- ✓ *real = 0.0;*
- ✓ *imaginary = 0.0;*

- ✓ *for (int s=0; s<NofXpixels; s++) {*
- ✓ *for (int p=0; p<NofYpixels; p++) {*

- ✓ *ds = ((int) s - NofXpixels/2);*
- ✓ *dp = ((int) p - NofYpixels/2);*

- ✓ *k3 = ((int)(dp*NofXpixels)+ds);*
- ✓ *t = ((p*NofXpixels)+s);*

- ✓ *phase = ((double) 2.0 * pi * k2 * k3 / (NofXpixels*NofYpixels));*

- ✓ *real += (double) *(kSpaceR+t) * cos((double) phase);*

- ✓ *imaginary -= (double) *(kSpaceI+t) * sin((double) phase);*

- ✓ }

- ✓ }

- ✓ **(reconSignal+w) = ((double) sqrt(((double)real*real + (double)imaginary*imaginary)));*

- ✓ **(reconSignal+w) /= (double)scale;*

- ✓ }

- ✓ }

void CPointSource2010Dlg::OnInverseFourierTransform()
{

    UpdateData(true);
    int NofXpixels = m_Xpixels, NofYpixels = m_Ypixels;
    int i, j, index;
    int dx, dy;
    int ds, dp;
    int k2, k3, w, t;

```
        double pi = 3.141592;
        double phase;

        //2010
        double emittingSource = 1000.0; // same as K in OnCalculateSignal();
        double scale = ((double)m_Xpixels*m_Ypixels*emittingSource);
        //2010

        FILE * logfile;
        char logfilename[128]="INV-FourierT.log";

        CString HelpMessage;

        FILE *image;
        char imageFilename[256];
        if ((logfile = fopen(logfilename,"w+"))==NULL)
        {
         // clear memory here not necessary here
         // because this if statement takes place
         // after blocks of memory have not been allocated.

         exit(0);

        } else { // allocate memory

            // 2010
            // The INV FT is calculated with data used with
            // the FT button, thus please make sure that data
            // now located in the edit boxes is consistent with
            // data used to calculate the FT.

        HelpMessage.Format("%s\n %s\n %s\n %s\n" , "The INV FT is calculated with data used with" , "the FT
        button, thus please make sure that data", "now located in the edit boxes is consistent with",
        "data used to calculate the FT.");
        MessageBox(HelpMessage);
            //2010
            if ((kSpaceR = (double *) calloc( NofXpixels*NofYpixels, sizeof(double)) ) == NULL)
            {
            fprintf(logfile,"%s\n", "Not enough memory to allocate Real Image data: Exit");
            exit(0);
            }
            if ((kSpaceI = (double *) calloc( NofXpixels*NofYpixels, sizeof(double)) ) == NULL)
            {
            fprintf(logfile,"%s\n", "Not enough memory to allocate Real Image data: Exit");
            // FIFO memory deallocation method
            free(kSpaceR);
            exit(0);
            }
            if ((reconSignal = (double *) calloc( NofXpixels*NofYpixels, sizeof(double)) ) == NULL)
            {
            fprintf(logfile,"%s\n", "Not enough memory to allocate Imaginary Image data: Exit");
            // FIFO memory deallocation method
            free(kSpaceR);
            free(kSpaceI);
            exit(0);
            }
```

```
} // allocate memory
//// read image data and initialize pointers
sprintf(imageFilename, "%s%s", "K-SpaceR-", m_ImageFile);

if ((image = fopen(imageFilename,"rb+"))==NULL)
{

    fprintf(logfile, "%s%s\n", "Cannot open Image File: ", imageFilename);
    // FIFO memory deallocation method
    free(kSpaceR);
    free(kSpaceI);
    free(reconSignal);

    exit(0);

} else { // read data and initialize pointers
    double number = 0.0;
    for (i=0; i<NofXpixels; i++)
    {
        for (j=0; j<NofYpixels; j++)
        {
            index = ((j*NofXpixels)+i);
            fread(&number,sizeof(double),1,image);
            *(kSpaceR+index) = (double) number;
        }

    }
    fclose(image);

}// read data and initialize pointers
char imageFilename2[256];
sprintf(imageFilename2, "%s%s", "K-SpaceI-", m_ImageFile);

if ((image = fopen(imageFilename2,"rb+"))==NULL)
{

    fprintf(logfile, "%s%s\n", "Cannot open Image File: ", imageFilename2);
    // FIFO memory deallocation method
    free(kSpaceR);
    free(kSpaceI);
    free(reconSignal);
    exit(0);

} else { // read data and initialize pointers
    double number = 0.0;

    for (i=0; i<NofXpixels; i++)
    {
        for (j=0; j<NofYpixels; j++)
        {
            index = ((j*NofXpixels)+i);
            fread(&number,sizeof(double),1,image);
            *(kSpaceI+index) = (double) number;
        }

    }
```

```
        fclose(image);

        for (i=0; i<NofXpixels; i++)
        {
            for (j=0; j<NofYpixels; j++)
            {
                index = ((j*NofXpixels)+i);
                *(reconSignal+index)= (double)0.0;
            }


        }
}// read data and initialize pointers
double real = 0.0, imaginary = 0.0;
///// INV Fourier Transform //////
for (i=0; i<NofXpixels; i++)
{ ///process k-space data
    for (j=0; j<NofYpixels; j++)
    {

        dx = ((int) i - NofXpixels/2);
        dy = ((int) j - NofYpixels/2);

        k2 = ((int)(dx*NofYpixels)+dy);
        w = ((j*NofXpixels)+i);

          real = 0.0;
          imaginary = 0.0;

          for (int s=0; s<NofXpixels; s++)
          { ///process k-space data
              for (int p=0; p<NofYpixels; p++)
              {

                    ds = ((int) s - NofXpixels/2);
                    dp = ((int) p - NofYpixels/2);

                    k3 = ((int)(dp*NofXpixels)+ds);

                    t = ((p*NofXpixels)+s);

                    phase = ((double) 2.0 * pi * k2 * k3 / (NofXpixels*NofYpixels) );

                    real += (double) *(kSpaceR+t) * cos( (double) phase );

                    imaginary -= (double) *(kSpaceI+t) * sin( (double) phase );

              }

          }///process k-space data
              *(reconSignal+w) = ((double) sqrt( ((double)real*real + (double)imaginary*imaginary) ) );

              *(reconSignal+w) /= (double)scale;


      }
} ///process k-space data
///// INV Fourier Transform //////
```

```
double savedata = 0.0;
FILE * pf;
char filename[128];
sprintf(filename, "%s%s", "reconSignal-", m_ImageFile);
fprintf(logfile, "%s\t%s\n", "Now Saving Reconstructed Signal in File: ", filename);

if ((pf = fopen(filename,"wb+"))==NULL)
{
fprintf(logfile, "%s\n", "Cannot open file to save K-Space Signal");
// FIFO memory deallocation method
free(kSpaceR);
free(kSpaceI);
free(reconSignal);
exit(0);

} else { // save data

for (i=0; i<NofXpixels; i++)
{ ///save k-space data
    for (j=0; j<NofYpixels; j++)
    {
        index = ((j*NofXpixels)+i);
        savedata = (double)*(reconSignal+index);
        fwrite(&savedata,sizeof(double),1,pf);
    }
} ///save k-space data
fprintf(logfile,"%s\n", "Reconstructed Signal Saved");

fclose (pf);
} // save data

fprintf(logfile,"%s\n", "Processing Completed");
fclose(logfile);
system( logfilename );

// FIFO memory deallocation method
free(kSpaceR);
free(kSpaceI);
free(reconSignal);

}
```

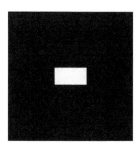

Figure 5: Inverse Fourier transformation of the real and imaginary components obtained Fourier transforming the rectangular object of size 16x32 that was seen in Fig. 2.b.

The core of the method called *void CPointSource2010Dlg::OnDisplayON()* is the function *LaunchOpenGL()*. The output of the method is the text file called *'imageDisplay.log'* which contains the 2D image resolution and matrix size. Such file is to the benefit of other functions that are not part of the main class *CPointSource2010Dlg* and is relevant to the import of resolution related data relevant to the image to display.

The text file *'imageDisplay.log'* is made by the method *void CPointSource2010Dlg::OnDisplayON()* upon pushing the button of the GUI called *'View Image'* and using the following instructions:

Computer Science Applications

- ✓ *char keaboard[128]="imageDisplay.log";*

- ✓ *if ((pointToKeaboardFile = fopen(keaboard,"w"))==NULL) {*

- ✓ *ExitMessage.Format("%s\n" , "Cannot Open File: imageDisplay.log; Exit");*
- ✓ *MessageBox(ExitMessage);*

- ✓ *exit(0);*

- ✓ *}else{*
- ✓ *fprintf(pointToKeaboardFile,"%d\n", rcxres);*
- ✓ *fprintf(pointToKeaboardFile,"%d\n", rcyres);*
- ✓ *fprintf(pointToKeaboardFile,"%lf\n", Xsize);*
- ✓ *fprintf(pointToKeaboardFile,"%lf\n", Ysize);*
- ✓ *fclose(pointToKeaboardFile);*

- ✓ *}*

Once the file '*imageDisplay.log*' is saved, the method *void CPointSource2010Dlg::OnDisplayON()* reads data into the program through the instruction '*ImageData = data(filename, rcyres, rcxres, datatype, logfile)*'. The float pointer '*(ImageData)*' is assigned with the output released from the method *float * CPointSource2010Dlg::data(char filename[], int rcyres, int rcxres, char datatype[], FILE * logfile)*, which takes as input the filename to read ('*char filename[]*'), which is identified through the variable '*filename*'. The number of pixels along the X direction ('*rcxres*'), which is identified through the variable '*rcxres*', the number of pixels along the Y direction ('*rcyres*'), which is identified through the variable '*rcyres*'. The data type contained inside the binary file to import ('*char datatype[]*'), identified through the variable '*datatype*', and the *log* file pointer '*FILE * logfile*' identified through the variable '*logfile*'. The output released from the method *float * CPointSource2010Dlg::data(char filename[], int rcyres, int rcxres, char datatype[], FILE * logfile)* is a float pointer containing the data to display which are made available as global variable to the instruction '*LaunchOpenGL()*', which is the routine that progresses to the display of the data with OpenGL ®. The *log* file is a text file where data relevant to processing is saved and made available to the user in the currect directory where the program runs. The instructions that are relevant to the *log* file are: '*FILE * logfile*', which is the declaration of the file pointer, '*sprintf(logfilename, "%s%s%s", "ImageDisplay-", m_VolumeFileName, ".log")*', which sets the *log* file name and store it into '*logfilename*', and finally '*logfile = fopen(logfilename,"w")*', which releases into the file pointer '*logfile*' the output of '*fopen(logfilename,"w")*'.

void CPointSource2010Dlg::OnDisplayON()
{

```
        UpdateData(true);
        // 2010
        CString HelpMessage, ExitMessage;
        if ( ImageData != NULL ) { free(ImageData); }
        static int rcxres = m_Xpixels;
        static int rcyres = m_Ypixels;
        char filename[256];
        char datatype[23];

        /// make the keaboard ///
        FILE * pointToKeaboardFile;
        char keaboard[128]="imageDisplay.log";

        if ((pointToKeaboardFile = fopen(keaboard,"w"))==NULL)
        { // 2010

        ExitMessage.Format("%s\n" , "Cannot Open File: imageDisplay.log; Exit" );
        MessageBox(ExitMessage);
```

```
    // clear memory here not necessary here
    // because this if statement takes place
    // after blocks of memory have not been allocated.
exit(0);


}else{

fprintf(pointToKeaboardFile,"%d\n", rcxres);
fprintf(pointToKeaboardFile,"%d\n", rcyres);
fprintf(pointToKeaboardFile,"%lf\n", Xsize);
fprintf(pointToKeaboardFile,"%lf\n", Ysize);
fclose(pointToKeaboardFile);

}


char logfilename[256];
FILE * logfile;
sprintf(logfilename, "%s%s%s", "ImageDisplay-", m_VolumeFileName, ".log");

if ((logfile = fopen(logfilename,"w"))==NULL)
{

    // clear memory here not necessary here
    // because this if statement takes place
    // after blocks of memory have not been allocated.
    exit(0);

}


fprintf(logfile,"%s\t %s\n", "Processing the Image File: ", m_VolumeFileName);
fprintf(logfile,"%s\t %d\n", "X Matrix Resolution: ", rcxres);
fprintf(logfile,"%s\t %d\n", "Y Matrix Resolution: ", rcyres);
fprintf(logfile,"%s\t %lf\n", "X Pixel Size: ", Xsize);
fprintf(logfile,"%s\t %lf\n", "Y Pixel Size: ", Ysize);
fprintf(logfile,"%s\t %s\n", "Data Type: ", "DOUBLE (Real 64 bits)" );
sprintf(filename,"%s", m_VolumeFileName);
sprintf(datatype, "%s", "DOUBLE");

ImageData = data(filename, rcyres, rcxres, datatype, logfile);
imEraseMemoryFlag = 0;
fclose(logfile);

CString ViewMessage;
ViewMessage.Format("%s\n" , "Ready to Launch OpenGL Visualization of the Image" );
AfxMessageBox(ViewMessage);

LaunchOpenGL();
// clear memory here not necessary here
// because this function allocates memory
// to be used in succeding OpenGL ® related
// routines.

}
```

Computer Science Applications

The method *void CPointSource2010Dlg::OnHelp()* is called upon pushing the button '*Help*' and saves in the local directory a log file named '*pointSource2010Help.log*' containing the information necessary to the user to properly interact with the entire Visual C++ ® application with commands given through the Graphical User Interface.

```
void CPointSource2010Dlg::OnHelp()
{

        CString HelpMessage;
        char logfilename[128];
        FILE *logfile;
        sprintf(logfilename,"%s","pointSource2010Help.log");

        if ((logfile = fopen(logfilename,"w"))==NULL)
        {

            HelpMessage.Format("%s\n %s\n" , " Cannot open log file", "Now Exit" );
            MessageBox(HelpMessage);
            exit(0);

        } else {
        // 2010
        fprintf(logfile,"%s\n", "Welcome to pointSource 2010");
        fprintf(logfile,"\n");
        fprintf(logfile,"%s\n", "Image Size:");
        fprintf(logfile,"%s\n", "Please set a Square Image Size (Number of pixels along X and Y) between 17 and
        129");
        fprintf(logfile,"%s\n", "The Image Size both along X and Y must be an odd number");
        fprintf(logfile,"\n");

        fprintf(logfile,"%s\n", "Object Size:");
        fprintf(logfile,"%s\n", "Please set the object Half size between 4 and 32 pixels for both X and Y");
        fprintf(logfile,"\n");

        fprintf(logfile,"%s\n", "Gaussian, Circular and Elliptical like Front Wave Light and Sampled Signal:");
        fprintf(logfile,"%s\n", "The Light Rate and the Sampling Rate have to be such to have Ratio greater than 1:2");
        fprintf(logfile,"%s\n", "to fulfill Nyquist Theorem");
        fprintf(logfile,"%s\n", "Possible Values: Light Rate (0.00017) and Sampling Rate (0.0017)");
        fprintf(logfile,"\n");

        fprintf(logfile,"%s\n", "Direct and Inverse Fourier Transforms:");
        fprintf(logfile,"%s\n", "Please make sure that the input file in the edit box is: sampledSignal.img:");
        fprintf(logfile,"%s\n", "This is necessary to insure Direct Fourier Transformation of the Object sampled with
                    the push button 'Calculate Signal';");
        fprintf(logfile,"%s\n", "And reconstruction, through Inverse Fourier Transform, of the object sampled with
                    the push button 'Calculate Signal'");
        fprintf(logfile,"\n");

        fprintf(logfile,"%s\n", "Images I/O:");
        fprintf(logfile,"%s\n", "All Images are saved in the local directory and the DataType is DOUBLE (64-bits
        Real)");
        fprintf(logfile,"\n");

        fprintf(logfile,"%s\n", "Please work with One Image Size at once, then to process and view");
        fprintf(logfile,"%s\n", "an Image set with different X and/or Y Size, please Exit the program and Run it
                    Again.");
        fprintf(logfile,"\n");
        fprintf(logfile,"%s\n", "THE PROGRAM WILL DISPLAY THE IMAGE DATA");
```

```
fprintf(logfile,"%s\n", "A single 2D Window will be shown");
fprintf(logfile,"%s\n", "Move the mouse arrow to give control to the window");
fprintf(logfile,"%s\n", "Press U and D keys to see the Image");
fprintf(logfile,"%s\n", "Press Esc key to Exit the program");
fprintf(logfile,"\n");

fprintf(logfile,"\n");
fprintf(logfile,"%s\n", "To Exit the program please perform the following steps:");
fprintf(logfile,"%s\n", "1. Close the Display Window where the Image data is seen");
fprintf(logfile,"%s\n", "2. Click on the Exit Button");
fprintf(logfile,"%s\n", "OR 3. Hit the Esc key when viewing the Display Window");
fclose(logfile);

HelpMessage.Format("%s\n %s\n %s\n %s\n %s\n %s\n %s\n" , " THE PROGRAM WILL DISPLAY
THE IMAGE DATA" , "A Single 2D Window will be displayed" , "Move the mouse arrow to give control to
the window" , "Use U and D keys to view the Image", "Press Esc key to quit OpenGL and to clear Memory" ,
"Please set the Light Rate and the Sampling Rate", "such to have Ratio greater than 1:2");

MessageBox(HelpMessage);

        }// else

}
```

The method *void CPointSource2010Dlg::OnExit()* quits the application after proper release of the pointers employed for dynamic memory allocation. Memory is released through the instructions *'free(ImageData)'* and *'free(pimage)'* upon proper check of the value assigned to the variables *'imEraseMemoryFlag'* and *'pEraseMemoryFlag'* respectively. The value of *'imEraseMemoryFlag = 0'* and *'pEraseMemoryFlag = 0'* is assigned inside the methods *void CPointSource2010Dlg::OnDisplayON()* and *void CPointSource2010Dlg::AllocateMemoryforOpenGLGraphics()* upon the allocation of the memory to the pointers *'*(ImageData)'* and *'*(pimage)'*.

void CPointSource2010Dlg::OnExit()
```
{
        //2010
        if (ImageData != NULL)
        {
            if (imEraseMemoryFlag == 0)
            {
                free(ImageData);
                imEraseMemoryFlag = 1;
            }

        }
        if (pimage != NULL)
        {
            if (pEraseMemoryFlag == 0)
            {
                free(pimage);
                pEraseMemoryFlag = 1;
            }

        }
        //2010
        exit(0);

}
```

Computer Science Applications

The method *void CPointSource2010Dlg::OnSamplekspace()* checks that the image size and the object size are within the limits permitted by the application then calculates a light source as function of space and time. The front wave of light in the 2D space imaging plane is composed of points. The origin of the light is located at the center of the 2D space plane.

The light source is calculated through the instruction: '*(lightSource+index) = ((double)2.0 * pi * d)', where 'd = ((double) sqrt(((double) dtx * dtx) + ((double) dty * dty))' is the radius of the circle (front wave). The values of 'dtx' and 'dty' are calculated through the instructions: 'dtx = (double) (NofXpixels/2.0) + sqrt(((double) radius*radius - ((double) j - NofYpixels/2.0)*((double) j - NofYpixels/2.0)))', 'dtx *= ((double)emittingSource)' and 'dty = (double) (NofYpixels/2.0) + sqrt(((double) radius*radius - ((double) i − NofXpixels/2.0)*((double) i - NofXpixels/2.0)))', 'dty *= ((double)emittingSource)' respectively. The complete set of instructions is:

- ✓ *for (i=0; i<NofXpixels; i++) {*
- ✓ *for (j=0; j<NofYpixels; j++) {*

- ✓ *index = ((j*NofXpixels)+i);*

- ✓ *double radius = ((double)sqrt(((double)NofXpixels*NofXpixels) + ((double)NofYpixels*NofYpixels)) / 2.0);*

- ✓ *dtx = (double) (NofXpixels/2.0) + sqrt(((double) radius*radius - ((double) j - NofYpixels/2.0)*((double) j - NofYpixels/2.0)));*

- ✓ *dtx *= ((double)emittingSource);*

- ✓ *dty = (double) (NofYpixels/2.0) + sqrt(((double) radius*radius - ((double) i - NofXpixels/2.0)*((double) i - NofXpixels/2.0)));*

- ✓ *dty *= ((double)emittingSource);*

- ✓ *double d = (double) sqrt(((double) dtx * dtx) + ((double) dty * dty));*

- ✓ **(lightSource+index) = ((double)2.0 * pi * d);*

- ✓ *}*

- ✓ *}*

Thereafter, the method *void CPointSource2010Dlg::OnSamplekspace()* samples the k-Space of such light source with the Whittaker-Shannon interpolation formula [2-4] and obtains the 'sampledSignal'. The inputs to the sinc functions 'sincx' and 'sincy' are 'dx = (double) pi * (2.0 * bandwidth * di - dtx)' and 'dy = (double) pi * (2.0 * bandwidth * dj - dty)', where: 'di = ((int) i - NofXpixels/2)', 'dtx = ((double)((int) i - NofXpixels/2) * m_TheSamplingRate)', 'dj = ((int) j - NofYpixels/2)' and 'dty = ((double)((int) j - NofYpixels/2) * m_TheSamplingRate)' respectively. The complete set of instructions is:

- ✓ *for (i=0; i<NofXpixels; i++) {*
- ✓ *for (j=0; j<NofYpixels; j++) {*

- ✓ *di = ((int) i - NofXpixels/2);*
- ✓ *dj = ((int) j - NofYpixels/2);*

- ✓ *dtx = ((double)((int) i - NofXpixels/2) * m_TheSamplingRate);*
- ✓ *dty = ((double)((int) j - NofYpixels/2) * m_TheSamplingRate);*

- ✓ *index = ((j*NofXpixels)+i);*

- ✓ **(sampledSignal+index) = (double)0.0;*

- ✓ *dx = (double) pi * (2.0 * bandwidth * di - dtx);*

✓ *dy = (double) pi * (2.0 * bandwidth * dj - dty);*

✓ *if ((double)fabs((double) dx) > toll)*

✓ *sincx = (double) sin((double) dx) / ((double) dx);*

✓ *else sincx = (double)1.0;*

✓ *if ((double)fabs((double) dy) > toll)*

✓ *sincy = (double) sin((double) dy) / ((double) dy);*

✓ *else sincy = (double)1.0;*

✓ **(sampledSignal+index) = ((double) *(lightSource + (j*NofXpixels)+i)) * sincx * sincy);*

✓ *}*

✓ *}*

After sampling, the real and imaginary components of the k-Space of '*sampledSignal*' are calculated with the direct Fourier transformation and they are shown in Fig. 6.c and 6.d. To perform such calculation, the method computes the phase as: '*((double) 2.0 * pi * k2 * k3 / (NofXpixels*NofYpixels))*', the real and imaginary counterparts as: '*complexR = (double) cos(phase)*' and '*complexI = - (double) sin(phase)*' respectively. These two components are summed up on a pixel-by-pixel basis through the formulas: '**(kSpaceR+w) += (double) *(sampledSignal+t) * complexR*' and '**(kSpaceI+w) += (double) *(sampledSignal+t) * complexI*' respectively, where: '**(kSpaceR)*' and '**(kSpaceI)*' are two pointers dynamically allocated. Noteworthy is the calculation of '*k2 = ((int)(dx*NofYpixels)+dy)*' and '*k3 = ((int)(dp*NofXpixels)+ds)*', where: '*dx = ((int) i - NofXpixels/2)*', '*dy = ((int) j - NofYpixels/2)*', '*ds = ((int) s - NofXpixels/2)*' and '*dp = ((int) p - NofYpixels/2)*'. The instructions are:

✓ *for (i=0; i<NofXpixels; i++) {*
✓ *for (j=0; j<NofYpixels; j++) {*

✓ *dx = ((int) i - NofXpixels/2);*
✓ *dy = ((int) j - NofYpixels/2);*
✓ *k2 = ((int)(dx*NofYpixels)+dy);*
✓ *w = ((j*NofXpixels)+i);*

✓ *for (int s=0; s<NofXpixels; s++) {*
✓ *for (int p=0; p<NofYpixels; p++) {*

✓ *ds = ((int) s - NofXpixels/2);*
✓ *dp = ((int) p - NofYpixels/2);*

✓ *k3 = ((int)(dp*NofXpixels)+ds);*

✓ *t = ((p*NofXpixels)+s);*

✓ *phase = ((double) 2.0 * pi * k2 * k3 / (NofXpixels*NofYpixels));*

✓ *complexR = (double) cos(phase);*

✓ *complexI = - (double) sin(phase);*

✓ **(kSpaceR+w) += (double) *(sampledSignal+t) * complexR;*

✓   **(kSpaceI+w) += (double) *(sampledSignal+t) * complexI;*

✓   }
✓   }

✓   }
✓   }

```
void CPointSource2010Dlg::OnSamplekspace()
{

        UpdateData(true);

        int NofXpixels = m_Xpixels, NofYpixels = m_Ypixels;
        double sincx, sincy, complexR, complexI, phase;
        int i, j, index, w;

        double pi = 3.141592;
        double toll = 0.000001;
        // 2010
        const int XobjectHalfSize = ((int)m_objectXSize/2);
        const int YobjectHalfSize = ((int)m_objectYSize/2);
        //2010
        //2010
        double emittingSource = 1.0; // not same as K in OnCalculateSignal();
        emittingSource = ((double)m_lightRate*emittingSource);
        // frequency (1/sec)
        // light (1.0) emitted at m_lightRate per sec. constantly.
        //2010

        // 2010
        double bandwidth = ((double)m_lightRate); // frequency (1/sec)
        // because the emitting source 'emittingsource' is emitting
        // constantly at the rate of m_lightRate per sec.
        double dtx, dty;
        int a, b;
        // 2010

        CString HelpMessage;
        FILE * logfile;
        char logfilename[128]="k-space.log";

        if ( (m_TheSamplingRate > 2.0*m_lightRate) )
        { // 2010
        // sampling the k-space of the signal 'emittingSource' with
        // Whittaker-Shannon interpolation formula
        if ((logfile = fopen(logfilename,"w+"))==NULL)
        {

        // clear memory here not necessary here
         // because this if statement takes place
         // after blocks of memory have not been allocated.
         exit(0);

        } else { // allocate memory and do tests
         //2010
```

```
if ( NofXpixels != NofYpixels || NofXpixels < 17 || NofXpixels > 129 ||
                          NofYpixels < 17 || NofYpixels > 129 )
{// test condition image size

    HelpMessage.Format("%s\n %s\n %s\n %s\n %s\n" , "Please set a Square Image Size", "Between 17
    and 129 Pixels", "The Image Width and Lengh", "must be both powers of 2, plus 1:", "Now Exit");

    MessageBox(HelpMessage);
    // clear memory here not necessary here
    // because this if statement takes place
    // after blocks of memory have not been allocated.

    exit(0);

}// test condition image size

if ( m_objectXSize < 4 || m_objectXSize > 32 || m_objectYSize < 4 || m_objectYSize > 32 )
{// test condition object size

HelpMessage.Format("%s\n %s\n %s\n" , "Please set the Object Half Size", "Between 4 and 32 Pixels",
"Now Exit");

MessageBox(HelpMessage);
// clear memory here not necessary here
// because this if statement takes place
// after blocks of memory have not been allocated.

exit(0);

}// test condition object size

else { // test condition object size (power of 2)

a = ((int)m_objectXSize % 2);
b = ((int)m_objectYSize % 2);

if ( a != 0  || b != 0 )
{// test condition object size even number of pixels

HelpMessage.Format("%s\n %s\n %s\n %s\n" , "Please set a Square or Rectangular", "Object Size with
Width and Lengh", " which must be both powers of 2", "Now Exit");
MessageBox(HelpMessage);
// clear memory here not necessary here
// because this if statement takes place
// after blocks of memory have not been allocated.

exit(0);

}// test condition object size even number of pixels
} // test condition object size (power of 2)

a = ((int)NofXpixels % 2);
b = ((int)NofYpixels % 2);
if ( a == 0  || b == 0 )
{// test condition image size odd number of pixels: powers of 2, plus 1
```

Computer Science Applications

```
        HelpMessage.Format("%s\n %s\n %s\n %s\n" , "Please set a Square Image Size", "The Image Width and
    Lengh", "must be both powers of 2, plus 1", "Now Exit");

            MessageBox(HelpMessage);
            // clear memory here not necessary here
            // because this if statement takes place
            // after blocks of memory have not been allocated.
            exit(0);

        }// test condition image size odd number of pixels: powers of 2, plus 1

        if ((kSpaceR = (double *) calloc( NofXpixels*NofYpixels, sizeof(double)) ) == NULL)
        {
            fprintf(logfile,"%s\n", "Not enough memory to allocate Real Image data: Exit");
            exit(0);
        }
        if ((kSpaceI = (double *) calloc( NofXpixels*NofYpixels, sizeof(double)) ) == NULL)
        {
            fprintf(logfile,"%s\n", "Not enough memory to allocate Real Image data: Exit");
            // FIFO memory deallocation method
            free(kSpaceR);
            exit(0);
        }
        if ((lightSource = (double *) calloc( NofXpixels*NofYpixels, sizeof(double)) ) == NULL)
        {
            fprintf(logfile,"%s\n", "Not enough memory to allocate Real Image data: Exit");
            // FIFO memory deallocation method
            free(kSpaceR);
            free(kSpaceI);
            exit(0);
        }
        if ((sampledSignal = (double *) calloc( NofXpixels*NofYpixels, sizeof(double)) ) == NULL)
        {
            fprintf(logfile,"%s\n", "Not enough memory to allocate Real Image data: Exit");
            // FIFO memory deallocation method
            free(kSpaceR);
            free(kSpaceI);
            free(lightSource);
            exit(0);
        }

            ////initialize pointers
            double number = 0.0;
            for (i=0; i<NofXpixels; i++)
            {
                for (j=0; j<NofYpixels; j++)
                {
                    index = ((j*NofXpixels)+i);
                    *(kSpaceR+index) = (double) 0.0;
                    *(kSpaceI+index) = (double) 0.0;
                    *(sampledSignal+index) = (double)0.0;
                }
            }

        }   ////initialize pointers and do tests

    } // allocate memory and do tests
```

```
/// (1) calculate Light Source as function of space and time
/// (begin)
for (i=0; i<NofXpixels; i++)
{
    for (j=0; j<NofYpixels; j++)
    {

        index = ((j*NofXpixels)+i);
        // 2010
        // Sampling points 'dtx' and 'dty' in the k-space
        // of the object. The sampling points are located
        // in the circle having center at the center of
        // the k-space (the center of the 2D imaging plane).
        // The circle of sampling points has per radius
        // the half diagonal of the object.
        // The circle of sampling points:

// ((double) i - NofXpixels/2.0)*((double) i - NofXpixels/2.0) +
// ((double) j - NofYpixels/2.0)*((double) j - NofYpixels/2.0) =
// (radius*radius);
// 2010
        // The half diagonal of the 2D imaging plane;
        double radius = ((double)sqrt( ((double)NofXpixels*NofXpixels) +
                                ((double)NofYpixels*NofYpixels) ) / 2.0);

// space (pixel coord 'x' on the circle of:
// space and time)

dtx = (double) (NofXpixels/2.0) + sqrt( ((double) radius*radius - ((double) j –
                NofYpixels/2.0)*((double) j - NofYpixels/2.0) ) );
dtx *= ((double)emittingSource);
// space (pixel) / time (sec) =
// space (pixel) * frequency (1/sec)
// space (pixel coord 'y' on the circle of:
// space and time)

dty = (double) (NofYpixels/2.0) + sqrt( ((double) radius*radius - ((double) i –
                NofXpixels/2.0)*((double) i - NofXpixels/2.0) ) );
dty *= ((double)emittingSource);
// space (pixel) / time (sec) =
// space (pixel) * frequency (1/sec)
// circular (x, y) point of space and time

double d = (double) sqrt( ((double) dtx * dtx) + ((double) dty * dty) );

        // 2010
        // Circular Light as function of
        // space and time. The front wave of light
        // in the 2D space imaging plane is composed of
        // points. The origin of the light is
        // located at the  center of the 2D space plane.
        // The light is emitting at the rate:
        // 'emittingSource' = emittingsource * m_lightRate,
        // per seconds.
        // Anywhere in the 2D plane the point of light
        // is distant from the center of:
```

```
                    // 'd' =((double) sqrt( ((double) dtx * dtx) +
                    //                    ((double) dty * dty) );
                    // 'd' is the radius of the circle:
                    // ((double)2.0 * pi * d)
                    *(lightSource+index) = ((double)2.0 * pi * d);
                    // 2010


            }
    } /// (1) calculate Light Source as function of space and time
     // (end)
    //2010
        int di ,dj;
        double dx, dy;


    // (2) Whittaker-Shannon sampling in space-time  (begin)//////
    // Build the space-time dimension (called k-space)
        for (i=0; i<NofXpixels; i++)
        { ////Sample Signal
            for (j=0; j<NofYpixels; j++)
            {

            di = ((int) i - NofXpixels/2);
            dj = ((int) j - NofYpixels/2);

            dtx = ((double)((int) i - NofXpixels/2) * m_TheSamplingRate); //space (pixel) * frequency (1/sec)
            dty = ((double)((int) j - NofYpixels/2) * m_TheSamplingRate); //space (pixel) * frequency (1/sec)

            index = ((j*NofXpixels)+i);

            *(sampledSignal+index) = (double)0.0;

            /// (2) Whittaker-Shannon interpolation formula
            dx = (double) pi * (2.0 * bandwidth * di - dtx);
            // Where 2.0 * bandwidth * di is:
            // frequency (1/sec) * space (pixel)
            dy = (double) pi * (2.0 * bandwidth * dj - dty);
            //  2.0 * bandwidth * dj is:
            // frequency (1/sec) * space (pixel)

            if ( (double)fabs( (double) dx ) > toll )
            sincx = (double) sin( (double) dx ) /  ((double) dx);

            else sincx = (double)1.0;

            if ( (double)fabs( (double) dy ) > toll )

            sincy = (double) sin( (double) dy ) /  ((double) dy);

            else sincy = (double)1.0;
            // The front wave (lightSource) is Circular.
            // Whittaker-Shannon sampling happppens on the
            // entire 2D imaging plane, which is space-time.
            // In this specific case, sampling takes place
            // in the space-time plane.

            *(sampledSignal+index) =
            ((double) *(lightSource + ((j*NofXpixels)+i) ) * sincx * sincy );
```

```
            /// (2) Whittaker-Shannon interpolation formula
                    }
        }
///// (2) Whittaker-Shannon sampling in space-time  (end)//////
//2010
/// (3) FT the space-time dimension (called k-space) to obtain
///  the FT of the k-space of the non uniform signal: (Circular Light).
/// (begin)
int k2, ds, dp, k3, t;

///// Fourier Transform //////
for (i=0; i<NofXpixels; i++)
{ ///calculate k-space data
    for (j=0; j<NofYpixels; j++)
       {
           dx = ((int) i - NofXpixels/2);
           dy = ((int) j - NofYpixels/2);

           k2 = ((int)(dx*NofYpixels)+dy);
           w = ((j*NofXpixels)+i);

           for (int s=0; s<NofXpixels; s++)
           { ///calculate k-space data
               for (int p=0; p<NofYpixels; p++)
               {
                   ds = ((int) s - NofXpixels/2);
                   dp = ((int) p - NofYpixels/2);

                   k3 = ((int)(dp*NofXpixels)+ds);

                   t = ((p*NofXpixels)+s);

// Fourier Theory demonstrates that given
// signal can be decomposed in an infinite
// sum of cosine and sine waves having 'phase'
// as argument. Euler formula permits to
// formalize Fourier Theory and associates
// the cosine to the real part of the single
// wave, and the sine to the imaginary part
// of the single wave. Thus 'phase' necessitates
// because of Euler formula, such to create
// the imaginary component.
phase = ((double) 2.0 * pi * k2 * k3 / (NofXpixels*NofYpixels) );

complexR = (double) cos( phase );
complexI = - (double) sin( phase );

*(kSpaceR+w) += (double) *(sampledSignal+t) * complexR;

*(kSpaceI+w) += (double) *(sampledSignal+t) * complexI;

               }
           }
        }
} ///// (3) FT the space-time dimension (called k-space)
//// to obtain the FT of the k-space (end)
```

```
double savedata = 0.0;
FILE * pf;
char filename[128];

sprintf(filename, "%s", "CircularLight.img");

fprintf(logfile, "%s\n%s\t%s\t\n", "Now Saving Circular Light Decaying",
                                    "as Function of Space and Time in File: ", filename);

if ((pf = fopen(filename,"wb+"))==NULL)
{
fprintf(logfile, "%s\n", "Cannot open file to save Light Signal");
// FIFO memory deallocation method
free(kSpaceR);
free(kSpaceI);
free(lightSource);
free(sampledSignal);
exit(0);
} else { // save data

for (i=0; i<NofXpixels; i++)
{ ///save k-space data
    for (j=0; j<NofYpixels; j++)
    {
        index = ((j*NofXpixels)+i);
        savedata = (double)*(lightSource+index);
        fwrite(&savedata,sizeof(double),1,pf);
    }
} ///save Light

fprintf(logfile,"%s\n", "Light Signal Saved");
fclose (pf);
} // save data
sprintf(filename, "%s", "SampledLight.img");

fprintf(logfile, "%s\n%s\t%s\t\n", "Now Saving Sampled Circular Light Decaying", "as Function of Space
and Time in File: ", filename);

if ((pf = fopen(filename,"wb+"))==NULL)
{

fprintf(logfile, "%s\n", "Cannot open file to save Sampled Light Signal");
// FIFO memory deallocation method
    free(kSpaceR);
    free(kSpaceI);
    free(lightSource);
    free(sampledSignal);
    exit(0);

} else { // save data

for (i=0; i<NofXpixels; i++)
{ ///save k-space data
    for (j=0; j<NofYpixels; j++)
    {
        index = ((j*NofXpixels)+i);
```

```
        savedata = (double)*(sampledSignal+index);
        fwrite(&savedata,sizeof(double),1,pf);
    }
} ///save Sampled Light

fprintf(logfile,"%s\n", "Sampled Light Signal Saved: This is k-space");

fclose (pf);
} // save data

sprintf(filename, "%s", "k-SpaceSamplingR.img");

fprintf(logfile, "%s\t%s\n", "Now Saving K-Space Signal (Real) in File: ", filename);

if ((pf = fopen(filename,"wb+"))==NULL)
{
 fprintf(logfile, "%s\n", "Cannot open file to save k-Space Signal (Real)");

    // FIFO memory deallocation method
    free(kSpaceR);
    free(kSpaceI);
    free(lightSource);
    free(sampledSignal);
    exit(0);
} else { // save data

for (i=0; i<NofXpixels; i++)
{ ///save k-space data
    for (j=0; j<NofYpixels; j++)
    {
        index = ((j*NofXpixels)+i);
        savedata = (double)*(kSpaceR+index);
        fwrite(&savedata,sizeof(double),1,pf);
    }
} ///save k-space data

fprintf(logfile,"%s\n", "k-Space Signal (Real) Saved");

fclose (pf);
} // save data

sprintf(filename, "%s", "k-SpaceSamplingI.img");
fprintf(logfile, "%s\t%s\n", "Now Saving K-Space Signal (Imaginary) in File: ", filename);
if ((pf = fopen(filename,"wb+"))==NULL)
{
 fprintf(logfile, "%s\n", "Cannot open file to save k-Space Signal (Imaginary)");

    // FIFO memory deallocation method
    free(kSpaceR);
    free(kSpaceI);
    free(lightSource);
    free(sampledSignal);
    exit(0);

} else { // save data
```

```
        for (i=0; i<NofXpixels; i++)
        { ///save k-space data
            for (j=0; j<NofYpixels; j++)
            {
                index = ((j*NofXpixels)+i);
                savedata = (double)*(kSpaceI+index);
                fwrite(&savedata,sizeof(double),1,pf);
            }
        } ///save k-space data

        fprintf(logfile,"%s\n", "k-Space Signal (Imaginary) Saved");
        fclose (pf);
        } // save data

        fprintf(logfile,"%s\n", "Processing Completed");
        fclose(logfile);
        system( logfilename );
            // FIFO memory deallocation method
            free(kSpaceR);
            free(kSpaceI);
            free(lightSource);
            free(sampledSignal);

        }// 2010
        else{
            HelpMessage.Format("%s\n %s\n %s\n %s\n %s\n" , "Please make sure that" , "lightRate and The Sam-
            plingRate", "fulfill the Nyquist Theorem." , "Rerun before proceeding" ,"to signal reconstruction");
            MessageBox(HelpMessage);
            }

}
```

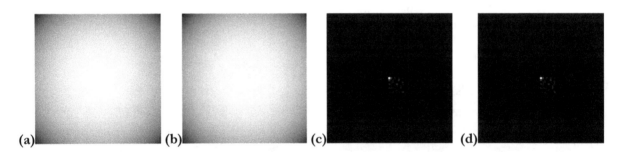

(a)   (b)   (c)   (d)

Figure 6: The circular light is generated and shown in (a). The sampled light (b) is obtained calculating the Whittaker-Shannon interpolation formula [2-4] on the source of light shown in (a). The direct Fourier transformation of the light seen in (b) yields the real and imaginary components of the k-Space as shown in (c) and (d) respectively.

The method *void CPointSource2010Dlg::OnReconstructObject()* is used to recontruct in image space an object which components are given in the real and imaginary parts in k-Space. The inverse Fourier transformation is the algorithm implemented here which accepts real and imaginary parts of the object ('*kSpaceR*' and '*kSpaceI*') and releases the output '*reconSignal*'. The method *void CPointSource2010Dlg::OnReconstructObject()* is called in when the user pushes the button '*Reconstruct*' of the Graphical User Interface.

Details of the inverse Fourier transformation were given above and herein recalled. The phase is calculated on a pixel-by-pixel basis with the formula: '*phase = ((double) 2.0 * pi * k2 * k3 / (NofXpixels*NofYpixels))*', which requires the calculation of '*k2*' and '*k3*' also on a pixel-by-pixel basis. Specifically, '*dx = ((int) i - NofXpixels/2)*' and '*dy = ((int) j - NofYpixels/2)*' are necessary to compute '*k2 = ((int)(dx*NofYpixels)+dy)*' and '*ds = ((int) s - NofXpixels/2)*' and '*dp = ((int) p - NofYpixels/2)*' are necessary to compute '*k3 = ((int)(dp*NofXpixels)+ds)*'. Once the phase is known, computing proceeds with the calculation of the summations of the real and imaginary components across the spectrum: '*real += (double)*

*(kSpaceR+t) * cos((double) phase)' and '*imaginary -= (double) *(kSpaceI+t) * sin((double) phase)*'. And the calculation of the reconstructed signal: '**(reconSignal+w) = ((double) sqrt(((double)real*real + (double)imaginary*imaginary)))*'. Since the sum comprises of the entire spatial extent of the planar image, the reconstructed signal needs scaling through the division of '**(reconSignal + w)*' by the factor '*scale = ((double)m_Xpixels*m_Ypixels*emittingSource)*'.

void CPointSource2010Dlg::OnReconstructObject()

```
{
        UpdateData(true);

        int NofXpixels = m_Xpixels, NofYpixels = m_Ypixels;
        int i, j, index;
        int dx, dy;
        int ds, dp;
        int k2, k3, w, t;
        double pi = 3.141592;
        double phase;
        //2010
        double emittingSource = 1.0; // not the same as K in OnCalculateSignal();
        double scale = ((double)m_Xpixels*m_Ypixels*emittingSource);
        //2010
        FILE * logfile;
        char logfilename[128]="k-space-INV-FourierT.log";

        CString HelpMessage;

        if ((logfile = fopen(logfilename,"w+"))==NULL)
        {
         // clear memory here not necessary here
         // because this if statement takes place
         // after blocks of memory have not been allocated.
         exit(0);
        } else { // allocate memory

            // 2010
            // Signal reconstruction is calculated with data used with
            // the Sample K-Space, thus please make sure that data
            // now located in the edit boxes is consistent with
            // data used to sample the k-space.

        HelpMessage.Format("%s\n %s\n %s\n %s\n" , "Signal reconstruction is calculated with data used with" ,
        "the Sample K-Space, thus please make sure that data", "now located in the edit boxes is consistent with", "data
        used to sample the k-space.");
        MessageBox(HelpMessage);
        //2010

        if ((kSpaceR = (double *) calloc( NofXpixels*NofYpixels, sizeof(double)) ) == NULL)
        {
            fprintf(logfile,"%s\n", "Not enough memory to allocate Real Image data: Exit");
            exit(0);
        }

        if ((kSpaceI = (double *) calloc( NofXpixels*NofYpixels, sizeof(double)) ) == NULL)
        {
            fprintf(logfile,"%s\n", "Not enough memory to allocate Real Image data: Exit");
            // FIFO memory deallocation method
            free(kSpaceR);
```

53

```
            exit(0);
      }

      if ((reconSignal = (double *) calloc( NofXpixels*NofYpixels, sizeof(double)) ) == NULL)
      {
          fprintf(logfile,"%s\n", "Not enough memory to allocate Imaginary Image data: Exit");
          // FIFO memory deallocation method
          free(kSpaceR);
          free(kSpaceI);
          exit(0);
      }
} // allocate memory
//// read image data and initialize pointers
FILE *image;
char imageFilename[128];

sprintf(imageFilename, "%s", "k-SpaceSamplingR.img");

if ((image = fopen(imageFilename,"rb+"))==NULL)
{
 fprintf(logfile, "%s%s\n", "Cannot open Image File: ", imageFilename);
  // FIFO memory deallocation method
 free(kSpaceR);
 free(kSpaceI);
 free(reconSignal);
 exit(0);

} else { // read data and initialize pointers
double number = 0.0;

     for (i=0; i<NofXpixels; i++)
     {
         for (j=0; j<NofYpixels; j++)
         {
             index = ((j*NofXpixels)+i);
             fread(&number,sizeof(double),1,image);
             *(kSpaceR+index) = (double) number;
         }

     }

     fclose(image);
 }// read data and initialize pointers

char imageFilename2[128];
sprintf(imageFilename2, "%s", "k-SpaceSamplingI.img");

 if ((image = fopen(imageFilename2,"rb+"))==NULL)
 {
 fprintf(logfile, "%s%s\n", "Cannot open Image File: ", imageFilename2);
 // FIFO memory deallocation method
 free(kSpaceR);
 free(kSpaceI);
 free(reconSignal);
 exit(0);
 } else { // read data and initialize pointers
```

```
        double number = 0.0;
        for (i=0; i<NofXpixels; i++)
        {
            for (j=0; j<NofYpixels; j++)
            {
                index = ((j*NofXpixels)+i);
                fread(&number,sizeof(double),1,image);
                *(kSpaceI+index) = (double) number;
            }

        }
        fclose(image);
        for (i=0; i<NofXpixels; i++)
        {
            for (j=0; j<NofYpixels; j++)
            {
                index = ((j*NofXpixels)+i);
                *(reconSignal+index)= (double)0.0;
            }
        }
}// read data and initialize pointers
double real = 0.0, imaginary = 0.0;

///// INV Fourier Transform //////
for (i=0; i<NofXpixels; i++)
{ ///process k-space data
    for (j=0; j<NofYpixels; j++)
    {
    dx = ((int) i - NofXpixels/2);
    dy = ((int) j - NofYpixels/2);

    k2 = ((int)(dx*NofYpixels)+dy);

    w = ((j*NofXpixels)+i);

    real = 0.0;
    imaginary = 0.0;

    for (int s=0; s<NofXpixels; s++)
    { ///process k-space data
        for (int p=0; p<NofYpixels; p++)
        {

    ds = ((int) s - NofXpixels/2);
    dp = ((int) p - NofYpixels/2);

    k3 = ((int)(dp*NofXpixels)+ds);

    t = ((p*NofXpixels)+s);

    phase = ((double) 2.0 * pi * k2 * k3 / (NofXpixels*NofYpixels) );

    // this 'phase' is conceptually the same as that seen
    // in OnSamplekSpace(), because Euler formula necessitates it.

    real += (double) *(kSpaceR+t) * cos( (double) phase );
```

```
            imaginary -= (double) *(kSpaceI+t) * sin( (double) phase );


         }
      }///process k-space data
      *(reconSignal+w) = ((double) sqrt( ((double)real*real + (double)imaginary*imaginary) ) );

      *(reconSignal+w) /= (double)scale;


    }
} ///process k-space data

///// INV Fourier Transform //////
double savedata = 0.0;
FILE * pf;
char filename[128];

sprintf(filename, "%s", "k-space-reconSignal.img");
fprintf(logfile, "%s\t%s\n", "Now Saving Reconstructed Signal in File: ", filename);

if ((pf = fopen(filename,"wb+"))==NULL)
{
 fprintf(logfile, "%s\n", "Cannot open file to save K-Space Signal");
 // FIFO memory deallocation method
 free(kSpaceR);
 free(kSpaceI);
 free(reconSignal);
 exit(0);
} else { // save data

for (i=0; i<NofXpixels; i++)
{ ///save k-space data
    for (j=0; j<NofYpixels; j++)
    {
        index = ((j*NofXpixels)+i);
        savedata = (double)*(reconSignal+index);
        fwrite(&savedata,sizeof(double),1,pf);
    }
} ///save k-space data
fprintf(logfile,"%s\n", "Reconstructed Signal Saved");
fclose (pf);
} // save data
    fprintf(logfile,"%s\n", "Processing Completed");
    fclose(logfile);
    system( logfilename );

// FIFO memory deallocation method
free(kSpaceR);
free(kSpaceI);
free(reconSignal);


}
```

Figure 7: The circular light shown in Fig. 6.a is reconstructed through the real and imaginary components of the k-Space shown in Fig. 6.c and 6.d.

The method *void CPointSource2010Dlg::OnSampleEllipticalLight()* is employed once the user pushes the button named '*Sample (Elliptical)*' and it differs from the push button '*Sample (Circular)*', because the front wave of light is elliptical. The push button named '*Sample (Circular)*' calls in the method previously seen *void CPointSource2010Dlg::OnSamplekspace().*

The functionality in the method *void CPointSource2010Dlg::OnSampleEllipticalLight()* is quite similar to that seen already in *void CPointSource2010Dlg::OnSamplekspace()* and so the order of processing is (i) Generation of a light source which is elliptical in its front wave:

- ✓ '**(lightSource+index) = (double) emittingSource * ((double) 1.0 / (1.0 + (d*d)))*'

- ✓ '*d = ((double) (((double) ((double) i - NofXpixels/2.0)/(ax*ax))**
  ((double) ((double) i - NofXpixels/2.0)/(ax*ax))
) +
  (((double) ((double) j - NofYpixels/2.0)/(bx*bx))*
  ((double) ((double) j - NofYpixels/2.0)/(bx*bx))
  ))'

- ✓ '*double ax = (double)m_ex/2.0*'

- ✓ '*double bx = (double)m_ey/2.0*'

(ii) Sampling takes place with the Whittaker-Shannon interpolation formula inside the object defined as: '*i <= ((int)NofXpixels/2.0 + (int)objectXSize) && i >= ((int)NofXpixels/2.0 - (int)objectXSize) && j <= ((int)NofYpixels/2.0 + (int)objectYSize) && j >= ((int)NofYpixels/2.0 - (int)objectYSize)*' (setting the elliptical front wave and giving '*dx*' and '*dy*' as input to the Sinc functions):

- ✓ '*dx = (double) pi * (2.0 * bandwidth * dti - dtx)*'

- ✓ '*dy = (double) pi * (2.0 * bandwidth * dtj - dty)*'

- ✓ '*dtj = sqrt((double) (bx*bx) * yEllipse)*'

- ✓ '*dti = sqrt((double) (ax*ax) * xEllipse)*'

- ✓ '*dtx = ((double) dti * m_TheSamplingRate)*'

- ✓ '*dty = ((double) dtj * m_TheSamplingRate)*'
- ✓ '*double xEllipse = ((double) 1.0 - (((double) ((double) j - NofYpixels/2.0)/(bx*bx))**
  ((double) ((double) j - NofYpixels/2.0)/(bx*bx))))'

- ✓ '*double yEllipse =((double) 1.0 - (((double) ((double) i - NofXpixels/2.0)/(ax*ax))**
  ((double) ((double) i - NofXpixels/2.0)/(ax*ax))))'
- ✓ '*double ax = (double)m_ex/2.0*'

- ✓ '*double bx = (double)m_ey/2.0*'

- ✓ '**(sampledSignal+w) = ((double) *(lightSource + w) * sincx * sincy)*'

(iii) Direct Fourier transformation of the sampled signal and related determination of the real and imaginary part of the k-Space signal (which is shown in Figs. 8.a and 8.b):

Computer Science Applications

- ✓ '$dx = ((int) \, i - NofXpixels/2)$'

- ✓ '$dy = ((int) \, j - NofYpixels/2)$'

- ✓ '$k2 = ((int)(dx*NofYpixels)+dy)$'

- ✓ '$ds = ((int) \, s - NofXpixels/2)$'

- ✓ '$dp = ((int) \, p - NofYpixels/2)$'

- ✓ '$k3 = ((int)(dp*NofXpixels)+ds)$'

- ✓ '$phase = ((double) \, 2.0 * pi * k2 * k3 \, / \, (NofXpixels*NofYpixels) \,)$'

- ✓ '$complexR = (double) \, cos(\, phase \,)$'

- ✓ '$complexI = -(double) \, sin(\, phase \,)$'

- ✓ '$*(kSpaceR+w) \mathrel{+}= (double) \, *(sampledSignal+t) * complexR$'

- ✓ '$*(kSpaceI+w) \mathrel{+}= (double) \, *(sampledSignal+t) * complexI$'

At this point the real and imaginary part of the signal can be summed up and saved into the output files.

void CPointSource2010Dlg::OnSampleEllipticalLight()

```
{

        UpdateData(true);
        int NofXpixels = m_Xpixels, NofYpixels = m_Ypixels;
        double sincx, sincy, complexR, complexI, phase;
        int i, j, index, w;

        double pi = 3.141592;
        double toll = 0.000001;
        int a, b;
        // 2010
        int objectXSize = ((int)m_objectXSize/2);
        int objectYSize = ((int)m_objectYSize/2);
        // 2010
        //2010
        double emittingSource = 1.0;
        emittingSource = ((double)m_lightRate*emittingSource);
        // frequency (1/sec)
        // light (1.0) emitted at m_lightRate per sec. constantly.
        //2010

        // 2010
        double bandwidth = ((double)m_lightRate); // frequency (1/sec)
        // because the emitting source 'emittingsource' is emitting
        // constantly at the rate of m_lightRate per sec.
        double dtx, dty;
        double dx, dy;
        double dtj, dti;
```

```
// 2010
CString HelpMessage;
FILE * logfile;
char logfilename[128]="k-space.log";

if ( (m_TheSamplingRate > 2.0*m_lightRate) )
{ // 2010
// sampling the k-space of the signal 'emittingSource' with
// Whittaker-Shannon interpolation formula
if ((logfile = fopen(logfilename,"w+"))==NULL)
{
 // clear memory here not necessary here
 // because this if statement takes place
 // after blocks of memory have not been allocated.
 exit(0);

} else { // allocate memory and do tests

//2010
if ( NofXpixels != NofYpixels || NofXpixels < 17 || NofXpixels > 129 ||
                                 NofYpixels < 17 || NofYpixels > 129 )
{// test condition image size

HelpMessage.Format("%s\n %s\n %s\n %s\n %s\n" , "Please set a Square Image Size", "Between 17 and
129 Pixels", "The Image Width and Lengh", "must be both powers of 2, plus 1:", "Now Exit");
   MessageBox(HelpMessage);

   // clear memory here not necessary here
   // because this if statement takes place
   // after blocks of memory have not been allocated.
   exit(0);

}// test condition image size

if ( m_objectXSize < 4 || m_objectXSize > 32 || m_objectYSize < 4 || m_objectYSize > 32 )
{// test condition object size

HelpMessage.Format("%s\n %s\n %s\n" , "Please set the Object Half Size", "Between 4 and 32 Pixels",
"Now Exit");

MessageBox(HelpMessage);
// clear memory here not necessary here
// because this if statement takes place
// after blocks of memory have not been allocated.
exit(0);
}// test condition object size

else { // test condition object size (power of 2)

a = ((int)m_objectXSize % 2);
b = ((int)m_objectYSize % 2);

 if ( a != 0  || b != 0 )
 {// test condition object size even number of pixels
```

```
        HelpMessage.Format("%s\n %s\n %s\n %s\n" , "Please set a Square or Rectangular", "Object Size with
        Width and Lengh", " which must be both powers of 2", "Now Exit");
        MessageBox(HelpMessage);

        // clear memory here not necessary here
        // because this if statement takes place
        // after blocks of memory have not been allocated.
        exit(0);

        }// test condition object size even number of pixels
        } // test condition object size (power of 2)
        a = ((int)NofXpixels % 2);
        b = ((int)NofYpixels % 2);

        if ( a == 0  || b == 0 )
        {// test condition image size odd number of pixels: powers of 2, plus 1

        HelpMessage.Format("%s\n %s\n %s\n %s\n" , "Please set a Square Image Size", "The Image Width and
        Lengh", "must be both powers of 2, plus 1", "Now Exit");

            MessageBox(HelpMessage);

            // clear memory here not necessary here
            // because this if statement takes place
            // after blocks of memory have not been allocated.
               exit(0);
        }// test condition image size odd number of pixels: powers of 2, plus 1
        if ((kSpaceR = (double *) calloc( NofXpixels*NofYpixels, sizeof(double)) ) == NULL)
        {
            fprintf(logfile,"%s\n", "Not enough memory to allocate Real Image data: Exit");
            exit(0);
        }
        if ((kSpaceI = (double *) calloc( NofXpixels*NofYpixels, sizeof(double)) ) == NULL)
        {
            fprintf(logfile,"%s\n", "Not enough memory to allocate Real Image data: Exit");
            // FIFO memory deallocation method
            free(kSpaceR);
            exit(0);
        }
        if ((lightSource = (double *) calloc( NofXpixels*NofYpixels, sizeof(double)) ) == NULL)
        {
            fprintf(logfile,"%s\n", "Not enough memory to allocate Real Image data: Exit");
            // FIFO memory deallocation method
            free(kSpaceR);
            free(kSpaceI);
            exit(0);
        }
        if ((sampledSignal = (double *) calloc( NofXpixels*NofYpixels, sizeof(double)) ) == NULL)
        {
            fprintf(logfile,"%s\n", "Not enough memory to allocate Real Image data: Exit");
            // FIFO memory deallocation method
            free(kSpaceR);
            free(kSpaceI);
            free(lightSource);
            exit(0);
        }
            ////initialize pointers
```

```
    double number = 0.0;
    for (i=0; i<NofXpixels; i++)
    {
        for (j=0; j<NofYpixels; j++)
        {
            index = ((j*NofXpixels)+i);
            *(kSpaceR+index) = (double) 0.0;
            *(kSpaceI+index) = (double) 0.0;
            *(sampledSignal+index) = (double)0.0;
        }

    }   ////initialize pointers and do tests
} // allocate memory and do tests
    double d;
    /// Ellipse
    double ax = (double)m_ex/2.0;
    double bx = (double)m_ey/2.0;
/// (1) calculate Light Source as function of space and time
/// (begin)
for (i=0; i<NofXpixels; i++)
{
    for (j=0; j<NofYpixels; j++)
    {
    index = ((j*NofXpixels)+i);

    /// The front wave (lightSource) is Elliptical.
    double xEllipse = ( (double) 1.0*1.0 -
    ( ((double) ((double) j - NofYpixels/2.0)/(bx*bx))*
      ((double) ((double) j - NofYpixels/2.0)/(bx*bx)) ) );

    double yEllipse = ( (double) 1.0*1.0 -
    ( ((double) ((double) i - NofXpixels/2.0)/(ax*ax))*
      ((double) ((double) i - NofXpixels/2.0)/(ax*ax)) ) );

    if ( yEllipse < 0 ) yEllipse = - yEllipse;
    else if ( yEllipse >= 0 ) double yEllipse = yEllipse;

    if ( xEllipse < 0 ) xEllipse = - xEllipse;
    else if ( xEllipse >= 0 ) double xEllipse = xEllipse;

    // space (pixel coord 'y' on the ellipse)
    dtj =  sqrt( (double) (bx*bx) * yEllipse );

    // space (pixel coord 'x' on the ellipse)
    dti =  sqrt( (double) (ax*ax) * xEllipse );
    /// Ellipse

    d = ((double) ( ((double) ((double) i - NofXpixels/2.0)/(ax*ax))*
                ((double) ((double) i - NofXpixels/2.0)/(ax*ax))
            ) +
            ( ((double) ((double) j - NofYpixels/2.0)/(bx*bx))*
                ((double) ((double) j - NofYpixels/2.0)/(bx*bx))
            ));

        // 2010
        // Elliptical Light as function of
```

```
            // space and time. The front wave of light
            // in the 2D space imaging plane is composed of
            // points. The origin of the light is
            // located at the  center of the 2D space plane.
            // The light is emitting at the rate:
            // 'emittingSource' = emittingsource * m_lightRate,
            // per seconds.
            *(lightSource+index) = (double) emittingSource * ( (double) 1.0 / (1.0 + (d*d)) );
            // 2010

        }
    } /// calculate Light Source as function of space and time
     /// (end)


        //2010
        /// (2) Whittaker-Shannon sampling in space-time //////
        /// Build the space-time dimension (called k-space)
        /// (begin)
        for (i=0; i<NofXpixels; i++)
        { ////Sample Signal

            for (j=0; j<NofYpixels; j++)
            {
        w = ((j*NofXpixels)+i);

        /// Ellipse
        double xEllipse = ( (double) 1.0 -
        ( ((double) ((double) j - NofYpixels/2.0)/(bx*bx))*
          ((double) ((double) j - NofYpixels/2.0)/(bx*bx))
        ) );

        double yEllipse = ( (double) 1.0 -
        ( ((double) ((double) i - NofXpixels/2.0)/(ax*ax))*
          ((double) ((double) i - NofXpixels/2.0)/(ax*ax))
        ) );
        if ( yEllipse < 0 ) yEllipse = - yEllipse;
        else if ( yEllipse >= 0 ) double yEllipse = yEllipse;

        if ( xEllipse < 0 ) xEllipse = - xEllipse;
        else if ( xEllipse >= 0 ) double xEllipse = xEllipse;

        // space (pixel coord 'y' on the ellipse)
        dtj = sqrt( (double) (bx*bx) * yEllipse );
        // space (pixel coord 'x' on the ellipse)
        dti = sqrt( (double) (ax*ax) * xEllipse );
        /// Ellipse

        dtx = ((double) dti * m_TheSamplingRate);
        //space (pixel) * frequency (1/sec)

        dty = ((double) dtj * m_TheSamplingRate);
        //space (pixel) * frequency (1/sec)
        /// Ellipse

        if ( i <= ((int)NofXpixels/2.0 + (int)objectXSize) &&

            i >= ((int)NofXpixels/2.0 - (int)objectXSize) &&
```

```
        j <= ((int)NofYpixels/2.0 + (int)objectYSize) &&

        j >= ((int)NofYpixels/2.0 - (int)objectYSize) )
        { // size the object

        /// (2) Whittaker-Shannon interpolation formula
        dx = (double) pi * (2.0 * bandwidth * dti - dtx);
        dy = (double) pi * (2.0 * bandwidth * dtj - dty);
        // Where 2.0 * bandwidth * di is: frequency (1/sec) * space (pixel)
        // 2.0 * bandwidth * dj is: frequency (1/sec) * space (pixel)

        if ( (double)fabs( (double) dx ) > toll )

        sincx = (double) sin( (double) dx ) /  ((double) dx);

        else sincx = (double)1.0;

        if ( (double)fabs( (double) dy ) > toll )

        sincy = (double) sin( (double) dy ) /  ((double) dy);
        else sincy = (double)1.0;

        // The front wave (lightSource) is Elliptical.
        // Whittaker-Shannon sampling happpens on the
        // spatial extent of the object size on the
        // 2D imaging plane, which is space-time.

        // sampling happens on elliptical paths:
        // (see: Ellipse)

*(sampledSignal+w) = ((double) *(lightSource + w) * sincx * sincy );
/// (2) Whittaker-Shannon interpolation formula

} else { // size the object

        *(sampledSignal+w) = (double) 0.0;

}// size the object

        }

    }   /// (2) Whittaker-Shannon sampling in space-time //////
        /// (end)
 //2010

/// (3) FT the space-time dimension (called k-space)
/// to obtain the FT of the k-space (begin)
int k2, ds, dp, k3, t;

///// Fourier Transform //////
for (i=0; i<NofXpixels; i++)
{ ///calculate k-space data
    for (j=0; j<NofYpixels; j++)
    {
        dx = ((int) i - NofXpixels/2);
        dy = ((int) j - NofYpixels/2);
```

```
            k2 = ((int)(dx*NofYpixels)+dy);

            w = ((j*NofXpixels)+i);

            for (int s=0; s<NofXpixels; s++)
            { ///calculate k-space data
                for (int p=0; p<NofYpixels; p++)
                {

                ds = ((int) s - NofXpixels/2);
                dp = ((int) p - NofYpixels/2);

                k3 = ((int)(dp*NofXpixels)+ds);

                t = ((p*NofXpixels)+s);
```

```
// Fourier Theory demonstrates that given
// signal can be decomposed in an infinite
// sum of cosine and sine waves having 'phase'
// as argument. Euler formula permits to
// formalize Fourier Theory and associates
// the cosine to the real part of the single
// wave, and the sine to the imaginary part
// of the single wave. Thus 'phase' necessitates
// because of Euler formula, such to create
// the imaginary component.
// 'phase' is the same to cosine and sine,
// which are de-phased of pi/2.

phase = ((double) 2.0 * pi * k2 * k3 / (NofXpixels*NofYpixels) );

complexR = (double) cos( phase );

complexI = -(double) sin( phase );

*(kSpaceR+w) += (double) *(sampledSignal+t) * complexR;

*(kSpaceI+w) += (double) *(sampledSignal+t) * complexI;

    }///calculate k-space data

}///calculate k-space data

    }
} ///calculate k-space data
/// (3) FT the space-time dimension (called k-space)
/// to obtain the FT of the k-space (end)

double savedata = 0.0;
FILE * pf;
char filename[128];
sprintf(filename, "%s", "EllipticalLight.img");
fprintf(logfile, "%s\n%s\t%s\t\n", "Now Saving Elliptical Light", "as Function of Space and Time in File: ",
filename);

if ((pf = fopen(filename,"wb+"))==NULL)
```

```
            {
            fprintf(logfile, "%s\n", "Cannot open file to save Light Signal");
                    // FIFO memory deallocation method
                    free(kSpaceR);
                    free(kSpaceI);
                    free(lightSource);
                    free(sampledSignal);
                    exit(0);
            } else { // save data

            for (i=0; i<NofXpixels; i++)
            { ///save k-space data
                    for (j=0; j<NofYpixels; j++)
                    {
                        index = ((j*NofXpixels)+i);
                        savedata = (double)*(lightSource+index);
                        fwrite(&savedata,sizeof(double),1,pf);
                    }
            } ///save Light
            fprintf(logfile,"%s\n", "Light Signal Saved");

            fclose (pf);
            } // save data

            sprintf(filename, "%s", "SampledLight.img");
            fprintf(logfile, "%s\n%s\t%s\t\n", "Now Saving Sampled Circular Light Decaying", "as Function of Space
                        and Time in File: ", filename);
            if ((pf = fopen(filename,"wb+"))==NULL)
            {
            fprintf(logfile, "%s\n", "Cannot open file to save Sampled Light Signal");
                    // FIFO memory deallocation method
                    free(kSpaceR);
                    free(kSpaceI);
                    free(lightSource);
                    free(sampledSignal);
                    exit(0);
            } else { // save data

            for (i=0; i<NofXpixels; i++)
            { ///save k-space data
                    for (j=0; j<NofYpixels; j++)
                    {
                        index = ((j*NofXpixels)+i);
                        savedata = (double)*(sampledSignal+index);
                        fwrite(&savedata,sizeof(double),1,pf);
                    }
            } ///save Sampled Light

            fprintf(logfile,"%s\n", "Sampled Light Signal Saved: This is k-space");

            fclose (pf);
            } // save data

            sprintf(filename, "%s", "k-SpaceSamplingR.img");
            fprintf(logfile, "%s\t%s\n", "Now Saving K-Space Signal (Real) in File: ", filename);
```

Computer Science Applications

```c
if ((pf = fopen(filename,"wb+"))==NULL)
{
fprintf(logfile, "%s\n", "Cannot open file to save k-Space Signal (Real)");
    // FIFO memory deallocation method
    free(kSpaceR);
    free(kSpaceI);
    free(lightSource);
    free(sampledSignal);
    exit(0);
} else { // save data
for (i=0; i<NofXpixels; i++)
{ ///save k-space data
    for (j=0; j<NofYpixels; j++)
    {
        index = ((j*NofXpixels)+i);
        savedata = (double)*(kSpaceR+index);
        fwrite(&savedata,sizeof(double),1,pf);
    }
} ///save k-space data
fprintf(logfile,"%s\n", "k-Space Signal (Real) Saved");
fclose (pf);
} // save data

sprintf(filename, "%s", "k-SpaceSamplingI.img");

fprintf(logfile, "%s\t%s\n", "Now Saving K-Space Signal (Imaginary) in File: ", filename);
if ((pf = fopen(filename,"wb+"))==NULL)
{
    fprintf(logfile, "%s\n", "Cannot open file to save k-Space Signal (Imaginary)");
    // FIFO memory deallocation method
    free(kSpaceR);
    free(kSpaceI);
    free(lightSource);
    free(sampledSignal);
    exit(0);
} else { // save data

for (i=0; i<NofXpixels; i++)
{ ///save k-space data
    for (j=0; j<NofYpixels; j++)
    {
        index = ((j*NofXpixels)+i);
        savedata = (double)*(kSpaceI+index);
        fwrite(&savedata,sizeof(double),1,pf);
    }
} ///save k-space data

fprintf(logfile,"%s\n", "k-Space Signal (Imaginary) Saved");

fclose (pf);
} // save data

fprintf(logfile,"%s\n", "Processing Completed");
fclose(logfile);
system( logfilename );
    // FIFO memory deallocation method
    free(kSpaceR);
```

```
        free(kSpaceI);
        free(lightSource);
        free(sampledSignal);

    }// 2010
    else{

        HelpMessage.Format("%s\n %s\n %s\n %s\n %s\n" , "Please make sure that" , "lightRate and The
        SamplingRate", "fulfill the Nyquist Theorem." , "Rerun before proceeding" ,"to signal reconstruction");
        MessageBox(HelpMessage);

    }

}
```

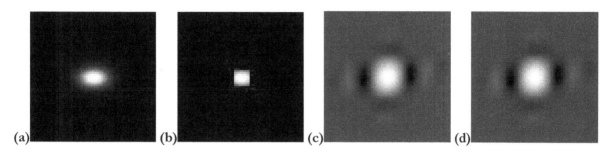

Figure 8: The elliptical light obtained calculating the light source as function of space and time with an ellipse size of 3.5x4.5 is shown in (a). The light sampled with the Whittaken-Shannon formula [2-4] is shown in (b), whilst (c) and (d) show respectively real and imaginary components of the k-Space once the sampled light is direct Fourier transformed.

The method *void CPointSource2010Dlg::OnSeeSamples()* shows sample images to the user through the use of the command '*system*' and is called in upon pushing the button named '*See Samples*' (see Fig. 3).

void CPointSource2010Dlg::OnSeeSamples()

```
{
    system("EllipticalLight.bmp");
}
```

Summary

This chapter has addressed a detailed description of the methods of the source code of a project named *point-Source2010*. This project is an implementation of the Whittaker-Shannon interpolation formula [2-4]. Also, an implementation of the Fourier Transformations in their direct and indirect formulation, k-Space sampling of artificial sources of light having circular or elliptical wave front. The project *pointSource2010* like many other programs in the book provides the students with the ease of understanding of how to implement OpenGL ® routines for data visualization and how to embed such routines in the Visual C++ ® programming environment.

References

[1] Shreiner, D., Woo, M., Neider, J., Davis, T. (2007). *OpenGL Programming Guide: The Official Guide to Learning OpenGL.* Version 2.1 (6th Edition), Addison-Wesley Professional.

[2] Whittaker, E. T. (1915). *On the functions which are represented by the expansions of interpolation theory.* Proceedings of the Royal Society Edinburgh, UK, Sec. A(35), 181-194.

[3] Whittaker, J. M. (1935). *Interpolatory Function Theory.* Cambridge Univ. Press, Cambridge, England.

[4] Shannon, C. E. (1998). *Communication in the Presence of Noise.* Prodeedings of the IEEE, 86(2) pp. 447-457.

CHAPTER 3

Sub-pixel Efficacy Region (SRE) Interpolation Functions' Validation

Introduction

The reader should be informed that each of the push buttons of the GUI interfaces with one of the programs employed for the validation of the SRE-based interpolation functions which are described elsewhere [1]. The source code is placed on the internet at the site www.sourcecodewebsiteCarloCiulla.com. In this chapter is given an outline on how to build flow chart diagrams which describe the Graphical User Interface (GUI) shown in Fig. 2 of chapter 1 in the present manuscript.

An overview on the hierarchy governing the GUI shows that the '*SRE - Graphical User Interface*' is placed at the top level from which it follows the second level from the top where the user finds the panel named '*Bivariate Linear Interpolation*' where the push buttons '*Single Processing*' and '*Multiple Processing*' are located. At the same level from the top, the user also finds the push buttons '*Quadratic B-Spline*', '*Cubic B-Spline*', '*Lagrange*' and '*Sinc*' which are all relevant to signal-image processing with classic and SRE-based interpolation. Additionally, at the same level two more push buttons are located and they are called: (i) '*Lagrange*' which relates to the classic trivariate cubic interpolation paradigm; and (ii) '*Image Viewer*' which is pertinent to data visualization.

The Flow Charts of the Graphical User Interface

In the hierarchy shown in Fig. 1 the GUI (magenta) is at the top level, and the box representing '*Bivariate Linear Interpolation*' is shown one layer down (see blue) while the boxes indicating '*Single Processing*' and '*Multiple Processing*' are two levels below (see plum). One layer down are the variables misplacement along X, Y and Z axis and number of voxels along X, Y and Z axis (see grey), and they are given as input to '*Single Processing*' and '*Multiple Processing*'.

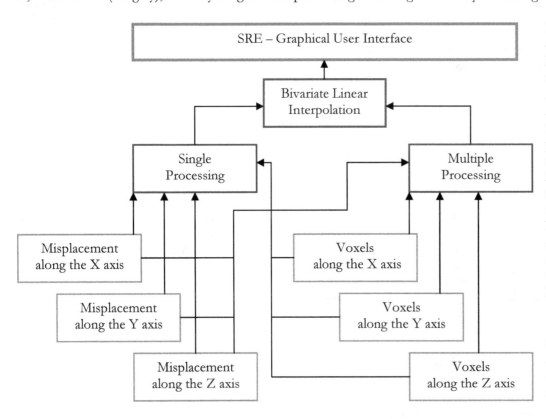

Figure 1: The flow chart of the bivariate liner interpolation in the two variants: '*Single Processing*' and '*Multiple Processing*'. In either of the two cases the misplacement along the three axis X, Y and Z is input along with the number of voxels along X, Y and Z. Both misplacement and number of voxels are set by the user through the sliders located in the GUI.

In Fig. 2 the difference between '*Single Processing*' and '*Multiple Processing*' is that the former processes an

image or a volume with a single misplacement, whereas the latter enforces processing with a set of misplacements. '*Multiple Processing*' is running the algorithm multiple times and recording for each iteration the value of the interpolation error in the two cases of classic bivariate liner interpolation and SRE-based bivariate linear interpolation.

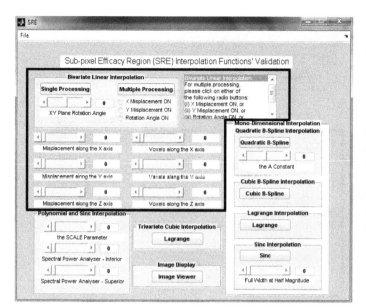

Figure 2: The part of the GUI inside the dark insert is represented with the flow chart shown in Fig. 1.

In the case of '*Single Processing*' the misplacement is set through a rotation angle (see slider which name is '*XY Plane Rotation Angle*'). In the case of '*Multiple Processing*' the user can chose as to if the misplacement along X and Y is determined through a rotation or through the misplacement along X and Y separately.

In Fig. 3 is shown the flow chart of the Quadratic B-Spline Interpolation in its relationship with the GUI and the input variables which are the same as those of the Bivariate Linear Interpolation except for the value of the 'a' constant.

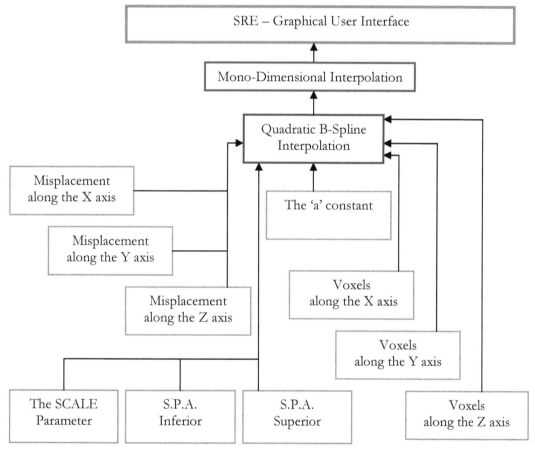

Figure 3: The flow chart of the '*Quadratic B-Spline*' shown in four layers. The top (see magenta) is where the GUI resides. One level down (see blue) is located the push button relevant to the calculation of the mono-dimensional interpolation functions. One level further down is the push button of the '*Quadratic B-Spline Interpolation*' (see plum). And one level further down (see grey) are located the input variables to the function. Such variables are the same as shown in figure 1 for the Bivariate

Linear Interpolation with the addition of the '*a*' *constant* which is a parameter relevant to the parametric B-Spline, the '*SCALE*' parameter and the '*Spectral Power Analyzer*' (S.P.A.) in its inferior and superior values [1].

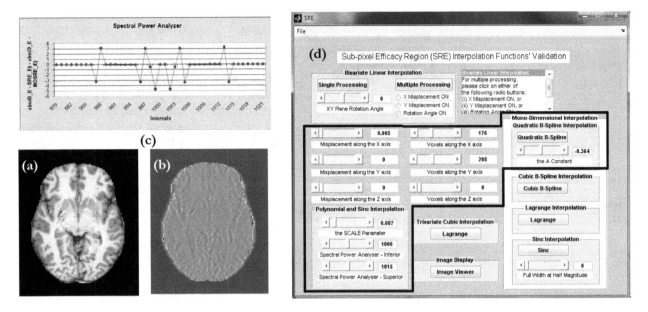

Figure 4: The frequency components of the interpolated image which match the most with the original image (a) are shown in (c). The novel recomputed sampling locations [1] are shown in (b). The part of the GUI inside the dark insert (d) is represented with the flow chart shown in figure 3.

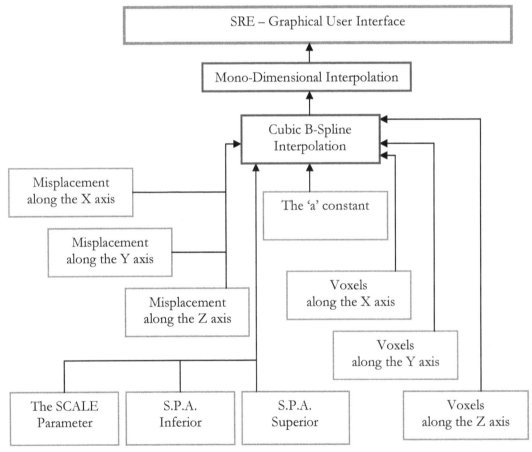

Figure 5: The flow chart of the Cubic Interpolation functions. Its similarity with figure 3 is remarkable as the input values are the same except for the value of the *'a' constant* which is missing in this chart.

While Figs. 3 and 5 show the flow chart of the GUI as pertaining to the *'Quadratic B-Spline'* processing and the *'Cubic B-Spline'* processing respectively, Figs. 4 and 6 show the results obtained while processing a Magnetic Resonance Imaging (MRI) 2D plane image with the two

SRE-based interpolation functions. The reader may appreciate that Fig. 3 relates to Fig. 4 in that the part of the GUI included in the dark insert. Similarly, Fig. 5 relates to Fig. 6 for the same reason. Also, Figs. 4 and 6 show the *'Spectral Power Analyzer'* (S.P.A.) resulting from processing and also the novel recomputed locations where adaptive SRE-based re-sampling takes place. The meaning of the *'Spectral Power Analyzer'* is that of showing the frequency components of the re-sampled MRI which closely match the frequency components of the original MRI (a).

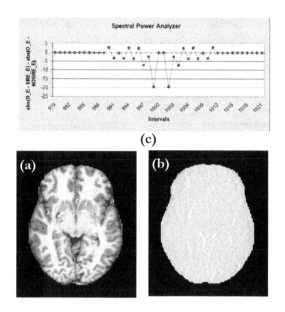

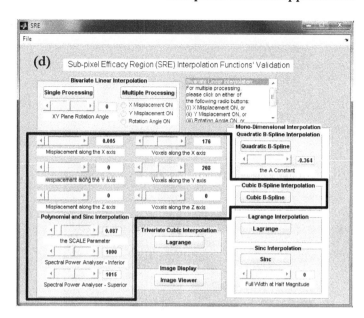

Figure 6: The frequency components of the interpolated image which match the most with the original image (a) are shown in (c). The novel recomputed sampling locations [1] are shown in (b). The part of the GUI inside the dark insert (d) is represented with the flow chart shown in figure 3.

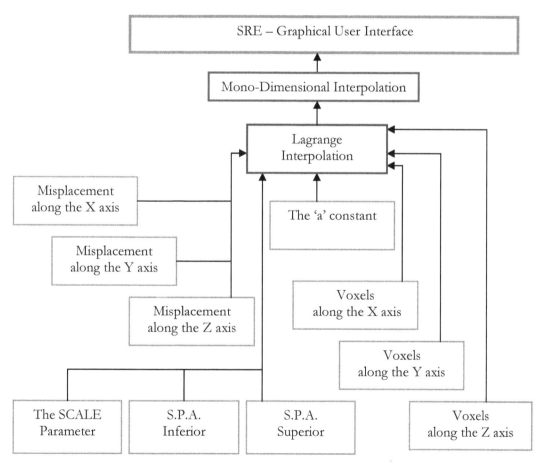

Figure 7: The part of the GUI which is relevant to processing with Lagrange interpolation both classic and SRE-based is illustrated as flow chart with emphasis on the variables (see grey) input to the push button (see plum).

The evolution of the S.P.A. shows negatives (SRE-based interpolation outperforming classic interpolation) and positives (classic interpolation outperforming SRE-based interpolation) [1]. The novel resampling locations show a considerable match with the anatomical features of the

MRI seen in Figs. 4.b, 6.b, and 8.b, and they are accountable for the reduced interpolation error. Figs. 3, 5, 7 and 9 show a variable called The *'SCALE'* Parameter which is the constant used to scale the convolutions of the polynomial interpolation functions. For more details on this parameter and its influence on the interpolation error the reader is referred to previously reported research [1].

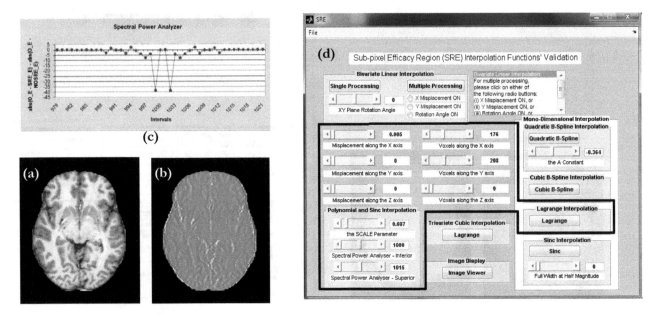

Figure 8: The original MRI and the novel re-sampling locations are shown in (a) and (b) respectively. The *Spectral Power Analyzer* is shown in (c). The part of the GUI in the dark insert (d) is relevant to the processing with Lagrange interpolation and the flow chart is shown in Fig. 7.

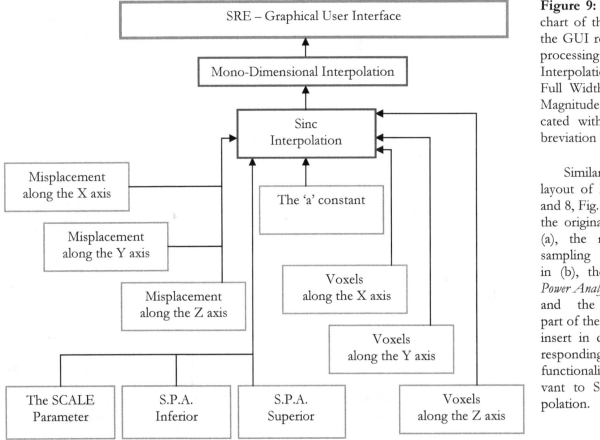

Figure 9: The flow chart of the part of the GUI relevant to processing with Sinc Interpolation. The Full Width at Half Magnitude is indicated with the abbreviation '*FWHM*'.

Similarly to the layout of Figs. 4, 6 and 8, Fig. 10 shows the original MRI in (a), the novel re-sampling locations in (b), the '*Spectral Power Analyzer*' in (c) and the selected part of the GUI (see insert in dark) corresponding to the functionality relevant to Sinc interpolation.

It is observable in the figures showing the GUI that there are two more push buttons. One is that relevant to the use of *ImageViewer* (in either of its versions: 2009 and 2010). This push button is important as it makes an interface between the Matlab ® GUI and the Visual C++ ® /OpenGL ® application. Also, the remaining push button is that one of the trivariate cubic interpolation function and this button calls in the program which reproduces the interpolation function in its classic form only.

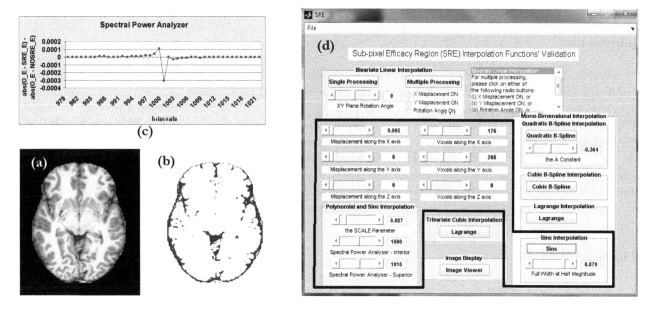

Figure 10: The original MRI is shown in (a) and the novel re-sampling locations obtained with SRE-based Sinc interpolation are shown (b). The Spectral Power Analyzer is shown in (c). The part of the GUI in the dark insert in (d) is relevant to the processing with Sinc interpolation (both classic and SRE-based) and the flow chart is shown in Fig. 9.

Summary

This chapter addresses the details of the programming environment built in order to validate the SRE-based interpolation functions [1] describing with flow charts the GUI which interface each of the programs used for validation. The chapter also reports some unpublished results obtainable with the SRE-based interpolation with specific mention on the '*Spectral Power Analyzers*' of the interpolated data and the maps of novel re-sampling locations determined through the adaptive re-sampling approach utilized and fully explored earlier across several interpolation paradigm covering three dimensions and three degrees of polynomial order [1].

References

[1] Ciulla, C. (2009). *Improved Signal and Image Interpolation in Biomedical Applications: The Case of Magnetic Resonance Imaging (MRI)* - Medical Information Science Reference - IGI Global Publisher, Hershey, PA, U.S.A.

[2] Shreiner, D., Woo, M., Neider, J., Davis, T. (2007). *OpenGL Programming Guide: The Official Guide to Learning OpenGL.* Version 2.1 (6th Edition), Addison-Wesley Professional.

Computer Science Applications

CHAPTER 4

The Visual C++ Implementation of the Booth Algorithm

Introduction

The Booth algorithm is implemented inside a C++ Graphical User Interface (GUI) called '*CSC239 Semester Project*'. As visible the GUI shows also three additional panels which are worth commenting before hand. The panel '*Sorting Algorithm*' has ten edit boxes accepting numbers inside it, along with the push button '*Sort*' which runs the sorting algorithm. The panel '*Binary Conversion*' has two edit boxes accepting numbers inside the range [-128, 127] which are fed as input to the push buttons named '*One's Complement*' and '*Two's Complement*'.

In reference to the Graphical User Interface which relates to the Booth algorithm for binary multiplication [1-2] it is worth mentioning that inside the panel named '*Booth Algorithm*' there are two edit boxes named '*[-8, 7]*' and two user input variables which correspond to the multiplicand and the multiplier and they are named '*m_BoothNumber*' and '*m_BoothNumberM*' respectively. The push button named '*Booth Multiplication*' is assigned to the method *void CCSC239ProjectDlg::OnBoothAlgorithm()*.

The Source Code

It is important to note that the line of code here reported are written for binary multiplications of integers in between the range [-8, 7]. That means each of multiplicand, two's complement of the multiplicand and multiplier will be converted in a binary number having four digits and the algorithm will run four iterations. This is consistent with what reported in Figs. 4 and 5 in the summary section of the present chapter. The instructions employed to convert the decimal number into a binary are:

```
✓  for (int i = 0; i <= 3; i++) {

✓  invert[i] = div % 2;
✓  q = ( (int) div / 2 );
✓  div = q;

✓  }
```

The instructions utilized to find the two' s complement of a binary number are:

```
✓  // find the Two's complement of the Multiplicand
✓  for (int j = 3; j >= 0; j--) {

✓  if ( invert[j] == 1 ) {

✓  p = j;
✓  index = j;

✓  for ( int s = p; s >= 0; s--) {

✓  if ( invert[s] != 1 ) {}
✓  else if ( invert[s] == 1 ) index = s;

✓  }

✓  break;

✓  }

✓  }
```

74

- ✓ *// Two's Complement bits flipping*
- ✓ *for (int s = 3; s > index; s--) {*

- ✓ *invert[s] = 1 - invert[s];*

- ✓ *}*

void CCSC239ProjectDlg::OnBoothAlgorithm()
```
{
        // TODO: Add your control notification handler code here
        UpdateData(true);
        int q, p, index=3;
        int div;
        int invert[9];

        CString MyMessage;

        if ( !( m_BoothNumber <= 7 && m_BoothNumber >= -8 ) ||
            !( m_BoothNumberM <= 7 && m_BoothNumberM >=- 8) ){

            MyMessage.Format("Please Enter an integer in the range [-8, 7]");
            AfxMessageBox(MyMessage);
        }

        if ( m_BoothNumber <= 7 && m_BoothNumber >= -8 &&
            m_BoothNumberM <= 7 && m_BoothNumberM >=- 8 )
        {// if [-8, 7]

            MyMessage.Format("Multiplicand = %d\n Multiplier = %d\n",
                            m_BoothNumber , m_BoothNumberM);
            AfxMessageBox(MyMessage);

        /// convert Multiplicand
        int A[9]; // multiplicand
        div = abs(m_BoothNumber);

        for (int i = 0; i <= 3;  i++)
        {
            invert[i] =  div % 2;
            q = ( (int) div / 2 );
            div  = q;
        }

        invert[4]=0;
        invert[5]=0;
        invert[6]=0;
        invert[7]=0;
        invert[8]=0;
        /// convert Multiplicand

        /// store Multiplicand in A
        A[0]=invert[3];
        A[1]=invert[2];
        A[2]=invert[1];
        A[3]=invert[0];

        for (i = 4; i < 9;  i++)
```

```
        {
             A[i] = invert[i];
        }

MyMessage.Format("Multiplicand:\n %d%d%d%d%d%d%d%d\t%d\n" ,
                 A[0], A[1], A[2], A[3], A[4], A[5], A[6], A[7], A[8] );
AfxMessageBox(MyMessage);

        // find Two's complement of the Multiplicand
        for (int j = 3; j >= 0;  j--)
        {

            if ( invert[j] == 1 )
            {

                p = j;
                index  = j;

                for ( int s = p; s >= 0; s--)
                {
                    if ( invert[s] != 1 ) {}
                        else if ( invert[s] == 1 ) index = s;
                }

                break;
            }

        }

        // Two's Complement  // flip bits
        for ( int s = 3; s > index; s--)
        {
            invert[s] = 1 - invert[s];
        }

// store S (TWO'S COMPLEMENT OF MULTIPLICAND)
int S[9];
for ( int w = 0; w < 9; w++ )
{
    S[w] = invert[w];
}

S[0]=invert[3];
S[1]=invert[2];
S[2]=invert[1];
S[3]=invert[0];

MyMessage.Format("Two's Complement of Multiplicand:\n %d%d%d%d%d%d%d%d\t%d\n" ,
S[0], S[1], S[2], S[3], S[4], S[5], S[6], S[7], S[8] );
AfxMessageBox(MyMessage);

/// convert Multiplier
int P[9]; // multiplier
div = abs(m_BoothNumberM);
```

```
for (i = 0; i <= 3;  i++)
{
    invert[i] =  div % 2;
    q = ( (int) div / 2 );
    div  = q;
}

invert[4]=0;
invert[5]=0;
invert[6]=0;
invert[7]=0;
invert[8]=0;
/// convert Multiplier

/// store Multiplicand in P
P[4]=invert[3];
P[5]=invert[2];
P[6]=invert[1];
P[7]=invert[0];
P[8]=invert[8];

for (i = 4; i < 8;  i++)
{
    P[i-4] = invert[i];
}

MyMessage.Format("Multiplier:\n %d%d%d%d%d%d%d%d\t%d\n" ,
                P[0], P[1], P[2], P[3], P[4], P[5], P[6], P[7], P[8] );
AfxMessageBox(MyMessage);

for (int m = 1; m <=4; m++)
{ // Booth Multiplication Loop

    if ( ( P[7]==0 && P[8]==0 ) || ( P[7]==1 && P[8]==1 ) )
    {
    // do nothing
    }

    else if (  P[7]==0 && P[8]==1  )
    { // P = P + A
        int carry  = 0;
    for (w = 8; w >= 0; w--)
    { // calculate product

        /// calculate sum
        if ( P[w]==0 && A[w]==0 && carry==0 )
        {
            P[w] = 0;
            carry = 0;
        }
        else if ( P[w]==1 && A[w]==0 && carry==0 ){
            P[w] = 1;
            carry = 0;
        }
        else if ( P[w]==0 && A[w]==1 && carry==0 ){

            P[w] = 1;
```

```
                  carry = 0;
              }
              else if ( P[w]==1 && A[w]==0 && carry==1 ){

                  P[w] = 0;
                  carry = 1;
              }
              else if ( P[w]==0 && A[w]==1 && carry==1 ){

                  P[w] = 0;
                  carry = 1;
              }
              else if ( P[w]==1 && A[w]==1 && carry==0 ){

                  P[w] = 0;
                  carry = 1;
              }
              else if ( P[w]==1 && A[w]==1 && carry==1 ){

                  P[w] = 1;
                  carry = 1;
              }
              else if ( P[w]==0 && A[w]==0 && carry==1 ){

                  P[w] = 1;
                  carry = 0;
              } /// calculate sum

      } // calculate product
      }// P = P + A
      else if (  P[7]==1 && P[8]==0  )
      { // P = P + S
          int carry  = 0;

      for (w = 8; w >= 0; w--)
      { // calculate product
          /// calculate sum
          if ( P[w]==0 && S[w]==0 && carry==0 )
          {
              P[w] = 0;
              carry = 0;
          }
          else if ( P[w]==1 && S[w]==0 && carry==0 ){

              P[w] = 1;
              carry = 0;
          }
          else if ( P[w]==0 && S[w]==1 && carry==0 ){
              P[w] = 1;
              carry = 0;
          }
          else if ( P[w]==1 && S[w]==0 && carry==1 ){

              P[w] = 0;
              carry = 1;
          }
```

```
        else if ( P[w]==0 && S[w]==1 && carry==1 ){

            P[w] = 0;
            carry = 1;
        }
        else if ( P[w]==1 && S[w]==1 && carry==0 ){

            P[w] = 0;
            carry = 1;
        }
        else if ( P[w]==1 && S[w]==1 && carry==1 ){

            P[w] = 1;
            carry = 1;
        }
        else if ( P[w]==0 && S[w]==0 && carry==1 ){

            P[w] = 1;
            carry = 0;
        } /// calculate sum

    } // calculate product

}// P = P + S

MyMessage.Format("P (before shift):\n %d%d%d%d%d%d%d%d\t%d\n" ,
                P[0], P[1], P[2], P[3], P[4], P[5], P[6], P[7], P[8] );
AfxMessageBox(MyMessage);
int store[9];
    for (w = 0; w < 9; w++)
    { // shift
        store[w] = P[w];
    }
    for (w = 0; w < 8; w++)
    { // shift
        P[w+1] = store[w];
    }

MyMessage.Format("P:\n %d%d%d%d%d%d%d%d\t%d\n" ,
                P[0], P[1], P[2], P[3], P[4], P[5], P[6], P[7], P[8] );
AfxMessageBox(MyMessage);

}// Booth Multiplication Loop


 // if either one of the two numbers is negative then the result is negative thus
 // DO TWO's COMPLEMENT OF THE RESULT
 // Two's Complement
if ( m_BoothNumberM < 0 || m_BoothNumber < 0  )
{// if
    index = 0;

    for (int j = 0; j < 8;  j++)
    {
        if ( P[j] == 1 )
        {
            p = j;
```

```
                index  = j;

                for ( int s = p; s < 8; s++)
                {
                    if ( P[s] != 1 ) {}
                        else if ( P[s] == 1 ) index = s;
                }
                break;
            }


        }

        // Two's Complement  // flip bits
        for ( int s = 0; s < index; s++ )
        {
            P[s] = 1 - P[s];
        }
    }// if
    else if ( m_BoothNumberM ==-8 && m_BoothNumber > 0 ) {}
    else if ( m_BoothNumberM < 0 && m_BoothNumber < 0 ) {}
    else if ( m_BoothNumberM > 0 && m_BoothNumber > 0 ) {}
    else if ( m_BoothNumberM == 0 && m_BoothNumber == 0 ) {}

    MyMessage.Format("Result of Booth Multiplication:\n %d%d%d%d%d%d%d%d\t%d\n" ,
                P[0], P[1], P[2], P[3], P[4], P[5], P[6], P[7], P[8] );
    AfxMessageBox(MyMessage);

    } // if [-8, 7]


}
```

Figs. 1 through 3 show the steps of the Booth multiplication 4*(-7). In Fig. 4, the algorithm is summarized and the example multiplication is between the numbers 3 and 5. The first four columns of 'A' from left are filled with the binary digits which make the multiplicand, the remaining four columns of 'A' from left are filled with zeros and so the column used for the shift (the 9th column). The first four columns of 'S' from left are filled with the two' complement of the multiplicand, the remaining four columns of 'S' are also filled with zeros and so the 9th column. Before the first of the four iterations, the first partial product 'P' is filled with four zeros in the first four columns from left and the next four columns from left will be filled with the binary digits which make the multiplier. The 9th column will be filled with a zero. Each of the four iterations' operation is determined by the content of the last two columns (the 8th and the 9th). If the last two bits of the partial product 'P' are 00 or 11 the algorithm does not sum up anything, and instead shifts 'P' to the right. If instead the last two bits of the partial product 'P' are 0 and 1 then the algorithm sums up 'P' and 'A' to have the new partial product and so it makes a shift to the right of the resulting 'P'. If the last two bits of the partial product 'P' are 1 and 0 then the algorithm sums up 'P' and 'S' then it makes a shift to the right.

Summary

This chapter illustrates the program that describes the Booth algorithm for binary multiplication and such program is embedded in a single method of a Visual C++ ® project which readily provides the students with a Graphical User Interface. The chapter details on one sample multiplication which, consistently with the set of educational slides presented in chapter 1, shows each of the steps of the Booth algorithm and the relevant results obtained through the GUI. The Booth algorithm implemented in combinational logic circuits and the slide set was possible to make combining the knowledge provided in [1-2] and www.wikipedia.org (see Figs. 4 and 5).

The Graphical User Interface seen at the top left of Fig. 4 was made with Visual C++ ® to convert decimals to binary along with the full implementation of the Booth Algorithm. It also includes the implementation of the sequential sorting algorithm, the calculation of the ones' complement and the two's complement. Materials presented in Figs. 1

through 5 might be useful to initiate a semester project and/or to hand in midterm or final exams in computer science major undergraduate courses.

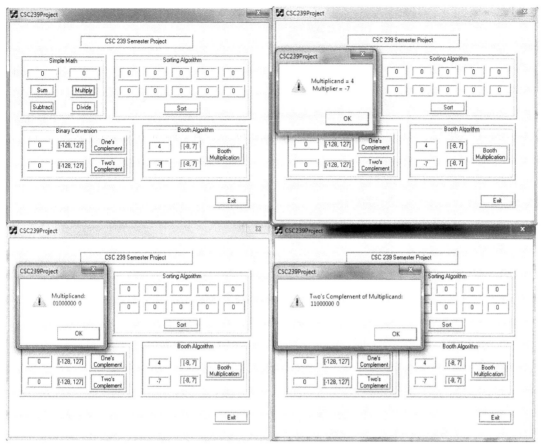

Figure 1: The Graphical User Interface of the Visual C++ ® implementation of the Booth algorithm [1-2] is shown in the upper left. The multiplicand and the multiplier in decimal format are shown in the upper right. The multiplicand (4) is shown in the lower left and the two's complement of the multiplicand is shown in the lower right of the figure.

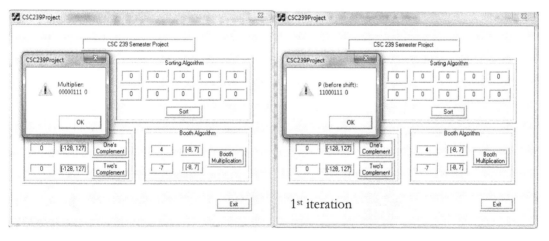

1ˢᵗ iteration

Figure 2: The absolute value of the multiplier (-7) is shown in the upper most left of the figure. The partial product 'P' of the multiplication before the shift is shown at the right of the upper most row of the figure.

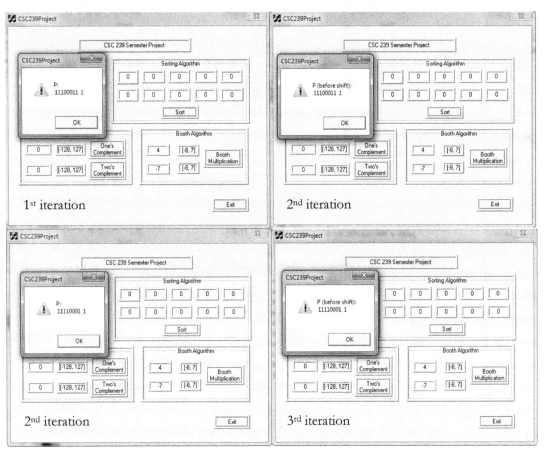

Figure 2 (Contd): The central and lower most rows of the figure show the partial product 'P' of the Booth multiplication [1-2] at the second and third iteration of the algorithm.

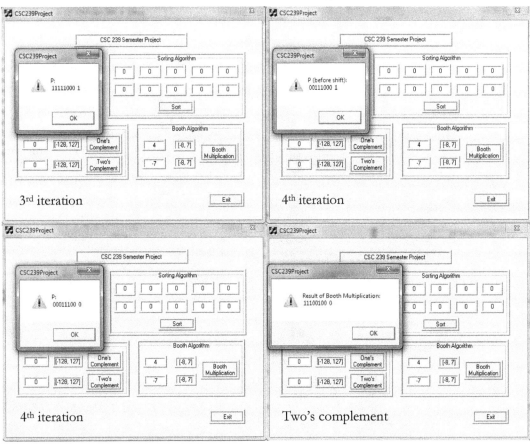

Figure 3: The final step of the Booth multiplication 4 * -7 [1-2] seen through the graphical user interface. The partial product 'P' of the multiplication of the third iteration is shown at the upper left, whereas the upper right shows the partial product of the fourth and final iteration before the shift. The lower row shows the partial product after the shift (see left) and the result of the Booth multiplication (see right).

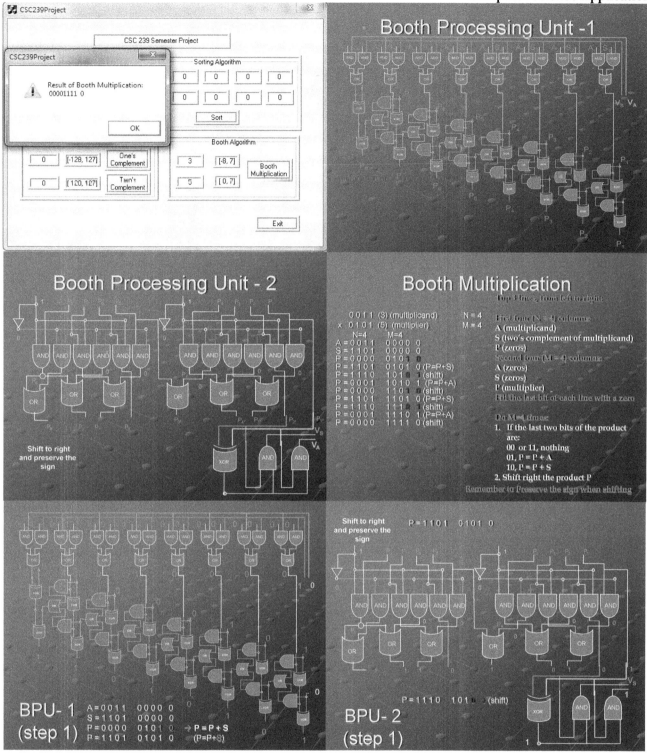

Figure 4: The Visual C++ implementation of the Booth algorithm [1-2] along with the educational slide showing the algorithm for a sample binary multiplication.

Computer Science Applications

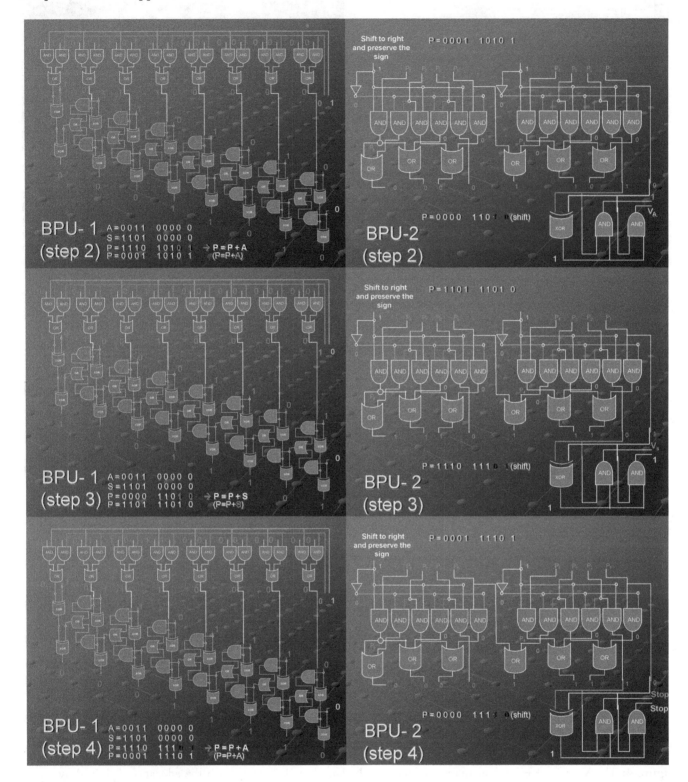

Figure 5: Educational slide sets © on logic gates and binary arithmetic of the Booth algorithm, the Booth processing unit: steps two through four.

References

[1] Null, L. & Lobur J. (2007). *The Essentials of Computer Organization and Architecture*, Second Edition. Jones and Bartlett Publishers. Sudbury, MA, U.S.A.

[2] Booth, A.D. (1951). *A Signed Binary Multiplication Algorithm*. Quarterly Journal of Mechanics and Applied Mathematics. Clarendon Press; Oxford University Press. England.

CHAPTER 5

The Source Code of ROTRA 2008

Introduction

This chapter begins introducing to the reader details of the variables and methods of the Graphical User Interface shown in Fig. 1. Likewise all of the chapters of this manuscript which report source code of Visual C++ ® programs, the variables with suffix '*m_*' at the beginning of their name are user input values introduced through the GUI.

The panel called '*Input the Rigid Body Transformation*' has six edit boxes and for each is declared a variable. Specifically: '*Rotation about the X Axis (deg)*', '*Rotation about the Y Axis (deg)*' and '*Rotation about the Z Axis (deg)*' link to the variables '*m_theta*', '*m_fi*' and '*m_psi*' respectively. And the edit boxes named '*X Translation (mm)*', '*Y Translation (mm)*' and '*Z Translation (mm)*' link to the variables '*m_Xt*', '*m_Yt*', and '*m_Zt*' respectively. In the same panel the push button named '*Calculate Transformation*' link to the method called *void CROTRA2008Dlg::OnCalculateRT()*.

The panel called '*Image Volumes Processing*' has three push buttons by the name of: '*Add Slices to the Image Volume*', '*Apply Transformation*' and '*Run Image Viewer*', which calls in the methods *void CROTRA2008Dlg::OnCreateVolume()*, *void CROTRA2008Dlg::OnApplyRT()* and *void CROTRA2008Dlg::OnImageViewer()* respectively. The variables in this panel are three and they are called: '*m_VS*', '*m_NofSlices*', and '*m_VolumeName*' and they are associated with the edit boxes called '*Add Slices*', '*Number of Slices*' and '*Image Volume*' respectively.

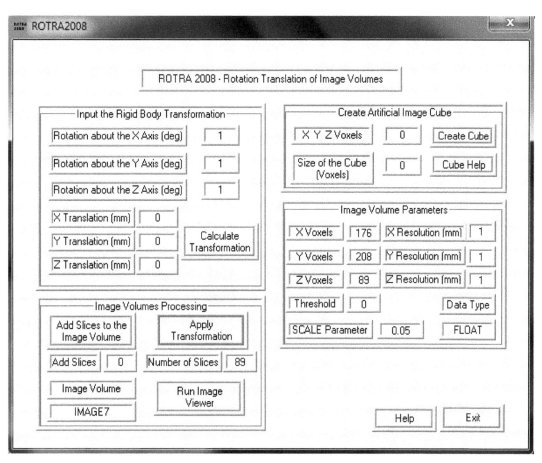

Figure 1: The GUI of *ROTRA 2008* as it appears before pushing the button '*Apply Transformation*' which calls in the method just above reported by the name of *void CROTRA2008Dlg::OnApplyRT()* and employed to apply the rotation of 1 deg about the three axis X, Y and Z of the coordinate system.

The panel named '*Create Artificial Image Cube*' has two edit boxes named: '*X Y Z Voxels*' and '*Size of the Cube (Voxels)*' and there are two variables associated with them and they are called: '*m_VolumeSize*' and '*m_CubeSize*'.

There are also two push buttons called: '*Create Cube*' and '*Cube Help*' which call in the methods *void CROTRA2008Dlg::OnCreatetheCube()* and *void CROTRA2008Dlg::OnHelpCube()*.

The panel named '*Image Volume Parameters*' has nine edit boxes called: '*X Voxels*', '*Y Voxels*', '*Z Voxels*', '*X Resolution (mm)*', '*Y resolution (mm)*', '*Z Resolution (mm)*', '*Threshold*', '*SCALE Parameter*' and '*Data Type*'. The variables associated with these nine edit boxes are called: '*m_rcxres*', '*m_rcyres*', '*m_numslice*', '*m_XRES*', '*m_YRES*', '*m_ZRES*', '*m_TH*', '*m_SCALE*', and '*m_DataType*' respectively. These details can be appreciated while looking at Fig. 1.

Computer Science Applications

The Source Code

The main class of this program is *CROTRA2008Dlg* and so all of the methods shown in this chapter belong to it. The instruction '*pointer = (float *) calloc(((numslice*rcyres*rcxres)+1), sizeof(float))*' dynamically allocates memory releasing a pointer containing the data volume. The method *void CROTRA2008Dlg::OnCreatetheCube()* creates a cube of a user given number of voxels ('*m_CubeSize*') inside a volume of zero value pixel intensity which size is also determined by the user. Data are initialized to zero values and then filled in with the pixel intensity value 150 but only in the portion of the volume occupied by the cube. The variable '*csize = ((int)m_CubeSize/2)*' defines the size of the cube. The instructions employed to initialize data and to create the cube are:

- ✓ *for(sl=1; sl<=numslice; sl++) {*
- ✓ *for(j=0; j<rcyres; j++) {*
- ✓ *for(i=0; i<rcxres; i++) {*

- ✓ *k2=(j*rcxres+i)+((sl-1)*rcyres*rcxres);*
- ✓ **(pointer+k2) = 0;*

- ✓ *}*
- ✓ *}*
- ✓ *}*

- ✓ *for(sl=((int)numslice/2 - csize); sl<=((int)numslice/2 + csize); sl++) {*
- ✓ *for(j=((int)rcyres/2 - csize); j<=((int)rcyres/2 + csize); j++) {*
- ✓ *for(i=((int)rcxres/2 - csize); i<=((int)rcxres/2 + csize); i++) {*

- ✓ *k2=(j*rcxres+i)+(sl*rcyres*rcxres);*
- ✓ **(pointer+k2) = 150;*

- ✓ *}*
- ✓ *}*
- ✓ *}*

The method *void CROTRA2008Dlg::OnCreatetheCube()* also calculates the center of mass of the cube inside the volume and saves data into a binary file of floating point (32 bits) numbers. The coordinates of the center of mass are identified through the variables '*comx*', '*comy*' and '*comz*'. The instructions employed are:

- ✓ *for(sl=1; sl<=numslice; sl++) {*
- ✓ *for(j=0; j<rcyres; j++) {*
- ✓ *for(i=0; i<rcxres; i++) {*

- ✓ *k2=(j*rcxres+i)+((sl-1)*rcyres*rcxres);*
- ✓ *count+=(*(pointer+k2));*

- ✓ *sumi = sumi + ((double)i)*(*(pointer+k2));*
- ✓ *sumj = sumj + ((double)j)*(*(pointer+k2));*
- ✓ *sumsl = sumsl + ((double)sl-1)*(*(pointer+k2));*

- ✓ *}*
- ✓ *}*
- ✓ *}*

- ✓ *comx = (double)sumi/(count);*
- ✓ *comy = (double)sumj/(count);*
- ✓ *comz = (double)sumsl/(count);*

To save the cube into a binary file where each pixel value is stored as a floating point number (32 bits Real) the program utilizes the following instructions. At the end of the process, the pointer '*(pointer)' containing the data is released from memory with the instruction '*free(pointer)*'.

- ✓ *if ((pf = fopen(filename,"wb+"))==NULL) {*

- ✓ *fprintf(logfile, "%s\n", "Cannot open file to save Cube Volume...Now Exit");*
- ✓ *exit(0);*

- ✓ *} else {*

- ✓ *for(sl=1; sl<=numslice; sl++) {*
- ✓ *for(j=0; j<rcyres; j++){*
- ✓ *for(i=0; i<rcxres; i++){*

- ✓ *k2=(j*rcxres+i)+((sl-1)*rcyres*rcxres);*
- ✓ *savedata=(float)*(pointer+k2);*
- ✓ *fwrite(&savedata,sizeof(float),1,pf);*

- ✓ *}*
- ✓ *}*
- ✓ *}*

- ✓ *fclose(pf);*
- ✓ *free(pointer);*

- ✓ *}*

void CROTRA2008Dlg::OnCreatetheCube()
{

```
    UpdateData(true);

    int sl, j, i, k2;
    float number = 0;
    float *pointer = 0;
    char filename[128];
    FILE *pf;
    int rcxres;
    int rcyres;
    int numslice;
    double count = 0;
    double comx = 0, comy = 0, comz = 0, sumi = 0, sumj = 0, sumsl = 0;
    int csize;
    FILE * logfile;
    char logfilename[128];
    CString Message;

    sprintf(logfilename, "%s%d%s%d%s", "CUBE", m_VolumeSize, "-", m_CubeSize, ".log");
    sprintf(filename, "%s%d%s%d", "CUBEIMAGE-", m_VolumeSize, "-", m_CubeSize);

    if ((logfile = fopen(logfilename,"w+"))==NULL)
    {
        Message.Format("%s\n%s\n%s\n" , "Cannot open file: ", logfilename, "Now Exit");
        AfxMessageBox(Message);
```

```
            exit(0);
      } else { // else

            fprintf(logfile,"%s%s\n", "Making the Cube in File: " , filename );
            fprintf(logfile,"%s%d\n", "Number of X, Y, Z Volume Voxels: " , m_VolumeSize );
            fprintf(logfile,"%s%d\n", "Cube Size along X, Y, Z in Voxels: " , m_CubeSize );
            fprintf(logfile,"%s\n" , "Now creating the cube");

      } // else

      rcxres = (int)m_VolumeSize;
      rcyres = (int)m_VolumeSize;
      numslice = (int)m_VolumeSize;
      csize = ((int)m_CubeSize/2);

         if ((pointer = (float *) calloc( ((numslice*rcyres*rcxres)+1), sizeof(float)) ) == NULL)
         {
              fprintf(logfile, "%s\n" , "Not enough memory to allocate the Cube data");
              exit(0);
         }

//fill the cube with zeros
for(sl=1 ;sl<=numslice; sl++) {
    for(j=0;j<rcyres;j++){
        for(i=0;i<rcxres;i++){

            k2=(j*rcxres+i)+((sl-1)*rcyres*rcxres);
            *(pointer+k2)=0;

        }
    }
}

/*these lines make the cube image data*/
for(sl=((int)numslice/2 - csize); sl<=((int)numslice/2 + csize); sl++) {
    for(j=((int)rcyres/2 - csize); j<=((int)rcyres/2 + csize); j++){
        for(i=((int)rcxres/2 - csize); i<=((int)rcxres/2 + csize); i++){

        k2=(j*rcxres+i)+(sl*rcyres*rcxres);
        *(pointer+k2)=150;

                }
            }
        }

      fprintf(logfile, "%s\n" ,"The cube is loaded in memory");
      fprintf(logfile,"%s\n" , "The program will find the Center of Mass (COM) of the cube");

      for(sl=1;sl<=numslice; sl++) {
          for(j=0;j<rcyres;j++){
              for(i=0;i<rcxres;i++){

              k2=(j*rcxres+i)+((sl-1)*rcyres*rcxres);
              count+=(*(pointer+k2));
              sumi = sumi + ((double)i)*(*(pointer+k2));
              sumj = sumj + ((double)j)*(*(pointer+k2));
```

```
                        sumsl = sumsl + ((double)sl-1)*(*(pointer+k2));

                                        }
                                    }
                                }

            comx = (double)sumi/(count);
            comy = (double)sumj/(count);
            comz = (double)sumsl/(count);

            fprintf(logfile, "%s%f\n", "The x coordinate of the COM: ", comx);
            fprintf(logfile, "%s%f\n", "The y coordinate of the COM: ", comy);
            fprintf(logfile, "%s%f\n", "The z coordinate of the COM: ", comz);

            /// save cube
            float savedata;
            fprintf(logfile, "%s%s\n", "Now Saving File: ", filename);

            if ((pf = fopen(filename,"wb+"))==NULL)
            {
                fprintf(logfile, "%s\n", "Cannot open file to save Cube Volume...Now Exit");
                exit(0);
            } else { // else

                for(sl=1;sl<=numslice; sl++) {
                    for(j=0;j<rcyres;j++){
                        for(i=0;i<rcxres;i++){

                            k2=(j*rcxres+i)+((sl-1)*rcyres*rcxres);
                            savedata=(float)*(pointer+k2);
                            fwrite(&savedata,sizeof(float),1,pf);

                                }
                            }
                        }
                fclose(pf);
                free(pointer);
            } // else

            fprintf(logfile, "%s%s\n", "Cube Saved in file: ", filename);
            fprintf(logfile, "%s\n", "DataType: Float (32-bits Real)");
            fclose(logfile);
            system(logfilename);

}
```

The method *void CROTRA2008Dlg::OnExit()* provides the user with safe exit upon pushing the button '*Exit*' located in the Graphical User Interface (See Fig. 1).

void CROTRA2008Dlg::OnExit()
```
{
        exit(0);
}
```
The method *void CROTRA2008Dlg::OnHelpCube()* is called upon pushing the button named '*Cube Help*' and suggests to the user to input the number of voxels along X, Y and Z directions as powers of 2. Also, the cube size is preferred to be a power of 2.

Computer Science Applications

void CROTRA2008Dlg::OnHelpCube()
{

      CString HelpMessage;

      HelpMessage.Format("%s\n%s\n" , "Please select X Y Z Voxels as powers of 2",
                              "Also, the Cube Size as power of 2");
      AfxMessageBox(HelpMessage);

}

The method *void CROTRA2008Dlg::OnCalculateRT()* calculates the rigid body transformation coefficients of a rotation-translation for given values of the three rotational angles: pitch (Rotation about the X-axis), roll (Rotation about the Y-axis), and yaw (Rotation about the Z-axis). And, also the three misplacements values of the center of mass of the digitized 3D volume. The values of sine and cosine are calculated for each of the three rotational angles. The rotation matrix is calculated multiplying rot X (pitch) * rot Y (roll) * rot Z (yaw), which is the rotation about the X axis times the rotation about the Y axis times the rotation about the Z axis. The 3x3 rotation matrix therefore comprises of nine coefficients:

- ✓ *a = ((float)costheta * cosfi)*   *b = -((float)cosfi * sentheta)*   *c = -((float)senfi)*

- ✓ *d = -((float)senpsi * senfi * costheta) + ((float)cospsi * sentheta)* *e= ((float)senpsi * senfi * sentheta) + ((float)cospsi * costheta)* *f = -((float)senpsi * cosfi)*

- ✓ *g = ((float)cospsi * senfi * costheta) + ((float)senpsi * sentheta)* *h = -((float)sentheta * cospsi * senfi) + ((float)senpsi * costheta)* *i = ((float)cosfi * cospsi)*

while the translation vector: ('Xt = (float)m_Xf', 'Yt = (float)m_Yf', 'Zt = (float)m_Zf') is made of three coefficients (the shift along the X, Y and Z axis respectively). Totaling twelve coefficients, the rotation-translation (rigid body) transformation is saved in a text file using the following instructions:

- ✓ *if ((pf = fopen(filename,"w+"))==NULL) {*

- ✓ *fprintf(logfile, "%s\n" , "Cannot open file RTMATRIX...Now Exit");*
- ✓ *exit(0);*

- ✓ *}else{*

- ✓ *fprintf(pf, "%f\n" , Xt);*
- ✓ *fprintf(pf, "%f\n" , Yt);*
- ✓ *fprintf(pf, "%f\n" , Zt);*
- ✓ *fprintf(pf, "%f\n" , a);*
- ✓ *fprintf(pf, "%f\n" , b);*
- ✓ *fprintf(pf, "%f\n" , c);*
- ✓ *fprintf(pf, "%f\n" , d);*
- ✓ *fprintf(pf, "%f\n" , e);*
- ✓ *fprintf(pf, "%f\n" , f);*
- ✓ *fprintf(pf, "%f\n" , g);*
- ✓ *fprintf(pf, "%f\n" , h);*
- ✓ *fprintf(pf, "%f\n" , i);*
- ✓ *fclose(pf);*
- ✓ *}*

void CROTRA2008Dlg::OnCalculateRT()
{

```
        UpdateData(true);
        char filename[128];

        float cosfi, cospsi, costheta, senfi, senpsi, sentheta;
        float a, b, c, d, e, f, g, h, i;
        float fi, theta, psi;
        FILE * pf;
        float Xt, Yt, Zt, RAD;
        FILE * logfile;
        char logfilename[128];

        CString Message;
        sprintf(logfilename, "%s", "RTMATRIX.log");
        sprintf(filename, "%s", "RTMATRIX.txt");

        if ((logfile = fopen(logfilename,"w+"))==NULL)
        {

            Message.Format("%s\n%s\n%s\n" , "Cannot open file: ", logfilename, "Now Exit");
            AfxMessageBox(Message);
            exit(0);

        } else { // else

            fprintf(logfile,"%s%s\n", "Calculating the Rigid Body Transformation: " , filename );

            //// RotX * RotY * RotZ ///
            psi = (float)m_theta;
            fi = (float)m_fi;
            theta = (float)m_psi;

            fprintf(logfile,"%s%f\n", "Pitch angle (Rotation about the X-axis): " , psi );
            fprintf(logfile,"%s%f\n", "Roll angle (Rotation about the Y-axis): ", fi );
            fprintf(logfile,"%s%f\n", "Yaw angle (Rotation about the Z-axis): " , theta );
            fprintf(logfile,"%s%f\n", "The Shift Along the X axis: " , m_Xt );
            fprintf(logfile,"%s%f\n", "The Shift Along the Y axis: " , m_Yt );
            fprintf(logfile,"%s%f\n", "The Shift Along the Z axis: " , m_Zt );

        } // else

            Xt = (float)m_Xt;
            Yt = (float)m_Yt;
            Zt = (float)m_Zt;

        /*Computation of the angles theta psi and fi*/
        RAD=(float)360;


        /*tranform in radiants*/
        fprintf(logfile,"%s\n", "The Angles in Radians: ");
        theta=((float)(2*3.14)/(RAD/theta));
        psi=((float)(2*3.14)/(RAD/psi));
        fi=((float)(2*3.14)/(RAD/fi));
```

```
//// RotX * RotY * RotZ ///
fprintf(logfile, "%s%f\n", "Pitch angle (Rotation about the X-axis): ", psi);
fprintf(logfile, "%s%f\n", "Roll angle (Rotation about the Y-axis): ", fi);
fprintf(logfile, "%s%f\n", "Yaw angle (Rotation about the Z-axis): ", theta);

costheta = (float)cos( (float)theta );
cospsi = (float)cos( (float)psi );
cosfi = (float)cos( (float)fi );

//// RotX * RotY * RotZ ///
fprintf(logfile, "%s%f\n", "Cosine Psi (Pitch angle): ", cospsi);
fprintf(logfile, "%s%f\n", "Cosine Fi (Roll angle): ", cosfi);
fprintf(logfile, "%s%f\n", "Cosine Theta (Yaw angle): ", costheta);

sentheta = (float)sin( (float)theta );
senpsi = (float)sin( (float)psi );
senfi = (float)sin( (float)fi );

//// RotX * RotY * RotZ ///
fprintf(logfile, "%s%f\n", "Sine Psi (Pitch angle): ", senpsi);
fprintf(logfile, "%s%f\n", "Sine Fi (Roll angle): ", senfi);
fprintf(logfile, "%s%f\n", "Sine Theta (Yaw angle): ", sentheta);

    /*Computation of the rotation Matrix*/
    //// RotX * RotY * RotZ ///
    a = ((float)costheta * cosfi);
    b = -((float)cosfi * sentheta);
    c = -((float)senfi);
    d = -((float)senpsi * senfi * costheta) + ((float)cospsi * sentheta);
    e = ((float)senpsi * senfi * sentheta) + ((float)cospsi * costheta);
    f = -((float)senpsi * cosfi);
    g = ((float)cospsi * senfi * costheta) + ((float)senpsi * sentheta);
    h = -((float)sentheta * cospsi * senfi) + ((float)senpsi * costheta);
    i = ((float)cosfi * cospsi);

    fprintf(logfile, "%s\n", "Rotation Matrix: ");
    fprintf(logfile, "a = %f\t b = %f\t c = %f\n", a, b, c);
    fprintf(logfile, "d = %f\t e = %f\t f = %f\n", d, e, f);
    fprintf(logfile, "g = %f\t h = %f\t i = %f\n", g, h, i);
    fprintf(logfile, "%s\n", "Shift Array: ");

    fprintf(logfile, "Xt = %f\n", Xt);
    fprintf(logfile, "Yt = %f\n", Yt);
    fprintf(logfile, "Zt = %f\n", Zt);

if ((pf = fopen(filename,"w+"))==NULL)
 {

    fprintf(logfile, "%s\n" , "Cannot open file RTMATRIX...Now Exit");
    exit(0);

}else{ // else

    fprintf(pf, "%f\n" , Xt);
    fprintf(pf, "%f\n" , Yt);
    fprintf(pf, "%f\n" , Zt);
```

```
            fprintf(pf, "%f\n" , a);
            fprintf(pf, "%f\n" , b);
            fprintf(pf, "%f\n" , c);
            fprintf(pf, "%f\n" , d);
            fprintf(pf, "%f\n" , e);
            fprintf(pf, "%f\n" , f);
            fprintf(pf, "%f\n" , g);
            fprintf(pf, "%f\n" , h);
            fprintf(pf, "%f\n" , i);

            fclose(pf);
    } // else

    fprintf(logfile, "%s\n" , "The Rigid Body Transformation Coefficients were saved in: ");
    fprintf(logfile, "%s\n" , filename);
    fclose(logfile);

    system(logfilename);

}
```

Given a 3D digital volume with a number of slices, the method *void CROTRA2008Dlg::OnCreateVolume()* allows the user to add slices below the last slice (bottom) and above the first slice (top) of the volume. Specifically, the user input variable *'m_VS'* represents the number of additional slices to add to the original image volume. The slices are totally empty thus having zero value in their pixels' intensity. Thus, *'m_VS/2'* slices will be added below the last slice and *'m_VS/2'* slices will be added above the first slice. Clearly *'m_VS'* is even number. The method uses three for loops to import the data into the program from a binary file which may contain pixels intensity values in the following formats: *'CHAR'*, *'SHORT'*, *'INT'*, or *'FLOAT'*. The outer most loop is *'for(sl=1; sl<=numslice-m_VS; sl++)'* where *'ls=(int)sl+((int)(m_VS/2))'* is used to place the rigid body in the middle of the total number of slices (*'numslice+VS'*), thus leaving (*'VS/2'*) empty slices below the last slice and above the first slice. The data type of the resulting volume is float (32-bits Real). The instructions utilized to read in data and to create the empty space above and below the rigid body are:

✓ *if ((pf = fopen(filename3,"rb+"))==NULL) {*

✓ *fprintf(logfile, "%s%s\n", "Cannot open Image Volume File: ", filename3);*
✓ *free(pointer);*
✓ *exit(0);*

✓ *}*

✓ *int ls=0; // to place the rigid body in the middle of the number of slices (numslice+VS),*
        // leaving (VS/2) empty slices below and above

✓ *unsigned char number3 = 1;*
✓ *short number1 = 1;*
✓ *int number2 = 1;*

✓ *for(sl=1; sl<=numslice-m_VS; sl++) {*
✓ *for(j=0; j<rcyres; j++){*
✓ *for(i=0; i<rcxres; i++){*

✓ *if(strcmp(DataType,"CHAR")==0) {*

✓ *fread(&number3,sizeof(unsigned char),1,pf);*

```
✓   number = (float)number3;

✓   }
✓   else if(strcmp(DataType,"SHORT")==0) {

✓   fread(&number1,sizeof(short),1,pf);
✓   number = (float)number1;

✓   }
✓   else if(strcmp(DataType,"INT")==0) {

✓   fread(&number2,sizeof(int),1,pf);
✓   number = (float)number2;

✓   }
✓   else if(strcmp(DataType,"FLOAT")==0) {

✓   fread(&number,sizeof(float),1,pf);
✓   number = (float)number;

✓   }

✓   ls=(int)sl+((int)(m_VS/2));   // to place the rigid body in the middle of the number of slices (numslice+VS),
                                   // leaving (VS/2) empty slices below and above

✓   k2=(j*rcxres+i)+((ls-1)*rcyres*rcxres);
✓   *(pointer+k2)= (float)number;

✓   }
✓   }
✓   }

✓   fclose (pf);
✓   fprintf(logfile, "%s%s\t%s\n", "Image Volume Data: ", filename3, "Loaded");
✓   fprintf(logfile, "%d\t%s\n", m_VS, "Slices were Added to the Volume");
```

void CROTRA2008Dlg::OnCreateVolume()

```
{
        UpdateData(true);
        char filename[260];
        char filename3[254];
        float *pointer = 0;
        float number = 0;
        int sl, j, i, k2;
        FILE *pf;
        int rcxres;
        int rcyres;
        int numslice;
        char DataType[30];
        CString Message;
        FILE * logfile;
        char logfilename[260];
        sprintf(filename3, "%s", m_VolumeName);
        sprintf(logfilename, "%s%s%s", "newVOL", filename3, ".log");
```

```
if ((logfile = fopen(logfilename,"w+"))==NULL)
{

Message.Format("%s\n%s\n%s\n" , "Cannot open file: ", logfilename, "Now Exit");
AfxMessageBox(Message);
exit(0);

} else { // load variables from user input and save to logfile
            rcxres = (int)m_rcxres;
            rcyres = (int)m_rcyres;
            numslice = (int)m_numslice + (int)m_VS;

            sprintf(DataType, "%s", m_DataType);

            Message.Format("%s\n%s\n%s\n%s\n%s\n" , "The Image Volume DataType is: ", DataType,
            "Is this the correct DataType?", "Please verify consistency", "at the end of processing");
            AfxMessageBox(Message);

            fprintf(logfile, "%s%s\n", "Image Volume being processed: ", filename3);
            fprintf(logfile, "%s%d\n", "Number of Voxels Along X: ", rcxres);
            fprintf(logfile, "%s%d\n", "Number of Voxels Along Y: ", rcyres);
            fprintf(logfile, "%s%d\n", "Number of Voxels Along Z: ", ((int)numslice-m_VS));
            fprintf(logfile, "%s%s\n", "DataType: ", DataType);

    } // load variables from user input and save to logfile

fprintf(logfile, "%s\n", "Now Loading the Image Volume Data");

if ((pointer = (float *) calloc( ((numslice*rcyres*rcxres)+1), sizeof(float)) ) == NULL)
{

fprintf(logfile, "%s\n", "Not enough memory to allocate Image Data...Now Exit");
exit(0);

} else { // else
        /// initialize pointer
        for(sl=1;sl<=numslice; sl++) {
            for(j=0;j<rcyres;j++){
                for(i=0;i<rcxres;i++){

                    k2=(j*rcxres+i)+((sl-1)*rcyres*rcxres);
                    *(pointer+k2)= (float)0;

                                }
                            }
                        }
    } // else
if ((pf = fopen(filename3,"rb+"))==NULL)
{
fprintf(logfile, "%s%s\n", "Cannot open Image Volume File: ", filename3);
free(pointer);
exit(0);
}
int ls=0; // to place the rigid body in the middle of the number of slices (numslice+VS),
        // leaving (VS/2) empty slices below and above
```

Computer Science Applications

```
/*these lines read the image data*/

unsigned char number3 = 1;
short number1 = 1;
int number2 = 1;

  for(sl=1 ;sl<=numslice-m_VS; sl++) {
      for(j=0;j<rcyres;j++){
          for(i=0;i<rcxres;i++){

  if(strcmp(DataType,"CHAR")==0)
  {
  fread(&number3,sizeof(unsigned char),1,pf);
  number = (float)number3;
  }

      else if(strcmp(DataType,"SHORT")==0)
      {
      fread(&number1,sizeof(short),1,pf);
      number = (float)number1;
      }

      else if(strcmp(DataType,"INT")==0)
      {
      fread(&number2,sizeof(int),1,pf);
      number = (float)number2;
      }

      else if(strcmp(DataType,"FLOAT")==0)
      {
       fread(&number,sizeof(float),1,pf);
       number = (float)number;
      }

          ls=(int)sl+((int)(m_VS/2));   // to place the rigid body in the middle of the number of slices
                                        // (numslice+VS), leaving (VS/2) empty slices below and above

      k2=(j*rcxres+i)+((ls-1)*rcyres*rcxres);
      *(pointer+k2)= (float)number;

                  }
                }
            }

    fclose (pf);
    fprintf(logfile, "%s%s\t%s\n", "Image Volume Data: ", filename3, "Loaded");
    fprintf(logfile, "%d\t%s\n", m_VS, "Slices were Added to the Volume");

      /// save new image
      float savedata = 0;
      sprintf(filename, "%s%s", "newVOL", filename3);
      fprintf(logfile, "%s%s\n", "Now Saving in File: ", filename);
      if ((pf = fopen(filename,"wb+"))==NULL)
      {

      fprintf(logfile, "%s\n", "Cannot open file to save Image Volume");
```

```
        exit(0);

    } else { // else
    for(sl=1;sl<=numslice; sl++) {
        for(j=0;j<rcyres;j++){
            for(i=0;i<rcxres;i++){

            k2=(j*rcxres+i)+((sl-1)*rcyres*rcxres);
            savedata=(float)*(pointer+k2);
            fwrite(&savedata,sizeof(float),1,pf);


                }
            }
        }

        fclose(pf);
        free(pointer);

    } // else

    fprintf(logfile, "%s%s\n", "3D Image Volume Saved in file: ", filename);
    fprintf(logfile, "%s\n", "DataType: Float (32-bits Real)");
    fclose(logfile);
    system(logfilename);
}
```

The method *void CROTRA2008Dlg::OnApplyRT()* is the core of the source code of the program implementation described in this chapter. The first two tasks performed are those of reading the 3D image volume from the binary file where this is contained and to calculate the coordinates of the center of mass of the volume. The rigid body transformation is then calculated as rot X (rotation about the X axis) * rot Y (rotation about the Y axis) * rot Z (rotation about the Z axis). The three rotational angles as well the three shifts of the coordinate of the center of mass of the volume are read in from the user input through the Graphical User Interface.

While processing, the source code shows that the information relevant to the operations performed is saved in a *'log'* file which will be available automatically readable from the user at the end of the routine because of the command *'system'*.

The method *void CROTRA2008Dlg::OnApplyRT()* here illustrated resolves an issue of relevance that comes to the attention when applying a rigid body transformation through the following formulas:

$$xnew = ((float)aa * (i-comx)) + ((float)ba * (j-comy)) + ((float)ca * ((sl-1)-comz)) + (float)xoa + (float)comx \quad (1)$$

$$ynew = ((float)da * (i-comx)) + ((float)ea * (j-comy)) + ((float)fa * ((sl-1)-comz)) + (float)yoa + (float)comy \quad (2)$$

$$znew = ((float)ga * (i-comx)) + ((float)ha * (j-comy)) + ((float)la * ((sl-1)-comz)) + (float)zoa + (float)comz \quad (3)$$

Where *'aa'*, *'ba'*, *'ca'*, *'da'*, *'ea'*, *'fa'*, *'ga'*, *'ha'* and *'la'* are the coefficients of the rotation matrix, *'xoa'*, *'yoa'* and *'zoa'* are the misplacements applied to the center of mass. And *'comx'*, *'comy'* and *'comz'* are the coordinates of the center of mass of the image volume. Equations (1), (2) and (3), introduce a misplacement of the center of mass. They are thus theoretically ill posed. In order to correct for such misplacement, the following adjustment is needed. In first instance the following variables are calculated:

✓ *xintegera = (int)(float)floor((float)comx)*   (4)

✓ *yintegera = (int)(float)floor((float)comy)*   (5)

✓ *zintegera = (int)(float)floor((float)comz)*   (6)

Computer Science Applications

Further, the following lines calculate the fractionals: '*fractionalx*', '*fractionaly*' and '*fractionalz*' of '*xcom*', '*ycom*' and '*zcom*' which are the cause of the misplacement of the center of mass. Such misplacement happens because the rotations about the X axis, about the Y axis and about the Z axis are not zero when using equations (1), (2) and (3).

✓   *float fractionalx = ((float) comx - (float)floor((float)comx))*   (7)

✓   *float fractionaly = ((float) comy - (float)floor((float)comy))*   (8)

✓   *float fractionalz = ((float) comz - (float)floor((float)comz))*   (9)

Therefore the corrected formulas are given substituting in equations (1), (2) and (3) the values of '*comx*', '*comy*' and '*comz*' with the values of '*xintegera*', '*yintegera*' and '*zintegera*' respectively. Also, in equations (1), (2) and (3), the values of '*fractionalx*', '*fractionaly*' and '*fractionalz*' are added to enforce the correction. Given this explanation, the reader is addressed to the source code of *void CROTRA2008Dlg::OnApplyRT()* to see the details of such substitution which is treated as single case, each depending on the rotation to be corrected.

Once the correction is made, the source code performs the interpolation of the data using the trivariate cubic paradigm. The coefficients of the interpolation paradigm are identified through the instructions '*LGR1 = ((float) ((1/2) * cubic_term) - quadratic_term - ((1/2) * power_one_term) + 1)*' and '*LGR2 = ((float) (-(1/6) * cubic_term) + quadratic_term - ((11/6) * power_one_term) + 1)*', where '*Mx = ((float)xnew) - (float)floor((float)xnew)*', '*My = ((float)ynew) - (float)floor((float)ynew)*', '*Mz = ((float)znew) - (float)floor((float)znew)*', and '*cubic_term = ((float) (Mx + My + Mz) * (Mx + My + Mz) * (Mx + My + Mz))*', '*quadratic_term = ((float) (Mx + My + Mz) * (Mx + My + Mz))*', '*power_one_term = ((float) (Mx + My + Mz))*'. The neighborhood chosen in order to calculate the coefficients of the trivariate cubic interpolation is defined through the following lines of code:

✓   *//Central 3 x 3 Sub-neighborhood of f (0, 0, 0)*

✓   *k1=(iynew*rcxres+ixnew)+((iznew-1)*rcyres*rcxres); //f000*

✓   *f000 = (float)*(pointer+k1);*

✓   *k2=(iynew*rcxres+(ixnew-1))+((iznew-1)*rcyres*rcxres); //fm100*

✓   *fm100 = (float)*(pointer+k2);*

✓   *k3=(iynew*rcxres+(ixnew+1))+((iznew-1)*rcyres*rcxres); //f100*

✓   *f100 = (float)*(pointer+k3);*

✓   *k4=(iynew*rcxres+(ixnew-1))+((iznew-2)*rcyres*rcxres); //fm10m1*

✓   *fm10m1 = (float)*(pointer+k4);*

✓   *k5=(iynew*rcxres+ixnew)+((iznew-2)*rcyres*rcxres); //f00m1*

✓   *f00m1 = (float)*(pointer+k5);*

✓   *k6=(iynew*rcxres+(ixnew+1))+((iznew-2)*rcyres*rcxres); //f10m1*

✓   *f10m1 = (float)*(pointer+k6);*

✓   *k7=(iynew*rcxres+(ixnew-1))+(iznew*rcyres*rcxres); //fm101*

✓   *fm101 = (float)*(pointer+k7);*

✓   *k8=(iynew*rcxres+ixnew)+(iznew*rcyres*rcxres); //f001*

- ✓ $f001 = (float)*(pointer+k8);$

- ✓ $k9=(iynew*rcxres+(ixnew+1))+(iznew*rcyres*rcxres);$ //f101

- ✓ $f101 = (float)*(pointer+k9);$

- ✓ // Outer-Right 3 x 3 Sub-neighborhood of f (0, 0, 0)

- ✓ $k10=((iynew-1)*rcxres+ixnew)+((iznew-1)*rcyres*rcxres);$ //f0m10

- ✓ $f0m10 = (float)*(pointer+k10);$

- ✓ $k11=((iynew-1)*rcxres+(ixnew-1))+((iznew-1)*rcyres*rcxres);$ //fm1m10

- ✓ $fm1m10 = (float)*(pointer+k11);$

- ✓ $k12=((iynew-1)*rcxres+(ixnew+1))+((iznew-1)*rcyres*rcxres);$ //f1m10

- ✓ $f1m10 = (float)*(pointer+k12);$

- ✓ $k13=((iynew-1)*rcxres+(ixnew-1))+(iznew-2)*rcyres*rcxres);$ //fm1m1m1

- ✓ $fm1m1m1 = (float)*(pointer+k13);$

- ✓ $k14=((iynew-1)*rcxres+ixnew)+(iznew-2)*rcyres*rcxres);$ //f0m1m1

- ✓ $f0m1m1 = (float)*(pointer+k14);$

- ✓ $k15=((iynew-1)*rcxres+(ixnew+1))+(iznew-2)*rcyres*rcxres);$ //f1m1m1

- ✓ $f1m1m1 = (float)*(pointer+k15);$

- ✓ $k16=((iynew-1)*rcxres+(ixnew-1))+(iznew*rcyres*rcxres);$ //fm1m11

- ✓ $fm1m11 = (float)*(pointer+k16);$

- ✓ $k17=((iynew-1)*rcxres+ixnew)+(iznew*rcyres*rcxres);$ //f0m11

- ✓ $f0m11 = (float)*(pointer+k17);$

- ✓ $k18=((iynew-1)*rcxres+(ixnew+1))+(iznew*rcyres*rcxres);$ //f1m11

- ✓ $f1m11 = (float)*(pointer+k18);$

- ✓ // Outer-Left 3 x 3 Sub-neighborhood of f (0, 0, 0)

- ✓ $k19=((iynew+1)*rcxres+ixnew)+(iznew-1)*rcyres*rcxres);$ //f010

- ✓ $f010 = (float)*(pointer+k19);$

- ✓ $k20=((iynew+1)*rcxres+(ixnew-1))+(iznew-1)*rcyres*rcxres);$ //fm110

- ✓ $fm110 = (float)*(pointer+k20);$

- ✓ $k21=((iynew+1)*rcxres+(ixnew+1))+(iznew-1)*rcyres*rcxres);$ //f110

- ✓ $f110 = (float)*(pointer+k21);$

- ✓ $k22=((iynew+1)*rcxres+(ixnew-1))+((iznew-2)*rcyres*rcxres); //fm11m1$

- ✓ $fm11m1 = (float)*(pointer+k22);$

- ✓ $k23=((iynew+1)*rcxres+ixnew)+((iznew-2)*rcyres*rcxres); //f01m1$

- ✓ $f01m1 = (float)*(pointer+k23);$

- ✓ $k24=((iynew+1)*rcxres+(ixnew+1))+((iznew-2)*rcyres*rcxres); //f11m1$

- ✓ $f11m1 = (float)*(pointer+k24);$

- ✓ $k25=((iynew+1)*rcxres+(ixnew-1))+(iznew*rcyres*rcxres); //fm111$

- ✓ $fm111 = (float)*(pointer+k25);$

- ✓ $k26=((iynew+1)*rcxres+ixnew)+(iznew*rcyres*rcxres); //f011$

- ✓ $f011 = (float)*(pointer+k26);$

- ✓ $k27=((iynew+1)*rcxres+(ixnew+1))+(iznew*rcyres*rcxres); //f111$

- ✓ $f111 = (float)*(pointer+k27);$

Further, the calculation of the center of mass' coordinates happen before and after the application of the rotation-translation to the grid. It is shown that the variation of center of mass position is the same for interpolated data and raw data. This particular is well visible in the '*log*' file displayed automatically at the end of processing (see Fig. 4). The variable '*TH*' is the threshold employed to select the pixel intensity values and is input by the user through the GUI panel called '*Image Volume Parameters*' (see Fig. 1). The lines of code employed to calculate the center of mass before and after the rigid body transformation are:

- ✓ $float\ intcomx = 0,\ intcomy = 0,\ intcomz = 0;$

- ✓ $for(sl=1;\ sl<=numslice;\ sl++)\ \{$
- ✓ $for(j=0;\ j<rcyres;\ j++)\ \{$
- ✓ $for(i=0;\ i<rcxres;\ i++)\ \{$
- ✓ $k2=(j*rcxres+i)+((sl-1)*rcyres*rcxres);$
- ✓ $if\ (\ *(interdata+k2) > TH\ )\ \{$

- ✓ $count++;$
- ✓ $sumi = sumi + ((float)i);$
- ✓ $sumj = sumj + ((float)j);$
- ✓ $sumsl = sumsl + ((float)sl-1);$

- ✓ $\}$

- ✓ $\}$
- ✓ $\}$
- ✓ $\}$

- ✓ $intcomx = ((float)sumi/count);$
- ✓ $intcomy = ((float)sumj/count);$
- ✓ $intcomz = ((float)sumsl/count);$

- ✓ *float NOTintcomx = 0, NOTintcomy = 0, NOTintcomz = 0;*

- ✓ *for(sl=1; sl<=numslice; sl++) {*
- ✓ *for(j=0; j<rcyres; j++) {*
- ✓ *for(i=0; i<rcxres; i++) {*

- ✓ *k2=(j*rcxres+i)+((sl-1)*rcyres*rcxres);*

- ✓ *if (*(originalData+k2) > TH) {*

- ✓ *count++;*
- ✓ *sumi = sumi + ((float)i);*
- ✓ *sumj = sumj + ((float)j);*
- ✓ *sumsl = sumsl + ((float)sl-1);*

- ✓ *}*

- ✓ *}*
- ✓ *}*
- ✓ *}*

- ✓ *NOTintcomx = ((float)sumi/ count);*
- ✓ *NOTintcomy = ((float)sumj/ count);*
- ✓ *NOTintcomz = ((float)sumsl/ count);*

void CROTRA2008Dlg::OnApplyRT()
{

```
    UpdateData(true);
    char filename[254];
    char filename3[254];
    float number = 0;
    float *pointer = 0;
    int sl, j, i;
    FILE *pf;
    float XRES, YRES, ZRES;
    int TH;
    int rcxres;
    int rcyres;
    int numslice;
    CString Message;
    FILE * logfile;
    char logfilename[270];
    char DataType[30];
    float comx=0, comy=0, comz=0, sumi=0, sumj=0, sumsl=0;
    float aa, ba, ca, da, ea, fa, ga, ha, la;
    float xoa, yoa, zoa;
    float fi, theta, psi;
    float Xt, Yt, Zt, RAD;
    float cosfi, cospsi, costheta, senfi, senpsi, sentheta;

    ///////////////////// trivariate cubic Lagrange interpolation variables/////////
    int k1, k2, k3, k4, k5, k6, k7, k8, k9, k10;
    int k11, k12, k13, k14, k15, k16, k17, k18, k19, k20;
    int k21, k22, k23, k24, k25, k26, k27;
```

101

```
float f000, fm101, f001, f101, fm100, f100, fm10m1, f00m1, f10m1, fm1m11, f0m11, f1m11, fm1m10, f0m10;
float f1m10, fm1m1m1, f0m1m1, f1m1m1, fm111, f011, f111, fm110, f010, f110, fm11m1, f01m1, f11m1;
float omega1, omega2, Mx, My, Mz, LGR1, LGR2;
float cubic_term, quadratic_term, power_one_term;
float SCALE;
int k0;
float tfLGR;
float convolution;
int xintegera, yintegera, zintegera;
///////////////////// trivariate cubic Lagrange interpolation variables/////////

        sprintf(filename3, "%s", m_VolumeName);
        sprintf(logfilename, "%s%s%s", "ROTRA", filename3, ".log");

        if ((logfile = fopen(logfilename,"w+"))==NULL)
        {

                Message.Format("%s\n%s\n%s\n" , "Cannot open file: ", logfilename, "Now Exit");
                AfxMessageBox(Message);
                exit(0);

        } else { // load variables from user input and save to logfile

                rcxres = (int)m_rcxres;
                rcyres = (int)m_rcyres;
                numslice = (int)m_NofSlices;
                sprintf(DataType, "%s", m_DataType);

        if(strcmp(DataType,"FLOAT")!=0)
        { // if

        Message.Format("%s\n%s\n%s\n%s\n" , "The Image Volume DataType is: ",
        DataType, "Please Change to FLOAT", "Now Exit");
        AfxMessageBox(Message);
        fprintf(logfile, "%s\n%s\n%s\n%s\n" , "The Image Volume DataType is: ",
        DataType, "Please Change to FLOAT", "Now Exit");
        exit(0);

        } // if

        //// RotX * RotY * RotZ ///
        psi = (float)m_theta;
        fi = (float)m_fi;
        theta = (float)m_psi;
        Xt = (float)m_Xt;
        Yt = (float)m_Yt;
        Zt = (float)m_Zt;
        XRES = (float)m_XRES;
        YRES = (float)m_YRES;
        ZRES = (float)m_ZRES;
        TH = (int)m_TH;
        SCALE = (float)m_SCALE;

        //// now save to logfile
        fprintf(logfile, "%s\n", "Now Loading the Image Volume Data");
        fprintf(logfile, "%s\n", "The program will find the Center of Mass (COM) of the Image Volume");
```

```
fprintf(logfile, "%s\n", "The program will apply the Rigid Body Tranformation to the Image Data");
fprintf(logfile, "%s%s\n", "Image Volume being processed: ", filename3);
fprintf(logfile, "%s%d\n", "Number of Voxels Along X: ", rcxres);
fprintf(logfile, "%s%d\n", "Number of Voxels Along Y: ", rcyres);
fprintf(logfile, "%s%d\n", "Number of Voxels Along Z: ", numslice);
fprintf(logfile, "%s%f\n", "Voxels' Size Along the X axis: ", XRES);
fprintf(logfile, "%s%f\n", "Voxels' Size Along the Y axis: ", YRES);
fprintf(logfile, "%s%f\n", "Voxels' Size Along the Z axis: ", ZRES);


//// RotX * RotY * RotZ ///
fprintf(logfile, "%s%f\n", "Rotation about the X-axis: ", psi);
fprintf(logfile, "%s%f\n", "Rotation about the Y-axis: ", fi);
fprintf(logfile, "%s%f\n", "Rotation about the Z-axis: ", theta);
fprintf(logfile, "%s%f\n", "The Shift Along the X axis: ", Xt);
fprintf(logfile, "%s%f\n", "The Shift Along the Y axis: ", Yt);
fprintf(logfile, "%s%f\n", "The Shift Along the Z axis: ", Zt);
fprintf(logfile, "%s%d\n", "The Threshold: ", TH);
fprintf(logfile, "%s%f\n", "The SCALE parameter: ", SCALE);

} // load variables from user input and save to logfile

if ((pointer = (float *) calloc( ((numslice*rcyres*rcxres)+1), sizeof(float)) ) == NULL)
{

    fprintf(logfile, "%s\n", "Not enough memory to allocate Image Data... Now Exit");
    exit(0);

} else { // initialize and read data
    /// initialize pointer
    for(sl=1;sl<=numslice; sl++) {
        for(j=0;j<rcyres;j++){
            for(i=0;i<rcxres;i++){

                k2=(j*rcxres+i)+((sl-1)*rcyres*rcxres);
                *(pointer+k2)= (float)0;
                            }
                        }
                    }

    if ((pf = fopen(filename3,"rb+"))==NULL)
    {

    fprintf(logfile, "%s%s\n", "Cannot open file: ", filename3);
    free(pointer);
    exit(0);

    }

    /*these lines read the image data*/
    for(sl=1; sl<=numslice; sl++) {
        for(j=0;j<rcyres;j++){
            for(i=0;i<rcxres;i++){

                fread(&number,sizeof(float),1,pf);
                k2=(j*rcxres+i)+((sl-1)*rcyres*rcxres);
                *(pointer+k2)= (float) number;
```

```
                                            }
                                        }
                                    }

        fclose (pf);
        fprintf(logfile, "%s%s%s\n", "The Image Data: ", filename3, " has been loaded");
} // initialize and read data

fprintf(logfile, "%s\n", "Now Calculating the Center of Mass (COM):");
long int count=0;

    for(sl=1;sl<=numslice; sl++) {
        for(j=0;j<rcyres;j++){
            for(i=0;i<rcxres;i++){

            k2=(j*rcxres+i)+((sl-1)*rcyres*rcxres);

            if ( *(pointer+k2) > TH )
            { // if

            count++;
            sumi = sumi + ((float)i);
            sumj = sumj + ((float)j);
            sumsl = sumsl + ((float)sl-1);

            }// if
                                    }
                                }
                            }

        comx = ((float)sumi/count);
        comy = ((float)sumj/count);
        comz = ((float)sumsl/count);
    fprintf(logfile, "%s%f\n", "The x coordinate of the COM: ", comx);
    fprintf(logfile, "%s%f\n", "The y coordinate of the COM: ", comy);
    fprintf(logfile, "%s%f\n", "The z coordinate of the COM: ", comz);

    ///// calculate rotation translation transformation
    fprintf(logfile, "%s\n", "Now Calculating the rigid body rotation translation transformation");
    RAD=(float)360;

/*tranform in radiants*/
fprintf(logfile,"%s\n", "The Angles in Radians: ");

theta=((float)(2*3.14)/(RAD/theta));
psi=((float)(2*3.14)/(RAD/psi));
fi=((float)(2*3.14)/(RAD/fi));

//// RotX * RotY * RotZ ///
fprintf(logfile, "%s%f\n", "Pitch angle (Rotation about the X-axis): ", psi);
fprintf(logfile, "%s%f\n", "Roll angle (Rotation about the Y-axis): ", fi);
fprintf(logfile, "%s%f\n", "Yaw angle (Rotation about the Z-axis): ", theta);

costheta = (float)cos( (float)theta );
cospsi = (float)cos( (float)psi );
cosfi = (float)cos( (float)fi );
```

```
//// RotX * RotY * RotZ ///
fprintf(logfile, "%s%f\n", "Cosine Psi (Pitch angle): ", cospsi);
fprintf(logfile, "%s%f\n", "Cosine Fi (Roll angle): ", cosfi);
fprintf(logfile, "%s%f\n", "Cosine Theta (Yaw angle): ", costheta);

sentheta = (float)sin( (float)theta );
senpsi = (float)sin( (float)psi );
senfi = (float)sin( (float)fi );

//// RotX * RotY * RotZ ///
fprintf(logfile, "%s%f\n", "Sine Psi (Pitch angle): ", senpsi);
fprintf(logfile, "%s%f\n", "Sine Fi (Roll angle): ", senfi);
fprintf(logfile, "%s%f\n", "Sine Theta (Yaw angle): ", sentheta);

        /*Computation of the rotation Matrix*/

        //// RotX * RotY * RotZ ///
        aa = ((float)costheta * cosfi);
        ba = -((float)cosfi * sentheta);
        ca = -((float)senfi);
        da = -((float)senpsi * senfi * costheta) + ((float)cospsi * sentheta);
        ea = ((float)senpsi * senfi * sentheta) + ((float)cospsi * costheta);
        fa = -((float)senpsi * cosfi);
        ga = ((float)cospsi * senfi * costheta) + ((float)senpsi * sentheta);
        ha = -((float)sentheta * cospsi * senfi) + ((float)senpsi * costheta);
        la = ((float)cosfi * cospsi);

        xoa = (float)Xt;
        yoa = (float)Yt;
        zoa = (float)Zt;

        fprintf(logfile, "%s\n", "The Rotation Matrix: ");
        fprintf(logfile, "%f\t%f\t%f\n", aa, ba, ca);
        fprintf(logfile, "%f\t%f\t%f\n", da, ea, fa);
        fprintf(logfile, "%f\t%f\t%f\n", ga, ha, la);
        fprintf(logfile, "%s\n", "The Shift Array: ");
        fprintf(logfile, "Xt = %f\t Yt = %f\t Zt = %f\n", xoa, yoa, zoa);
        float savedata = 0;
        sprintf(filename, "%s%s", filename3, "INT");

float *interdata=0;
if ((interdata = (float *) calloc( ((numslice*rcyres*rcxres)+1), sizeof(float)) ) == NULL)
{

    fprintf(logfile, "%s\n", "Not enough memory to allocate fMRI data: Exit");
    free(pointer);
    exit(0);

} else { // else

        /// initialize interdata
        for(sl=1;sl<=numslice; sl++) {
            for(j=0;j<rcyres;j++){
                for(i=0;i<rcxres;i++){

                k2=(j*rcxres+i)+((sl-1)*rcyres*rcxres);
```

```
                        *(interdata+k2)= (float)0;


                                          }
                                   }
                            }
        } // else


float *originalData=0;
if ((originalData = (float *) calloc( ((numslice*rcyres*rcxres)+1), sizeof(float)) ) == NULL)
{

        fprintf(logfile, "%s\n", "Not enough memory to allocate fMRI data: Exit");
        free(pointer);
        free(interdata);
        exit(0);

} else { // else

                /// initialize originalData
                for(sl=1;sl<=numslice; sl++) {
                        for(j=0;j<rcyres;j++){
                                for(i=0;i<rcxres;i++){

                                k2=(j*rcxres+i)+((sl-1)*rcyres*rcxres);
                                *(originalData+k2)= (float)0;


                                        }
                                }
                        }
        } // else
        /// the following lines calculate the fractionals of xcom, ycom and zcom that are the cause of the
        ///  misplacement of the center of mass.
        /// This misplacement happens because of rotations (rot x, rot y, or rot z) !=0

        xintegera = (int)(float)floor((float)comx);
        yintegera = (int)(float)floor((float)comy);
        zintegera = (int)(float)floor((float)comz);

        float fractionalx = ((float) comx - (float)floor((float)comx));
        float fractionaly = ((float) comy - (float)floor((float)comy));
        float fractionalz = ((float) comz - (float)floor((float)comz));

///////////////////////data re-sampling/////////////////////////
                fprintf(logfile, "%s\n", "Now applying the 3D transformation (rotation-translation)");
                fprintf(logfile, "%s\n", "to the Image Volume, and interpolating data with the");
                fprintf(logfile, "%s\n", "Trivariate Cubic Lagrange Interpolation Function.");
                fprintf(logfile, "%s\n", "Now Resampling...");

                int ixnew = 0, iynew = 0, iznew = 0;
                int kk;
                float xnew = 0, ynew = 0, znew = 0;

                for(sl=1;sl<=numslice; sl++) {
                        for(j=0;j<rcyres;j++){
                                for(i=0;i<rcxres;i++){
```

$$k0=(j*rcxres+i)+((sl-1)*rcyres*rcxres);$$

// the shift along x y or z is determined here because of the coefficients of the
// rotation matrix that means that below lines in between are theoretically ill posed!
// also when this formula is used to correct for motion, another misplacement along
// x, y and z is introduced and that makes the motion correction paradigm theoretically ill posed!

```
/*
        xnew = ((float)aa * (i-comx)) +
               ((float)ba * (j comy)) +
               ((float)ca * ((sl-1)-comz)) +
               (float)xoa + (float)comx;

        ynew = ((float)da * (i-comx)) +
               ((float)ea * (j-comy)) +
               ((float)fa * ((sl-1)-comz)) +
               (float)yoa + (float)comy;

        znew  = ((float)ga * (i-comx)) +
               ((float)ha * (j-comy)) +
               ((float)la * ((sl-1)-comz)) +
               (float)zoa + (float)comz;
*/

  if ( psi == 0 && fi == 0 && theta == 0 ) {
  // if RotX == 0 && RotY == 0 && RotZ == 0

     xnew =      ((float)aa * (float)(i-xintegera)) +
                 ((float)ba * (float)(j-yintegera)) +
                 ((float)ca * (float)((sl-1)-zintegera)) +
                 (float)xoa + (float)comx;

     ynew =      ((float)da * (float)(i-xintegera)) +
                 ((float)ea * (float)(j-yintegera)) +
                 ((float)fa * (float)((sl-1)-zintegera)) +
                 (float)yoa + (float)comy;

  } else if( psi == 0 && fi == 0 && theta != 0 ) {
  // if RotX == 0 && RotY == 0 && RotZ != 0

     xnew =      ((float)aa * (float)(i-xintegera)) +
                 ((float)ba * (float)(j-yintegera)) +
                 ((float)ca * (float)((sl-1)-zintegera)) +
                 (float)xoa + (float)comx + (float)fractionalx;

     ynew =      ((float)da * (float)(i-xintegera)) +
                 ((float)ea * (float)(j-yintegera)) +
                 ((float)fa * (float)((sl-1)-zintegera)) +
                 (float)yoa + (float)comy + (float)fractionaly;

  } else if ( psi != 0 && fi == 0 && theta == 0 ) {
  // if RotX != 0 && RotY == 0 && RotZ == 0

     xnew =      ((float)aa * (float)(i-xintegera)) +
                 ((float)ba * (float)(j-yintegera)) +
                 ((float)ca * (float)((sl-1)-zintegera)) +
```

```
                        (float)xoa + (float)comx;

    ynew =              ((float)da * (float)(i-xintegera)) +
                        ((float)ea * (float)(j-yintegera)) +
                        ((float)fa * (float)((sl-1)-zintegera)) +
                        (float)yoa + (float)comy + (float)fractionaly;

    } else if ( psi != 0 && fi == 0 && theta != 0 ) {
    // if RotX != 0 && RotY == 0 && RotZ != 0

    xnew =              ((float)aa * (float)(i-xintegera)) +
                        ((float)ba * (float)(j-yintegera)) +
                        ((float)ca * (float)((sl-1)-zintegera)) +
                        (float)xoa + (float)comx + (float)fractionalx;

    ynew =              ((float)da * (float)(i-xintegera)) +
                        ((float)ea * (float)(j-yintegera)) +
                        ((float)fa * (float)((sl-1)-zintegera)) +
                        (float)yoa + (float)comy + (float)fractionaly;

    } else if ( psi == 0 && fi != 0 && theta == 0 ) {
    // if RotX == 0 && RotY != 0 && RotZ == 0

    xnew =              ((float)aa * (float)(i-xintegera)) +
                        ((float)ba * (float)(j-yintegera)) +
                        ((float)ca * (float)((sl-1)-zintegera)) +
                        (float)xoa + (float)comx + (float)fractionalx;

    ynew =              ((float)da * (float)(i-xintegera)) +
                        ((float)ea * (float)(j-yintegera)) +
                        ((float)fa * (float)((sl-1)-zintegera)) +
                        (float)yoa + (float)comy;

    } else if ( psi == 0 && fi != 0 && theta != 0 ) {
    // if RotX == 0 && RotY != 0 && RotZ != 0

    xnew =              ((float)aa * (float)(i-xintegera)) +
                        ((float)ba * (float)(j-yintegera)) +
                        ((float)ca * (float)((sl-1)-zintegera)) +
                        (float)xoa + (float)comx + (float)fractionalx;

    ynew =              ((float)da * (float)(i-xintegera)) +
                        ((float)ea * (float)(j-yintegera)) +
                        ((float)fa * (float)((sl-1)-zintegera)) +
                        (float)yoa + (float)comy + (float)fractionaly;

    } else if ( psi != 0 && fi != 0 && theta == 0 ) {
    // if RotX != 0 && RotY != 0 && RotZ == 0

      xnew = ((float)aa * (float)(i-xintegera)) +
                        ((float)ba * (float)(j-yintegera)) +
                        ((float)ca * (float)((sl-1)-zintegera)) +
                        (float)xoa + (float)comx + (float)fractionalx;

      ynew = (float)da * (float)(i-xintegera)) +
                        ((float)ea * (float)(j-yintegera)) +
```

```
                    ((float)fa * (float)((sl-1)-zintegera)) +
                    (float)yoa + (float)comy + (float)fractionaly;

} else if ( psi != 0 && fi != 0 && theta != 0 ) {
// if RotX != 0 && RotY != 0 && RotZ != 0

xnew =          ((float)aa * (float)(i-xintegera)) +
                ((float)ba * (float)(j-yintegera)) +
                ((float)ca * (float)((sl-1)-zintegera)) +
                (float)xoa + (float)comx + (float)fractionalx;

ynew =          ((float)da * (float)(i-xintegera)) +
                ((float)ea * (float)(j-yintegera)) +
                ((float)fa * (float)((sl-1)-zintegera)) +
                (float)yoa + (float)comy + (float)fractionaly;
}

znew =          ((float)ga * (float)(i-xintegera)) +
                ((float)ha * (float)(j-yintegera)) +
                ((float)la * (float)((sl-1)-zintegera)) +
                (float)zoa + (float)comz;

ixnew = (int) (float)floor((float)xnew);
iynew = (int) (float)floor((float)ynew);
iznew = (int) (float)floor((float)znew);


if( (ixnew>=1)&&(ixnew<rcxres-2)&&
    (iynew>=1)&&(iynew<rcyres-2)&&
    (iznew>=2)&&(iznew<=numslice-2) // (1)
){
        //Central 3 x 3 Sub-neighborhood of f (0, 0, 0)

        k1=(iynew*rcxres+ixnew)+((iznew-1)*rcyres*rcxres); //f000

        f000 = (float)*(pointer+k1);

        k2=(iynew*rcxres+(ixnew-1))+((iznew-1)*rcyres*rcxres); //fm100

        fm100 = (float)*(pointer+k2);

        k3=(iynew*rcxres+(ixnew+1))+((iznew-1)*rcyres*rcxres); //f100

        f100 = (float)*(pointer+k3);

        k4=(iynew*rcxres+(ixnew-1))+( (iznew-2)*rcyres*rcxres ); //fm10m1

        fm10m1 = (float)*(pointer+k4);

        k5=(iynew*rcxres+ixnew)+( (iznew-2)*rcyres*rcxres); //f00m1

        f00m1 = (float)*(pointer+k5);

        k6=(iynew*rcxres+(ixnew+1))+( (iznew-2)*rcyres*rcxres); //f10m1

        f10m1 = (float)*(pointer+k6);
```

```
k7=(iynew*rcxres+(ixnew-1))+( iznew*rcyres*rcxres); //fm101

fm101 = (float)*(pointer+k7);

k8=(iynew*rcxres+ixnew)+( iznew*rcyres*rcxres); //f001

f001 = (float)*(pointer+k8);

k9=(iynew*rcxres+(ixnew+1))+( iznew*rcyres*rcxres); //f101

f101 = (float)*(pointer+k9);

// Outer-Right 3 x 3 Sub-neighborhood of f (0, 0, 0)

k10=((iynew-1)*rcxres+ixnew)+((iznew-1)*rcyres*rcxres); //f0m10

f0m10 = (float)*(pointer+k10);

k11=((iynew-1)*rcxres+(ixnew-1))+((iznew-1)*rcyres*rcxres); //fm1m10

fm1m10 = (float)*(pointer+k11);

k12=((iynew-1)*rcxres+(ixnew+1))+((iznew-1)*rcyres*rcxres); //f1m10

f1m10 = (float)*(pointer+k12);
k13=((iynew-1)*rcxres+(ixnew-1))+( iznew-2)*rcyres*rcxres ); //fm1m1m1

fm1m1m1 = (float)*(pointer+k13);

k14=((iynew-1)*rcxres+ixnew)+( iznew-2)*rcyres*rcxres ); //f0m1m1

f0m1m1 = (float)*(pointer+k14);

k15=((iynew-1)*rcxres+(ixnew+1))+( iznew-2)*rcyres*rcxres ); //f1m1m1

f1m1m1 = (float)*(pointer+k15);

k16=((iynew-1)*rcxres+(ixnew-1))+( iznew*rcyres*rcxres ); //fm1m11

fm1m11 = (float)*(pointer+k16);

 k17=((iynew-1)*rcxres+ixnew)+( iznew*rcyres*rcxres ); //f0m11

f0m11 = (float)*(pointer+k17);

k18=((iynew-1)*rcxres+(ixnew+1))+( iznew*rcyres*rcxres ); //f1m11

f1m11 = (float)*(pointer+k18);

// Outer-Left 3 x 3 Sub-neighborhood of f (0, 0, 0)

k19=((iynew+1)*rcxres+ixnew)+( iznew-1)*rcyres*rcxres ); //f010

f010 = (float)*(pointer+k19);

k20=((iynew+1)*rcxres+(ixnew-1))+( iznew-1)*rcyres*rcxres ); //fm110
```

```
        fm110 = (float)*(pointer+k20);

        k21=((iynew+1)*rcxres+(ixnew+1))+( (iznew-1)*rcyres*rcxres ); //f110

        f110 = (float)*(pointer+k21);

        k22=((iynew+1)*rcxres+(ixnew-1))+( (iznew-2)*rcyres*rcxres ); //fm11m1

        fm11m1 = (float)*(pointer+k22);

        k23=((iynew+1)*rcxres+ixnew)+( (iznew-2)*rcyres*rcxres); //f01m1

        f01m1 = (float)*(pointer+k23);

        k24=((iynew+1)*rcxres+(ixnew+1))+( (iznew-2)*rcyres*rcxres); //f11m1

        f11m1 = (float)*(pointer+k24);

        k25=((iynew+1)*rcxres+(ixnew-1))+( iznew*rcyres*rcxres); //fm111

        fm111 = (float)*(pointer+k25);

        k26=((iynew+1)*rcxres+ixnew)+( iznew*rcyres*rcxres); //f011
        f011 = (float)*(pointer+k26);

        k27=((iynew+1)*rcxres+(ixnew+1))+( iznew*rcyres*rcxres); //f111

        f111 = (float)*(pointer+k27);

 omega1 = ( (float) fm101 + fm100 + f100 + f10m1 + fm1m11 + fm1m10 + f1m10 + f1m1m1 +
              fm111 + fm110 + f110 + f11m1 );

 omega2 = ( (float) fm101 + f001 + f101 + fm100 + f100 + fm10m1 + f00m1 + f10m1 +
              fm1m11 + f0m11 + f1m11 + fm1m10 + f0m10 + f1m10 + fm1m1m1 +
              f0m1m1 + f1m1m1 + fm111 + f011 + f111 + fm110 + f010 + f110 +
              fm11m1 + f01m1 + f11m1 );

   Mx = ((float)xnew) - (float)floor((float)xnew);
   My = ((float)ynew) - (float)floor((float)ynew);
   Mz = ((float)znew) - (float)floor((float)znew);

cubic_term = ( (float) ( Mx + My + Mz ) * ( Mx + My + Mz ) * ( Mx + My + Mz ) );
quadratic_term = ( (float) ( Mx + My + Mz ) * ( Mx + My + Mz ) );
power_one_term = ( (float) ( Mx + My + Mz ) );

LGR1 = ( (float) ( (1/2) * cubic_term ) - quadratic_term - ( (1/2) * power_one_term ) + 1 );
LGR2 = ( (float) ( -(1/6) * cubic_term ) + quadratic_term - ( (11/6) * power_one_term ) + 1 );

   convolution = ( (float) omega1 * LGR1 + omega2 * LGR2 );

 if ( convolution == 0 )
 tfLGR = (float)0;
 else
 tfLGR = ( (float) SCALE / ( -convolution ) );
 tfLGR *= ( (float) 1 / (XRES * YRES * ZRES) );
 kk=(j*rcxres+i)+((sl-2)*rcyres*rcxres);
```

```
        if ( sl >= 2 )
        {

            *(interdata+kk) = ((float) f000 + tfLGR );
            *(originalData+kk) = ((float) f000);
            if ( *(interdata+kk) <= (TH + tfLGR) ) *(interdata+kk) = ((float)0);

        }
                    } // (1)

                } // for loop
            } // for loop
        } // for loop

    fprintf(logfile, "%s\n", "Resampling Completed.");
    /// save new image
    fprintf(logfile, "%s%s\n", "Now Saving New Interpolated Image Volume: ", filename);

    if ((pf = fopen(filename,"wb+"))==NULL)
    {

        fprintf(logfile, "%s", "Cannot open file to save 3D Transformed Image Volume");
        exit(0);

    }else{ // else save
            for(sl=1;sl<=numslice; sl++) {
                for(j=0;j<rcyres;j++){
                    for(i=0;i<rcxres;i++){

                    k2=(j*rcxres+i)+((sl-1)*rcyres*rcxres);

                    savedata=(float)*(interdata+k2);

                    fwrite(&savedata,sizeof(float),1,pf);

                            }
                        }
                    }
    fclose(pf);
    }// else save

    fprintf(logfile, "%s%s\n", "Data has been Interpolated and Saved in file: ", filename);
    fprintf(logfile, "%s\n", "DataType: Float (32-bits Real)");
    fprintf(logfile, "%s\n", "Now Calculating the Center of Mass (COM after truncation)");
    fprintf(logfile, "%s\n", "of the 3D Transformed Image Volume (interpolated data)");

    count=0;
    sumi = (float)0;
    sumj = (float)0;
    sumsl = (float)0;

    float intcomx = 0, intcomy = 0, intcomz = 0;

        for(sl=1;sl<=numslice; sl++) {
            for(j=0;j<rcyres;j++){
                for(i=0;i<rcxres;i++){
```

```
                    k2=(j*rcxres+i)+((sl-1)*rcyres*rcxres);

                    if ( *(interdata+k2) > TH )
                    //// shows the effect of the truncation of the new coordinates while re-slicing the grid
                    { // if
                        count++;
                        sumi = sumi + ((float)i);
                        sumj = sumj + ((float)j);
                        sumsl = sumsl + ((float)sl-1);
                    }// if
                                                        }
                                            }
                                }

intcomx = ((float)sumi/count);
intcomy = ((float)sumj/count);
intcomz = ((float)sumsl/count);

fprintf(logfile, "%s%f\n", "The x coordinate of the COM: ", intcomx);
fprintf(logfile, "%s%f\n", "The y coordinate of the COM: ", intcomy);
fprintf(logfile, "%s%f\n", "The z coordinate of the COM: ", intcomz);

fprintf(logfile, "%s\n%s\n", "Before and After the Application of the Rotation Translation to the Grid",
                    "The Variation of Center of Mass Position is: ");

fprintf(logfile, "%s%f\n", "xCOM - x_interpolated_COM: ", (comx - intcomx) );
fprintf(logfile, "%s%f\n", "yCOM - y_interpolated_COM: ", (comy - intcomy) );
fprintf(logfile, "%s%f\n", "zCOM - z_interpolated_COM: ", (comz - intcomz) );

  /// save new image
  sprintf(filename, "%s%s", filename3, "RAW");
  fprintf(logfile, "%s%s\n", "Now Saving New Image Volume (Not Interpolated): ", filename);

  if ((pf = fopen(filename,"wb+"))==NULL)
  {

  fprintf(logfile, "%s\n", "Cannot open file to save 3D Transformed (Not Interpolated) Image Volume");
  exit(0);

  } else { // else save

          for(sl=1;sl<=numslice; sl++) {
              for(j=0;j<rcyres;j++){
                  for(i=0;i<rcxres;i++){

                  k2=(j*rcxres+i)+((sl-1)*rcyres*rcxres);
                  savedata=(float)*(originalData+k2);
                  fwrite(&savedata,sizeof(float),1,pf);

                                        }
                              }
                  }
          fclose(pf);

  } // else save
```

```
fprintf(logfile, "%s%s\n", "Not Interpolated Data Saved in: ", filename);
fprintf(logfile, "%s\n", "DataType: Float (32-bits Real)");
fprintf(logfile, "%s\n", "Now Calculating the Center of Mass (COM after truncation)");
fprintf(logfile, "%s\n", "of the 3D Transformed Image Volume (NOT interpolated data)");

count=0;
sumi = (float)0;
sumj = (float)0;
sumsl = (float)0;
float NOTintcomx = 0, NOTintcomy = 0, NOTintcomz = 0;

        for(sl=1;sl<=numslice; sl++) {
            for(j=0;j<rcyres;j++){
                for(i=0;i<rcxres;i++){

                k2=(j*rcxres+i)+((sl-1)*rcyres*rcxres);
                if ( *(originalData+k2) > TH )
                //// shows the effect of the truncation of the new coordinates while re-slicing the grid
                { // if

                    count++;
                    sumi = sumi + ((float)i);
                    sumj = sumj + ((float)j);
                    sumsl = sumsl + ((float)sl-1);

                }// if
                                            }
                                    }
                            }

NOTintcomx = ((float)sumi/count);
NOTintcomy = ((float)sumj/count);
NOTintcomz = ((float)sumsl/count);

fprintf(logfile, "%s%f\n", "The x coordinate of the COM: ", NOTintcomx);
fprintf(logfile, "%s%f\n", "The y coordinate of the COM: ", NOTintcomy);
fprintf(logfile, "%s%f\n", "The z coordinate of the COM: ", NOTintcomz);
fprintf(logfile, "%s\n%s\n", "Before and After the Application of the Rotation Translation to the Grid",
                "The Variation of Center of Mass Position is: ");

fprintf(logfile, "%s%f\n", "xCOM - x_NOTinterpolated_COM: ", (comx - NOTintcomx) );
fprintf(logfile, "%s%f\n", "yCOM - y_NOTinterpolated_COM: ", (comy - NOTintcomy) );
fprintf(logfile, "%s%f\n", "zCOM - z_NOTinterpolated_COM: ", (comz - NOTintcomz) );
///////////////////////data re-sampling///////////////////////

free(pointer);
free(interdata);
free(originalData);
fclose(logfile);
system(logfilename);


}
```

The method *void CROTRA2008Dlg::OnImageViewer()* allows viewing the results of processing with the program called *ImageViewer 2009*. Pushing the button named *'Run Image Viewer'* located in the panel named *'Image Volumes Processing'* runs the executable *ImageViewer.exe* through the use of the command *'system'*.

```
void CROTRA2008Dlg::OnImageViewer()
{
        system("ImageViewer.exe");
}
```

The method *void CROTRA2008Dlg::OnHelp()* is written in order to save in the local directory the text file named '*Help.log*' where the user finds information relevant to the proper usage of *ROTRA 2008*.

```
void CROTRA2008Dlg::OnHelp()
{

        CString HelpMessage;
        FILE * logfile;
        char logfilename[128];

        sprintf(logfilename,"%s","Help.log");

        if ((logfile = fopen(logfilename,"w"))==NULL)
        {
        HelpMessage.Format("%s\n%s\n" , "Cannot save the file Help.log" , "Now Click to Exit the program" );
        MessageBox(HelpMessage);
        exit(0);

        } else{ // else

        HelpMessage.Format("%s\n%s\n%s\n%s\n" , "Welcome to ROTRA2008",
                        "Please Read the Help.log file", "Created under the current", "work directory");
        AfxMessageBox(HelpMessage);

        fprintf(logfile, "%s\n", "Welcome to ROTRA2008");
        fprintf(logfile, "\n");
        fprintf(logfile, "%s\n", "Following is the description of the functionality offered through this Graphical User
                        Interface (GUI).");
        fprintf(logfile, "\n");
        fprintf(logfile, "%s\n", "1. The panel named: Create Artificial Image Cube");
        fprintf(logfile, "\n");

        fprintf(logfile, "%s\n", "The push button named Create Cube takes two input parameters: ");
        fprintf(logfile, "%s\n", "a. The size of the Volume (X Y Z Voxels) and b. The Size of the Cube.");
        fprintf(logfile, "%s\n", "Both a. and b. have to be integer numbers, specifically powers of 2.");
        fprintf(logfile, "%s\n", "The program then creates a volume that includes a cube inside it.");
        fprintf(logfile, "\n");

        fprintf(logfile, "%s\n", "2. The panel named: Input the Rigid Body Transformation");
        fprintf(logfile, "\n");

        fprintf(logfile, "%s\n", "Please input the 6 parameters defining the 6 degrees of freedom of the rigid object in
                        3D.");
        fprintf(logfile, "%s\n", "They are: ");
        fprintf(logfile, "%s\n", "Pitch angle (Rotation about the X-axis)");
        fprintf(logfile, "%s\n", "Roll angle (Rotation about the Y-axis)");
        fprintf(logfile, "%s\n", "Yaw angle (Rotation about the Z-axis)");
        fprintf(logfile, "%s\n", "The Shift Along the X axis");
        fprintf(logfile, "%s\n", "The Shift Along the Y axis");
        fprintf(logfile, "%s\n", "The Shift Along the Z axis");
        fprintf(logfile, "%s\n", "The push button named Calculate Rigid Body Transformation");
```

```
        fprintf(logfile, "%s\n", "will generate the Rotation Translation (RT) parameters:");
        fprintf(logfile, "%s\n", "6 entries of the Rotation Matrix and 3 entries of the Translation Array.");
        fprintf(logfile, "%s\n", "Data is saved in file: RTMATRIX.txt");
        fprintf(logfile, "\n");
        fprintf(logfile, "%s\n", "3. The panel named: Image Volume Parameters");
        fprintf(logfile, "\n");
        fprintf(logfile, "%s\n", "Please input all of the parameters before using any of the push buttons of the panel
                named:");
        fprintf(logfile, "%s\n", "Image Volumes Processing");
        fprintf(logfile, "%s\n", "X Voxels, Y Voxels, Z Voxels: the number  of voxels of the Image Volume along X, Y
                and Z axis.");
        fprintf(logfile, "%s\n", "X Resolution (mm), Y Resolution (mm), Z Resolution (mm) define the size of the 3D
                Image Voxels.");
        fprintf(logfile, "%s\n", "The Threshold: it is used to calculate the Center of Mass (COM).");
        fprintf(logfile, "%s\n", "The SCALE Parameter is used to scale the convolution of the Trivariate Cubic
                Interpolation Function.");
        fprintf(logfile, "%s\n", "The DataType:");
        fprintf(logfile, "%s\n", "Please set this as: CHAR or SHORT or INT or FLOAT before pushing the button
                named");
        fprintf(logfile, "%s\n", "Add Slices to the Image Volume.");
        fprintf(logfile, "\n");
        fprintf(logfile, "%s\n", "4. The panel named: Image Volumes Processing");
        fprintf(logfile, "\n");
        fprintf(logfile, "%s\n", "When using the push button named Add Slices to the Image Volume,");
        fprintf(logfile, "%s\n", "a new Image Volume will be generated with a given number of empty slices.");
        fprintf(logfile, "%s\n", "Please set this number in the edit box positioned just below the push button,");
        fprintf(logfile, "%s\n", "and make sure this number is even.");
        fprintf(logfile, "%s\n", "The edit box just below the caption named Image Volume");
        fprintf(logfile, "%s\n", "indicates the file name of the Volume that will be processed when using the push
                buttons:");
        fprintf(logfile, "%s\n", "a. Add Slices to the Image Volume and b. Apply Rotation Translation");
        fprintf(logfile, "\n");
        fprintf(logfile, "%s\n", "When using the push button named Apply Rotation Translation,");
        fprintf(logfile, "%s\n", "the Image Volume identified with the file name typed in the edit box just below the
                caption named Image Volume,");
        fprintf(logfile, "%s\n", "will be processed. Before using this push button, please make sure that the Panels
                named:");
        fprintf(logfile, "%s\n", "a. Input the Rigid Body Transformation and b. Image Volume Parameters");
        fprintf(logfile, "%s\n", "are properly initialized. Specifically, the only DataType accepted by the push button
                named Apply Rotation Translation,");
        fprintf(logfile, "%s\n", "is FLOAT. Two new image volumes will be created: One is re-sliced after
                interpolation, its file name ends with 'INT'");
        fprintf(logfile, "%s\n", "and one is re-sliced without interpolation and its file name ends with 'RAW'.");
        fprintf(logfile, "\n");

        fprintf(logfile, "%s\n", "Every program of the GUI saves the corresponding .log file where processing is
                decribed.");
        fprintf(logfile, "\n");
        fprintf(logfile, "%s\n", "5. The push button named: Run Image Viewer, prompt the user to another GUI that
        can be used to view the Image Volumes.");
        fprintf(logfile, "\n");
        fclose(logfile);
        }//else

}
```

Summary

This chapter has presented the source code of a project named *ROTRA 2008* (see Figs. 2, 3 and 4) which can be utilized to create artificial data (a cube inside a three dimensional volume), to apply rigid-body transformations to 3D data sets and interpolate data after the application of the transformation composite 2D views [1-2] in three instances: plane, sagittal and coronal views (see Fig. 3).

ROTRA 2008 also provides the students with the possibility to add slices to a 3D data set and to view the data with OpenGL ®. The program addresses an issue of relevance in signal processing which is manifest when applying a rigid-body transformation to a digitized 3D volume. Specifically, a shift along X, Y or Z is determined because of the coefficients of the rotation matrix, which means that the lines of code employed to rotate each voxel (three dimensional pixel) are theoretically ill posed and they are in need of a correction. Such correction happens by means of three fractionals (one for each of the three directions of the three dimensional coordinate system), which are calculated and applied to the rigid body transformation. *ROTRA 2008* demonstrates that the application of such fractionals result in the interpolated data having the same center of mass' coordinates of non-interpolated data.

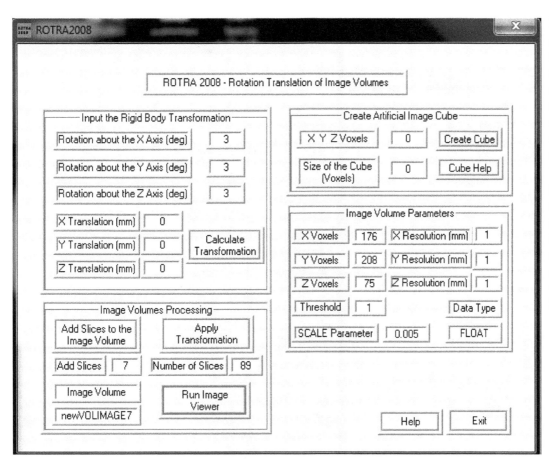

Figure 2: Seven empty slices below the last slice and above the first slice are added to the original image volume made of 75 slices to obtain a new volume called '*newVOLIMAGE7*' and totaling 89 slices. The rotation transformation of 3 deg about the three axis of the coordinate system is applied to the new volume and the result is shown in Fig. 3.

Computer Science Applications

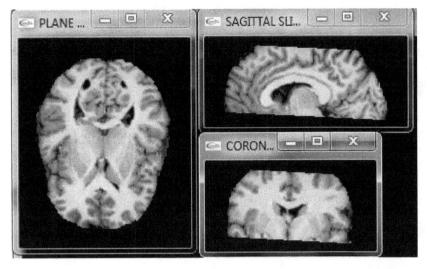

Figure 3 (left) : The result MRI . This volume [3-8] differs from '*newVOLI-MAGE7*' (see Fig. 2) because of the rotation of 3 deg about the three axis of the coordinate system.

Figure 4 (next page): The application of the rotation to the 3D image volume automatically provides to the user information about processing readable from the '*log*' file. Worth noting the variation of the center of mass ('*COM*') before and after the application of the rigid body transformation shows the values: -0.150940, -0.213509, 0.394314 along X, Y and Z respectively. And this is demonstrates the effect of the existing rotational

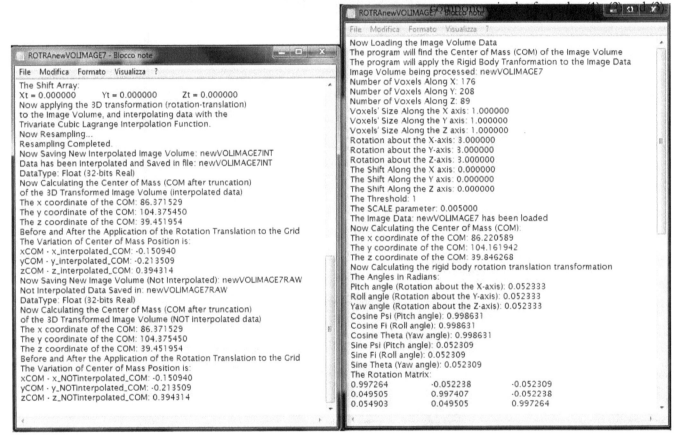

References

[1] Ciulla, C. (2000). *Development and Characterization of Techniques for Neuroimaging Alignment.* Master's Thesis, New Jersey Institute of Technology, Newark, NJ, USA.

[2] Ciulla, C. (2008). *AUTOALIGN: Methodology and Technology for the Alignment of Functional Magnetic Resonance Imaging Time Series. Image Registration: The case of Functional MRI.* VDM Verlag Dr. Müller.

[3] Buckner, R. L., Head, D., Parker, J., Fotenos, A. F., Marcus, D., Morris, J. C., & Snyder, A. Z. (2004). *A unified approach for morphometric and functional data analysis in young, old, and demented adults using automated atlas-based head size normalization: Reliability and validation against manual measurement of total intracranial volume.* Neuroimage, 23(2), 724-738.

[4] Fotenos, A. F., Snyder, A. Z., Girton, L. E., Morris, J. C., & Buckner, R. L. (2005). *Normative estimates of cross-sectional and longitudinal brain volume decline in aging and AD.* Neurology, 64, 1032-1039.

[5] Marcus, D. S., Wang, T. H., Parker, J., Csernansky, J. G., Morris, J. C., & Buckner, R. L. (2007). *Open Access Series of*

Imaging Studies (OASIS): Cross-sectional MRI data in young, middle aged, nondemented, and demented older adults. Journal of Cognitive Neuroscience, 19(9), 1498-1507.

[6] Morris, J. C. (1993). *The clinical dementia rating (CDR): current version and scoring rules.* Neurology, 43(11), 2412b-2414b.

[7] Rubin, E. H., Storandt, M., Miller, J. P., Kinscherf, D. A., Grant, E. A., Morris, J. C., & Berg, L. A. (1998). *A prospective study of cognitive function and onset of dementia in cognitively healthy elders.* Archives of Neurology, 55(3), 395-401.

[8] Zhang, Y., Brady, M., & Smith, S. (2001). *Segmentation of brain MR images through a hidden markov random field model and the expectation maximization algorithm.* IEEE Transactions on Medical Imaging, *20*(1), 45-57.

CHAPTER 6

The Source Code of ObjNet and ANN98

Introduction

The source code of *ObjNet* is here reported as sample that can be utilized as executable to run behind one of the push buttons of the Graphical User Interface called *ANN98*. The methods of *ANN98* are reported in part II of this chapter. The method that runs *ObjNet* is called *void CANN98Dlg::OnRunObjNet98()*. As a note to the reader the source code of *NET98* and *TESTNET*, which can be called in through the push buttons of *ANN98*, was employed in [1] and is available as freeware at the internet site www.sourcecodewebsiteCarloCiulla.com.

The Source Code

Part I: ObjNet

The data structure of *ObjNet* is '*learning_set*', whereas the classes are: '*files_management*', '*patterns_management*', '*backpropagation*', '*initialise_a_net*', '*neural_net*' and '*syncronise*'. The data structure contains the neural network variables specifically the number of patterns to process ('*T*'), the number of input neurons ('*INP*'), the number of neurons in the hidden layer of the network ('*HID*'), the number of output neurons ('*OUT*'), the learning rate ('*RATE*'), the smoothing factor ('*SMOOF*'), the tolerance of the learning process ('*TOLL*') and the number of iterations before printing out the error of fit ('*ITE*').

The class '*files_management*' is called at the beginning of the program before the start of the neural network learning process and uses the method *void files_management::set_learning_variables(char path_store[80])* to set the internal variables of the network. Once the program is aware of how is possible to discriminate between types of patterns on the basis of the file name extension, the method *int files_management::find_requested_files(char selector[10], char current_dir[80])* opens the local directory where the program is running to find the number of patterns of each type to be included in the learning process.

The class '*patterns_management*' is a collection of methods that are devoted to the employment of the patterns in the learning process. This class comes into play with methods like *void patterns_management::pattern_normaliser(char filename[128], float *p1, float *p2, int x)* used to scale data in the range [0, 1]. Also, to mention are methods *int patterns_management::first_layer_connections_saver(float * x1, int p, int q)*, *int patterns_management::second_layer_connections_saver(float * x2, int r, int v)* and *int patterns_management::range_saver(float * f1, float * f2, int r)* employed to save data at the end of the learning process.

The class '*backpropagation*' is a collection of methods that are used to run the back-propagation algorithm [2] across the neural network. To mention, the methods *void backpropagation::second_layer_weight_adjustment(float * b1, float * b2, float r1, float s1, int p, int q)*, *void backpropagation::first_layer_weight_adjustment(float * b4, float * b5, float r1, float s1, int p, int r)* and *void backpropagation::weight_adjustment(initialise_a_net& obj)* are employed during the learning process for the calculation of the weights' adjustment. There are also two pointers named '*float * transit3*' and '*float * transit4*' employed to collect the corrections to the weighting connections for each iteration of the back-propagation algorithm and to make them available to the next iteration such to calculate the weights adjustment [2].

Among the methods of the class '*initialise_a_net*' are: *void initialise_a_net::first_layer_random_weigth_generator(int r, int v)* and *void initialise_a_net::second_layer_random_weigth_generator(int v, int q)*, utilized to initialize the neural network along with the other variables and method of the class. Particularly, these two methods are devoted to the generation of random values for the weighting connections between the input layer and the hidden layer, and between the hidden layer and the output layer of the network.

The class '*neural_net*' is a collection of methods that enforce the back-propagation rule while crossing the neural network. The method *void neural_net::cross_the_net(float * first_layer_connections, float * second_layer_connections, float * pattern_user, float * output, int inde, float * transit2, float * transit1)* takes as input pointers which through dynamic allocation of data are organized such that a pattern, along with the weighting connections, produce the output on the basis of the input. The methods *void neural_net::second_layer_correction_calculator(float * l7, float * l8, int r, int q)* and *void neural_net::first_layer_correction_calculator(float * l12, float * l13, int q, int p)* determine the correction to the weights of the network, whereas the methods *void neural_net::delta2(float * l4, float * l5, float * l6, int q, int b)* and *void neural_net::delta1(float * l9, float * l10, float * l11, int q, int b)* calculate the actual numerical value of the correction to apply to the weights following the math of the delta rule [2].

Finally the class *'syncronise'* is a collection of methods which handle the weights and their update at each of the iterations of the learning process. To view the mathematics of the neural network here presented the reader is referred to previous research [1-2].

```
#define  LOWEST    -500000
#define  HIGHEST    500000
#define  INPUT      100
#define  STEP       50
```

struct learning_set
```
{

    unsigned int  T ;
    int INP ;
    int HID ;
    int OUT ;
    float RATE ;
    float SMOOF ;
    float TOLL ;
    unsigned int ITE ;

} set;

    char buff[INPUT][10];

    float * make_desidered_output(int q, float * op);

    int indexx(float * l7, unsigned int c);

    float error_calculator(float * a1 , float * a2, int q ,int b);

    float * zeroes_generator(int r , int q);

    float * output_nodes_producer(float * l1 ,float * l2 ,int p ,int r);

    float * F_net (float * l3 ,int q);

    float multiplier(float m);

    float sigmoid(float input);
```

class files_management
```
{

    char string[80];
    float * dim;

    public:
    char * get_a_path();

    void set_learning_variables(char path_store[80]);

    int find_requested_files(char selector[10], char current_dir[80]);

    float * get_dim() { return dim; };

    char *  give_a_path() { return string; }
```

```
        void free_memory () { delete dim; }

    };

class patterns_management
{

        float * pattern;
        float * pattern_normalised;

        float * smallest;
        float * biggest;

        public:

        void pattern_handler(char filename[128],int x);

        float normalise(float value, float min, float max);

        char * take_a_filename(char selector[10], char current_dir[80], unsigned int r, unsigned int p);

        void pattern_normaliser(char filename[128], float *p1 ,float * p2 , int x);

        void data_scanner(float * y_output, char current_dir[80]);

        void get_a_pattern(unsigned int t,float * out,char current_dir[80]);

        float * give_a_pattern() { return pattern_normalised;}

        float * get_max_range() { return biggest; }

        float * get_min_range() { return smallest; }

        int first_layer_connections_saver(float * x1, int p, int q);

        int second_layer_connections_saver(float * x2, int r, int v );

        int range_saver(float * f1 , float * f2 , int r );

        void free_memory() { delete biggest;
                             delete smallest; }

    };

class backpropagation
{

        float * transit3;
        float * transit4;
        public:
        void second_layer_weight_adjustment( float * b1, float * b2, float r1, float s1 ,int p ,int q );

        void first_layer_weight_adjustment( float * b4, float * b5, float r1, float s1, int p ,int r);

        void weight_adjustment(initialise_a_net& obj);

        float * get_transit3() { return transit3; }
```

122

```
        float * get_transit4() { return transit4; }

};

class initialise_a_net
{

        float * first_layer_connections;
        float * second_layer_connections;

        float * first_layer_change;
        float * second_layer_change;

        float * def1;
        float * def2;
        float * transit1;
        float * transit2;

        public:

        void first_layer_random_weigth_generator(int r,int v);

        void second_layer_random_weigth_generator(int v,int q);

        void net_setup (void);

        void transit (void);

        float * get_conn1() { return first_layer_connections; }
        float * get_conn2() { return second_layer_connections; }

        float * get_def1() { return def1; }
        float * get_def2() { return def2; }

        float * get_transit1() { return transit1; }
        float * get_transit2() { return transit2; }

        float * get_change1() { return first_layer_change; }
        float * get_change2() { return second_layer_change; }

        friend class syncronise;

        friend void backpropagation::weight_adjustment(initialise_a_net& obj);

        void free_memory1(){  delete first_layer_connections;
                              delete second_layer_connections;
                              delete first_layer_change;
                              delete second_layer_change;
                              delete def1;
                              delete def2;
                          }
        void free_memory2() { delete transit1;
                              delete transit2;
                          }

};
```

Computer Science Applications

```
class neural_net
{
        float   * transfer_hidden ;
        float   * transfer_output ;

        float   * function_net1;
        float   * function_net2;

        float   * delta2_store;
        float   * delta1_store;

        float  * corr1;
        float  * corr2;

        public:
        void cross_the_net(float * first_layer_connections,
                float * second_layer_connections,
                float * pattern_user,
                float * output,
                int inde,
                float * transit2,
                float * transit1);

        void delta2 (float * l4,float * l5 ,float * l6,int q ,int b);

        void second_layer_correction_calculator(float * l7,float * l8,int r,int q);

        void first_layer_correction_calculator(float * l12,float * l13,int q,int p);

        void delta1 (float * l9,float * l10,float * l11,int q,int b);

        float * get_net_output() { return transfer_output; }

        void free_memory(){ delete transfer_hidden ;
                        delete transfer_output ;
                        delete function_net1;
                        delete function_net2;
                        delete delta2_store;
                        delete delta1_store;
                }

};

class syncronise
{
        public:
        void syncro1(initialise_a_net& obj);

        void syncro2(initialise_a_net& obj);

        void syncro11(initialise_a_net& obj);

        void syncro22(initialise_a_net& obj);

};
```

The instruction '*fm.set_learning_variables(fm.get_a_path())*' consists of a message sent to the method *void files_management::set_learning_variables(char path_store[80])* which takes as input the path where the patterns' files are located. The path is obtained through the message '*fm.get_a_path()*' sent to the method *char * files_management::get_a_path()*.

The instruction '*output = (*fp1) (set.OUT, fm.get_dim())*' is possible because the declaration '*float * (*fp1) (int q, float * op) = &make_desidered_output*' through which the float pointer '*(*fp1)*' becomes the recipient what's released by the function *float * make_desidered_output(int q, float * op)*. This function takes two inputs, specifically the integer '*q*', which is the number of output neurons of the neural network ('*set.OUT*'), and the float pointer '*(*op)*', which is obtained through the message '*fm.get_dim()*' returning the float pointer '*(*dim)*'. The pointer '*(*dim)*' contains the number of patterns to be learned for each class type. The instruction '*output= (*fp1) (sct.OUT, fm.get_dim())*' determines the neural network desired output for each class type.

The instruction '*pm.data_scanner(output, fm.give_a_path())*' is a message sent to the method *void patterns_management::data_scanner(float * y_output, char current_dir[80])* which receives two input variables. The variables are the float pointer '*(*output)*' which contains the neural network desired output, and the message '*fm.give_a_path()*' sent to the method *char * files_management::give_a_path()* in order to give the path ('*char current_dir[80]*') where is stored the data set to be employed for the learning process. The method *void patterns_management::data_scanner(float * y_output, char current_dir[80])* has three main functionalities: (i) to read all of the patterns and show them on the screen to the user, (ii) to find minimum and maximum of each of the parameters across all the patterns (the number of parameters is given by the number of values of which a single pattern is made of), (iii) to scale the patterns inside the range [0, 1] and (iv) to search for mismatching cases which would prevent the convergence of the learning process, and in such case to provide the user with safe exit from the program.

The message '*ian.net_setup()*' is sent to the method *void initialise_a_net::net_setup (void)*, which functionalities are those of the initialization of the weighting connections of the neural network through the allocation of memory cells accessed by float pointers and filled initially with zeros (before the beginning of the neural network learning process). The message '*ian.transit()*' is sent to the method *void initialise_a_net::transit(void)* which task is that of initializing with zeros the memory cells accessed through the float pointers '*(*transit1)*' and '*(*transit2)*'. The float pointers '*(*transit1)*' and '*(*transit2)*' serve as containers for the current value of the weighting connections between input and hidden layer and hidden and output layer respectively.

The message '*pm.get_a_pattern(gt, output, fm.give_a_path())*' is the first one of the learning process and takes three inputs: (i) the index '*gt*', identifier of the pattern that has to be processed, (ii) the float pointer '*(*output)*' which contains the neural network desired output, and (iii) the message '*fm.give_a_path()*' which is given to the method *char * files_management::give_a_path()* in order to feed the path where the entire learning process data set is located. The outcome of the message '*pm.get_a_pattern(gt, output, fm.give_a_path())*' is to return to the neural network the pattern for processing.

The instruction '*user = pm.give_a_pattern()*' is an assignment given to the float pointer '*(*user)*' through a message sent to the method *float * patterns_management::give_a_pattern()* which returns the float pointer '*(*pattern_normalised)*'. The instruction '*inde = (*fp2) (output, gt)*' is possible because of the declaration '*int (*fp2) (float * l7, unsigned int c) = &indexx*' of the float pointer '*(*fp2)*' containing the address of the output released from the function '*int indexx(float * l7, unsigned int c)*'. Such function '*int indexx(float * l7, unsigned int c)*' takes as input the float pointer '*(*output)*' ('*(*l7)*') which is the neural network desired output, and the integer '*gt*' ('*c*') which is the identifier of the pattern being processed. The outcome of the instruction '*inde = (*fp2) (output, gt)*' is that of assigning to the variable '*inde*' (integer) the index necessary to identify the pattern being processed inside the full database containing the training set to be processed by the neural network.

The message '*nn.cross_the_net(ian.get_conn1(), ian.get_conn2(), user, output, inde, ian.get_transit2(), ian.get_transit1())*' is given to the method *void neural_net::cross_the_net(float * first_layer_connections, float * second_layer_connections, float * pattern_user, float * output, int inde, float * transit2, float * transit1)* which takes the following inputs.
The float pointer '*(*first_layer_connections)*', which contains the neural network weighting connections between the input layer and the hidden layer. This input is given through the message '*ian.get_conn1()*' to the method *float * initialise_a_net:: get_conn1()*. The float pointer '*(*second_layer_connections)*', which contains the neural network weighting connections between the hidden layer and the output layer. This input is given through the message '*ian.get_conn2()*' to the method *float * initialise_a_net:: get_conn2()*. The float pointers '*(*pattern_user)*' and '*(*output)*' containing the pattern to be processed and the desired output respectively. The integer '*inde*', which identifies the pattern inside the database, and the float pointers '*(*transit1)*', '*(*transit2)*', which contain the current value of the weighting connections between input layer

125

Computer Science Applications

and hidden layer and hidden layer and output layer respectively. The pointers '*(transit1)' and '*(transit2)' are fed as inputs through the messages 'ian.get_transit1()' and 'ian.get_transit2()' respectively.

At the first iteration of the learning process the pointers '*(first_layer_connections)', '*(second_layer_connections)', '*(transit1)' and '*(transit2)' contain zeros as per initialization. The outcome of the method *void neural_net::cross_the_net(float * first_layer_connections, float * second_layer_connections, float * pattern_user, float * output, int inde, float * transit2, float * transit1)* is in the instructions '*(transit1 + k1) = ((*(transit1 +k1)) + (*(corr1 + k1)))' and '*(transit2 + k1) = ((*(transit2 +k1)) + (*(corr2 + k1)))', which consist in the assignment of the updated weighting connections of the neural network, between the input layer and the hidden layer ('*(transit1)') and between the hidden layer and the output layer ('*(transit2)').

The instruction 'cumulate = (*fp3) (nn.get_net_output(), output, set.OUT, inde)' is possible because of the declaration *'float (*fp3) (float * a1, float * a2, int q, int b) = &error_calculator*, where the float number 'cumulate' is assigned the content of the float pointer '(*fp3)' which is released from the function *float error_calculator(float * a1 , float * a2, int q, int b)*. The function *float error_calculator(float * a1 , float * a2, int q, int b)* takes as input two float pointers named respectively '*(a1)', which is 'nn.get_net_output()' and '*(a2)', which is '*(output)'. Worth noting that 'nn.get_net_output()' is a pointer although the syntax is that of a message. Specifically, the method *float * neural_net::get_net_output()* returns the pointer '*(transfer_output)' (see its declaration). The variable 'cumulate' contains the actual error of fit of the current iteration, for the given pattern of the training set.

The two messages 'syn.syncro1(ian)' and 'syn.syncro2(ian)' have the meaning of storing the neural network internal connections between the input layer and the hidden layer ('syn.syncro1(ian)'), and the hidden layer and the output layer ('syn.syncro2(ian)') respectively. The message 'bp.weight_adjustment(ian)' has the meaning to adjust and correct the weighting connections of the neural network. Details of such process can be found later in this chapter where the explanation of the functionality of the method *void backpropagation::weight_adjustment(initialise_a_net& obj)* is given. The two messages 'syn.syncro11(ian)' and 'syn.syncro22(ian)' have the meaning of storing the change (due to the adjustment) determined for the neural network internal connections between the input layer and the hidden layer ('syn.syncro11(ian)'), and the hidden layer and the output layer ('syn.syncro22(ian)') respectively. These two messages are the last ones employed iteratively at each step of the neural network learning process.

At the end of the neural network learning process the following messages are given in the program. The message 'pm.first_layer_connections_saver(ian.get_def1(), set.HID, set.INP)' is given to the method *int patterns_management::first_layer_connections_saver(float * x1, int p, int q)*, which receives the following three inputs. The float pointer '*(x1)' given through the message 'ian.get_def1()' to the method *float * initialise_a_net:: get_def1()*. The integer numbers 'p' and 'q', which are the number of neurons in the hidden layer 'set.HID' and the number of neurons in the input layer 'set.INP' respectively. The functionality of the method *int patterns_management::first_layer_connections_saver(float * x1, int p, int q)* is that of saving in a text file the weighting connections between the input layer and the hidden layer of the neural network.

The message 'pm.second_layer_connections_saver(ian.get_def2(), set.HID, set.OUT)' is given to the method *int patterns_management::second_layer_connections_saver(float * x2, int r, int v)*, which receives the following three inputs. The float pointer '*(x2)' given through the message 'ian.get_def2()' to the method *float * initialise_a_net:: get_def2()*. The integer numbers 'r' and 'v', which are the number of neurons in the hidden layer 'set.HID' and the number of neurons in the output layer 'set.OUT' respectively. The functionality of the method *int patterns_management::second_layer_connections_saver(float * x2, int r, int v)* is that of saving in a text file the weighting connections between the hidden layer and the output layer of the neural network.

The message 'pm.range_saver(pm.get_max_range(), pm.get_min_range(), set.INP)' is given to the method *int patterns_management::range_saver(float * f1, float * f2, int r)*, which receives the following three inputs. The float pointer '*(f1)', which is received through the message 'pm.get_max_range()' given to the method *float * patterns_management:: get_max_range()* returning the float pointer '*(biggest)'. The float pointer '*(f2)', which is received through the message 'pm.get_min_range()' given to the method *float * patterns_management:: get_min_range()* returning the float pointer '*(smallest)', and the integer 'r' which indicates the number of parameters which a pattern is made of ('set.INP'). The functionality of the method *int patterns_management::range_saver(float * f1, float * f2, int r)* is that of saving in a text file the range (minimum and maximum) employed to scale each of the parameters contained in a pattern. The file contains a number of numerical values that are two times the number of parameters which a pattern is made of.

126

```
void main (void)
{

        char ch;
        float * output;
        float * user;
        unsigned int gt;
        int learning=0,counter=0,inde;
        float erro, cumulate;


        float * (*fp1) (int q, float * op) = &make_desidered_output;
        int (*fp2) (float * l7, unsigned int c) = &indexx;
        float (*fp3) (float * a1,float * a2,int q,int b) = &error_calculator;


        files_management       fm;
        patterns_management   pm;
        initialise_a_net       ian;
        neural_net            nn;
        syncronise            syn;
        backpropagation       bp;

        fm.set_learning_variables(fm.get_a_path());

        cout << "DIGIT Y to CONTINUE or N to quit" << endl;
        while((ch!='Y')&&(ch!='N')){
        cin >> ch;
        ch=toupper(ch);
                                }

        switch(ch){

        case 'N':
        fm.free_memory();
        exit(0);

        case 'Y':
        cout << "\n" << endl;
        cout << "LEARNING SET STORED" << endl;
        cout << "THE NET WILL MAKE A RANGE FOR NORMALISATION" << endl;
        break;
        }

        output= (*fp1) (set.OUT,fm.get_dim());

        pm.data_scanner(output,fm.give_a_path());

        cout << "No mismatching cases found" << endl;
        cout << "DIGIT L to START THE LEARNING PROCESS or Q to quit" << endl;

        while((ch!='L')&&(ch!='Q')){
        cin >> ch;
        ch=toupper(ch);
                                }

        switch(ch){
```

Computer Science Applications

```
case 'Q':
delete output;
fm.free_memory();
exit(0);

case 'L':
cout << "THE NET WILL DISPLAY THE ERROR OF FIT" << endl;
break;

        }

   ian.net_setup();

do{

   gt=0;
   erro=0.0;

   ian.transit();

do{

pm.get_a_pattern(gt,output,fm.give_a_path());

user = pm.give_a_pattern();

inde = (*fp2) (output,gt);

nn.cross_the_net(ian.get_conn1(),
         ian.get_conn2(),
         user,
         output,
         inde,
         ian.get_transit2(),
         ian.get_transit1() );

cumulate = (*fp3) (nn.get_net_output(),output,set.OUT,inde);
erro = erro + cumulate;

delete user;

nn.free_memory();

gt++;

}while(gt<(set.T)) ;

counter++;

if(counter>(set.ITE))
{
printf("ERROR=%.6lf\n",(erro*0.5) );
counter=0;
learning++;
}
```

128

```
        syn.syncro1(ian);
        syn.syncro2(ian);

        bp.weight_adjustment(ian);

        syn.syncro11(ian);
        syn.syncro22(ian);

        ian.free_memory2();

        if(learning>STEP)
        {

        learning=0;
        ch='S';
        printf("DIGIT M to CONTINUE THE LEARNING PROCESS or Q to STOP IT\n");

        while((ch!='M')&&(ch!='Q')){
        cin >> ch;
        ch=toupper(ch);

                                }
}
}while( (ch!='Q')&&((erro*0.5)>=(set.TOLL)) );


        cout << "REQUESTED BOTTOM REACHED" << endl;
        cout << "SAVING DATA..." << endl;

        if( (pm.first_layer_connections_saver(ian.get_def1(),set.HID,set.INP) ) == 1 ){

        cout << "FIRST LAYER WEIGHT SAVED" << endl;

        } else

        cout << "WARNING FIRST LAYER WEIGHT NOT SAVED" << endl;

        if( (pm.second_layer_connections_saver(ian.get_def2(),set.HID,set.OUT) ) == 1 ){

        cout << "SECOND LAYER WEIGHT SAVED" << endl;

        } else

        cout << "WARNING SECOND LAYER WEIGHT NOT SAVED" << endl;


        if( (pm.range_saver(pm.get_max_range(),pm.get_min_range(),set.INP) ) == 2 ){

        cout << "RANGE FOR NORMALISATION SAVED" << endl;

        } else

        cout << "WARNING RANGE FOR NORMALISATION NOT SAVED" << endl;

        delete output;
        fm.free_memory();
        pm.free_memory();
```

```
        ian.free_memory1();
        cout << "END" << endl;


}
```

The method *int patterns_management::first_layer_connections_saver(float * x1, int p, int q)* is employed at the end of the learning process to save the weighting connections between the input layer and the hidden layer of the neural network. The method requires to the user to have available a drive named '*C*' where the text file '*WEIGHT.A1*' will be saved.

int patterns_management::first_layer_connections_saver(float * x1, int p, int q)
```
 {

        int j , k1, ok, k6;
        FILE * sl;

        if ((sl = fopen("C:\\WEIGHT.A1","w+"))==NULL)
        {

        ok = 0 ;

        } else  ok=1;
           for(j=1;j<p+1;j++){

             for(k1=0;k1<q+1;k1++){

             k6=(k1 +((q+1)*(j-1)) );

             fprintf(sl,"%f\n",*(x1 + k6));

                        }

                }
           fclose(sl);
           return ok;


}
```

Likewise the method *int patterns_management::first_layer_connections_saver(float * x1, int p, int q)*, the method *int patterns_management::second_layer_connections_saver(float * x2, int r, int v)* saves the weighting connections existing between the hidden layer and the output layer. The output file is called '*WEIGHT.A2*'. It is worth noting that the two computational layers of the neural network are the hidden and the output layers, whereas the input layer is not.

int patterns_management::second_layer_connections_saver(float * x2, int r, int v)
```
 {

        int j , k1, ok, k6;
        FILE * sl;

        if ((sl = fopen("C:\\WEIGHT.A2","w+"))==NULL)

        {

        ok = 0 ;

        } else  ok=1;
```

```
        for(k1=0;k1<r+1;k1++){

            for(j=1;j<v+1;j++){


            k6=( (j-1)+(k1*v) );

            fprintf(sl,"%f\n",*(x2 + k6));

                        }

                    }
        fclose(sl);


        return ok;


    }
```

The method *int patterns_management::range_saver(float * f1, float * f2, int r)* saves the maximum and minimum value of each input variable to the neural network across the entire set of patterns of the training set. These maximum and minimum numbers represent the actual range employed for the scaling the data inside [0, 1]. The two output text files are: *'BIGGEST.A1'* and *'SMALLEST.A1'*.

```
int patterns_management::range_saver(float * f1, float * f2, int r)
 {

        int j,ok,ko;
        FILE * sl;

        if ((sl = fopen("C:\\BIGGEST.A1","w+"))==NULL)
        {

        ok = 0 ;

        } else  ok=1;

         for(j=1;j<r+1;j++){

            fprintf(sl,"%f\n",*(f1 + j));

                        }
          fclose(sl);

        if ((sl = fopen("C:\\SMALLEST.A1","w+"))==NULL)
        {

        ko = 0 ;

        } else  ko=1;

         for(j=1;j<r+1;j++){

            fprintf(sl,"%f\n",*(f2 + j));

                        }
          fclose(sl);
```

return (ok+ko);

}

The method *void syncronise::syncro1(initialise_a_net& obj)* has the role to store the weighting connections between the input layer and the hidden layer (*"*(first_layer_connections)"*). The method is utilized iteratively in order to store the current connections. The assignment *'*(obj.get_def1()+k6) = *(obj.get_conn1()+k6)'* determines the actual storage, specifically the message *'obj.get_conn1()'* gets the connections from the float pointer called *"*(first_layer_connections)'* into the float pointer called *"*(def1)'* through the message *'obj.get_def1()'*. The index *'k6'* spans across the set of connections.

void syncronise::syncro1(initialise_a_net& obj)
{

int k1,k6,k4;

for(k4=1;k4<((set.HID)+1);k4++){

for(k1=0;k1<((set.INP)+1);k1++){

k6=(k1 +(((set.INP)+1)*(k4-1)));

*(obj.get_def1()+k6) = *(obj.get_conn1()+k6);

}

}

}

Similarly, the method *void syncronise::syncro2(initialise_a_net& obj)* stores the connections (*"*(second_layer_connections)'*) existing between the hidden layer and the output layer, iteratively during the learning process. The assignment *'*(obj.get_def2()+k6) = *(obj.get_conn2()+k6)'* makes use of the message *'obj.get_conn2()'* which brings the connections from the float pointer called *"*(second_layer_connections)'* into the float pointer called *"*(def2)'* through the message *'obj.get_def2()'*.

void syncronise::syncro2(initialise_a_net& obj)
{

int k1,k4,k6;

for(k1=0;k1<((set.HID)+1);k1++){

for(k4=1;k4<((set.OUT)+1);k4++){

k6=((k4-1) + (k1*(set.OUT)));

*(obj.get_def2()+k6) = *(obj.get_conn2()+k6);

}

}

}

The method *void syncronise::syncro11(initialise_a_net& obj)* stores the change in the connections between the input layer and the hidden layer, iteratively during the learning process. The assignment *'*(obj.get_change1()+k6) = *(obj.get_transit1()+k6)'* makes use of the message *'obj.get_change1()'* which brings the connections into the float pointer called *"*(first_layer_change)'* from the float pointer called *"*(transit1)'* through the message *'obj.get_transit1()'*.

void syncronise::syncro11(initialise_a_net& obj)
{

        int k3,k1,k6;

        for(k3=1;k3<((set.HID)+1);k3++){

          for(k1=0;k1<((set.INP)+1);k1++){

           k6=(k1 +(((set.INP)+1)*(k3-1)));

           *(obj.get_change1()+k6) = *(obj.get_transit1()+k6);

           }

          }

}

The method *void syncronise::syncro22(initialise_a_net& obj)* stores the change in the connections between the hidden and the output layer, iteratively during the learning process. The assignment '*(obj.get_change2()+k2) = *(obj.get_transit2()+k2)'* makes use of the message '*obj.get_change2()*' which brings the connections into the float pointer called '*(second_layer_change)*' from the float pointer called '*(transit2)*' through the message '*obj.get_transit2()*'.

void syncronise::syncro22(initialise_a_net& obj)
{

        int k1,k3,k2;

        for(k1=0;k1<((set.HID)+1);k1++){

        for(k3=1;k3<((set.OUT)+1);k3++){

          k2=((k1*(set.OUT))+k3);

          *(obj.get_change2()+k2) = *(obj.get_transit2()+k2);

          }

          }

}

The method *void backpropagation::weight_adjustment(initialise_a_net& obj)* determines the adjustment to the weighting connections of the entire neural network.

The instruction '*second_layer_weight_adjustment(obj.get_transit2(), obj.get_change2(), set.RATE, set.SMOOF, set.HID, set.OUT)*' takes as input two float pointers '*(transit2)*' and '*(second_layer_change)*' through the input messages '*obj.get_transit2()*' and '*obj.get_change2()*' respectively. The float pointer '*(second_layer_connections)*' is then assigned the sum contained in the two float pointers '*(def2)*' and '*(transit3)*', and this is achieved through the assignment '*(obj.get_conn2()+k4) = ((*(obj.get_def2()+k4)) + (*(transit3+k4)))*'. Specifically, the message '*obj.get_conn2()*' reaches the pointer '*(second_layer_connections)*' and the message '*obj.get_def2()*' reaches the pointer '*def2*'.

The instruction '*first_layer_weight_adjustment(obj.get_transit1(), obj.get_change1(), set.RATE, set.SMOOF, set.HID, set.INP)*' takes as input two float pointers '*(transit1)*' and '*(first_layer_change)*' through the input messages '*obj.get_transit1()*' and '*obj.get_change1()*' respectively. The float pointer '*(first_layer_connections)*' is then assigned the sum contained in the two float pointers '*(def1)*' and '*(transit4)*', and this is achieved through the assignment '*(obj.get_conn1()+k4) = ((*(obj.get_def1()+k4)) + (*(transit4+k4)))*'. Specifically, the message '*obj.get_conn1()*' reaches the pointer '*(first_layer_connections)*' and the message '*obj.get_def1()*' reaches the pointer '*(def1)*'.

Computer Science Applications

```
void backpropagation::weight_adjustment(initialise_a_net& obj)
{

        int k1,k6,k4;

        second_layer_weight_adjustment(obj.get_transit2(),obj.get_change2(),
                            set.RATE,set.SMOOF,set.HID,set.OUT);

            for(k1=0;k1<((set.HID)+1);k1++){

                for(k6=1;k6<((set.OUT)+1);k6++){

                k4=( (k6-1) + (k1*(set.OUT)) );
                *(obj.get_conn2()+k4) = ( (*(obj.get_def2()+k4) ) + (*(transit3+k4) ) );

                                                }

                                        }
        delete transit3;

            first_layer_weight_adjustment(obj.get_transit1(),obj.get_change1(),set.RATE,set.SMOOF,set.HID,set.INP);
            for(k6=1;k6<((set.HID)+1);k6++){

                for(k1=0;k1<((set.INP)+1);k1++){

            k4=( k1+ (((set.INP)+1) * (k6-1) ) );
            *(obj.get_conn1()+k4) = ( (*(obj.get_def1()+k4) ) + (*(transit4+k4) ) );

                                        }

                                }
        delete transit4;

}
```

The method *void backpropagation::second_layer_weight_adjustment(float * b1, float * b2, float r1, float s1 , int p, int q)* calculates the weights' adjustment of the current neural network iteration for the connections between the hidden layer and the output layer. The calculation is made through the instruction '*(transit3+k6) = ((r1 * (*(b1+k1))) + (s1 * (*(b2+k1))))*', by means of which, the float pointer '*(transit3)*' becomes the recipient of the sum of the two float pointers '*(b1)*' and '*(b2)*' which are input to the method. While the pointer '*(b1)*' is multiplied times the coefficient 'r1', the pointer '*(b2)*' is multiplied times the coefficient 's1'.

void backpropagation::second_layer_weight_adjustment(float * b1, float * b2, float r1, float s1 , int p, int q)

```
{

        int k1,k6,i,j;

        if (!(transit3 = new float[((p+1)*(q+1))*sizeof(float)]))
        {
        cout << "Not enough memory to allocate adjustments" << endl;
        exit(1);
        } else


        for(i=0;i<p+1;i++){
            for(j=1;j<q+1;j++){
```

```
                    k1=((i*q)+j);
                    k6= k1-1;
                    *(transit3+k6) =  ( (r1 * (*(b1+k1)) )  +  (s1 * (*(b2+k1)) ) );


               }
          }

}
```

The method *void backpropagation::first_layer_weight_adjustment(float * b4, float * b5, float r1, float s1, int p, int r)* calculates the weights' adjustment of the current neural network iteration for the connections between the input layer and the hidden layer. The calculation is made through the instruction '*(transit4+k6) = ((r1 * (*(b4+k6))) + (s1 * (*(b5+k6))))*', by means of which, the float pointer '*(transit4)*' becomes the recipient of the sum of the two float pointers '*(b4)*' and '*(b5)*' which are input to the method. While the pointer '*(b4)*' is multiplied times the coefficient '*r1*', the pointer '*(b5)*' is multiplied times the coefficient '*s1*'.

```
void backpropagation::first_layer_weight_adjustment( float * b4, float * b5, float r1, float s1, int p, int r)
{
        int k6,i,j;

        if (!(transit4 = new float[((p+1)*(r+1))*sizeof(float)]))
        {
        cout << "Not enough memory to allocate adjustments" << endl;
        exit(1);
        } else

        for(j=1;j<p+1;j++){

            for(i=0;i<r+1;i++){

                    k6=(i + ((r+1)*(j-1)) );
                    *(transit4+k6) =  ( (r1 * (*(b4+k6)) )  +  (s1 * (*(b5+k6)) ) );


               }

            }

}
```

The function *float error_calculator(float * a1, float * a2, int q, int b)* is employed at each iteration of the learning process to calculate the error of fit between the current network output and the desired output. The function *float multiplier(float m)* correlates with the calculation of the correction term of the delta rule at the output layer. The correction term is the partial derivative of the error of fit and is given by: the current output ('*m*'), times one minus the current output, times the difference between the desired output and the current output. The function *float sigmoid(float input)* calculates the sigmoid of the current input, fed to either the hidden layer or the output layer, through the instruction '*(float)1 / (1+exp((double)-input))*' such to determine the current output.

```
float error_calculator(float * a1, float * a2, int q, int b)
{

        int i,w;
        float fog;

        fog=0;
         for(i=1;i<q+1;i++){

        w=(q+i+(q*b));
```

```
          fog = fog + (  ( ( *(a1 + i) ) - ( *(a2 + w) ) ) * ( ( *(a1 + i) ) - ( *(a2 + w) ) )  );

                    }

      return fog;

}
```

float multiplier(float m)

```
{

      return ( m * float(1-m) );

}
```

float sigmoid(float input)

```
{

      float activate;

      activate=(float)1/(1+exp((double)-input));

      return activate;

}
```

The function *float * output_nodes_producer(float * l1, float * l2, int p, int r)* calculates the current value of the output at the node of the output layer. This operation is determined in two steps. One step consists of the calculation of the running sum (*'top'*), which is made by the multiplication of the weighting connection '*(l1+k6)*' times the input to the output node '*(l2+i)*'. And this sum is given by the instruction '*top = top + ((*(l1+k6)) * (*(l2+i)))*'. The second step consists of the calculation of the sigmoid function of the final sum through the instruction '*sigmoid(top)*'. The function *float * output_nodes_producer(float * l1, float * l2, int p, int r)* takes two float pointers as input and they are: the weighting connections '*(l1)*' and the input to the output node '*(l2)*'.

float * output_nodes_producer(float * l1, float * l2, int p, int r)

```
{

      float * y ;
      float top ;
      int i,j,k6;

      if (!(y = new float[(p+1)*sizeof(float)]))
      {
      cout << "Not enough memory to allocate output_nodes" << endl;
      exit(1);
      } else

        for(j=1;j<p+1;j++){
                top=0;

        for(i=0;i<r+1;i++){

        k6=(i+((r+1)*(j-1)));
        top  = top + ( (*(l1+k6) ) * ( *(l2+i) ) );

                    }
```

```
                *(y+j) = sigmoid( top );

                        }
        return y;

}
```

The function *float * F_net (float * l3, int q)* correlates with the calculation of the correction term of the delta rule at the output layer. Specifically, this function calculates the term one minus the current output (*'m'*), through the instruction *'multiplier(net)'*, which calls in the function *float multiplier(float m)*.

float * F_net (float * l3, int q)

```
{

        float * f1;
        float net ;
        int j ;

        if (!(f1 = new float[(q+1)*sizeof(float)]))
        {
        cout << "Not enough memory to allocate F_net" << endl;
        exit(1);
        } else

        for(j=1;j<q+1;j++){

        net= *(l3+j);
        *(f1+j) = multiplier ( net );

                        }
        return f1;

}
```

The method *void neural_net::delta2 (float * l4, float * l5, float * l6, int q, int b)* relates to the delta rule [2]. Particularly, to understand the functionality of this method, the following instructions are relevant: *'function_net2 = F_net (transfer_output, set.OUT)'* and *'delta2(output, transfer_output, function_net2, set.OUT, inde)'*. The first instruction calls in the function *float * F_net (float * l3, int q)* which takes in as input the float pointer *'*(transfer_output)'*. This is a pointer containing the current neural network output to the given pattern and it is calculated through the assignment *'transfer_output = output_nodes_producer(second_layer_connections, transfer_hidden, set.OUT, set.HID)'*. The second instruction (*'delta2(output, transfer_output, function_net2, set.OUT, inde)'*) takes as input the following float pointers: *'*(output)'*, which is the neural network desired output; *'*(transfer_output)'*, which is the neural network current output; and *'*(function_net2)'*, which is released from the function *float * F_net (float * l3, int q)*.

The instruction *'*(delta2_store+j) = ((*(l4+a)) - (*(l5+j))) * (*(l6+j))'* correlates the pointer *'*(l4)'* to the pointer *'*(output)'*, the pointer *'*(l5)'* to the pointer *'*(transfer_output)'* and the pointer *'*(l6)'* to the pointer *'*(function_net2)'*. The result of the instruction *'*(delta2_store+j) = ((*(l4+a)) - (*(l5+j))) * (*(l6+j))'* is therefore the j-th output neuron's multiplicative term: the difference between desired output and current output, times one minus the current output.

void neural_net::delta2 (float * l4, float * l5, float * l6, int q, int b)

```
{

        int a ,j ;

        if (!(delta2_store = new float[(q+1)*sizeof(float)]))
        {
        cout << "Not enough memory to allocate delta2" << endl;
```

```
        exit(1);
        } else
        for(j=1;j<q+1;j++){

        a=(q+j+(q*b));
        *(delta2_store+j) = ( (*(l4+a)) - (*(l5+j)) ) * ( *(l6+j) );

                            }


}
```

The method *void neural_net::second_layer_correction_calculator(float * l7, float * l8, int r, int q)* is involved in the calculation of the full delta rule [2] correction term to the weighting connections between the hidden layer and the output layer. The method is invoked (*'second_layer_correction_calculator(delta2_store, transfer_hidden, set.HID, set.OUT)'*) inside the method *void neural_net::cross_the_net(float * first_layer_connections, float * second_layer_connections, float * pattern_user, float * output, int inde, float * transit2, float * transit1)* and takes as inputs the float pointers '*(delta2_store)*' and '*(transfer_hidden)*'.

The pointer '*(delta2_store)*' is the j-th output neuron's term: difference between desired output and current output, times one minus the current output. The full delta rule correction term comprises of the multiplication between '*(delta2_store)*' and the term released into the pointer '*(transfer_hidden)*' from the assignment *'transfer_hidden = output_nodes_producer (first_layer_connections, pattern_user, set.HID, set.INP)'*. Such assignment calculates the convolution of weighting connections (between the input layer and the hidden layer) and inputs to the hidden layer. The weighting connections between the input layer and the hidden layer are stored in the float pointer '*(first_layer_connections)*' whereas the inputs to the hidden layer proceed directly from the non-computational input layer and they are stored in the float pointer '*(pattern_user)*', they are the inputs to the neural network.

void neural_net::second_layer_correction_calculator(float * l7, float * l8, int r, int q)
```
{

        int n,i,j;

        if (!(corr2 = new float[((r+1)*(q+1))*sizeof(float)]))
        {
        cout << "Not enough memory to allocate corrections" << endl;
        exit(1);

        } else

        for(i=0;i<r+1;i++){

            for(j=1;j<q+1;j++){

        n = ((i*q)+j);

        *(corr2+n) =  ( (*(l7+j) ) * ( *(l8+i) ) );

                            }

                        }


}
```

The method *void neural_net::delta1 (float * l9, float * l10, float * l11, int q, int b)* is involved in the calculation of the delta rule [2] correction term to the weighting connections between the input layer and the hidden layer. The method is invoked (*'delta1 (delta2_store, second_layer_connections, function_net1, set.HID, set.OUT)'*) inside the method *void neural_net::cross_the_net (float * first_layer_connections, float * second_layer_connections, float * pattern_user, float * output, int inde, float * transit2, float * transit1)*. There are three float pointers as input to *void neural_net::delta1 (float * l9, float * l10, float * l11, int q, int b)* and they are: '*(delta2_store)*' , '*(second_layer_connections)*' and '*(function_net1)*'. The running sum of the multiplication '*(delta2_store)*' times '*(second_layer_connections)' is cumulated till its total and then multiplied times '*(function_net1)'. Where the float pointer '*(function_net1)' is released from the assignment 'function_net1 = F_net (transfer_hidden, set.HID)', which calculates for the j-th neuron of the hidden layer the multiplicative term: difference between desired output and current output, times one minus the current output. This process allows to back-propagate the weights correction term back to the neurons of the hidden layer.

The method *void neural_net::first_layer_correction_calculator(float * l12, float * l13, int q, int p)* is involved in the calculation of the full delta rule [2] correction term to the weighting connections between the input layer and the hidden layer. The method is invoked ('first_layer_correction_calculator(delta1_store, pattern_user, set.HID, set.INP)') inside the method *void neural_net::cross_the_net(float * first_layer_connections, float * second_layer_connections, float * pattern_user, float * output, int inde, float * transit2, float * transit1)* and takes as inputs the float pointers '*(delta1_store)' and '*(pattern_user)'. Inside the method *void neural_net::first_layer_correction_calculator(float * l12, float * l13, int q, int p)*, the assignment '*(corr1 +n) = ((*(l12 +j)) * (*(l13 +i)))' correlates the pointer '*(l12)' to the pointer '*(delta1_store)', and the pointer '*(l13)' to the pointer '*(pattern_user)', which comprises of the input to the neural network.

```
void neural_net::first_layer_correction_calculator( float * l12, float * l13, int q, int p)
{

    int n,i,j;

    if (!(corr1 = new float[((p+1)*(q+1))*sizeof(float)]))
    {
    cout << "Not enough memory to allocate corrections" << endl;
    exit(1);
    } else

    for(j=1;j<q+1;j++){

        for(i=0;i<p+1;i++){

    n = ( ((j-1)*(p+1)) + i );
    *(corr1+n) =   ( (*(l12 +j) ) * ( *(l13 +i) ) );

                }

            }

}


void neural_net::delta1 ( float * l9, float * l10,  float * l11, int q, int b)
{

    int i,j,n ;
    float sop;
    if (!(delta1_store = new float[(q+1)*sizeof(float)]))
    {
     cout << "Not enough memory to allocate delta1" << endl;
    exit(1);
    } else
     for(j=1;j<q+1;j++){
            sop=0;

    for(i=1;i<b+1;i++){

    n=( i + (q*(i-1)) + j - 1 );
    sop = sop + ( ( (*(l9 + i)) * (*(l10 + n)) ) );

            }
```

```
        *(delta1_store+j) = sop * ( *(l11 + j) ) ;

                            }


}
```

The method *void neural_net::second_layer_correction_calculator(float * l7, float * l8, int r, int q)* produces as ultimate outcome the correction terms to the weights connecting the hidden layer to the output layer and these correction terms are stored into the float pointer '*(corr2)'. The numerical value contained in this pointer is summed at each iteration of the learning process to the current value of the weights ('*(transit2)') and this is visible through the instruction '*(transit2 + k1) =((*(transit2 +k1)) + (*(corr2 + k1)))' reported inside the method *void neural_net::cross_the_net(float * first_layer_connections, float * second_layer_connections, float * pattern_user, float * output, int inde, float * transit2, float * transit1)*.

Like wise, the method *void neural_net::first_layer_correction_calculator(float * l12, float * l13, int q, int p)* produces as ultimate outcome the correction terms to the weights connecting the input layer to the hidden layer and these correction terms are stored into the float pointer '*(corr1)'. The numerical value contained in this pointer is summed at each iteration of the learning process to the current value of the weights ('*(transit1)') and this is visible through the instruction '*(transit1 + k1) =((*(transit1 +k1)) + (*(corr1 + k1)))' reported inside the method *void neural_net::cross_the_net(float * first_layer_connections, float * second_layer_connections, float * pattern_user, float * output, int inde, float * transit2, float * transit1)*.

```
void neural_net::cross_the_net(float * first_layer_connections, float * second_layer_connections,
                    float * pattern_user, float * output, int inde, float * transit2, float * transit1)
{

    int k4,k6,k1;

    transfer_hidden = output_nodes_producer(first_layer_connections, pattern_user,set.HID,set.INP);

    *(transfer_hidden)= 1.0 ;

    function_net1 = F_net (transfer_hidden,set.HID);

    transfer_output = output_nodes_producer(second_layer_connections, transfer_hidden,set.OUT,set.HID);

    function_net2 = F_net (transfer_output,set.OUT);

    delta2(output,transfer_output,function_net2,set.OUT,inde);

    second_layer_correction_calculator(delta2_store,transfer_hidden, set.HID,set.OUT);

        for(k4=0;k4<((set.HID)+1);k4++){

        for(k6=1;k6<((set.OUT)+1);k6++){

            k1 = ((k4*(set.OUT))+k6);
            *(transit2 + k1) =( ( *(transit2 +k1) ) + ( *(corr2 + k1) ) );

                            }

                        }
    delete corr2;

    delta1(delta2_store,second_layer_connections,function_net1,set.HID,set.OUT);

    first_layer_correction_calculator(delta1_store,pattern_user,set.HID,set.INP);

        for(k4=1;k4<((set.HID)+1);k4++){
```

```
for(k6=0;k6<((set.INP)+1);k6++){

    k1 = ( ((k4-1)*((set.INP)+1)) + k6 );
    *(transit1 + k1) =( ( *(transit1 +k1) ) + ( *(corr1 + k1) ) );


                    }
                }
        delete corr1;


}
```

The method *void initialise_a_net::net_setup (void)* has the capability to initialize the neural network before the beginning of the learning process. The set of instructions are: '*first_layer_random_weigth_generator(set.INP, set.HID)*', employed to generate random values for the weighting connections between the input layer and the hidden layer; and '*second_layer_random_weigth_generator(set.HID, set.OUT)*', employed to generate random values for the weighting connections between the hidden layer and the output layer.

Also, the instruction '*first_layer_change = zeroes_generator(set.INP, set.HID)*' is employed to generate zeros for the initial values of the change to apply to the weighting connections between the input layer and the hidden layer; and the instruction '*second_layer_change = zeroes_generator(set.HID, set.OUT)*' is employed to generate zeros for the initial values of the change to apply to the weighting connections between the hidden layer and the output layer. Finally, the instructions '*def1 = zeroes_generator(set.HID, set.INP)*' and '*def2 = zeroes_generator(set.HID, set.INP)*' are employed to generate zeros for the values of the containers ('*(def1)*') and ('*(def2)*') of the final numerical values of the weights.

void initialise_a_net::net_setup (void)
```
{

        first_layer_random_weigth_generator(set.INP,set.HID);

        second_layer_random_weigth_generator(set.HID,set.OUT);

        first_layer_change=zeroes_generator(set.INP,set.HID);

        second_layer_change = zeroes_generator(set.HID,set.OUT);

        def1 = zeroes_generator(set.HID,set.INP);

        def2 = zeroes_generator(set.HID,set.INP);

}
```

The method *void initialise_a_net::transit(void)* has the capability to initializes with zero values the float pointers '*(transit1)*' and '*(transit2)*' at the beginning of the learning process. The initialization take place through the assignments '*transit1 = zeroes_generator(set.HID, set.INP)*' and '*transit2 = zeroes_generator(set.HID, set.OUT)*'. The float pointers '*(transit1)*' and '*(transit2)*' serve as containers for the current value of the weighting connections between input and hidden layers and hidden and output layers respectively.

void initialise_a_net::transit(void)
```
{

        transit1=zeroes_generator(set.HID,set.INP);
        transit2=zeroes_generator(set.HID,set.OUT);

}
```
Like wise the methods *void initialise_a_net::first_layer_random_weigth_generator(int r, int v)* and *void initialise_a_net::second_layer_random_weigth_generator(int v, int q)* have the capability to initialize the float pointers '*(first_layer_connections)*' and '*(second_layer_connections)*'. While the pointers '*(transit1)*' and '*(transit2)*' serve as containers

Computer Science Applications

for the current value of the weighting connections, the pointers '*(first_layer_connections)' and '*(second_layer_connections)' are employed in the calculations during each iteration of the learning process.

void initialise_a_net::first_layer_random_weigth_generator(int r, int v)
```
{

        int s;
        int k6,i,j;

        if (!(first_layer_connections = new float[((r+1)*(v+1))*sizeof(float)]))
        {
        cout << "Not enough memory to allocate first_layer" << endl;
        exit(1);
        } else

                for(j=1;j<v+1;j++){

                for(i=0;i<r+1;i++){

                s=rand() %10;
                k6=( i+ ((r+1)*(j-1)) );
                *(first_layer_connections+k6)=(float)s*0.001;

                                        }

                                        }

}
```

void initialise_a_net::second_layer_random_weigth_generator(int v, int q)
```
{

        int s;
        int k6,i,j;

        if (!(second_layer_connections = new float[((q+1)*(v+1))*sizeof(float)]))
        {
        cout << "Not enough memory to allocate second_layer" << endl;
        exit(1);
        } else

                for(i=0;i<v+1;i++){

                for(j=1;j<q+1;j++){

                s=rand() %10;
                k6=( (j-1) + (i*q) );
                *(second_layer_connections+k6)=(float)s*0.001;

                                        }

                                        }

}
```

The function *float * zeroes_generator(int r , int q)* is employed inside the methods *void initialise_a_net::net_setup(void)* and *void initialise_a_net::transit(void)* to fill in memory with zero values. This is visible in the instructions '*def1 = ze-*

roes_generator(set.HID, set.INP)', 'def2 = zeroes_generator(set.HID, set.INP)', 'transit1 = zeroes_generator(set.HID, set.INP)' and 'transit2 = zeroes_generator(set.HID, set.OUT)'.

float * zeroes_generator(int r , int q)
```
{

        int i;
        float * g;

        if (!(g = new float[((r+1)*(q+1))*sizeof(float)]))
        {
        cout << "Not enough memory to allocate zeroes" << endl;
        exit(1);
        } else
                for(i=0;i<(r+1)*(q+1);i++){

                *(g+i)=0.0;

                                                        }
        return g;

}
```

The function *float * make_desidered_output(int q, float * op)* is employed to make and store, prior to the beginning of the learning process, the desired neural network output. This function is called inside the *main* of the program with the instruction *'output= (*fp1) (set.OUT, fm.get_dim())'* upon proper declaration: *'float * (*fp1) (int q, float * op) = &make_desidered_output'*. The declaration shows the float pointer *'(*fp1)'* is the recipient of what is delivered from the function, which takes as input the integer *'q'* and the float pointer *'*(op)'*. The instruction *'output= (*fp1) (set.OUT, fm.get_dim())'* shows that the float pointer input to the function is given by the message *'fm.get_dim()'* by means of which the function *float * get_dim()* returns the float pointer *'*(dim)'* as input to the function. This pointer contains the number of patterns be learned for each class type and this is manifest through the instruction *'*(dim+l) = find_requested_files(buff[l], path_store)'* located in the method *void files_management::set_learning_variables(char path_store[80])*. In this particular instruction, the number of classes of the training set is associated to the counter *'l'* in *'*(dim+l)'*.

In general, the desired output of the neural network is a string of zeros with the value *'1'* assigned to the active neuron delegated to the recognition of the pattern type. For example, the string [1, 0, 0, 0] is a desired output that assigns to the first neuron (see value *'1'*) the task of recognizing the given pattern type which is set to be associated to the string [1, 0, 0, 0]. At the end of a successful training process, feeding to the network the pattern which was associated to the string [1, 0, 0, 0], requires that the first neuron responds with the value *'1'* and the remaining three neurons respond with the value *'0'*.

float * make_desidered_output(int q, float * op)
```
{

        float * y_output;
        int k5,k1,as;
        int k2;

        if (!(y_output= new float[((q*q)+(q+1))*sizeof(float)]))
        {
        cout << "Not enough memory to allocate output" << endl;
        exit(1);
        }

        *(y_output)=*(op);

        for(k5=1;k5<=q;k5++){
```

```
        *(y_output+k5) = ( (*(op+k5)) + (*(y_output+k5-1)) );

                              }

     k5=0;

     for(k2=0;k2<q;k2++){

     k5++;

     for(k1=0;k1<q;k1++){

         as=(q+1)+k1+(k2*q);

         if( k1==(k5-1) ) {

         *(y_output+as)=1.0;

                         } else  *(y_output+as)=0.0;

                      }

                      }

     return y_output;

}
```

Prior to the beginning of the learning process, the neural network has to be given the correct set of variables. Specifically: the total number of patterns comprising the training set, the number of patterns for each class type, the number of input neurons, the number of neurons in the hidden layer and the number of neurons in the output layer (this number is the same as the number of pattern types to classify). Also, the directory where the training data set is located, the learning rate, the smoothing factor to the iterative weights' adjustment, the tolerance of the training process, the number of iterations before the error of fit can be printed out to the screen.

The method *void files_management::set_learning_variables(char path_store[80])* fulfills all of these tasks with the assistance of the user interaction. The user is prompted automatically by the program to insert the aforementioned variables.

void files_management::set_learning_variables(char path_store[80])
```
{

        FILE * sc;

        char first_file[80];
        int k1=0,l;
        float cs;
        unsigned int  k2=0;
        char s1[5]="\\";
        double a,b;
        DIR *dir;
        struct dirent *ent;
    if ((dir = opendir(path_store)) == NULL)
    {
      perror("Unable to open directory");
      exit(1);
    }
```

```
for(l=1;l<=3;l++){

if((ent = readdir(dir)) != NULL)
{

if(l==3){

cout << "\n" << endl;

cout << "FIRST FILE OF THE LIST: " << ent->d_name << endl;

k2++;

}

} else{

cout << "cannot find FIRST FILE of the list " << endl;
exit(1);

        }

   }

    strcpy(first_file,path_store);
    strcat(first_file,s1);
    strcat(first_file,ent->d_name);
    cout << "entry: " << first_file << endl;

  if((sc=fopen(first_file,"r"))==NULL){

  cout << "cannot open first file of the list" << endl;

  exit(1);
                                        }

  while(!feof(sc)){

  k1++;
  fscanf(sc,"%f\n",&cs);

              }

  while ((ent = readdir(dir)) != NULL)
  {
   cout << "" << ent->d_name << endl;
   k2++;
  }

  if (closedir(dir) != 0)
  {

  perror("Unable to close directory");

  }
  cout << "INPUT NEURONS = " << k1 << endl;
```

```
set.INP=k1;
cout << "LEARNING PATTERNS = " << k2 << endl;

set.T=k2;

cout << "INSERT number of classes to discriminate"  "(OUTPUT NEURONS)" << endl;

cin >> k1;

set.OUT=k1;

if (!(dim= new float[(k1+1)*sizeof(float)]))
{
cout << "Not enough memory to allocate output limits" << endl;
exit(1);
}

*(dim)=0;
for(l=1;l<=k1;l++){

cout << "\n" << endl;

cout << "INSERT file extention [letter,number] of class " << l << endl;

cin >> buff[l];

*(dim+l) = find_requested_files(buff[l],path_store);

        }

cout << "\n" << endl;

a=sqrt( (set.INP)*(set.OUT) );
b=2*sqrt( (set.INP)+(set.OUT) );

cout << "set the number of HIDDEN NEURONS:" << endl;
cout << "following values are suggested:" << endl;
cout << "HID= " <<  (int)(float)a << endl;
cout << "HID= " <<  (int)(float)b << endl;

cout << "INSERT NUMBER of HIDDEN NEURONS" << endl;
cin >> k1;
set.HID=k1;

cout << "INSERT LEARNING RATE [0...1]" << endl;
cin >> cs;
set.RATE=cs;

cout << "INSERT SMOOTHING FACTOR [0...1]" << endl;
cin >> cs;
set.SMOOF=cs;

cout << "INSERT LEARNING PROCESS TOLERANCE"  << endl;
cin >> cs;
set.TOLL=cs;
cout << "INSERT ITERATION COUNTER VALUE (integer)" << endl;
cin >> k1;
```

146

```
set.ITE=k1;

cout << "CHECK if the learning set is currently correct" << endl;
cout << "\n" << endl;

cout << "T= " << set.T << endl;
cout << "INP= " << set.INP << endl;
cout << "HID= " << set.HID << endl;
cout << "OUT= " << set.OUT << endl;
cout << "RATE= " << set.RATE << endl;
cout << "SMOOF= " << set.SMOOF << endl;
cout << "TOLL= " << set.TOLL << endl;
cout << "ITE= " << set.ITE << endl;

}
```

Worth noting that the system is instructed to find automatically the number of patterns that belong to each class, in the directory where data resides. This is possible because each class type differs from another because of the extension of the file name. This is a requirement of the learning process. For instance, the classes having file name extension '.A1' and '.A2' identify two different pattern types. The user is requested to store and name the data for training according to this logic before the learning process begins. The task of identification of the patterns and their class type is performed by the method *int files_management::find_requested_files(char selector[10], char current_dir[80])*. The method *char * files_management::get_a_path()* receives from the user the path where the data set to be employed for the learning process is located.

int files_management::find_requested_files(char selector[10], char current_dir[80])

```
{

        unsigned int  k3=0;
        const char * a;
        const char * b;

        DIR *dir;
        struct dirent *ent;

          if ((dir = opendir(current_dir)) == NULL)
          {

          perror("Unable to open directory");
          exit(1);

          }else{

            b=selector;

            while ((ent = readdir(dir)) != NULL)
            {
            a=ent->d_name;

            if( (strstr(a,b))!=NULL ){

            k3++;
            cout << "" << ent->d_name << endl;
                                }
            }
            }
```

```
      if (closedir(dir) != 0)
      {

      perror("Unable to close directory");

      }

      cout << " \n" << endl;
      cout <<"FILES FOUND: " << k3 << endl;

      return k3;

}
```

char * files_management::get_a_path()
```
{

      cout << "INSERT LEARN DIRECTORY" << endl;
      cin >> string;
      return string;

}
```

The method *void patterns_management::get_a_pattern(unsigned int t, float * out, char current_dir[80])* retrieves a given pattern from the database where all files are located. This task is performed on the basis of the following three input variables. The integer *'t'*, which identifies the pattern being processed by the neural network. The float pointer *'*(out)'*, which contains the desired network output (see the message *'pm.get_a_pattern(gt, output, fm.give_a_path())'*) and the name of the directory containing the database *'current_dir[80]'*.

The method *void patterns_management::get_a_pattern(unsigned int t, float * out, char current_dir[80])* uses the following instructions to retrieve the pattern from the database. In first instance, the instruction *'inde = indexx(out, t)'* assigns an index to the integer pointer *'inde'*. The index is determined on the basis of the desired output *'*(out)'* corresponding to the pattern being processed, and also on the basis of the index *'t'*, which actually identifies the current pattern being processed. Worth noting that the instruction *'inde = indexx(out, t)'* has its declaration in *'int (*fp2) (float * l7, unsigned int c) = &indexx'*. The second instruction is *'select = (int)(*(out+inde))'*, which assigns (through the integer pointer *'inde'*) the value of the desired output being determined, to the integer variable *'select'*. Finally, the filename of the pattern being retrieved from the database is determined through the instruction *'name = take_a_filename(buff[inde+1], current_dir, select, t)'*, which makes use of the method *char * patterns_management::take_a_filename(char selector[10], char current_dir[80], unsigned int r, unsigned int p)*.

In other word, the desired output and the index of the pattern being processed determine the value of the variable *'inde'*. The value of the variable *'inde'* determines the value of desired output for the pattern being processed and places such value into the variable *'select'*. The variable *'select'* can be used in the method *char * patterns_management::take_a_filename(char selector[10], char current_dir[80], unsigned int r, unsigned int p)* to find the pattern into the database through the instruction *'name = take_a_filename(buff[inde+1], current_dir, select, t)'*.

void patterns_management::get_a_pattern(unsigned int t, float * out, char current_dir[80])
```
{

      int inde;
      unsigned int select;
      char *name, filename[128];

      inde=indexx(out,t);
      select=(int)(*(out+inde));

      name=take_a_filename(buff[inde+1],current_dir,select,t);
      strcpy(filename,name);
```

pattern_normaliser(filename,smallest,biggest,set.INP);

}

The methods *void patterns_management::pattern_handler(char filename[128], int x), float patterns_management::normalise(float value, float min, float max)* and *void patterns_management::pattern_normaliser(char filename[128], float *p1, float *p2, int x)* have the capability to manage the access to the patterns' data contained into the text files and the capability of scaling the parameters which each pattern is made of. While the method *void patterns_management::pattern_handler(char filename[128], int x)* makes available the pattern to processing, the methods *patterns_management::normalise(float value, float min, float max)* and *void patterns_management::pattern_normaliser(char filename[128], float *p1, float *p2, int x)* initiate the pattern to be a suitable neural network input through the scaling of its data inside the range [0, 1]. In this regard, the method *void patterns_management::pattern_normaliser(char filename[128], float *p1, float *p2, int x)* receives as input two float pointers '*(p1)' and '*(p2)' which address the range utilized for scaling.

void patterns_management::pattern_handler(char filename[128], int x)

```
{

        FILE *pf;
        int k2;
        float number;

        if (!(pattern = new float[(x+1)*sizeof(float)]))
        {
        cout << "Not enough memory to allocate pattern" << endl;
        exit(1);
        }

        if ((pf = fopen(filename,"r"))==NULL)
        {
        cout << "Cannot open file: " << filename << endl;
        delete pattern;
        exit(1);
        }

        *(pattern) = 1.0;

        for(k2=1;k2<x+1;k2++){

        fscanf(pf,"%f\n",&number);

        *(pattern+k2)=number;

                                }

        fclose (pf);

  }
```

float patterns_management::normalise(float value, float min, float max)

```
{

        float norm;
        norm = float(value-min)/(max-min);
        return norm;

}
```

Computer Science Applications

```
void  patterns_management::pattern_normaliser(char filename[128], float *p1, float *p2, int x)
{

        FILE *pf;
        int k2;
        float number;

        if (!(pattern_normalised = new float[(x+1)*sizeof(float)]))
        {
        cout << "Not enough memory to allocate pattern" << endl;
        exit(1);
        } else

        if ((pf = fopen(filename,"r"))==NULL)
        {

        cout << "Cannot open file: " << filename << endl;
        delete pattern_normalised;
        exit(1);

        }else
           *(pattern_normalised) = 1.0;

           for(k2=1;k2<x+1;k2++){

           fscanf(pf,"%f\n",&number);
            *(pattern_normalised+k2)=normalise( number,*(p1+k2),*(p2+k2) );

                                  }

        fclose (pf);


}
```

The instructions '*inde = indexx(y_output, j)*', '*select = (int)(*(y_output+inde))*' and '*name = take_a_filename(buff[inde+1], current_dir, select, j)*' found in the method *void patterns_management::data_scanner(float * y_output, char current_dir[80])* shred light on how a pattern is selected from the database containing all text files. This is done on the basis on two indexes: '*select*' and '*j*'. The index '*j*' spans across the full data set of patterns and the instruction '*inde=indexx(y_output, j)*' takes '*j*' as input along with the float pointer '**(y_output)*'. As it can be seen from the implementation of the function *int indexx(float * l7, unsigned int c)* the returning value is still an index ('*inde*') determined on the basis of the integer '*c*' which is '*j*' and the float pointer '*(l7)*' which is '**(y_output)*'. The float pointer '**(y_output)*' is made by the function *float * make_desidered_output(int q, float * op)* and comprises of the desired neural network output associated with the pattern being selected. On the basis of the index '*inde*' a new index called '*select*' is made from the instruction '*select = (int)(*(y_output+inde))*', which is still using the neural network desired output. At this point the method *char * patterns_management::take_a_filename(char selector[10], char current_dir[80], unsigned int r, unsigned int p)* uses the two indexes '*j*' and '*inde*' (see instruction '*name=take_a_filename(buff[inde+1], current_dir, select, j)*') to retrieve the file name associated with the pattern being selected from the database.

This approach to the selection of a pattern from the database is employed inside the method *void patterns_management::data_scanner(float * y_output, char current_dir[80])* for two main purposes. One is that of determining the range to be used for scaling the patterns into the range [0, 1]. In this regard, the set of instructions '*inde = indexx(y_output, j)*', '*select = (int)(*(y_output+inde))*', '*name = take_a_filename(buff[inde+1], current_dir, select, j)*', '*strcpy(filename, name)*' and '*pattern_handler(filename, set.INP)*' is employed in order to scan all patterns, to read from their text files the raw data and to determine the range to be used for the scaling (minimum and maximum for each of the parameters of which the pattern is made of). The second purpose is to scale the data contained inside the text files utilizing the range. In this regard the set of instructions is: '*inde = indexx(y_output, j)*', '*select = (int)(*(y_output+inde))*', '*name = take_a_filename(buff[inde+1], current_dir, select, j)*', '*strcpy(filename, name)*' and '*pattern_normaliser(filename, smallest, biggest,* *set.INP)*. The difference between the two set of instructions is in the use of '*pattern_handler(filename, set.INP)*' to determine the range and '*pattern_normaliser(filename, smallest, biggest, set.INP)*' to scale the patterns.

The last task performed by the method *void patterns_management::data_scanner(float * y_output, char current_dir[80])* is that of searching inside the data set for cases of patterns that are the same (they have the same numerical values inside their files). These cases might be quite detrimental to the neural network learning process. Assume for example that two patterns are the same but they are assigned by mistake to two different classes (pattern types). In such case the neural network will generate desired outputs which are different although the data (patterns) have the same numerical values. This incongruence will make impossible for the learning process to reach convergence which is to minimize the error of fit. The method *void patterns_management::data_scanner(float * y_output, char current_dir[80])* provides the user a safe exit in case two patterns are found the same regardless to their type (class).

char * patterns_management::take_a_filename(char selector[10], char current_dir[80], unsigned int r, unsigned int p)

```
{

            char klf[80];
            char s1[5]="\\";
            const char * a;
            const char * b;
            int stop=0,stop1;
            char * name;

            DIR *dir;
            struct dirent *ent;

            strcpy(klf,current_dir);

            strcat(klf,s1);

              if ((dir = opendir(current_dir)) == NULL)
              {
                perror("Unable to open directory");
                exit(1);
              }else{

              b=selector;
              while(stop==0){

              if((ent = readdir(dir)) != NULL)
              {

                  a=ent->d_name;

                  if( (strstr(a,b))!=NULL )
                  {

                  stop=1;

                  }

              }

                             }
              stop1=1;
              while(stop1<=(p-r)){

              if((ent = readdir(dir)) != NULL)
```

```
            {

        a=ent->d_name;

        if( (strstr(a,b))!=NULL )
        {

        stop1++;

        }

        }

                            }

        strcat(klf,ent->d_name);

        }

    name=klf;

    if (closedir(dir) != 0)
    {
    perror("Unable to close directory");
    }
    return name;

}

int indexx(float * l7, unsigned int c)
{

        int i,k2;

        k2=0 ;
        for(i=0;((int)(*(l7+i)))<=c;i++){

        k2++;
                                        }

        return k2-1;

}

void patterns_management::data_scanner(float * y_output, char current_dir[80])
{

        unsigned int select;
        unsigned int j,gt;
        char filename[128],FILENAME[128],ch;
        float wekk[INPUT+1],sery[INPUT+1];
        int alt,k1,k2;
        int inde;
        char * name;

        for(j=0;j<(set.T);j++){

        inde=indexx(y_output,j);
```

```
select=(int)(*(y_output+inde));

name=take_a_filename(buff[inde+1],current_dir,select,j);

strcpy(filename,name);

pattern_handler(filename,set.INP);


for(k1=0;k1<((set.INP)+1);k1++){

cout << "Pattern[" << j << "]" << "[" << k1 << "]=" << *(pattern+k1) << endl;

                            }
delete pattern;

                  }

for(k2=1;k2<((set.INP)+1);k2++){

    wekk[k2]=LOWEST;
    sery[k2]=HIGHEST;

                  }

for(j=0;j<(set.T);j++){

inde=indexx(y_output,j);

select=(int)(*(y_output+inde));

name=take_a_filename(buff[inde+1],current_dir,select,j);

strcpy(filename,name);

pattern_handler(filename,set.INP);

for(k2=1;k2<((set.INP)+1);k2++){

if( (*(pattern+k2) )   > ( wekk[k2] ) ){
wekk[k2] = *(pattern+k2) ;
                            }

if( ( *(pattern+k2) )   < ( sery[k2] ) ){
sery[k2] = *(pattern+k2) ;
                            }

                  }
delete pattern;
          }

cout << "RANGE FOR NORMALISATION" << endl;
cout << "\n" << endl;
for(k2=1;k2<((set.INP)+1);k2++){

    printf("MAX[%d]=%f \t MIN[%d]=%f\n ",k2,wekk[k2],k2,sery[k2]);
```

```
                                    }

            cout << "DIGIT N to NORMALISE PATTERNS or Q to quit" << endl;

while((ch!='Q')&&(ch!='N')){
cin >> ch;
ch=toupper(ch);
                                    }

switch(ch){
case 'Q':
exit(0);

case 'Y':
cout << "ALL PATTERNS WILL BE NORMALISED" << endl;
cout << "\n" << endl;
break;
            }

if (!(biggest = new float[(set.INP+1)*sizeof(float)]))
{
cout << "Not enough memory to allocate biggest" << endl;
exit(1);
} else
if (!(smallest = new float[(set.INP+1)*sizeof(float)]))
{
cout << "Not enough memory to allocate smallest" << endl;
exit(1);
} else

   for(k2=1;k2<((set.INP)+1);k2++){

   *(biggest+k2)=wekk[k2];
   *(smallest+k2)=sery[k2];

                                    }
for(j=0;j<(set.T);j++){

inde=indexx(y_output,j);

select=(int)(*(y_output+inde));

name=take_a_filename(buff[inde+1],current_dir,select,j);

strcpy(filename,name);

pattern_normaliser(filename,smallest,biggest,set.INP);

for(k2=0;k2<((set.INP)+1);k2++){

printf("IO[%d][%d]=%f\n",j,k2,*(pattern_normalised+k2) );

                                    }
cout << "\n" << endl;

delete pattern_normalised;
```

```
                              }

    alt=0;

    for(j=0;j<(set.T);j++){

    inde=indexx(y_output,j);

    select=(int)(*(y_output+inde));

    name=take_a_filename(buff[inde+1],current_dir,select,j);

    strcpy(filename,name);

    pattern_normaliser(filename,smallest,biggest,set.INP);

        for(k2=1;k2<((set.INP)+1);k2++){

        if( ( *(pattern_normalised+k2) )>1){
    printf("WARNING IO[%d][%d]=%f\n",j,k2,*(pattern_normalised+k2) );
    printf("It is from file %s\n",filename);

    alt++;
                                        }

                                  }

    delete pattern_normalised;

                }

    if(alt!=0){

    exit(0);

        } else

    cout << "All inputs correctly normalised" << endl;
    cout << "NOW THE NET WILL SEARCH FOR MISMATCHING CASES" << endl;
    cout << "please WAIT..." << endl;

    for(gt=0;gt<(set.T);gt++){

    inde=indexx(y_output,gt);

    select=(int)(*(y_output+inde));

    name=take_a_filename(buff[inde+1],current_dir,select,gt);

    strcpy(filename,name);

    pattern_normaliser(filename,smallest,biggest,set.INP);

    for(j=gt+1;j<(set.T);j++){

    inde=indexx(y_output,j);
```

```
        select=(int)(*(y_output+inde));

        name=take_a_filename(buff[inde+1],current_dir,select,j);

        strcpy(FILENAME,name);
        pattern=pattern_normalised;
        pattern_normaliser(FILENAME,smallest,biggest,set.INP);

        if(gt!=j){

           k2=-1;
           alt=-1;

        do{

           k2++;

        if( k2<((set.INP)+1) ){

        if( (*(pattern+k2) )== (*(pattern_normalised+k2) ) ){

        alt=alt+1;
                                                       }
                            }

        }while(k2<((set.INP)+1));

        if(alt==(set.INP)){

        cout << "WARNING!! :" << filename << "is MISMATCHING: " << FILENAME << endl;

        for(k2=0;k2<((set.INP)+1);k2++){

        printf("IO=%f   IO=%f\n",*(pattern_normalised+k2),  *(pattern+k2)  );

                            }

        delete pattern;
        delete pattern_normalised;
        exit(0);

               }   else

                  delete pattern;
           }

        }

        delete pattern_normalised;

        }

}
```

The methods outlined in part II are those which class container is '*CANN98Dlg*', which relates to the Graphical User Interface of the project *ANN98*. As already mentioned *ANN98* is a GUI running executables artificial neural networks (see for example the method called *void CANN98Dlg::OnRunObjNet98()* here reported as an example. The actual implementation of the push button that runs '*ObjNet.EXE*' also is located in chapter 7 within the project named *SPACE 2010*. It is here reported a description of the methods included into the GUI of *ANN98*. The method *void CANN98Dlg::OnParametersRange()* is employed to view text files relevant to the data range through the command '*system*'. The method *void CANN98Dlg::OnNetworkWeights()* uses the same command to view the weighting connections' values at the end of the learning process, and the method *void CANN98Dlg::OnNetworkClassification()* does view the network classification obtained after training the network, specifically during the test sessions.

```
void CANN98Dlg::OnParametersRange()
{

        CString ViewMessage;

        char outputFile[123];

        sprintf(outputFile, "%s", "BIGGEST.txt");
        ViewMessage.Format("%s\n%s\n" , "Ready to Display Output File:" , outputFile);
        AfxMessageBox(ViewMessage);
        system(outputFile);

        sprintf(outputFile, "%s", "SMALLEST.txt");
        ViewMessage.Format("%s\n%s\n" , "Ready to Display Output File:" , outputFile);
        AfxMessageBox(ViewMessage);
        system(outputFile);

}


void CANN98Dlg::OnNetworkWeights()
{

        CString ViewMessage;
        char outputFile[123];

        sprintf(outputFile, "%s", "WEIGHT1.txt");
        ViewMessage.Format("%s\n%s\n" , "Ready to Display Output File:" , outputFile);
        AfxMessageBox(ViewMessage);
        system(outputFile);

        sprintf(outputFile, "%s", "WEIGHT2.txt");
        ViewMessage.Format("%s\n%s\n" , "Ready to Display Output File:" , outputFile);
        AfxMessageBox(ViewMessage);
        system(outputFile);

}


void CANN98Dlg::OnNetworkClassification()
{

        CString ViewMessage;

        char outputFile[123];

        sprintf(outputFile, "%s", "RESPONSE.txt");
```

```
ViewMessage.Format("%s\n%s\n" , "Ready to Display Output File:" , outputFile);
AfxMessageBox(ViewMessage);
system(outputFile);

}
```

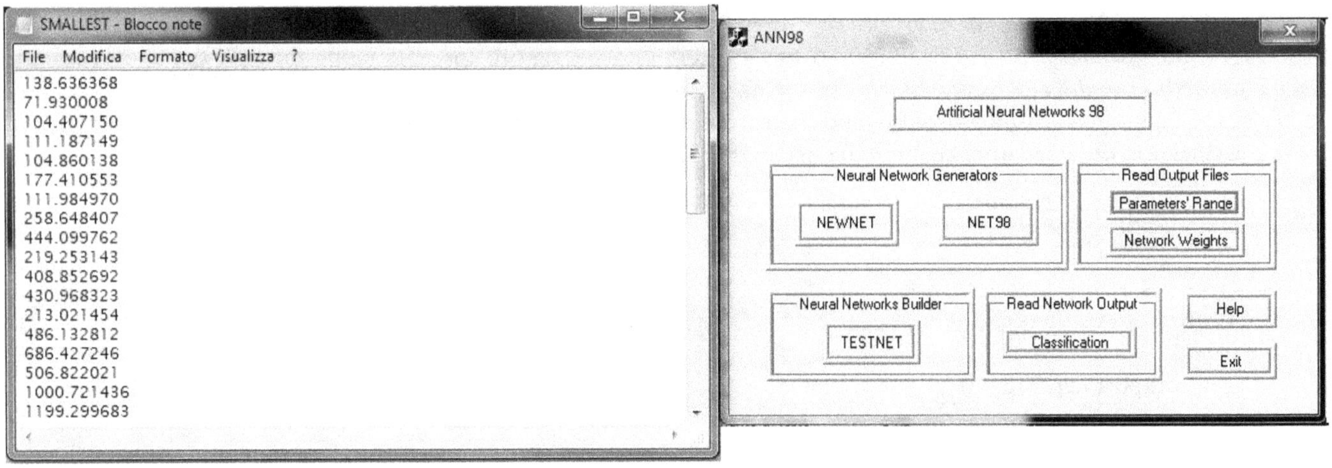

Figure 1: The Graphical User Interface of *ANN98* and the text file containing the minimum values of the patterns' parameters. The text file is displayed upon pushing the button '*Parameters' Range*' inside the panel named '*Read Output Files*'.

The Graphical User Interface of the project *ANN98* is here described (see Fig. 1). In the panel named '*Neural Network Generators*' are located two push buttons called '*NEWNET*' and '*NET98*', they are associated to the methods *void CANN98Dlg::OnNewnet()* and *void CANN98Dlg::OnNet98()* respectively, employed to run the programs '*NEWNET.EXE*' and '*NET98.EXE*'. The panel named '*Read Output Files*' contains the push buttons named '*Parameters' Range*' and '*Network Weights*' which are associated to the methods *void CANN98Dlg::OnParametersRange()* and *void CANN98Dlg::OnNetworkWeights()*. These methods have the capability to show to the user the text files containing the minimum and maximum of the patterns' parameters across the full data set, and the text files containing the neural network weighting connections.

The panel named '*Neural Network Builder*' contains the push button '*TESTNET*' which is associated to the method called *void CANN98Dlg::OnRunTESTNET()* to run the program '*TESTNET.EXE*'. The panel named '*Read Network Output*' contains the push button called '*Classification*' which is associated to the method *void CANN98Dlg::OnNetworkClassification()* employed to show to the user the classification of the patterns performed through the program '*TESTNET.EXE*'. Worth noting that the program '*TESTNET.EXE*' is a neural network builder, which means, it does not perform any learning process, instead builds the neural network on the basis of the weighting connections made by one of '*NEWNET.EXE*' or '*NET98.EXE*' at the end of their learning processes. Finally, the GUI shows the push button '*Help*' and the push button '*Exit*', which are associated to the methods *void CANN98Dlg::OnHelp()* and *void CANN98Dlg::OnExit()*. The method *void CANN98Dlg::OnHelp()* saves a text file named '*Help.log*' which can be viewed by the user before using the GUI. The method *void CANN98Dlg::OnExit()* provides safe exit to the program.

void CANN98Dlg::OnNewnet()
```
{
        system( "NEWNET.EXE" );
}
```

void CANN98Dlg::OnNet98()
```
{
        system( "NET98.EXE" );
}
```

void CANN98Dlg::OnRunTESTNET()
{
      system("TESTNET.EXE");
}

void CANN98Dlg::OnHelp()
{

      char logfilename[128];

      CString HelpMessage;

      FILE * logfile;

      sprintf(logfilename,"%s","Help.log");

      if ((logfile = fopen(logfilename,"w"))==NULL)
      {

      HelpMessage.Format("%s\n%s\n" , "Cannot save the file Help.log" , "Now Click to Exit the program");
      MessageBox(HelpMessage);
      exit(0);

      } else {

        fprintf(logfile,"%s\n", "Welcome to Artificial Neural Networks 98");
        fprintf(logfile,"%s\n", "There are three programs that you can run:");
        fprintf(logfile,"\n");

        fprintf(logfile,"%s\n", "1. NET98:");
        fprintf(logfile,"%s\n", "Artificial Neural Network generator with added capability to adapt");
        fprintf(logfile,"%s\n", "the Hidden Layer Architecture to the given patter recognition problem.");
        fprintf(logfile,"%s\n", "This program has been devised not to have restrictions on the maximum number
               of output neurons.");
        fprintf(logfile,"%s\n", "However in order to be compatible with TESTNET please run NET98 with 2, 3
               or 4 output neurons.");
        fprintf(logfile,"\n");

        fprintf(logfile,"%s\n", "2. NEWNET:");
        fprintf(logfile,"%s\n", "Artificial Neural Network generator with a fixed Architecture for the Hidden
               Layer.");
        fprintf(logfile,"%s\n", "This program has been devised to have 2, 3 or 4 output neurons.");
        fprintf(logfile,"\n");

        fprintf(logfile,"%s\n", "NET98 and NEWNET might produce two completely different architectures.");
        fprintf(logfile, "%s\n","This can be seen given that if the number of Hidden and Output neurons are the
               same for both");
        fprintf(logfile,"%s\n", "programs, the weighting connections of NET98 and NEWNET");
        fprintf(logfile, "%s\n","(in both input and output layers) might be different.");
        fprintf(logfile, "%s\n","This happens because of the capability of NET98 to re-train neurons during the
               learning process.");
        fprintf(logfile,"\n");
        fprintf(logfile,"%s\n", "NET98 and NEWNET produce 4 output files called:");
        fprintf(logfile,"%s\n", "'BIGGEST.A1', 'SMALLEST.A1' (which contain maximum and minimum values
               for each parameter)");
        fprintf(logfile,"%s\n", "'WEIGHT.A1', 'WEIGHT.A2' (which contain hidden and output network layers
               weighting connections)");

```
            fprintf(logfile,"%s\n", "These 4 output files are saved in the same folder where the programs run.");
            fprintf(logfile,"\n");

            fprintf(logfile,"%s\n", "3. TESTNET:");
            fprintf(logfile,"%s\n", "Artificial Neural Network used to validate the non linear separation achieved
                        through NEWNET or NET98.");
            fprintf(logfile,"\n");
            fprintf(logfile,"%s\n", "TESTNET produces the output file called 'RESPONSE.A1', which is placed in the
                        same folder where the program runs.");
            fprintf(logfile,"\n");

            fprintf(logfile,"%s\n", "The three programs run on the system command window.");
            fprintf(logfile,"\n");
            fprintf(logfile,"%s\n", "Before running either of the three programs please do the following:");
            fprintf(logfile,"\n");
            fprintf(logfile,"%s\n", "Preferably, confirm that your computer has available a drive named C:");
            fprintf(logfile,"%s\n", "Create a directory under the C: drive and remember to input the directory");
            fprintf(logfile,"%s\n", "name to any of the three programs when prompted to enter it.");
            fprintf(logfile,"%s\n", "Each of the files under the directory identifies a given pattern");
            fprintf(logfile,"%s\n", "Each of the files' extension (e.g. .A1, .A2, etc...) identifies a different class of the
                        pattern recognition problem.");
            fprintf(logfile,"\n");

            fprintf(logfile,"%s\n", "Other relevant information:");
            fprintf(logfile,"\n");
            fprintf(logfile,"%s\n", "When running NET98 please do interact with the Learning process to select");
            fprintf(logfile,"%s\n", "the desired Network internal architecture to achieve the desired minimum");
            fprintf(logfile,"%s\n", "at the end of the Learning Process.");
            fprintf(logfile,"\n");
            fprintf(logfile,"%s\n", "When running NEWNET the program suggests the number of neurons of the
                        Hidden Layer");
            fprintf(logfile,"%s\n", "which may provide a suitable Network internal architecture to achieve the desired
                        minimum");
            fprintf(logfile,"%s\n", "at the end of the Learning Process.");
            fprintf(logfile,"\n");
            fprintf(logfile,"%s\n", "When running TESTNET please set the number of Hidden neurons equal to that
                        of NEWNET or NET98");
            fprintf(logfile,"%s\n", "so to match the Neural Network Architecture generated through NEWNET or
                        NET98.");
            fprintf(logfile,"\n");
            fclose(logfile);
            HelpMessage.Format("%s\n%s\n" , "Please read the file Help.log just saved.",
                                            "Before using this Graphical Interface");
            MessageBox(HelpMessage);

        }//else

}


void CANN98Dlg::OnExit()
{
        exit(0);
}
```

Summary

This chapter has shown to the readers the source code of *ObjNet* and the GUI called *ANN98* (see Fig. 1) which are two programs implementing a project relating to artificial neural networks for pattern recognition. The program called *ObjNet* is object oriented and constitutes a good exercise for what relates to the study of basic concepts of the C++ programming language applied to the development of the artificial neural network in the specific case. The mathematics of the neural network were presented earlier [2].

The program called *ANN98* is a Graphical User Interface to several programs calling in neural networks one of which was employed in [1]. The programming details given in this chapter provide the students with methods embedded in C++ classes which are relevant to the random initialization of the network, the crossing of a pattern inside the network (from the input layer through the hidden layer and the output layer), and also the iterative correction of the weighting connections of the neural network on the basis of the back-propagation algorithm and the delta rule [2].

References

[1] Ciulla, C. (2009). *Improved Signal and Image Interpolation in Biomedical Applications: The Case of Magnetic Resonance Imaging (MRI)* - Medical Information Science Reference - IGI Global Publisher, Hershey, PA, U.S.A.

[2] Werbos, P. J. (1990). *Backpropagation through time: what it does and how to do it.* Proceedings of the IEEE, 78(10), 1550-1560.

CHAPTER 7

The Source Code of SPACE 2010

Introduction

SPACE 2010 is a collection of executables which run under the Graphical User Interface (GUI) devised for this project. As it can be seen in Fig. 1, *SPACE 2010* has a panel called '*Artificial Neural Networks*' where two push buttons by the name of '*ANN98*' and '*OBJNET*' are located. Using the push button named '*ANN98*' will bring up the GUI visible in Fig. 1. To mention that the source code of *ObjNet* is located in chapter 6 along with the source code of *ANN98*. Using the push button named '*OBJNET*' will run the executable *OBJNET.EXE*.

The panel called '*Signal Processing Applications*' has two push buttons by the name of '*InvertImage 2010*' and '*Image-Viewer 2010*', and they are associated with the methods called *void CSPACE2010Dlg::OnInvertImage2010()* and *void CSPACE2010Dlg::OnImageViewer()* respectively. The two push buttons run the programs *Invert Image 2010* and *Image-Viewer 2010* respectively.

The panel called '*Signal Processing Applications*' contains also edit boxes and push buttons relevant to the method called *void CSPACE2010Dlg::OnIntensityCurvatureFunctional()*. In order for this method to run properly, there are values to assign to five edit boxes corresponding to the following labeling: (i) '*X*', (ii) '*Y*', (iii) '*File Name*', (iv) '*X Misplacement*' and (v) '*Y Misplacement*'. The variables corresponding to the aforementioned labels are identified in the source code as: (i) '*m_rcxres*', (ii) '*m_rcyres*', (iii) '*m_FileName*', (iv) '*m_MisX*' and (v) '*m_MisY*'. The two push buttons are called '*Intensity Curvature Functional*' and '*Help ICF*' respectively. The push button '*Intensity Curvature Functional*' calls the method *void CSPACE2010Dlg::OnIntensityCurvatureFunctional()*. The push button '*Help ICF*' calls the method *void CSPACE2010Dlg::OnHelpIntCurvFunct()* and displays to the user the information useful to interact with the program. The outcome of the method *void CSPACE2010Dlg::OnIntensityCurvatureFunctional()* was shown in Fig. 7 of chapter 1 for a Magnetic Resonance Imaging (MRI) slice of the human brain and it pertains to the calculation of the Intensity Curvature Functional [1].

The panel called '*Whittaker Shannon Sampling and Fourier Theory*' contains a push button by the name of '*pointSource 2010*', which is associated to the method *void CSPACE2010Dlg::OnpointSource2010()* and runs the program *pointSource 2010* which GUI is visible in Fig. 2.

The Source Code

The function *void display(void)* belong to the OpenGL ® coding for display and contains the code '*glClear(GL_COLOR_BUFFER_BIT)*' [2] to clear the window display. The method *void CSPACE2010Dlg::init()* (function which belongs to the major class container '*CSPACE2010Dlg*') makes use of the I/O file '*keyboard.txt*' to import the variables related to the resolution of the image display. The instructions employed are:

- ✓ *FILE * pointTokeyboardFile;*

- ✓ *char keyboard[128]="keyboard.txt";*

- ✓ *if ((pointTokeyboardFile = fopen(keyboard,"r"))==NULL) {*

- ✓ *CString ExitMessage;*

- ✓ *ExitMessage.Format("%s\n" , "Cannot Open File: keyboard.txt: Exit");*

- ✓ *AfxMessageBox(ExitMessage);*

- ✓ *exit(0);*

- ✓ *}else{*

- ✓ *fscanf(pointTokeyboardFile,"%d\n", &rcxres);*
- ✓ *fscanf(pointTokeyboardFile,"%d\n", &rcyres);*

- ✓ *fscanf(pointTokeyboardFile,"%f\n", &PSPX);*
- ✓ *fscanf(pointTokeyboardFile,"%f\n", &PSPY);*
- ✓ *fclose(pointTokeyboardFile);*

- ✓ *}*

Also, in *void CSPACE2010Dlg::init()* we find OpenGL ® instructions [2] apt to set the color (*'glClearColor(0.0, 0.0, 0.0, 0.0)'*), to set the shading of the image display (*'glShadeModel(GL_FLAT)'*), to set the viewport size (*'glViewport(0, 0, (GLsizei)winx, (GLsizei)winy)'*), to load the identity matrix (*'glLoadIdentity()'*), and to set the orthogonal 2D view size (*'gluOrtho2D(0.0, (GLdouble)winx, 0.0, (GLdouble)winy)'*).

The function *void keyboard(unsigned char key, int x, int y)* is the main OpenGL ® routine which makes possible the interactive graphics in this collection called *SPACE 2010*. The function makes use of the I/O file *'keyboard.txt'* and considers two main cases associated with the keys *'1'* and *'2'* respectively, which the user may hit from the keyboard. In either of the two cases *'1'* or *'2'*, the routine displays a plane image by making use of dynamic allocation techniques which rely on pointers and additional instructions. The pointers are: *'(*planeWindowImage)'* and *'(GLfloat) *(imdata1)'*, *'(GLfloat) *(EIN)'* (both of them global to the extent of the source code herein reported). The image display happens upon filling the memory cells pointed by *'(*planeWindowImage)'* with the data pixels located inside the memory cells pointed by *'(GLfloat) *(imdata1)'* (*'case '1''*) or *'(GLfloat) *(EIN)'* (*'case '2''*). The instructions are:

- ✓ *case '1':*

- ✓ *for(j=0; j<rcyres; j++) {*
- ✓ *for(i=0; i<rcxres; i++) {*

- ✓ *k3 = (j*rcxres+i);*

- ✓ **(planeWindowImage + k3) = (GLfloat) *(imdata1+k3)/255;*
- ✓ **(planeWindowImage + k3*2) = (GLfloat) *(imdata1+k3)/255;*
- ✓ **(planeWindowImage + k3*3) = (GLfloat) *(imdata1+k3)/255;*
- ✓ **(planeWindowImage + k3*4) = (GLfloat) *(imdata1+k3)/255;*

- ✓ *}*
- ✓ *}*

- ✓ *case '2':*

- ✓ *for(j=0; j<rcyres; j++) {*
- ✓ *for(i=0; i<rcxres; i++) {*

- ✓ *k3 = (j*rcxres+i);*

- ✓ **(planeWindowImage + k3) = (GLfloat) *(EIN+k3)/255;*
- ✓ **(planeWindowImage + k3*2) = (GLfloat) *(EIN+k3)/255;*
- ✓ **(planeWindowImage + k3*3) = (GLfloat) *(EIN+k3)/255;*
- ✓ **(planeWindowImage + k3*4) = (GLfloat) *(EIN+k3)/255;*

- ✓ *}*
- ✓ *}*

The additional instructions [2] determine the following tasks: (i) to draw the buffer, (ii) to set the raster position, (iii) to zoom the pixel, (iv) to draw the pixel, and (v) to flush the display. Specifically, these instructions are: *'glDrawBuffer(GL_FRONT)'*, *'glRasterPos2i(0, 0)'*, *'glPixelZoom((GLfloat) PSPX, (GLfloat) PSPY)'*, *'glDrawPixels((GLsizei)rcxres, (GLsizei)rcyres, GL_LUMINANCE, GL_FLOAT, planeWindowImage)'* and *'glFlush()'* [2]. The instruction *'*(planeWindowImage + k3) = (GLfloat) *(imdata1+k3)/255'* assigns to the pointer of global visibility the content that needs to be seen on display through the function which draw each pixel: *'glDrawPixels((GLsizei)rcxres, (GLsizei)rcyres,*

Computer Science Applications

GL_LUMINANCE, GL_FLOAT, *planeWindowImage)*'. Similarly, the instruction '*(planeWindowImage + k3) = (GLfloat) *(EIN+k3)/255*' assigns to '*(planeWindowImage)*' the pixel data which will be on display through that same instruction '*glDrawPixels((GLsizei)rcxres, (GLsizei)rcyres, GL_LUMINANCE, GL_FLOAT, planeWindowImage)*'. Data in '*(imdata1)*' and '*(GLfloat) *(EIN)*' is scaled inside the range [0, 255] and so is divided by 255 such to be acceptable by '*glDrawPixels*', which process data in the range [0, 1]. Worth commenting the '*case 27*' indicated below as the case of hitting the '*ESC*' key to quit the OpenGL ® application.

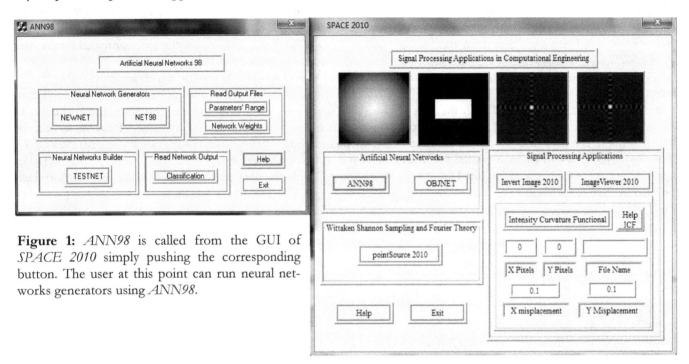

Figure 1: *ANN98* is called from the GUI of *SPACE 2010* simply pushing the corresponding button. The user at this point can run neural networks generators using *ANN98*.

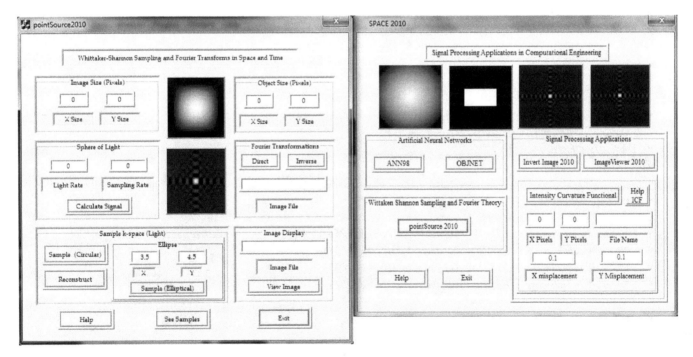

Figure 2: *pointSource 2010* is called from the GUI of *SPACE 2010* allowing the user to use the functionalities of direct and inverse Fourier transformations, Whittaker-Shannon sampling [3] and sampling in k-Space.

The function *void reshape(int w, int h)* is also part of the interactive graphics routines of the OpenGL ® portion of this program and makes use of the I/O file '*keyboard.txt*', in reading (before display), and in saving (after the change of display) the change of the resolution information determined by the user when changing the size of the 2D window. Once data is read in from '*keyboard.txt*', the routine performs the following tasks: (i) setting the viewport size, (ii) loading the identity matrix and (iii) setting the orthogonal 2D view size. The instructions that perform these operations are [2]: '*glViewport(0, 0, (GLsizei)w, (GLsizei)h)*', '*glLoadIdentity()*' and '*gluOrtho2D(0.0, (GLdouble)w, 0.0, (GLdouble)h)*'. Then, the I/O file '*keyboard.txt*' is updated and serves the purpose of storage for any functions not belonging to the main class container, thus engineering the purpose of exchanging variables between a function and a method (function inside the class).

The method *void CSPACE2010Dlg::LaunchOpenGL()* reads from the I/O file '*keyboard.txt*' then allocates dynamically the memory for OpenGL ® with the instruction '*AllocateMemoryforOpenGLGraphics()*' calling in the method *void CSPACE2010Dlg::AllocateMemoryforOpenGLGraphics()*. At this point the '*glut*' main loop is ready to be set through the following set of instructions [2]: '*glutInitDisplayMode(GLUT_SINGLE | GLUT_RGB)*', '*glutInitWindowSize(winx,winy)*', '*glutInitWindowPosition(100, 100)*', '*pw = glutCreateWindow("XY VIEW")*', '*init()*', '*glutDisplayFunc(display)*', '*glutReshape-Func(reshape)*', '*glutKeyboardFunc(keyboard)*', '*glutMainLoop()*'. These instructions perform the following tasks: (i) to set the window size, (ii) to set the window position, (iii) to create the window, (iv) to initialize the window, (v) to display the window, (vi) to manage the window reshape, and (vii) to manage the keyboard usage.

The method *void CSPACE2010Dlg::AllocateMemoryforOpenGLGraphics()* performs dynamic memory allocation through the instruction that uses the function '*malloc*', which is '*planeWindowImage = (float *) mal-loc(rcyres*rcxres*4*sizeof(float))*'. By doing so, the method *void CSPACE2010Dlg::AllocateMemoryforOpenGLGraphics()* has the pointer '**(planeWindowImage)*' as the available container of the data for 2D display which can be used inside the function *void keyboard(unsigned char key, int x, int y)*.

The purpose of the method *float * CSPACE2010Dlg::data(char filename[258], int rcyres, int rcxres)* is that of reading in the data and scaling it inside the range [0, 255] for processing. This method also uses dynamic allocation technique which, making use of a pointer, returns conveniently data within the global extent of the program here presented. Data returned through *float * CSPACE2010Dlg::data(char filename[258], int rcyres, int rcxres)* are thus made available to all of the functions and the methods herein discussed. The relevant instructions are:

- ✓ *if ((pf = fopen(filename,"rb+"))==NULL) {*

- ✓ *fprintf(logfile, "%s\n", "Not enough memory to allocate Image data");*
- ✓ *free(pointer1);*
- ✓ *exit(0);*

- ✓ *}*

- ✓ *for(j=0; j<rcyres; j++) {*
- ✓ *for(i=0; i<rcxres; i++) {*

- ✓ *fread(&number,sizeof(float),1,pf);*
- ✓ *k2=(j*rcxres+i);*
- ✓ **(pointer1+k2) = number;*

- ✓ *}*
- ✓ *}*

- ✓ *fclose (pf);*

- ✓ *for(i=0; i<rcxres*rcyres; i++) {*

- ✓ *if(*(pointer1+i)>max) {*

- ✓ *max=*(pointer1+i);*

- ✓ *}*

- ✓ *if(*(pointer1+i)<min) {*
- ✓ *min=*(pointer1+i);*

✓ }

✓ }

✓ *for(j=0; j<rcyres; j++){*
✓ *for(i=0; i<rcxres; i++){*

✓ *k2=(j*rcxres+i);*

✓ *if (max==min)*
✓ **(pointer1+k2)=(float)max;*
✓ *else *(pointer1+k2)=(float)(((float)*(pointer1+k2)-min)/((float)max-min))*255;*

✓ }
✓ }

For what relates to the push button named '*Intensity Curvature Functional*' located in the panel named '*Signal Processing Applications*', the relevant methods are: *(i) float * CSPACE2010Dlg::EIN_image(float * ImageData, int rcyres, int rcxres)*, (ii) *void CSPACE2010Dlg::OnIntensityCurvatureFunctional()* and (iii) *void CSPACE2010Dlg::OnHelpIntCurvFunct()*. As largely outlined elsewhere [1], the Intensity Curvature Functional is a measure of the image energy for signal processing applications like interpolation. The routines here reported constitutes of the coding of the formulation given earlier in [1].

The method *float * CSPACE2010Dlg::EIN_image(float * ImageData, int rcyres, int rcxres)* allocates a float pointer named '**(IntCurvIN)*' with the instruction '*IntCurvIN = (float *) calloc(((rcyres*rcxres)+1), sizeof(float))*'. The memory cells pointed by '**(ImageData)*' contain the two dimensional image and they are given as input to the method and thus employed for the calculation of the Intensity Curvature Functional with the following instructions:

✓ *for(j=0; j<rcyres; j++){*
✓ *for(i=0; i<rcxres; i++){*

✓ *k2=(j*rcxres+i);*

✓ *k7=((j*rcxres+i)+1);*

✓ *k8=((j+1)*(rcxres)+(i+1));*

✓ *k9=((j+1)*(rcxres)+(i));*

✓ *thetax = ((float)*(ImageData+k7) - (float)*(ImageData+k2));*

✓ *thetay = ((float)*(ImageData+k9) - (float)*(ImageData+k2));*

✓ *omega = (float)*(ImageData+k8) + (float)*(ImageData+k2) - (float)*(ImageData+k7) - (float)*(ImageData+k9);*

✓ *Hxy = ((float)*(ImageData+k2) * Mis_X * Mis_Y) +*

        ((float)(Mis_X * Mis_X * Mis_Y * thetax)/2.0) +

        ((float)(Mis_X * Mis_Y *Mis_Y * thetay)/2.0) +

        ((float)(Mis_X * Mis_Y *Mis_X * Mis_Y * omega)/4.0);

✓ **(IntCurvIN + k2) = ((float)2.0 * Hxy * omega);*

✓ }
✓ }

The method *void CSPACE2010Dlg::OnIntensityCurvatureFunctional()* performs the following tasks. Initially, the method writes the text file named '*keyboard.txt*', which contains the image matrix resolution information. This text file will serve the I/O operations in support also to the functions of the project which do not belong to the main class container '*CSPACE2010Dlg*' such as for example *void keyboard(unsigned char key, int x, int y)* and *void reshape(int w, int h)*. The instructions are:

- ✓ FILE * *pointTokeyboardFile;*
- ✓ *char keyboard[128]="keyboard.txt";*
- ✓ *if ((pointTokeyboardFile = fopen(keyboard,"w"))==NULL) {*

- ✓ *CString ExitMessage;*
- ✓ *ExitMessage.Format("%s\n" , "Cannot Open File: keyboard.txt: Exit");*
- ✓ *AfxMessageBox(ExitMessage);*
- ✓ *exit(0);*

- ✓ *}else{*

- ✓ *fprintf(pointTokeyboardFile,"%d\n", rcxres);*
- ✓ *fprintf(pointTokeyboardFile,"%d\n", rcyres);*
- ✓ *fprintf(pointTokeyboardFile,"%f\n", PSPX);*
- ✓ *fprintf(pointTokeyboardFile,"%f\n", PSPY);*
- ✓ *fclose(pointTokeyboardFile);*

- ✓ *}*

Subsequently, the method *void CSPACE2010Dlg::OnIntensityCurvatureFunctional()* employs the two instructions '*imdata1 = data(filename1, rcyres, rcxres)*' and '*EIN = EIN_image(imdata1, rcyres, rcxres)*' to load the image data into the pointer '*(imdata1)*' through the method *float * CSPACE2010Dlg::data(char filename[258], int rcyres, int rcxres)* and to calculate the Intensity Curvature Functional [1] through the method *float * CSPACE2010Dlg::EIN_image(float * ImageData, int rcyres, int rcxres)*, which takes as input the pointer '*(imdata1)*'. The latter method releases the processed image into the pointer '*(EIN)*'. Both pointers '*(imdata1)*' and '*(EIN)*' will be available for display inside the function *void keyboard(unsigned char key, int x, int y)*. The method *void CSPACE2010Dlg::OnIntensityCurvatureFunctional()* writes into the '*log*' file the information relevant to the image processing and also displays such information to the user for immediate view through the command '*system(logfileName)*'. After the user reads the information of the '*log*' file, the instruction '*LaunchOpenGL()*' sets the program into the display mode by calling the method *void CSPACE2010Dlg::LaunchOpenGL()*.

The method *void CSPACE2010Dlg::OnHelpIntCurvFunct()* serves the purpose to help the user set up the GUI before pushing the button named '*Intensity Curvature Functional*'. The methods *void CSPACE2010Dlg::OnOBJNET()*, *void CSPACE2010Dlg::OnANN98()*, *void CSPACE2010Dlg::OnpointSource2010()*, *void CSPACE2010Dlg::OnInvertImage2010()* and *void CSPACE2010Dlg::OnImageViewer()*, run through the command '*system*' the programs *OBJNET.EXE*, *ANN98.EXE*, *pointSource2010.EXE*, *InvertImage.EXE* and *ImageViewer.EXE* respectively. The method *void CSPACE2010Dlg::OnHelp()* is called upon pushing the button '*Help*' and recalls to the user that each application included in *SPACE 2010* saves the relevant help information in separate '*log*' files. The method *void CSPACE2010Dlg::OnExit()* provides the project with safe exit after release of the memory dynamically allocated.

```
// methods that cannot be included in any class because of the syntax required from OpenGL ® Libraries
void display(void);
void keyboard(unsigned char key, int x, int y);
void reshape(int w, int h);
// global variables
float * imdata1 = 0;
float * EIN = 0;
char logfileName[125]="IntCurvFunct.log";
FILE * logfile;
GLfloat  * planeWindowImage = NULL;
int pw;
```

167

Computer Science Applications

```
void display(void)
{
        glClear(GL_COLOR_BUFFER_BIT);
}

void CSPACE2010Dlg::init()
{

        int winx, winy;
        int rcxres;
        int rcyres;
        float PSPY;
        float PSPX;

        // Once the windows' size is changed:
        // read keyboard.txt containing the modified values of
        // the variables to use to display image data
        FILE * pointTokeyboardFile;
        char keyboard[128]="keyboard.txt";

        if ((pointTokeyboardFile = fopen(keyboard,"r"))==NULL)
        {

        CString ExitMessage;
        ExitMessage.Format("%s\n" , "Cannot Open File: keyboard.txt: Exit" );
        AfxMessageBox(ExitMessage);
        exit(0);

        }else{
        fscanf(pointTokeyboardFile,"%d\n", &rcxres);
        fscanf(pointTokeyboardFile,"%d\n", &rcyres);
        fscanf(pointTokeyboardFile,"%f\n", &PSPX);
        fscanf(pointTokeyboardFile,"%f\n", &PSPY);
        fclose(pointTokeyboardFile);
        }

        winx=(int)rcxres*PSPX;
        winy=(int)rcyres*PSPY;

        glClearColor(0.0, 0.0, 0.0, 0.0);
        glShadeModel(GL_FLAT);

        glViewport(0, 0, (GLsizei)winx, (GLsizei)winy);
        glLoadIdentity();
        gluOrtho2D(0.0, (GLdouble)winx, 0.0, (GLdouble)winy);

}

void keyboard(unsigned char key, int x, int y)
{

        int j,i,k3;
        float PSPX, PSPY;
        FILE * pointTokeyboardFile;
        char keyboard[128]="keyboard.txt";
        int rcxres, rcyres;
```

```
if ((pointTokeyboardFile = fopen(keyboard,"r"))==NULL)
{

CString ExitMessage;
 ExitMessage.Format("%s\n" , "Cannot Open File: keyboard.txt: Exit" );
AfxMessageBox(ExitMessage);

exit(0);

}else{

fscanf(pointTokeyboardFile,"%d\n", &rcxres);
fscanf(pointTokeyboardFile,"%d\n", &rcyres);
fscanf(pointTokeyboardFile,"%f\n", &PSPX);
fscanf(pointTokeyboardFile,"%f\n", &PSPY);
fclose(pointTokeyboardFile);

}

key=toupper(key);
switch(key){

case '1':

for(j=0;j<rcyres;j++){
  for(i=0;i<rcxres;i++){

    k3 = (j*rcxres+i) ;

    *(planeWindowImage + k3)   = (GLfloat) *(imdata1+k3)/255;
    *(planeWindowImage + k3*2) = (GLfloat) *(imdata1+k3)/255;
    *(planeWindowImage + k3*3) = (GLfloat) *(imdata1+k3)/255;
    *(planeWindowImage + k3*4) = (GLfloat) *(imdata1+k3)/255;

                  }
                }

glDrawBuffer(GL_FRONT);
glRasterPos2i(0,0);
glPixelZoom((GLfloat) PSPX, (GLfloat) PSPY);
glDrawPixels((GLsizei)rcxres, (GLsizei)rcyres, GL_LUMINANCE, GL_FLOAT, planeWindowImage);
glFlush();

break;

case '2':
for(j=0;j<rcyres;j++){
    for(i=0;i<rcxres;i++){

k3 = (j*rcxres+i) ;

*(planeWindowImage + k3)   = (GLfloat) *(EIN+k3)/255;
*(planeWindowImage + k3*2) = (GLfloat) *(EIN+k3)/255;
*(planeWindowImage + k3*3) = (GLfloat) *(EIN+k3)/255;
*(planeWindowImage + k3*4) = (GLfloat) *(EIN+k3)/255;
```

```
                    }
                }

glDrawBuffer(GL_FRONT);
glRasterPos2i(0,0);
glPixelZoom((GLfloat) PSPX, (GLfloat) PSPY);
glDrawPixels((GLsizei)rcxres, (GLsizei)rcyres, GL_LUMINANCE, GL_FLOAT, planeWindowImage);
glFlush();
break;

case 27:

free(imdata1);
free(EIN);
free(planeWindowImage);
CString ExitMessage;
ExitMessage.Format("%s\n" , "Now Leaving SPACE 2010: Exit");
AfxMessageBox(ExitMessage);
exit(0);

break;

    }

}

void reshape(int w, int h)
{

        /// read the keyboard matrix resolution///
        FILE * pointTokeyboardFile;
        char keyboard[128]="keyboard.txt";

        float PSPY, PSPX;

        int rcxres, rcyres;

        if ((pointTokeyboardFile = fopen(keyboard,"r"))==NULL)
        {

        CString ExitMessage;

        ExitMessage.Format("%s\n" , "Cannot Open File: keyboard.txt: Exit" );
        AfxMessageBox(ExitMessage);

        exit(0);
        }else{

        fscanf(pointTokeyboardFile,"%d\n", &rcxres);
        fscanf(pointTokeyboardFile,"%d\n", &rcyres);
        fscanf(pointTokeyboardFile,"%f\n", &PSPX);
        fscanf(pointTokeyboardFile,"%f\n", &PSPY);
        fclose(pointTokeyboardFile);

        }
```

```
glViewport(0, 0, (GLsizei)w, (GLsizei)h);
glLoadIdentity();
gluOrtho2D(0.0, (GLdouble)w, 0.0, (GLdouble)h);

if(glutGetWindow() == pw)
{
PSPX=((float)w/rcxres);
PSPY=((float)h/rcyres);
}

// Once the windows' size is changed:
// re-write keyboard.txt containing the modified values of
// the variables to use to image display

if ((pointTokeyboardFile = fopen(keyboard,"w"))==NULL)
{

CString ExitMessage;
ExitMessage.Format("%s\n" , "Cannot Open File: keyboard.txt: Exit" );
AfxMessageBox(ExitMessage);
exit(0);

}else{

fprintf(pointTokeyboardFile,"%d\n", rcxres);
fprintf(pointTokeyboardFile,"%d\n", rcyres);
fprintf(pointTokeyboardFile,"%f\n", PSPX);
fprintf(pointTokeyboardFile,"%f\n", PSPY);
fclose(pointTokeyboardFile);

}

}

void CSPACE2010Dlg::LaunchOpenGL()
{

UpdateData(true);
int winx, winy;
int rcxres;
int rcyres;
float PSPY, PSPX;

// Read keyboard.txt containing the modified values of
// the variables to use to display image data

FILE * pointToKeyboardFile;
char keyboardFile[128]="keyboard.txt";

if ((pointToKeyboardFile = fopen(keyboardFile,"r"))==NULL)
{

CString ExitMessage;
ExitMessage.Format("%s\n" , "Cannot Open File: keyboard.txt: Exit" );
AfxMessageBox(ExitMessage);
exit(0);
```

```
        }else{

        fscanf(pointToKeyboardFile,"%d\n", &rcxres);
        fscanf(pointToKeyboardFile,"%d\n", &rcyres);
        fscanf(pointToKeyboardFile,"%f\n", &PSPX);
        fscanf(pointToKeyboardFile,"%f\n", &PSPY);
        fclose(pointToKeyboardFile);

        }

        winx=(int)rcxres*PSPX;
        winy=(int)rcyres*PSPY;

        AllocateMemoryforOpenGLGraphics();

        glutInitDisplayMode(GLUT_SINGLE | GLUT_RGB);
        glutInitWindowSize(winx,winy);
        glutInitWindowPosition(100,100);
        pw = glutCreateWindow("XY VIEW");

        init();

        glutDisplayFunc(display);
        glutReshapeFunc(reshape);
        glutKeyboardFunc(keyboard);
        glutMainLoop();

}

void CSPACE2010Dlg::AllocateMemoryforOpenGLGraphics()
{

        UpdateData(true);
        int rcxres = m_rcxres;
        int rcyres = m_rcyres;

        //// memory allocation to data to display ///
        if ( planeWindowImage == NULL )
        {

            planeWindowImage = (float *) malloc(rcyres*rcxres*4*sizeof(float));

        if ( planeWindowImage == NULL )
        {
            CString ExitMessage;
            ExitMessage.Format("%s\n" , "Cannot Allocate Data for Display: Exit");
            AfxMessageBox(ExitMessage);
            free(imdata1);
            free(EIN);
            exit(0);
        }

        }
        //// memory allocation to data to display ///

}
```

172

```
float * CSPACE2010Dlg::data(char filename[258], int rcyres, int rcxres)
{

        FILE *pf;

        int j,i,k2;
        float number=1;
        float *pointer1=0;

        float max=-5000000000000;
        float min=5000000000000;

        if ((pointer1 = (float *) calloc( ((rcyres*rcxres)+1), sizeof(float)) ) == NULL)
        {
            fprintf(logfile,"%s\n" , "Not enough memory to allocate Image data");
            exit(0);
        }

        if ((pf = fopen(filename,"rb+"))==NULL)
        {
            fprintf(logfile, "%s\n", "Not enough memory to allocate Image data");
            free(pointer1);
            exit(0);
        }

        for(j=0;j<rcyres;j++){
            for(i=0;i<rcxres;i++){

            fread(&number,sizeof(float),1,pf);
            k2=(j*rcxres+i);
            *(pointer1+k2) = number;

                            }
                        }
            fclose (pf);

        /* scale in range 0-255*/
        ///compute max and min of data
        for(i=0;i<rcxres*rcyres;i++){ // for

            if( *(pointer1+i)>max ){

                max=*(pointer1+i);

                            }

            if( *(pointer1+i)<min ){

                min=*(pointer1+i);

                            }

                        } // for

        //// convert data into analog scale and store into pointer1
```

```
            for(j=0;j<rcyres;j++){
                for(i=0;i<rcxres;i++){

                    k2=(j*rcxres+i);

                    if (max==min)
                    *(pointer1+k2)=(float)max;
                    else
                    *(pointer1+k2)=(float)(((float)*(pointer1+k2)-min)/((float)max-min))*255;

                    }
                }

    return pointer1;


}

float * CSPACE2010Dlg::EIN_image(float * ImageData, int rcyres, int rcxres)
{

        UpdateData(true);
        float *IntCurvIN=0, omega, thetax, thetay, Hxy;
        int k2, k7, k8, i, j, k9;

        float Mis_X = m_MisX, Mis_Y = m_MisY;
        // these two locate (x,y)
        // thus changing the intensity curvature functional
        // and the resulting image

        if ((IntCurvIN = (float *) calloc( ((rcyres*rcxres)+1), sizeof(float)) ) == NULL)
        {
            fprintf(logfile, "%s\n" ,"Not enough memory to allocate Image data");
            exit(0);
        }

        for(j=0;j<rcyres;j++){
            for(i=0;i<rcxres;i++){

        k2=(j*rcxres+i);

        k7=((j*rcxres+i)+1);
        k8=((j+1)*(rcxres)+(i+1));
        k9=((j+1)*(rcxres)+(i));

        thetax = ( (float)*(ImageData+k7) - (float)*(ImageData+k2) );
        thetay = ( (float)*(ImageData+k9) - (float)*(ImageData+k2) );

        omega = (float)*(ImageData+k8) + (float)*(ImageData+k2) -
                (float)*(ImageData+k7) - (float)*(ImageData+k9);

        Hxy = ((float)*(ImageData+k2) * Mis_X * Mis_Y) +

            ((float)(Mis_X * Mis_X * Mis_Y * thetax)/2.0) +

            ((float)(Mis_X * Mis_Y *Mis_Y * thetay)/2.0) +
```

```
                ((float)(Mis_X * Mis_Y *Mis_X * Mis_Y * omega)/4.0);

             *(IntCurvIN + k2) = ((float)2.0 * Hxy * omega);

                             }
                           }

        return IntCurvIN;

}

void CSPACE2010Dlg::OnIntensityCurvatureFunctional()
{

        UpdateData(true);

        char filename1[258];

        int rcxres = m_rcxres;
        int rcyres = m_rcyres;

        /// start up values of the pixel size x and y
        float PSPY = 1, PSPX = 1;

        sprintf(filename1, "%s", m_FileName);

        if ((logfile = fopen(logfileName,"w"))==NULL)
        {
         exit(0);
        }


         /// write the keyboard matrix resolution///
        FILE * pointTokeyboardFile;
        char keyboard[128]="keyboard.txt";
        if ((pointTokeyboardFile = fopen(keyboard,"w"))==NULL)
        {

        CString ExitMessage;
        ExitMessage.Format("%s\n" , "Cannot Open File: keyboard.txt: Exit" );
        AfxMessageBox(ExitMessage);
        exit(0);

        }else{

        fprintf(pointTokeyboardFile,"%d\n", rcxres);
        fprintf(pointTokeyboardFile,"%d\n", rcyres);
        fprintf(pointTokeyboardFile,"%f\n", PSPX);
        fprintf(pointTokeyboardFile,"%f\n", PSPY);
        fclose(pointTokeyboardFile);

        }

        imdata1 = data(filename1, rcyres, rcxres);

        EIN = EIN_image(imdata1, rcyres, rcxres);
```

```
    /// open logfile to write data///
    fprintf(logfile,"%s\n", filename1);
    fprintf(logfile,"%s\n", "LOADING DATA");

    fprintf(logfile,"%s\t %d\n", "Pixels Along X =", rcxres);
    fprintf(logfile,"%s\t %d\n", "Pixels Along Y =", rcyres);
    fprintf(logfile,"%s\t %f\n", "Pixel Size X: =", PSPX);
    fprintf(logfile,"%s\t %f\n", "Pixel Size Y: =", PSPY);
    fprintf(logfile,"\n");
    fprintf(logfile,"%s\n" , "THE PROGRAM DISPLAY 2 IMAGES");
    fprintf(logfile,"%s\n" , "Use 1 key to see The Image");
    fprintf(logfile,"%s\n" , "Use 2 key to see The Intensity Curvature Functional EIN");
    fprintf(logfile,"%s\n" , "The Esc key will Quit SPACE 2010");
    fprintf(logfile,"\n");
    fprintf(logfile,"%s\n", "Data Loaded in Memory");

    fclose(logfile);
    system(logfileName);

    CString ViewMessage;
    ViewMessage.Format("%s\n%s\n%s\n" ,
    "Ready to Launch OpenGL Visualization" ,
    "Please Remember to close the XY View",
    "Window Before Exiting the Program.");

    AfxMessageBox(ViewMessage);

    LaunchOpenGL();

}

void CSPACE2010Dlg::OnHelpIntCurvFunct()
{

    CString HelpMessage;
    HelpMessage.Format("%s\n%s\n%s\n%s\n%s\n%s\n%s\n",
    "Please Set X and Y Misplacements", "in the Range [0, 1].",
    "IntensityCurvatureFunctional", "reads only Image Data in the Format:",
    "FLOAT (32 bits real).", "Should you need to convert your", "Data, please use ROTRA2008.");
    AfxMessageBox(HelpMessage);

}

void CSPACE2010Dlg::OnOBJNET()
{
    system("OBJNET.exe");
}

void CSPACE2010Dlg::OnANN98()
{
    system("ANN98.exe");
}
```

```
void CSPACE2010Dlg::OnpointSource2010()
{
        system("pointSource2010.exe");
}


void CSPACE2010Dlg::OnInvertImage2010()
{
        system("InvertImage.exe");
}


void CSPACE2010Dlg::OnImageViewer()
{
        system("ImageViewer.exe");
}


void CSPACE2010Dlg::OnHelp()
{

        CString HelpMessage;
        HelpMessage.Format("%s\n%s\n" , "Please View Help.log File" , "Relevant to Any Applications.");
        AfxMessageBox(HelpMessage);

}


void CSPACE2010Dlg::OnExit()
{

        if (planeWindowImage != NULL) { free(planeWindowImage); }
        exit(0);

}
```

Summary

This chapter has presented the source code of *SPACE 2010* which is a Visual C++ ® application collecting under the same GUI a set of executables: *ANN98, ObjNet, Invert Image 2010, ImageViewer 2010* (which is an upgrade of *ImageViewer 2009*), *pointSource 2010*, and *Intensity Curvature Functional* [1]. There are two main notions that the students can learn from this chapter. One is that it turns to be quite simple and easy in Visual C++ ® to interface an executable file to run under the same GUI and the other is the detail of the method called *float * CSPACE2010Dlg::EIN_image(float * ImageData, int rcyres, int rcxres)* which is a math instrument to measure the energy level of an image subject to the interpolation process [1].

References

[1] Ciulla, C. (2009). *Improved Signal and Image Interpolation in Biomedical Applications: The Case of Magnetic Resonance Imaging (MRI)* - Medical Information Science Reference - IGI Global Publisher, Hershey, PA, U.S.A.

[2] Shreiner, D., Woo, M., Neider, J., Davis, T. (2007). *OpenGL Programming Guide: The Official Guide to Learning OpenGL.* Version 2.1 (6th Edition), Addison-Wesley Professional.

[3] Whittaker, E. T. (1915). *On the functions which are represented by the expansions of interpolation theory.* Proceedings of the Royal Society Edinburgh, UK, Sec. A(35), 181-194.

CHAPTER 8

The Source Code of Image Viewer 2009 and Image Tool 2009

Introduction

This chapter introduces methods and variables of the programs associated with push buttons and edit boxes located in the Graphical User Interfaces of *Image Viewer 2009* and *Image Tool 2009*. *Image Viewer 2009* presents six edit boxes in the panel named '*Image Resolution*' and these are called: '*X Voxels*', '*Y Voxels*', '*Z Voxels*', '*X Voxel Size (mm)*', '*Y Voxel Size (mm)*' and '*Z Voxel Size (mm)*'. The variables associated with them are called: '*m_rcxres*', '*m_rcyres*', '*m_numslice*', '*m_Xsize*', '*m_Ysize*' and '*m_Zsize*' respectively (see Fig. 1).

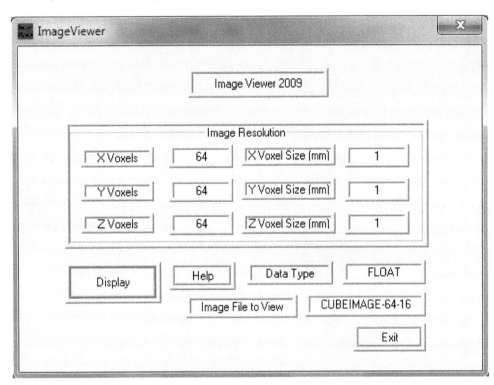

Figure 1: The Graphical User Interface of *Image Viewer 2009*. The panel '*Image Resolution*' contains six edit boxes dedicated to the resolution parameters. The '*Display*' button activates OpenGL ®. The '*Help*' button creates a file in the same directory where the program runs. This file contains information for the user on how to interact with the program. The two edit boxes: '*Data Type*' and '*Image File to View*', accept variables relevant to the image/volume display. The push button '*Exit*' provides safe exit to the program.

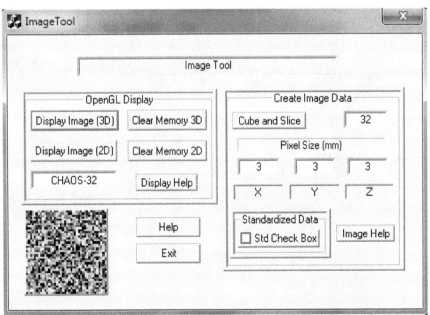

Figure 2: The Graphical User Interface of *Image Tool 2009*. The OpenGL ® display is active in 2D and 3D (composite 2D views) through the push buttons named '*Display Image 2D*' and '*Display Image 3D*'. The memory is cleared through the push buttons named: '*Clear Memory 2D*' and '*Clear Memory 3D*'. The panel '*Create Image Data*' is dedicated: (i) to the resolution parameters (see the four edit boxes), (ii) to produce a cube and a slice of random data and (iii) to chose through the check box as to if the data has to be standardized or not. The help '*log*' file is saved in the same directory where the program runs after pushing the '*Help*' button. The '*Exit*' button provides the user with a safe exit.

In the lower part of the GUI in *Image Viewer 2009* are located three push buttons and two edit boxes. The push buttons are: '*Display*', '*Help*' and '*Exit*'. These push buttons are related to the following methods: *void CImageViewerDlg::OnImageDisplay(), void CImageViewerDlg::OnHelp()* and *void CImageViewerDlg::OnExit()*. The two edit boxes are: '*Data Type*' and '*Image File to View*'; and they related to the following variables: '*m_DataType*' and '*m_VolumeFileName*' respectively.

Looking at the GUI of *Image Tool 2009* two panels are clearly distinguishable (see Fig. 2). One is by the name of '*OpenGL Display*' and the other one is by the name of '*Create Image Data*'. While in the former we distinguish five push buttons and one single edit box, in the latter we distinguish two push buttons, four edit boxes and one check box.

For what concerns the panel '*OpenGL Display*', the push buttons are called: '*Display Image 3D*', '*Display Image 2D*', '*Clear Memory 3D*', '*Clear Memory 2D*' and '*Display Help*'; and the methods associated with the push buttons are called: *void CImageToolDlg::OnDisplayImage(), void CImageToolDlg::OnDisplay2D(), void CImageToolDlg::OnClearMemory3D(), void CImageToolDlg::OnClearMemory2D()* and *void CImageToolDlg::OnHelpDisplay()* respectively. The edit box is associated with the program variable called '*m_VolumeFileName*'. The reader should note that *Image Viewer 2009* and *Image Tool 2009* are two distint applications and so are their variables even in the case they carry the same name.

For what concerns the panel '*Create Image Data*', the two push buttons are called: '*Cube and Slice*' and '*Image Help*'; and they are associated to the methods named: *void CImageToolDlg::OnCreatetheCube()* and *void CImageToolDlg::OnHelpCube()*. The four edit boxes in this panel are associated with the following program variables: '*m_VolumeSize*', '*m_PSizeX*', '*m_PSizeY*' and '*m_PSizeZ*' respectively. Finally, the check box in this panel has the variable '*m_StdLabel*' associated with it.

To the right of the image icon in the GUI, just below the panal named '*OpenGL Display*', are located two more push buttons by the name of '*Help*' and '*Exit*' and the methods they call in are named: *void CImageToolDlg::OnHelp()* and *void CImageToolDlg::OnExit()*.

The Source Code

The first method to comment on is *void CImageViewerDlg::init()*. This method is part of the OpenGL ® routines and is delegated to the initialization of three composite 2D views of the image display. The instructions [1] '*glClearColor(0.0, 0.0, 0.0, 0.0)*' and '*glShadeModel(GL_FLAT)*' clear the color and set the shading of the window display. The instructions '*glutGetWindow() == planeWindow*', '*glutGetWindow() == pw*', '*glutGetWindow() == sw*' and '*glutGetWindow() == cw*' are designed to identify the current window to work with and they do so through the integer variables: '*planeWindow*' (plane window for 2D display) '*pw*' (plane window for 3D display), '*sw*' (sagittal window) and '*cw*' (coronal window). Once the window is identified, additional instructions [1] take place on their benefit and they relates: (i) to set the viewport size ('*glViewport(0, 0, (GLsizei)winx, (GLsizei)winy)*'), (ii) to load the identity matrix ('*glLoadIdentity()*'), and (iii) to set the orthogonal 2D view size ('*gluOrtho2D(0.0, (GLdouble)winx, 0.0, (GLdouble)winy)*'). In order to clear the window display, the function *void display(void)* is available to use for each of the three windows.

Part I: Image Viewer 2009

```
#define WINX 300
#define WINY 300
#define WINZ 300

int ox = 360, oy = 360, oz = 360, z;

float *fMRIdata=0;
float *TwoDdata = 0;

int Slice=0, sagSlice=-1, corSlice=-1;

int pw, sw, cw, planeWindow;
float PSPX, PSPY;
float PSCX, PSCZ;
float PSSY, PSSZ;
int count=-1;

char datatype[12];
```

```
        FILE * logfile;

        GLfloat  * pimage = NULL;
        GLfloat  * simage = NULL;
        GLfloat  * cimage = NULL;

        GLfloat  * planeWindowImage = NULL;

        // methods that cannot be included in any class
        // bacause of the syntax required from OpenGL ® Libraries
        void display(void);
        void keyboard(unsigned char key, int x, int y);
        void reshape(int w, int h);
        void TwoDdisplay(void);

void CImageViewerDlg::init()
{

        int winx, winy, winz;

        static int rcxres = m_rcxres;
        static int rcyres = m_rcyres;
        static int numslice = m_numslice;


        /// read the keyboard matrix resolution///
        FILE * pointToKeyboardFile;
        char keyboardFile[128]="keyboard.txt";


        if ((pointToKeyboardFile = fopen(keyboardFile,"r"))==NULL)
        {

        CString ExitMessage;
        ExitMessage.Format("%s\n" , "Cannot Open File: keyboard.txt: Exit" );
        AfxMessageBox(ExitMessage);
        exit(0);

        }else{

        fscanf(pointToKeyboardFile,"%d\n", &numslice);
        fscanf(pointToKeyboardFile,"%d\n", &rcxres);
        fscanf(pointToKeyboardFile,"%d\n", &rcyres);
        fscanf(pointToKeyboardFile,"%f\n", &PSPX);
        fscanf(pointToKeyboardFile,"%f\n", &PSPY);
        fscanf(pointToKeyboardFile,"%f\n", &PSSZ);
        fclose(pointToKeyboardFile);

        }

        PSCZ = (float)PSSZ;
        PSSY = (float)PSPY;
        PSCX = (float)PSPX;
```

```
        winx=(int)rcxres*PSPX;
        winy=(int)rcyres*PSPY;
        winz=(int)numslice*PSSZ;

        glClearColor(0.0, 0.0, 0.0, 0.0);
        glShadeModel(GL_FLAT);

        if(glutGetWindow() == planeWindow)
        {

            glViewport(0, 0, (GLsizei)winx, (GLsizei)winy);
            glLoadIdentity();
            gluOrtho2D(0.0, (GLdouble)winx, 0.0, (GLdouble)winy);

        }

        if(glutGetWindow() == pw)
        {

            glViewport(0, 0, (GLsizei)winx, (GLsizei)winy);
            glLoadIdentity();
            gluOrtho2D(0.0, (GLdouble)winx, 0.0, (GLdouble)winy);

        }

        if(glutGetWindow() == sw)
        {

            glViewport(0, 0, (GLsizei)winy, (GLsizei)winz);
            glLoadIdentity();
            gluOrtho2D(0.0, (GLdouble)winy, 0.0, (GLdouble)winz);

        }

        if(glutGetWindow() == cw)
        {

            glViewport(0, 0, (GLsizei)winx, (GLsizei)winz);
            glLoadIdentity();
            gluOrtho2D(0.0, (GLdouble)winx, 0.0, (GLdouble)winz);

        }

}

void display(void)
{
        glClear(GL_COLOR_BUFFER_BIT);
}
```

The function *void keyboard(unsigned char key, int x, int y)* is designed in a similar way in all of the projects outlined in this manuscript. This function uses the I/O file '*keaboard.txt*' to import the image resolution data. The instructions are:

- ✓ *FILE * pointToKeyboardFile;*
- ✓ *char keyboardFile[128]="keyboard.txt";*
- ✓ *if ((pointToKeyboardFile = fopen(keyboardFile,"r"))==NULL)*

- ✓ {

- ✓ *CString ExitMessage;*
- ✓ *ExitMessage.Format("%s\n" , "Cannot Open File: keyboard.txt: Exit");*
- ✓ *AfxMessageBox(ExitMessage);*

- ✓ *exit(0);*

- ✓ *}else{*

- ✓ *fscanf(pointToKeyboardFile,"%d\n", &numslice);*
- ✓ *fscanf(pointToKeyboardFile,"%d\n", &rcxres);*
- ✓ *fscanf(pointToKeyboardFile,"%d\n", &rcyres);*
- ✓ *fscanf(pointToKeyboardFile,"%f\n", &PSPX);*
- ✓ *fscanf(pointToKeyboardFile,"%f\n", &PSSY);*
- ✓ *fscanf(pointToKeyboardFile,"%f\n", &PSCZ);*
- ✓ *fclose(pointToKeyboardFile);*

- ✓ }

The difference visible in this program with respect to other programs concerned with the display of a single 2D window is that more keys are available to the user to hit from the keyboard in order to slide the data display. In fact, the use of three composite 2D views relates to the display of three dimensional data. Specifically, the function void *keyboard(unsigned char key, int x, int y)* reported here uses the keys 'U' and 'D' to slide the plane views, 'L' and 'R' to slide the sagittal views and 'F' and 'B' to slide the coronal views.

Data display happens through the use of pointers employed in dynamic memory allocation management. The pointers employed are three and each corresponding to a different window: '*(pimage)*', '*(simage)*' and '*(cimage)*' and they are connected to the three windows' identifiers '*pw*', '*sw*' and '*cw*'. These pointers receive the data from the float pointer '*(GLfloat) *(fMRIdata)*' which is globally visible to entire extent of the program. The variable '*Slice*' controls which of plane views of the stack will be on display.

Further, the image display happens in each window with the additional instructions [1]: *glDrawBuffer(GL_FRONT)*, *glRasterPos2i(0, 0)*, *glPixelZoom((GLfloat) PSPX, (GLfloat) PSPY)*, *glDrawPixels((GLsizei)rcxres, (GLsizei)rcyres, GL_LUMINANCE, GL_FLOAT, pimage)* and *glFlush()*. These instructions are relevant to the window display and they perform the action of: (i) drawing the buffer, (ii) setting the raster position, (iii) zooming the pixel, (iv) drawing the pixel and (v) flushing the display. Data is given for display from the pointer container '*(GLfloat) *(fMRIdata)*' which is released from the method *float * CImageViewerDlg::data(char filename[], int numslice, int rcyres, int rcxres, char datatype[])*, as it shall be seen in subsequent sections of this chapter. Data contained into '*(GLfloat) *(fMRIdata)*' is inside the range [0, 255] and is scaled inside the range [0, 1] at the time of the transfer to the pointers '*(pimage)*', '*(simage)*' and '*(cimage)*'. Data transfer and display across sections of the plane view ('*case 'U'*', '*case 'D'*' and '*(pimage)*') happens because of the instructions:

- ✓ *case 'U':*
- ✓ *if((Slice>=0)&&(Slice<numslice))*
- ✓ *{*
- ✓ *Slice++;*

- ✓ *for(j=0; j<rcyres; j++) {*
- ✓ *for(i=0; i<rcxres; i++) {*

- ✓ *k2=(j*rcxres+i)+((Slice-1)*rcyres*rcxres);*
- ✓ *k3 = (j*rcxres+i);*
- ✓ *(pimage + k3)   = (GLfloat) *(fMRIdata+k2)/255;*
- ✓ *(pimage + k3*2) = (GLfloat) *(fMRIdata+k2)/255;*
- ✓ *(pimage + k3*3) = (GLfloat) *(fMRIdata+k2)/255;*

- ✓ }

- ✓ }

- ✓ *glDrawBuffer(GL_FRONT);*
- ✓ *glRasterPos2i(0,0);*
- ✓ *glPixelZoom((GLfloat) PSPX, (GLfloat) PSPY);*
- ✓ *glDrawPixels((GLsizei)rcxres, (GLsizei)rcyres, GL_LUMINANCE, GL_FLOAT, pimage);*
- ✓ *glFlush();*

- ✓ }
- ✓ *break;*

- ✓ *case 'D':*
- ✓ *if((Slice>1)&&(Slice<=numslice))*
- ✓ *{*
- ✓ *Slice--;*

- ✓ *for(j=0; j<rcyres; j++){*
- ✓ *for(i=0; i<rcxres; i++){*

- ✓ *k2=(j*rcxres+i)+((Slice-1)*rcyres*rcxres);*
- ✓ *k3 = (j*rcxres+i);*

- ✓ **(pimage + k3)   = (GLfloat) *(fMRIdata+k2)/255;*
- ✓ **(pimage + k3*2) = (GLfloat) *(fMRIdata+k2)/255;*
- ✓ **(pimage + k3*3) = (GLfloat) *(fMRIdata+k2)/255;*

- ✓ }
- ✓ }

- ✓ *glDrawBuffer(GL_FRONT);*
- ✓ *glRasterPos2i(0,0);*
- ✓ *glPixelZoom((GLfloat) PSPX, (GLfloat) PSPY);*
- ✓ *glDrawPixels((GLsizei)rcxres, (GLsizei)rcyres, GL_LUMINANCE, GL_FLOAT, pimage);*
- ✓ *glFlush();*

- ✓ }
- ✓ *break;*

```
void keyboard(unsigned char key, int x, int y)
{

        int sl,j,i,k2,k3;

        static int rcxres;
        static int rcyres;
        static int numslice;

        float PSCZ, PSSZ, PSPY, PSSY, PSPX, PSCX;

        /// read the keyboard matrix resolution///
        FILE * pointToKeyboardFile;
        char keyboardFile[128]="keyboard.txt";

        if ((pointToKeyboardFile = fopen(keyboardFile,"r"))==NULL)
        {
```

```
CString ExitMessage;
ExitMessage.Format("%s\n" , "Cannot Open File: keyboard.txt: Exit" );
AfxMessageBox(ExitMessage);

exit(0);

}else{

fscanf(pointToKeyboardFile,"%d\n", &numslice);
fscanf(pointToKeyboardFile,"%d\n", &rcxres);
fscanf(pointToKeyboardFile,"%d\n", &rcyres);
fscanf(pointToKeyboardFile,"%f\n", &PSPX);
fscanf(pointToKeyboardFile,"%f\n", &PSSY);
fscanf(pointToKeyboardFile,"%f\n", &PSCZ);
fclose(pointToKeyboardFile);

}

PSSZ = (float)PSCZ;
PSPY = (float)PSSY;
PSCX = (float)PSPX;

key=toupper(key);

if(glutGetWindow() == pw)
{

switch(key){

case 'U':
if( (Slice>=0)&&(Slice<numslice) )
{
Slice++;

for(j=0;j<rcyres;j++){
    for(i=0;i<rcxres;i++){

    k2=(j*rcxres+i)+((Slice-1)*rcyres*rcxres);
    k3 = (j*rcxres+i);

    *(pimage + k3)   = (GLfloat) *(fMRIdata+k2)/255;
    *(pimage + k3*2) = (GLfloat) *(fMRIdata+k2)/255;
    *(pimage + k3*3) = (GLfloat) *(fMRIdata+k2)/255;

                        }
                    }


glDrawBuffer(GL_FRONT);
glRasterPos2i(0,0);
glPixelZoom((GLfloat) PSPX, (GLfloat) PSPY);
glDrawPixels((GLsizei)rcxres, (GLsizei)rcyres, GL_LUMINANCE, GL_FLOAT, pimage);
glFlush();

}
break;
```

```
case 'D':
if( (Slice>1)&&(Slice<=numslice) )
{
Slice--;

 for(j=0;j<rcyres;j++){
  for(i=0;i<rcxres;i++){

    k2=(j*rcxres+i)+((Slice-1)*rcyres*rcxres);
    k3 = (j*rcxres+i);

    *(pimage + k3)   = (GLfloat) *(fMRIdata+k2)/255;
    *(pimage + k3*2) = (GLfloat) *(fMRIdata+k2)/255;
    *(pimage + k3*3) = (GLfloat) *(fMRIdata+k2)/255;

                            }
                        }

glDrawBuffer(GL_FRONT);
glRasterPos2i(0,0);
glPixelZoom((GLfloat) PSPX, (GLfloat) PSPY);
glDrawPixels((GLsizei)rcxres, (GLsizei)rcyres, GL_LUMINANCE, GL_FLOAT, pimage);
glFlush();

}
break;

default:
break;

}///switch

}///if
if(glutGetWindow() == sw)
{

switch(key){

case 'L':
if( (sagSlice>=-1)&&(sagSlice<rcxres-1) )
{
sagSlice++;

for(sl=1;sl<=numslice; sl++) {
 for(j=0;j<rcyres;j++){

    k2=(j*rcxres+sagSlice)+((sl-1)*rcyres*rcxres);
    k3 = ((sl-1)*rcyres+j);

    *(simage + k3)   = (GLfloat) *(fMRIdata+k2)/255;
    *(simage + k3*2) = (GLfloat) *(fMRIdata+k2)/255;
    *(simage + k3*3) = (GLfloat) *(fMRIdata+k2)/255;

                            }
                        }
```

185

```
glDrawBuffer(GL_FRONT);
glRasterPos2i(0,0);
glPixelZoom((GLfloat) PSSY, (GLfloat) PSSZ);
glDrawPixels((GLsizei)rcyres, (GLsizei)numslice, GL_LUMINANCE, GL_FLOAT, simage);
glFlush();

}
break;

case 'R':
if( (sagSlice>0)&&(sagSlice<=rcxres-1) )
{
sagSlice--;

for(sl=1;sl<=numslice; sl++) {
 for(j=0;j<rcyres;j++){

     k2=(j*rcxres+sagSlice)+((sl-1)*rcyres*rcxres);
     k3 = ((sl-1)*rcyres+j);

     *(simage + k3)   = (GLfloat) *(fMRIdata+k2)/255;
     *(simage + k3*2) = (GLfloat) *(fMRIdata+k2)/255;
     *(simage + k3*3) = (GLfloat) *(fMRIdata+k2)/255;

                              }
                      }

glDrawBuffer(GL_FRONT);
glRasterPos2i(0,0);
glPixelZoom((GLfloat) PSSY, (GLfloat) PSSZ);
glDrawPixels((GLsizei)rcyres, (GLsizei)numslice, GL_LUMINANCE, GL_FLOAT, simage);
glFlush();

}
break;

default:
break;

}///switch

}///if
if(glutGetWindow() == cw)
{

switch(key){
case 'F':
if( (corSlice>=-1)&&(corSlice<rcyres-1) )
{
corSlice++;

for(sl=1;sl<=numslice; sl++) {
    for(i=0;i<rcxres;i++){

     k2=(corSlice*rcxres+i)+((sl-1)*rcyres*rcxres);
     k3 = ((sl-1)*rcxres+i);
```

186

```
              *(cimage + k3)   = (GLfloat) *(fMRIdata+k2)/255;
              *(cimage + k3*2) = (GLfloat) *(fMRIdata+k2)/255;
              *(cimage + k3*3) = (GLfloat) *(fMRIdata+k2)/255;


                                  }
                              }

      glDrawBuffer(GL_FRONT);
      glRasterPos2i(0,0);
      glPixelZoom((GLfloat) PSCX, (GLfloat) PSCZ),
      glDrawPixels((GLsizei)rcxres, (GLsizei)numslice, GL_LUMINANCE, GL_FLOAT, cimage);
      glFlush();


      }
      break;


      case 'B':
      if( (corSlice>0)&&(corSlice<=rcyres-1) )
      {
      corSlice--;

      for(sl=1;sl<=numslice; sl++) {
        for(i=0;i<rcxres;i++){

            k2=(corSlice*rcxres+i)+((sl-1)*rcyres*rcxres);
            k3 = ((sl-1)*rcxres+i);

            *(cimage + k3)   = (GLfloat) *(fMRIdata+k2)/255;
            *(cimage + k3*2) = (GLfloat) *(fMRIdata+k2)/255;
            *(cimage + k3*3) = (GLfloat) *(fMRIdata+k2)/255;

                                  }
                              }

      glDrawBuffer(GL_FRONT);
      glRasterPos2i(0,0);
      glPixelZoom((GLfloat) PSCX, (GLfloat) PSCZ);
      glDrawPixels((GLsizei)rcxres, (GLsizei)numslice, GL_LUMINANCE, GL_FLOAT, cimage);
      glFlush();


      }

      break;
      default:
      break;

            }///switch

      }///if


}
```

The function *void reshape(int w, int h)* is intended to import data which relates to the image resolution and implement the interactive graphics available through OpenGL ®. This is performed by making storage of the change in the size of the 2D windows. Specifically, the I/O file *'keaboard.txt'* is employed to read the image resolution. The instructions are:

Computer Science Applications

- ✓ FILE *pointToKeyboardFile;
- ✓ char keyboardFile[128]="keyboard.txt";

- ✓ if ((pointToKeyboardFile = fopen(keyboardFile,"r"))==NULL)
- ✓ {

- ✓ CString ExitMessage;
- ✓ ExitMessage.Format("%s\n" , "Cannot Open File: keyboard.txt: Exit");
- ✓ AfxMessageBox(ExitMessage);
- ✓ exit(0);

- ✓ }else{

- ✓ fscanf(pointToKeyboardFile,"%d\n", &numslice);
- ✓ fscanf(pointToKeyboardFile,"%d\n", &rcxres);
- ✓ fscanf(pointToKeyboardFile,"%d\n", &rcyres);
- ✓ fscanf(pointToKeyboardFile,"%f\n", &valueX);
- ✓ fscanf(pointToKeyboardFile,"%f\n", &valueY);
- ✓ fscanf(pointToKeyboardFile,"%f\n", &valueZ);
- ✓ fclose(pointToKeyboardFile);

- ✓ }

The instructions [1] '*glViewport(0, 0, (GLsizei)w, (GLsizei)h)*', '*glLoadIdentity()*', '*gluOrtho2D(0.0, (GLdouble)w, 0.0, (GLdouble)h)*' perform the task of: (i) setting the viewport size, (ii) load the identity matrix and (iii) setting the orthogonal 2D view size. The pixel size is scaled to the number of pixels which the image is made of. Specifically, for the plane windows identified through '*glutGetWindow() == planeWindow*' and '*glutGetWindow() == pw*', the pixel size is determined by the instructions '*PSPX=((float)w/rcxres)*' and '*PSPY=((float)h/rcyres)*'. For the sagittal window identified through '*glutGetWindow() == sw*', the pixel size is determined by the instructions '*PSSY=((float)w/rcyres)*' and '*PSSZ=((float)h/numslice)*'. For the coronal window identified through '*glutGetWindow() == cw*', the pixel size is determined by the instructions '*PSCX=((float)w/rcxres)*' and '*PSCZ=((float)h/numslice)*'. The instructions are here reported:

- ✓ if(glutGetWindow() == planeWindow)
- ✓ {

- ✓ PSPX=((float)w/rcxres);
- ✓ PSPY=((float)h/rcyres);

- ✓ }

- ✓ if(glutGetWindow() == pw)
- ✓ {
- ✓ PSPX=((float)w/rcxres);
- ✓ PSPY=((float)h/rcyres);

- ✓ }

- ✓ if(glutGetWindow() == sw)
- ✓ {

- ✓ PSSY=((float)w/rcyres);
- ✓ PSSZ=((float)h/numslice);

- ✓ }

- ✓ *if(glutGetWindow() == cw)*
- ✓ *{*

- ✓ *PSCX=((float)w/ rcxres);*
- ✓ *PSCZ=((float)h/ numslice);*

- ✓ *}*

Worth noting that the variables 'PSPX', 'PSPY', 'PSSY', 'PSSZ', 'PSCX' and 'PSCZ' are global variables of the program. When the windows' size is changed by the user the text file *'keyboard.txt'* is updated with the following instructions:

- ✓ *if ((pointToKeyboardFile = fopen(keyboardFile,"w"))==NULL) {*

- ✓ *CString ExitMessage;*
- ✓ *ExitMessage.Format("%s\n" , "Cannot Open File: keyboard.txt: Exit");*
- ✓ *AfxMessageBox(ExitMessage);*
- ✓ *exit(0);*

- ✓ *}else{*

- ✓ *fprintf(pointToKeyboardFile,"%d\n", numslice);*
- ✓ *fprintf(pointToKeyboardFile,"%d\n", rcxres);*
- ✓ *fprintf(pointToKeyboardFile,"%d\n", rcyres);*

- ✓ *if(glutGetWindow() == planeWindow) {*

- ✓ *fprintf(pointToKeyboardFile,"%f\n", PSPX);*
- ✓ *fprintf(pointToKeyboardFile,"%f\n", PSPY);*
- ✓ *fprintf(pointToKeyboardFile,"%f\n", valueZ);*

- ✓ *}*

- ✓ *if(glutGetWindow() == pw) {*

- ✓ *fprintf(pointToKeyboardFile,"%f\n", PSPX);*
- ✓ *fprintf(pointToKeyboardFile,"%f\n", PSPY);*
- ✓ *fprintf(pointToKeyboardFile,"%f\n", valueZ);*

- ✓ *}*

- ✓ *if(glutGetWindow() == sw) {*
- ✓ *fprintf(pointToKeyboardFile,"%f\n", valueX);*
- ✓ *fprintf(pointToKeyboardFile,"%f\n", PSSY);*
- ✓ *fprintf(pointToKeyboardFile,"%f\n", PSSZ);*

- ✓ *}*

- ✓ *if(glutGetWindow() == cw) {*

- ✓ *fprintf(pointToKeyboardFile,"%f\n", PSCX);*
- ✓ *fprintf(pointToKeyboardFile,"%f\n", valueY);*
- ✓ *fprintf(pointToKeyboardFile,"%f\n", PSCZ);*

- ✓ *}*

Computer Science Applications

   ✓   *fclose(pointToKeyboardFile);*

   ✓   }

```
void reshape(int w, int h)
{

        static int rcxres;
        static int rcyres;
        static int numslice;

        float valueX = 0, valueY = 0, valueZ = 0;

        /// read the keyboard matrix resolution///
        FILE * pointToKeyboardFile;
        char keyboardFile[128]="keyboard.txt";

        if ((pointToKeyboardFile = fopen(keyboardFile,"r"))==NULL)
        {

        CString ExitMessage;
        ExitMessage.Format("%s\n" , "Cannot Open File: keyboard.txt: Exit" );
        AfxMessageBox(ExitMessage);
        exit(0);

        }else{

        fscanf(pointToKeyboardFile,"%d\n", &numslice);
        fscanf(pointToKeyboardFile,"%d\n", &rcxres);
        fscanf(pointToKeyboardFile,"%d\n", &rcyres);
        fscanf(pointToKeyboardFile,"%f\n", &valueX);
        fscanf(pointToKeyboardFile,"%f\n", &valueY);
        fscanf(pointToKeyboardFile,"%f\n", &valueZ);
        fclose(pointToKeyboardFile);

        }
        //// initialize variables: PSPX, PSPY, PSSZ
        PSPX = (float)valueX;
        PSPY = (float)valueY;
        PSSZ = (float)valueZ;

        glViewport(0, 0, (GLsizei)w, (GLsizei)h);
        glLoadIdentity();
        gluOrtho2D(0.0, (GLdouble)w, 0.0, (GLdouble)h);

        if(glutGetWindow() == planeWindow)
        {

            PSPX=((float)w/rcxres);
            PSPY=((float)h/rcyres);

        }

        if(glutGetWindow() == pw)
        {
```

```
        PSPX=((float)w/rcxres);
        PSPY=((float)h/rcyres);

}

if(glutGetWindow() == sw)
{

        PSSY=((float)w/rcyres);
        PSSZ=((float)h/numslice);

}

if(glutGetWindow() == cw)
{

        PSCX=((float)w/rcxres);
        PSCZ=((float)h/numslice);

}

// Once the windows' size is changed:
// re-write keyboard.txt containing the modified values of
// the variables: float PSPX; float PSPY; float PSSZ;

if ((pointToKeyboardFile = fopen(keyboardFile,"w"))==NULL)
{

CString ExitMessage;
ExitMessage.Format("%s\n" , "Cannot Open File: keyboard.txt: Exit" );
AfxMessageBox(ExitMessage);
exit(0);

}else{

fprintf(pointToKeyboardFile,"%d\n", numslice);
fprintf(pointToKeyboardFile,"%d\n", rcxres);
fprintf(pointToKeyboardFile,"%d\n", rcyres);

if(glutGetWindow() == planeWindow)
{

        fprintf(pointToKeyboardFile,"%f\n", PSPX);
        fprintf(pointToKeyboardFile,"%f\n", PSPY);
        fprintf(pointToKeyboardFile,"%f\n", valueZ);

}

if(glutGetWindow() == pw)
{

        fprintf(pointToKeyboardFile,"%f\n", PSPX);
        fprintf(pointToKeyboardFile,"%f\n", PSPY);
        fprintf(pointToKeyboardFile,"%f\n", valueZ);

}
```

```
        if(glutGetWindow() == sw)
        {

            fprintf(pointToKeyboardFile,"%f\n", valueX);
            fprintf(pointToKeyboardFile,"%f\n", PSSY);
            fprintf(pointToKeyboardFile,"%f\n", PSSZ);

        }

        if(glutGetWindow() == cw)
        {

            fprintf(pointToKeyboardFile,"%f\n", PSCX);
            fprintf(pointToKeyboardFile,"%f\n", valueY);
            fprintf(pointToKeyboardFile,"%f\n", PSCZ);

        }

        fclose(pointToKeyboardFile);

    }

}
```

The method *void TwoDdisplay(void)* is the input to the instruction *'glutDisplayFunc(TwoDdisplay)'* inside the method *void CImageViewerDlg::LaunchOpenGL()*. The purpose of the method *void TwoDdisplay(void)* is that of setting ready the pointer *'*(planeWindowImage)'* for 2D display with OpenGL ®. The pointer *'*(planeWindowImage)'* receives image data from the pointer *'(GLfloat) *(TwoDdata)'* which is released by the method *void CImageViewerDlg::OnImageDisplay()* through the instruction *'TwoDdata = data(filename, numslice, rcyres, rcxres, datatype)'*. The instructions employed to set the OpenGL ® display are:

- ✓ *if(glutGetWindow() == planeWindow) {*

- ✓ *for(j=0; j<rcyres; j++) {*
- ✓ *for(i=0; i<rcxres; i++) {*

- ✓ *k3 = (j*rcxres+i);*

- ✓ **(planeWindowImage + k3)   = (GLfloat) *(TwoDdata+k3)/255;*
- ✓ **(planeWindowImage + k3*2) = (GLfloat) *(TwoDdata+k3)/255;*
- ✓ **(planeWindowImage + k3*3) = (GLfloat) *(TwoDdata+k3)/255;*

- ✓ *}*
- ✓ *}*

- ✓ *glDrawBuffer(GL_FRONT);*
- ✓ *glRasterPos2i(0,0);*
- ✓ *glPixelZoom((GLfloat) PSPX, (GLfloat) PSPY);*
- ✓ *glDrawPixels((GLsizei)rcxres, (GLsizei)rcyres, GL_LUMINANCE, GL_FLOAT, planeWindowImage);*
- ✓ *glFlush();*

- ✓ *}*

```
void TwoDdisplay(void)
{

        // variables that are locally employed and are static within
        // the scope of the method
        int i, j, k3;

        // Variables can be retrieved from file:
        // "keyboard.txt".
        int rcxres;
        int rcyres;


        // The function:
        // keyboard(unsigned char key, int x, int y) is not active
        // inside the scope of the user-application interaction
        // while displaying 2D images. Specifically:
        // void TwoDdisplay(void) runs within the glutMainLoop().

        float PSPY;
        float PSPX;

        // these two variables are not relevant
        // to the scope of the function
        // however read from file "keyboard.txt"
        int numslice;
        float PSSZ;

        /// now read the keyboard matrix resolution///
        FILE * pointToKeyboardFile;
        char keyboard[128]="keyboard.txt";

        if ((pointToKeyboardFile = fopen(keyboard,"r"))==NULL)
        {

        CString ExitMessage;
        ExitMessage.Format("%s\n" , "Cannot Open File: keyboard.txt: Exit" );
        AfxMessageBox(ExitMessage);

        exit(0);
        }else{

        fscanf(pointToKeyboardFile,"%d\n", &numslice);
        fscanf(pointToKeyboardFile,"%d\n", &rcxres);
        fscanf(pointToKeyboardFile,"%d\n", &rcyres);
        fscanf(pointToKeyboardFile,"%f\n", &PSPX);
        fscanf(pointToKeyboardFile,"%f\n", &PSPY);
        fscanf(pointToKeyboardFile,"%f\n", &PSSZ);

        fclose(pointToKeyboardFile);

        }

        glClear(GL_COLOR_BUFFER_BIT);
```

```
        if(glutGetWindow() == planeWindow)
        {

            for(j=0;j<rcyres;j++){
                for(i=0;i<rcxres;i++){

                k3 = (j*rcxres+i);

                *(planeWindowImage + k3)   = (GLfloat) *(TwoDdata+k3)/255;
                *(planeWindowImage + k3*2) = (GLfloat) *(TwoDdata+k3)/255;
                *(planeWindowImage + k3*3) = (GLfloat) *(TwoDdata+k3)/255;

                            }
                        }

        glDrawBuffer(GL_FRONT);
        glRasterPos2i(0,0);
        glPixelZoom((GLfloat) PSPX, (GLfloat) PSPY);
        glDrawPixels((GLsizei)rcxres, (GLsizei)rcyres, GL_LUMINANCE, GL_FLOAT, planeWindowImage);
        glFlush();

        }

}
```

The method *void CImageViewerDlg::OnImageDisplay()* performs the task of creating the I/O file '*keaboard.txt*' which is employed to read the image resolution into the functions that are not part of the class container '*CImageViewerDlg*'. The instructions are:

✓   *FILE * pointTokeyboardFile;*
✓   *char keyboard[128]="keyboard.txt";*

✓   *if ((pointTokeyboardFile = fopen(keyboard,"w"))==NULL)*
✓   *{*

✓   *CString ExitMessage;*
✓   *ExitMessage.Format("%os\n" , "Cannot Open File: keyboard.txt: Exit");*
✓   *MessageBox(ExitMessage);*

✓   *exit(0);*

✓   *}else{*

✓   *fprintf(pointTokeyboardFile,"%od\n", m_numslice);*
✓   *fprintf(pointTokeyboardFile,"%od\n", m_rcxres);*
✓   *fprintf(pointTokeyboardFile,"%od\n", m_rcyres);*
✓   *fprintf(pointTokeyboardFile,"%olf\n", m_Xsize);*
✓   *fprintf(pointTokeyboardFile,"%olf\n", m_Ysize);*
✓   *fprintf(pointTokeyboardFile,"%olf\n", m_Zsize);*

✓   *fclose(pointTokeyboardFile);*

✓   *}*

Text data which relates to processing is saved into a '*log*' text file which is readily available to view for the user at the end of the image display and is located in the current directory where the program runs. The core of the method *void CImageViewerDlg::OnImageDisplay()* consists in three principal instructions: (i) '*fMRIdata = data(filename, numslice, rcyres, rcxres, datatype)*' which brings in the 3D image data into the program, (ii) '*TwoDdata = data(filename, numslice, rcyres, rcxres, datatype)*' which brings in the 2D image data into the program, and (iii) '*LaunchOpenGL()*' which allows the use of the method *void CImageViewerDlg::LaunchOpenGL()* to start OpenGL ®. In more details, '**(fMRIdata)*' and '**(TwoDdata)*' are pointers enforcing dynamic memory allocation management, receiving memory from the method *float * CImageViewerDlg::data(char filename[], int numslice, int rcyres, int rcxres, char datatype[])*, and storing data to display. '**(fMRIdata)*' and '**(TwoDdata)*' are pointers with global visibility which therefore can be used by functions like *void keyboard(unsigned char key, int x, int y)* and *void TwoDdisplay(void)* to act in favor to the display through the OpenGL ® interactive graphics.

```
void CImageViewerDlg::OnImageDisplay()
{

    UpdateData(true);

    if (fMRIdata != NULL)
    {
        free(fMRIdata);
    }

    if (TwoDdata != NULL)
    {
        free(TwoDdata);
    }

    static int rcxres=m_rcxres;
    static int rcyres=m_rcyres;
    static int numslice=m_numslice;

    char filename[128];

    /// make the keyboard ///
    FILE * pointTokeyboardFile;
    char keyboard[128]="keyboard.txt";

    if ((pointTokeyboardFile = fopen(keyboard,"w"))==NULL)
    {
    CString ExitMessage;
    ExitMessage.Format("%s\n" , "Cannot Open File: keyboard.txt: Exit" );
    MessageBox(ExitMessage);
    exit(0);

    }else{

    fprintf(pointTokeyboardFile,"%d\n", m_numslice);
    fprintf(pointTokeyboardFile,"%d\n", m_rcxres);
    fprintf(pointTokeyboardFile,"%d\n", m_rcyres);
    fprintf(pointTokeyboardFile,"%lf\n", m_Xsize);
    fprintf(pointTokeyboardFile,"%lf\n", m_Ysize);
    fprintf(pointTokeyboardFile,"%lf\n", m_Zsize);

    fclose(pointTokeyboardFile);

    }
```

```
        char logfilename[300];

        sprintf(logfilename, "%s%s%s", "ImageViewer", m_VolumeFileName, ".log");

        if ((logfile = fopen(logfilename,"w"))==NULL)
        {

         exit(0);

        }

        fprintf(logfile,"%s\t %s\n", "Processing the Image Volume Number: ", m_VolumeFileName);
        fprintf(logfile,"%s\t %d\n", "Number of Slices: ", m_numslice);
        fprintf(logfile,"%s\t %d\n", "X Matrix Resolution: ", m_rcxres);
        fprintf(logfile,"%s\t %d\n", "Y Matrix Resolution: ", m_rcyres);
        fprintf(logfile,"%s\t %lf\n", "X Pixel Size: ", m_Xsize);
        fprintf(logfile,"%s\t %lf\n", "Y Pixel Size: ", m_Ysize);
        fprintf(logfile,"%s\t %lf\n", "Z Pixel Size: ", m_Zsize);
        fprintf(logfile,"%s\t %s\n", "Data Type: ", m_DataType);
        sprintf(filename,"%s%s", "" , m_VolumeFileName);
        sprintf(datatype, "%s", m_DataType);

        if ( m_numslice > 1 )
        {
            fMRIdata = data(filename, numslice, rcyres, rcxres, datatype);
        } else if ( m_numslice == 1 ) {
            TwoDdata = data(filename, numslice, rcyres, rcxres, datatype);
        }

        fclose(logfile);

        CString ViewMessage;
        ViewMessage.Format("%s\n%s\n%s\n" , "Ready to Launch OpenGL Visualization" ,
        "to View Image, please remember to close" , "the Window(s) before exiting the program.");
        AfxMessageBox(ViewMessage);

        LaunchOpenGL();

}
```

The method *void CImageViewerDlg::LaunchOpenGL()* has two main functionalities. One is that of calling the method *void CImageViewerDlg::AllocateMemoryforOpenGLGraphics()* and the other is to start the main OpenGL ® loop. Memory allocation is performed dynamically as it shall be seen subsequently. Four pointers are declared globally to the use of the entire program and they are: '*GLfloat * planeWindowImage*', '*(GLfloat * pimage)*', '*(GLfloat * simage)*' and '*(GLfloat * cimage)*'. These pointers are dynamically allocated through the method *void CImageViewerDlg::AllocateMemoryforOpenGLGraphics()*. Once the memory is allocated for display the '*glut*' main loop will be launched for a single window (the plane view) making use of the following set of instructions [1]:

✓   *if (numslice == 1)   {*

✓   *glutInitWindowSize(winx,winy);*
✓   *glutInitWindowPosition(100,100);*
✓   *planeWindow = glutCreateWindow("XY VIEW");*
✓   *init();*
✓   *glutDisplayFunc(TwoDdisplay);*

✓   *glutReshapeFunc(reshape);*

✓   *}*

These instructions [1] perform the following tasks: (i) to set the window size, (ii) to set the window position, (iii) to create the window, (iv) to initialize the window, (v) to display the window, (vi) to manage the reshape of the window. This set of instructions is the same as seen in chapter 7 and is repeated in other projects reported in this manuscript when the '*glut*' main loop is initialized for any windows display.

As visible in *void CImageViewerDlg::LaunchOpenGL()*, the instructions seen for the plane view, which is identified by '*pw=glutCreateWindow("PLANE SLICES")*', are repeated for the sagittal view ('*sw=glutCreateWindow("SAGITTAL SLICES")*') and the coronal view ('*cw=glutCreateWindow("CORONAL SLICES")*'). The instructions relevant to plane sagittal and coronal views [1], which take place when the variable '*m_numslice*' is greater than one (stack of slices) are:

✓   *else if (numslice > 1) {*

✓   *// plane window*
✓   *glutInitWindowSize(winx,winy);*
✓   *glutInitWindowPosition(100,100);*
✓   *pw=glutCreateWindow("PLANE SLICES");*
✓   *init();*
✓   *glutDisplayFunc(display);*
✓   *glutKeyboardFunc(keyboard);*
✓   *glutReshapeFunc(reshape);*

✓   *// sagittal window*
✓   *glutInitWindowSize(winy,winz);*
✓   *glutInitWindowPosition(200,200);*
✓   *sw=glutCreateWindow("SAGITTAL SLICES");*
✓   *init();*
✓   *glutDisplayFunc(display);*
✓   *glutKeyboardFunc(keyboard);*
✓   *glutReshapeFunc(reshape);*

✓   *// coronal window*
✓   *glutInitWindowSize(winx,winz);*
✓   *glutInitWindowPosition(300,300);*
✓   *cw=glutCreateWindow("CORONAL SLICES");*
✓   *init();*
✓   *glutDisplayFunc(display);*
✓   *glutKeyboardFunc(keyboard);*
✓   *glutReshapeFunc(reshape);*

✓   *}*

void CImageViewerDlg::LaunchOpenGL()
{

       UpdateData(true);
       int winx, winy, winz;
       int rcxres = m_rcxres;
       int rcyres = m_rcyres;
       int numslice = m_numslice;

       /// read the keyboard matrix resolution///
       FILE * pointToKeyboardFile;

Computer Science Applications

```
char keyboardFile[128]="keyboard.txt";

if ((pointToKeyboardFile = fopen(keyboardFile,"r"))==NULL)
{

CString ExitMessage;
ExitMessage.Format("%s\n" , "Cannot Open File: keyboard.txt: Exit" );
AfxMessageBox(ExitMessage);

exit(0);

}else{

fscanf(pointToKeyboardFile,"%d\n", &numslice);
fscanf(pointToKeyboardFile,"%d\n", &rcxres);
fscanf(pointToKeyboardFile,"%d\n", &rcyres);
fscanf(pointToKeyboardFile,"%f\n", &PSPX);
fscanf(pointToKeyboardFile,"%f\n", &PSPY);
fscanf(pointToKeyboardFile,"%f\n", &PSSZ);

fclose(pointToKeyboardFile);

}

PSCZ = (float)PSSZ;
PSSY = (float)PSPY;
PSCX = (float)PSPX;

winx=(int)rcxres*PSPX;
winy=(int)rcyres*PSPY;
winz=(int)numslice*PSSZ;

glutInitDisplayMode(GLUT_SINGLE | GLUT_RGB);

AllocateMemoryforOpenGLGraphics();

if ( numslice == 1 )
{ // if plane window

glutInitWindowSize(winx,winy);
glutInitWindowPosition(100,100);
planeWindow = glutCreateWindow("XY VIEW");
init();
glutDisplayFunc(TwoDdisplay); // 2D display
glutReshapeFunc(reshape);

} // if plane window

else if ( numslice > 1 )
{ // if volume

//plane window
glutInitWindowSize(winx,winy);
glutInitWindowPosition(100,100);
pw=glutCreateWindow("PLANE SLICES");
init();
```

```
        glutDisplayFunc(display);
        glutKeyboardFunc(keyboard);
        glutReshapeFunc(reshape);

        //sagittal window
        glutInitWindowSize(winy,winz);
        glutInitWindowPosition(200,200);
        sw=glutCreateWindow("SAGITTAL SLICES");
        init();
        glutDisplayFunc(display);
        glutKeyboardFunc(keyboard);
        glutReshapeFunc(reshape);

        //coronal window
        glutInitWindowSize(winx,winz);
        glutInitWindowPosition(300,300);
        cw=glutCreateWindow("CORONAL SLICES");
        init();
        glutDisplayFunc(display);
        glutKeyboardFunc(keyboard);
        glutReshapeFunc(reshape);

        } // if volume

        glutMainLoop();

}
```

The method *float * CImageViewerDlg::data(char filename[], int numslice, int rcyres, int rcxres, char datatype[])* is employed to read into the program the data to display. The formats which can be read in are: '*CHAR*', '*SHORT*', '*INT*', '*FLOAT*' and '*DOUBLE*'. The method makes use of dynamic memory allocation management and realeses at the end of processing a pointer which is the data storage. Data is returned through the float pointer '**(bdata)*', which is allocated through the instruction '*bdata = (float *) calloc(((numslice*rcyres*rcxres)+1), sizeof(float))*'.

To read data in, for instance, in the case of the '*SHORT*' data format, the method uses the instruction '*pointer1 = (short *) calloc(((numslice*rcyres*rcxres)+1), sizeof(short))*' to allocate the memory cells before using the following instructions:

✓ *for(sl=1; sl<=numslice; sl++) {*
✓ *for(j=0; j<rcyres; j++) {*
✓ *for(i=0; i<rcxres; i++) {*

✓ *fread(&number1,sizeof(short),1,pf);*
✓ *k2=(j*rcxres+i)+((sl-1)*rcyres*rcxres);*
✓ **(pointer1+k2)=number1;*

✓ *}*
✓ *}*
✓ *}*

Setting the data, which was read in, available to use for the entire program, is done inside the method *void CImageViewerDlg::OnImageDisplay()* through the assignment '*fMRIdata = data(filename, numslice, rcyres, rcxres, datatype)*', given that the pointer '**(fMRIdata)*' has global visibility. This can happen after the data has been returned by *float * CImageViewerDlg::data(char filename[], int numslice, int rcyres, int rcxres, char datatype[])*.

Because the OpenGL ® instructions: '**(pimage + k3) = (GLfloat) *(fMRIdata+k2)/255*', '**(cimage + k3) = (GLfloat) *(fMRIdata+k2)/255*', '**(simage + k3) = (GLfloat) *(fMRIdata+k2)/255*' (located into the function *void keyboard(unsigned char key, int x, int y)*) determine that the pixel intensity is scaled in the range [0, 1], data is preliminarily scaled inside the

Computer Science Applications

range [0, 255] (once is read in through *float * CImageViewerDlg::data(char filename[], int numslice, int rcyres, int rcxres, char datatype[])*). The pointer '*(bdata)*' serves as container of the scaled data:

- ✓ *max=-5000000000000000000;*
- ✓ *min=5000000000000000000;*

- ✓ *for(i=0; i<rcxres*rcyres*numslice; i++) {*

- ✓ *if(*(pointer1+i)>max){*
- ✓ *max=*(pointer1+i);*
- ✓ *}*

- ✓ *if(*(pointer1+i)<min){*
- ✓ *min=*(pointer1+i);*
- ✓ *}*

- ✓ *}*

- ✓ *for(sl=1; sl<=numslice; sl++) {*
- ✓ *for(j=0; j<rcyres; j++) {*
- ✓ *for(i=0; i<rcxres; i++) {*

- ✓ *k2=(j*rcxres+i)+((sl-1)*rcyres*rcxres);*
- ✓ *if (max == min)*
- ✓ **(bdata+k2)=(float) max;*
- ✓ *else *(bdata+k2)=(float)(((float)*(pointer1+k2)-min)/((float)max-min))*255;*

- ✓ *}*
- ✓ *}*
- ✓ *}*

The pixel intensity scaled in the range [0, 1] is necessary to the instructions: '*glDrawPixels((GLsizei)rcxres, (GLsizei)rcyres, GL_LUMINANCE, GL_FLOAT, pimage)*', '*glDrawPixels((GLsizei)rcxres, (GLsizei)rcyres, GL_LUMINANCE, GL_FLOAT, cimage)*' and '*glDrawPixels((GLsizei)rcxres, (GLsizei)rcyres, GL_LUMINANCE, GL_FLOAT, simage)*' located inside the function *void keyboard(unsigned char key, int x, int y)*.

float * CImageViewerDlg::data(char filename[], int numslice, int rcyres, int rcxres, char datatype[])
{

```
        FILE *pf;
        int sl,j,i,k2;
        unsigned char number=1;
        short number1=1;
        int number2=1;
        float number3=1;
        double number4=1;
        unsigned char *pointer=0;
        short *pointer1=0;
        int *pointer2=0;
        float *pointer3=0;
        double *pointer4=0;
        float * bdata;
        double max, min;
```

```
if ((pf = fopen(filename,"rb+"))==NULL)
{
fprintf(logfile,"%s%s\n", "Cannot open file: " , filename );
exit(1);
}
if(strcmp(datatype,"CHAR")==0)
{

if ((pointer = (unsigned char *) calloc( ((numslice*rcyres*rcxres)+1), sizeof(unsigned char)) ) == NULL)
{
fprintf(logfile,"%s\n", "Not enough memory to allocate fMRI data");
exit(1);
}

for(sl=1 ;sl<=numslice; sl++) {
    for(j=0;j<rcyres;j++){
        for(i=0;i<rcxres;i++){

fread(&number,sizeof(unsigned char),1,pf);
k2=(j*rcxres+i)+((sl-1)*rcyres*rcxres);
*(pointer+k2)=number;


                }
            }
        }
fclose (pf);
if ((bdata = (float *) calloc( ((numslice*rcyres*rcxres)+1), sizeof(float)) ) == NULL)
{
fprintf(logfile,"%s\n", "Not enough memory to allocate fMRI data");
free(pointer);
exit(1);
}

for(sl=1 ;sl<=numslice; sl++) {
    for(j=0;j<rcyres;j++){
        for(i=0;i<rcxres;i++){

k2=(j*rcxres+i)+((sl-1)*rcyres*rcxres);
*(bdata+k2) = (float) *(pointer+k2);


                }
            }
        }

fprintf(logfile,"%s\n", "IMAGE DATA LOADED AND CONVERTED");
free(pointer);

} else if(strcmp(datatype,"SHORT")==0)
{
if ((pointer1 = (short *) calloc( ((numslice*rcyres*rcxres)+1), sizeof(short)) ) == NULL)
{
fprintf(logfile,"%s\n", "Not enough memory to allocate fMRI data");
exit(1);
}

for(sl=1 ;sl<=numslice; sl++) {
```

```
        for(j=0;j<rcyres;j++){
            for(i=0;i<rcxres;i++){

fread(&number1,sizeof(short),1,pf);
k2=(j*rcxres+i)+((sl-1)*rcyres*rcxres);
*(pointer1+k2)=number1;

                            }
                        }
                    }
fclose (pf);
if ((bdata = (float *) calloc( ((numslice*rcyres*rcxres)+1), sizeof(float)) ) == NULL)
{
fprintf(logfile,"%s\n", "Not enough memory to allocate fMRI data");
free(pointer1);
exit(1);
}

/*compute max and min of data*/
max=-5000000000000000000;
min=5000000000000000000;

for(i=0;i<rcxres*rcyres*numslice;i++){

if( *(pointer1+i)>max ){
max=*(pointer1+i);
                        }
if( *(pointer1+i)<min ){
min=*(pointer1+i);
                        }
                            }

/*convert data into analog scale and store into bdata*/
for(sl=1;sl<=numslice; sl++) {
    for(j=0;j<rcyres;j++){
        for(i=0;i<rcxres;i++){

        k2=(j*rcxres+i)+((sl-1)*rcyres*rcxres);
        if (max == min)
        *(bdata+k2)=(float) max;
        else *(bdata+k2)=(float)((((float)*(pointer1+k2)-min)/((float)max-min))*255;

                        }
                    }
                }

fprintf(logfile,"%s\n", "IMAGE DATA LOADED AND CONVERTED");
free(pointer1);

}else if(strcmp(datatype,"INT")==0)
{
if ((pointer2 = (int *) calloc( ((numslice*rcyres*rcxres)+1), sizeof(int)) ) == NULL)
{
fprintf(logfile,"%s\n", "Not enough memory to allocate fMRI data");
exit(1);
}
```

```
for(sl=1; sl<=numslice; sl++) {
  for(j=0;j<rcyres;j++){
      for(i=0;i<rcxres;i++){

  fread(&number2,sizeof(int),1,pf);
  k2=(j*rcxres+i)+((sl-1)*rcyres*rcxres);
  *(pointer2+k2)=number2;

                }
            }
        }

  fclose (pf);
  if ((bdata = (float *) calloc( ((numslice*rcyres*rcxres)+1), sizeof(float)) ) == NULL)
  {
  fprintf(logfile,"%s\n", "Not enough memory to allocate fMRI data");
  free(pointer2);
  exit(1);
  }

  /*compute max and min of data*/
  max=-5000000000000000000;
  min=5000000000000000000;

  for(i=0;i<rcxres*rcyres*numslice;i++){

  if( *(pointer2+i)>max ){
  max=*(pointer2+i);
            }
  if( *(pointer2+i)<min ){
  min=*(pointer2+i);
            }
                }

  /*convert data into analog scale and store into bdata*/
  for(sl=1;sl<=numslice; sl++) {
    for(j=0;j<rcyres;j++){
      for(i=0;i<rcxres;i++){

      k2=(j*rcxres+i)+((sl-1)*rcyres*rcxres);
      if (max == min)
      *(bdata+k2)=(float) max;
      else *(bdata+k2)=(float)(((float)*(pointer2+k2)-min)/((float)max-min))*255;

                }
            }
        }

  fprintf(logfile,"%s\n", "IMAGE DATA LOADED AND CONVERTED");
  free(pointer2);

  }else if(strcmp(datatype,"FLOAT")==0)
  {

  if ((pointer3 = (float *) calloc( ((numslice*rcyres*rcxres)+1), sizeof(float)) ) == NULL)
  {
```

```
fprintf(logfile,"%s\n", "Not enough memory to allocate fMRI data");
exit(1);
}

for(sl=1;sl<=numslice; sl++) {
    for(j=0;j<rcyres;j++){
        for(i=0;i<rcxres;i++){

fread(&number3,sizeof(float),1,pf);
k2=(j*rcxres+i)+((sl-1)*rcyres*rcxres);
*(pointer3+k2)=number3;

                }
            }
        }

fclose (pf);
if ((bdata = (float *) calloc( ((numslice*rcyres*rcxres)+1), sizeof(float)) ) == NULL)
{
fprintf(logfile,"%s\n", "Not enough memory to allocate fMRI data");
free(pointer3);
exit(1);
}

/*compute max and min of data*/
max=-5000000000000000000;
min=5000000000000000000;

for(i=0;i<rcxres*rcyres*numslice;i++){

if( *(pointer3+i)>max ){
max=*(pointer3+i);
                }
if( *(pointer3+i)<min ){
min=*(pointer3+i);
                }
                        }


/*convert data into analog scale and store into bdata*/
for(sl=1;sl<=numslice; sl++) {
    for(j=0;j<rcyres;j++){
        for(i=0;i<rcxres;i++){

            k2=(j*rcxres+i)+((sl-1)*rcyres*rcxres);
            if (max == min) *(bdata+k2)=(float) max;
            else *(bdata+k2)=(float)(((float)*(pointer3+k2)-min)/((float)max-min))*255;

                }
            }
        }

fprintf(logfile,"%s\n", "IMAGE DATA LOADED AND CONVERTED");
free(pointer3);

}else if(strcmp(datatype,"DOUBLE")==0)
```

```
{
if ((pointer4 = (double *) calloc( ((numslice*rcyres*rcxres)+1), sizeof(double)) ) == NULL)
{
fprintf(logfile,"%s\n", "Not enough memory to allocate fMRI data");
exit(1);
}

for(sl=1;sl<=numslice; sl++) {
    for(j=0;j<rcyres;j++){
        for(i=0;i<rcxres;i++){

fread(&number4,sizeof(double),1,pf);
k2=(j*rcxres+i)+((sl-1)*rcyres*rcxres);
*(pointer4+k2)=number4;

                }
            }
        }

fclose (pf);
if ((bdata = (float *) calloc( ((numslice*rcyres*rcxres)+1), sizeof(float)) ) == NULL)
{
fprintf(logfile,"%s\n", "Not enough memory to allocate fMRI data");
free(pointer4);
exit(1);
}

/*compute max and min of data*/
max=-5000000000000000000;
min=5000000000000000000;
for(i=0;i<rcxres*rcyres*numslice;i++){

if( *(pointer4+i)>max ){
max=*(pointer4+i);
                }
if( *(pointer4+i)<min ){
min=*(pointer4+i);
                }
                    }

/*convert data into analog scale and store into bdata*/
for(sl=1;sl<=numslice; sl++) {
    for(j=0;j<rcyres;j++){
        for(i=0;i<rcxres;i++){

        k2=(j*rcxres+i)+((sl-1)*rcyres*rcxres);
        if (max == min)
        *(bdata+k2)=(float) max;
        else *(bdata+k2)=(float)(((float)*(pointer4+k2)-min)/((float)max-min))*255;

                }
            }
        }

fprintf(logfile,"%s\n", "IMAGE DATA LOADED AND CONVERTED");
free(pointer4);
```

```
        }

        return bdata;

}
```

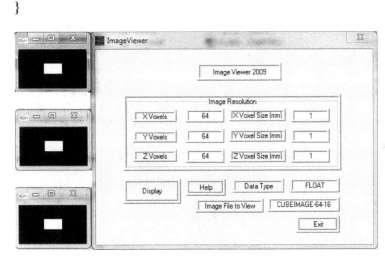

Figure 3: *ImageViewer 2009* employed to visualize artificial data (a cube of 16 pixels along the three edges inside a volume of 64 pixels). Composite 2D views (plane, coronal and sagittal) make the 3D visualization [2-3].

The method called *void CImageViewerDlg::AllocateMemoryforOpenGLGraphics()* acts through the function *'malloc'* to allocate memory for display in composite 2D windows. This is done through the instructions: *'pimage = (float *) malloc(rcyres*rcxres*3*sizeof(float))'*, *'planeWindowImage=(float *) malloc(rcyres*rcxres*3*sizeof(float))'*

(plane windows), *'cimage = (float *) malloc(rcyres*rcxres*3*sizeof(float))'* (coronal window) and *'simage = (float *) malloc(rcyres*rcxres*3*sizeof(float))'* (sagittal window), where *'*(planeWindowImage)'*, *'*(pimage)'*, *'*(cimage)'* and *'*(simage)'* are the four pointers recipients of the data allocated through the function *'malloc'*. For instance, in the case of the plane window for 2D image data allocation, the complete set of instructions is:

- ✓ *if (numslice == 1) {*
- ✓ *if (planeWindowImage == NULL) {*
- ✓ *planeWindowImage = (float *) malloc(rcyres*rcxres*3*sizeof(float));*
- ✓ *if (planeWindowImage == NULL) {*
- ✓ *CString ExitMessage;*
- ✓ *ExitMessage.Format("%s\n" , "Cannot Allocate Data for Display: Exit");*
- ✓ *AfxMessageBox(ExitMessage);*
- ✓ *free(TwoDdata);*
- ✓ *exit(0);*
- ✓ *}*
- ✓ *}*
- ✓ *}*

void CImageViewerDlg::AllocateMemoryforOpenGLGraphics()
```
{

        UpdateData(true);

        int rcxres=m_rcxres;
        int rcyres=m_rcyres;
        int numslice=m_numslice;

        float valueToDiscard = 0;
```

```
/// read the keyboard matrix resolution///
FILE * pointToKeyboardFile;
char keyboard[128]="keyboard.txt";

if ((pointToKeyboardFile = fopen(keyboard,"r"))==NULL)
{

CString ExitMessage;
ExitMessage.Format("%s\n" , "Cannot Open File: keyboard.txt: Exit" );
AfxMessageBox(ExitMessage);
exit(0);

}else{

fscanf(pointToKeyboardFile,"%d\n", &numslice);
fscanf(pointToKeyboardFile,"%d\n", &rcxres);
fscanf(pointToKeyboardFile,"%d\n", &rcyres);
fscanf(pointToKeyboardFile,"%f\n", &valueToDiscard);
fscanf(pointToKeyboardFile,"%f\n", &valueToDiscard);
fscanf(pointToKeyboardFile,"%f\n", &valueToDiscard);

fclose(pointToKeyboardFile);

}

if ( numslice == 1 )
{//// memory allocation for fMRI data to display ///

if ( planeWindowImage == NULL )
{

    planeWindowImage = (float *) malloc(rcyres*rcxres*3*sizeof(float));

if ( planeWindowImage == NULL )
{

    CString ExitMessage;
    ExitMessage.Format("%s\n" , "Cannot Allocate Data for Display: Exit");
    AfxMessageBox(ExitMessage);
    free(TwoDdata);

    exit(0);

}

}

} //// 2D data memory allocation to display ///

else if ( numslice > 1 )
{//// memory allocation to 3D data to display ///

if ( pimage == NULL )
{

    pimage = (float *) malloc(rcyres*rcxres*3*sizeof(float));

if ( pimage == NULL )
{
```

```
        CString ExitMessage;
        ExitMessage.Format("%s\n" , "Cannot Allocate Data for Display: Exit");
        AfxMessageBox(ExitMessage);
        free(fMRIdata);

        exit(0);

    }

    }

    if ( simage == NULL )
    {
        simage = (float *) malloc(rcyres*numslice*3*sizeof(float));

    if ( simage == NULL )
    {
        CString ExitMessage;
        ExitMessage.Format("%s\n" , "Cannot Allocate Data for Display: Exit");
        AfxMessageBox(ExitMessage);
        free(fMRIdata);

        exit(0);

    }

    }

    if ( cimage == NULL )
    {
        cimage = (float *) malloc(rcxres*numslice*3*sizeof(float));
    if ( cimage == NULL )
    {
        CString ExitMessage;
        ExitMessage.Format("%s\n" , "Cannot Allocate Data for Display: Exit");
        AfxMessageBox(ExitMessage);
        free(fMRIdata);

        exit(0);

    }

    }

    }//// memory allocation to 3D data to display ///

}
```

The method *void CImageViewerDlg::OnExit()* provides the program with the release of the dynamically allocated memory before the exit. The method *void CImageViewerDlg::OnHelp()* saves a text file called '*Help.log*' in the local directory where the program runs and this file is accessible to the view of the user at anytime.

void CImageViewerDlg::OnExit()
```
{
        if (fMRIdata != NULL)
```

```
        {
            free(fMRIdata);
        }
        if (TwoDdata != NULL)
        {
            free(TwoDdata);
        }
        if ( pimage != NULL )
        {
            free(pimage);
        }
        if ( simage != NULL )
        {
            free(simage);
        }
        if ( cimage != NULL )
        {
            free(cimage);
        }
        if ( planeWindowImage != NULL )
        {
            free(planeWindowImage);
        }
        exit(0);

}

void CImageViewerDlg::OnHelp()
{

        char logfilename[128];
        sprintf(logfilename,"%s","Help.log");
        if ((logfile = fopen(logfilename,"w"))==NULL)
        {
         exit(0);
        } else {

            fprintf(logfile,"%s\n", "Welcome to Image Viewer 2009");
            fprintf(logfile,"\n");
            fprintf(logfile,"%s\n", "Please remember to set for X, Y, and Z, the Image data
                                Resolution, Voxel Size (mm) and to specify the DataType");
            fprintf(logfile,"%s\n", "The Data Types available are: CHAR, SHORT, INT, FLOAT and DOUBLE");
            fprintf(logfile,"\n");
            fprintf(logfile,"%s\n", "THE PROGRAM WILL DISPLAY THE IMAGE DATA");
            fprintf(logfile,"%s\n", "Windows for 2D Plane Sagittal and Coronal Sections will be displayed");
            fprintf(logfile,"%s\n", "Move the mouse arrow to give control to the windows");
            fprintf(logfile,"%s\n", "Press U and D keys to see Plane sections");
            fprintf(logfile,"%s\n", "Press L and R keys to see Sagittal sections");
            fprintf(logfile,"%s\n", "Press F and B keys to see Coronal sections");
            fprintf(logfile,"\n");
            fprintf(logfile,"%s\n", "Please work with One single Image (2D or 3D) at once, then to process");
            fprintf(logfile,"%s\n", "a different Image, Exit the program and Run it Again.");
            fprintf(logfile,"\n");
            fprintf(logfile,"%s\n", "To Exit the program please perform the following steps:");
            fprintf(logfile,"%s\n", "1. Close all of the Display Windows where the Image data is seen");
            fprintf(logfile,"%s\n", "2. Click on the Exit Button");
```

```
        fclose(logfile);

        CString HelpMessage;

        HelpMessage.Format("%s\n %s\n %s\n %s\n %s\n %s\n %s\n %s\n %s\n" ,
        "Please place your Image Data",
        "Under the same directory where the program runs" ,
        "THE PROGRAM WILL DISPLAY THE IMAGE DATA" ,
        "Windows of 2D Plane Sagittal and Coronal Sections will be displayed",
        "Move the mouse arrow to give control to the windows" ,
        "Use U and D keys to see Plane sections" ,
        "Use L and R keys to see Sagittal sections" ,
        "Use F and B keys to see Coronal sections" ,
        "Also Please read the file Help.log before using the program");

        MessageBox(HelpMessage);

    }//else


}
```

Part II: Image Tool 2009

The application named *Image Tool 2009* is employed to visualize 2D and 3D (three composite 2D views) data and also to create randomized artificial data. To begin the explanation of the code it is worth noting that the pointers '*(GLfloat * pimage)*', '*(GLfloat * simage)*' and '*(GLfloat * cimage)*' are employed for 3D visualization and the pointer '*(GLfloat * planeWindowImage)*' is employed for single 2D image visualization. The variable named '*WhoIsONDisplay*' is employed to distinguish a 2D display session from a 3D display session. Visible also are the two pointers named '**(Imagedata)*' and '**(TwoDdata)*' which are employed to store data for 3D and 2D visualization respectively.

```
        #define WINX 300
        #define WINY 300
        #define WINZ 300

        int ox = 360, oy = 360, oz = 360, z;

        float *Imagedata = 0;
        float *TwoDdata = 0;
        int Slice=0, sagSlice=-1, corSlice=-1;

        int pw, sw, cw, view, planeWindow;

        int count=-1;

        char datatype[47];
        FILE * logfile;

        GLfloat  * pimage = NULL;
        GLfloat  * simage = NULL;
        GLfloat  * cimage = NULL;
        GLfloat  * planeWindowImage = NULL;

        // methods that cannot be included in any class
        // bacause of the syntax required from OpenGL ® Libraries
        void display(void);
```

```
        void keyboard(unsigned char key, int x, int y);
        void reshape(int w, int h);
        void TwoDdisplay(void);

        int WhoIsONDisplay = 0;
        int plEraseMemoryFlag = 0;
        int tEraseMemoryFlag = 0;
```

While the method *void CImageToolDlg::OnExit()* provides the program with the exit, the method *void CImage-ToolDlg::OnHelp()* provides the user with help through the text file *'Help.log'* which is saved in the local directory where the program runs, upon pushing the button named *'Help'* (see Fig. 2). This text file contains comprehensive information on how to interact with *Image Tool 2009*.

void CImageToolDlg::OnExit()
```
{
    exit(0);
}
```

void CImageToolDlg::OnHelp()
```
{

        char logfilename[128];

        sprintf(logfilename,"%s","Help.log");
        if ((logfile = fopen(logfilename,"w"))==NULL)
        {
         exit(0);
        } else{

            fprintf(logfile,"%s\n", "Welcome to Image Tool 2009");
            fprintf(logfile,"\n");
            fprintf(logfile,"%s\n", "This Application reads and display 2D and 3D Image Data.");
            fprintf(logfile,"%s\n", "Chaotic Image Data can be created employing randomization with");
            fprintf(logfile,"%s\n", "the push button named: Cube and Slice. Image Data conforming");
            fprintf(logfile,"%s\n", "with the header format can also be imported into this application.");

            fprintf(logfile,"\n");
            fprintf(logfile,"%s\n", "To display an Image either in 2D or 3D:" );
            fprintf(logfile,"%s\n", "Simply push the Buttons named Display Image (2D) or Display Image (3D).");
            fprintf(logfile,"\n");

            fprintf(logfile,"%s\n", "The program will read the Image Header, transparently to the user.");
            fprintf(logfile,"\n");

            fprintf(logfile,"%s\n", "The Image Header Information is in the following order:");
            fprintf(logfile,"%s\n", "X, Y, and Z Matrix Sizes; X, Y, and Z Pixel Size [mm]; DataType; StdLabel.");
            fprintf(logfile,"%s\n", "The Data Types available are: CHAR, SHORT, INT, FLOAT and DOUBLE.");
            fprintf(logfile,"%s\n", "The StdLabel is either Y or N to indicate as to if the Image
                                Data is in Standardized form or not.");
            fprintf(logfile,"\n");

            fprintf(logfile,"%s\n", "Multiple sessions are allowed. Please make sure that Memory
                                is Cleared after Display, either 2D or 3D.");
            fprintf(logfile,"%s\n", "Specifically: Clear Memory 2D after 2D Display");
            fprintf(logfile,"%s\n", "and Clear Memory 3D after 3D Display.");
            fprintf(logfile,"\n");
```

```
        fprintf(logfile,"%s\n", "Should you want to import Image Data with Header
                        Information conforming with this application,");
        fprintf(logfile,"%s\n", "it is not necessary to keep the Std Check Box checked.");
        fprintf(logfile,"\n");

        fprintf(logfile,"%s\n", "Should you want to create Standardized Image Data,");
        fprintf(logfile,"%s\n", "Please keep the Std Check Box checked before pushing the
                        button named: Cube and Slice.");
        fprintf(logfile,"\n");

        fprintf(logfile,"%s\n", "THE PROGRAM WILL DISPLAY THE IMAGE DATA");
        fprintf(logfile,"%s\n", "Windows for 2D Plane Sagittal and Coronal Sections will be displayed");
        fprintf(logfile,"%s\n", "Move the mouse arrow to give control to the windows");
        fprintf(logfile,"%s\n", "Press U and D keys to see Plane sections");
        fprintf(logfile,"%s\n", "Press L and R keys to see Sagittal sections");
        fprintf(logfile,"%s\n", "Press F and B keys to see Coronal sections");
        fprintf(logfile,"%s\n", "When viewing an Image Volume, once one Window is reshaped," );
        fprintf(logfile,"%s\n", "then Please Reshape the other Two also.");
        fprintf(logfile,"\n");
        fprintf(logfile,"%s\n", "To Exit the program please perform the following steps:");
        fprintf(logfile,"%s\n", "1. Close all of the Display Windows where the Image data is seen");
        fprintf(logfile,"%s\n", "2. Click on the Exit Button");
        fclose(logfile);

        CString HelpMessage;

                HelpMessage.Format("%s\n %s\n %s\n %s\n %s\n %s\n %s\n
                                %s\n %s\n %s\n %s\n %s\n %s\n" ,
                "Please place your Image Data",
                "Under the same directory where the program runs" ,
                "THE PROGRAM WILL DISPLAY 2D or 3D IMAGE DATA" ,
                "When Viewing 3D Data, Windows of 2D Plane Sagittal" ,
                "and Coronal Sections will be displayed" ,
                "Move the mouse arrow to give control to the windows" ,
                "Use U and D keys to see Plane sections" ,
                "Use L and R keys to see Sagittal sections" ,
                "Use F and B keys to see Coronal sections" ,
                "Once one Window is Reshaped, then Please Reshape" ,
                "the other Two Windows. Also, when Viewing 2D Data," ,
                "a single 2D Plane Window will be displayed" ,
                "Please read the file Help.log before using the program.");
                MessageBox(HelpMessage);

        }//else

}
```

The method *void CImageToolDlg::OnDisplayImage()* acts in two major steps. In first instance the method reads in data with the instruction '*Imagedata=data(filename)*' which calls in the method *float * CImageToolDlg::data(char filename[])*. The variable '*filename*' is input to *float * CImageToolDlg::data(char filename[])* from the Graphical User Interface to the program and is called '*m_VolumeFileName*'. Data is released to the storage pointer called '**(Imagedata)*' which is visible globally within the application. In second instance, *void CImageToolDlg::OnDisplayImage()* calls in the method *void CImageToolDlg::LaunchOpenGL()* to start the visualization with the instruction '*LaunchOpenGL()*'. The variable '*WhoIsONDisplay*' is set equal to the value '*3*' to indicate three dimensional visual display.

void CImageToolDlg::OnDisplayImage()
{

      UpdateData(true);

      char filename[128];
      sprintf(filename, "%s", m_VolumeFileName);

      Imagedata=data(filename);

      WhoIsONDisplay = 3;

      LaunchOpenGL();

}

The method *void CImageToolDlg::LaunchOpenGL()* is very much alike the ones so far seen for what concerns the OpenGL ® instructions [1], with the difference that the variable '*WhoIsONDisplay*' is checked as to if its value is equal to '*2*' or equal to '*3*'. In the former case the method *void CImageToolDlg::AllocateMemoryforOpenGLGraphics2D()* is called in for 2D visualization with the instruction '*AllocateMemoryforOpenGLGraphics2D()*', whereas in the latter case, the method *void CImageToolDlg::AllocateMemoryforOpenGLGraphics3D()* is called in for 3D visualization with the instruction '*AllocateMemoryforOpenGLGraphics3D()*'.

    The OpenGL ® instructions are written in order: (i) to set the window size, (ii) to set the window position, (iii) to create the window, (iv) to initialize the window, (v) to display the window, (vi) to manage the keyboard, (vii) to manage the window reshape. For the 2D display they are [1]:

- ✓ *glutInitWindowSize(winx,winy)*
- ✓ *glutInitWindowPosition(100,100)*
- ✓ *planeWindow = glutCreateWindow("XY VIEW")*
- ✓ *init()*
- ✓ *glutDisplayFunc(TwoDdisplay)*
- ✓ *glutReshapeFunc(reshape)*

For the 3D display the instructions are repeated each time for each of the three windows (plane, coronal and sagittal). Those relevant to the plane window are [1]:

- ✓ *glutInitWindowSize(winx,winy);*
- ✓ *glutInitWindowPosition(100,100);*
- ✓ *pw=glutCreateWindow("PLANE SLICES");*
- ✓ *init();*
- ✓ *glutDisplayFunc(display)*
- ✓ *glutKeyboardFunc(keyboard)*
- ✓ *glutReshapeFunc(reshape)*

The two dimensional case presents a difference versus the three dimensional case which is that '*glutDisplayFunc(TwoDdisplay)*' (two dimensional case) replaces '*glutDisplayFunc(display)*' and '*glutKeyboardFunc(keyboard)*' (three dimensional case). As the reader shall note in the subsequent sections of part II in this chapter, the function *void TwoDdisplay(void)* makes use of the instruction '*glutGetWindow() == planeWindow*' to identify the window, the instruction '**(planeWindowImage + k3) = (GLfloat) *(TwoDdata+k3)/255*' to assign the value of the pixel intensity to the pointer '**(planeWindowImage)*' and also the set of instructions [1] employed: (i) to draw the buffer, (ii) to set the raster position, (iii) to zoom the pixel, (iv) to draw the pixel and (v) to flush the display:

- ✓ *glDrawBuffer(GL_FRONT)*
- ✓ *glRasterPos2i(0,0)*
- ✓ *glPixelZoom((GLfloat) PSPX, (GLfloat) PSPY)*

Computer Science Applications

- ✓ *glDrawPixels((GLsizei)rcxres, (GLsizei)rcyres, GL_LUMINANCE, GL_FLOAT, planeWindowImage)*
- ✓ *glFlush()*

Whereas, in the three dimensional case the aforementioned instructions are placed inside the function *void keyboard(unsigned char key, int x, int y)*.

void CImageToolDlg::LaunchOpenGL()

```
{

        int winx, winy, winz;
        // variables that are locally employed and are non static within
        // the scope of the method because of the OpenGL ® interactive graphics
        int rcxres;
        int rcyres;
        int numslice;
        float PSSZ;
        float PSPY;
        float PSPX;
        /// read the keyboard matrix resolution///
        FILE * pointToKeyboardFile;
        char keyboardFile[128]="keyboard.txt";

        if ((pointToKeyboardFile = fopen(keyboardFile,"r"))==NULL)
        {

        CString ExitMessage;
        ExitMessage.Format("%s\n" , "Cannot Open File: keyboard.txt: Exit" );
        AfxMessageBox(ExitMessage);
        exit(0);

        }else{

        fscanf(pointToKeyboardFile,"%d\n", &numslice);
        fscanf(pointToKeyboardFile,"%d\n", &rcxres);
        fscanf(pointToKeyboardFile,"%d\n", &rcyres);
        fscanf(pointToKeyboardFile,"%f\n", &PSPX);
        fscanf(pointToKeyboardFile,"%f\n", &PSPY);
        fscanf(pointToKeyboardFile,"%f\n", &PSSZ);
        fclose(pointToKeyboardFile);

        }

        winx=(int)rcxres*PSPX;
        winy=(int)rcyres*PSPY;
        winz=(int)numslice*PSSZ;

        if ( WhoIsONDisplay == 2 )
            AllocateMemoryforOpenGLGraphics2D();

        else if ( WhoIsONDisplay == 3 )
            AllocateMemoryforOpenGLGraphics3D();

        glutInitDisplayMode(GLUT_SINGLE | GLUT_RGB);
        if ( numslice == 1 )
        { // if plane window
```

```
glutInitWindowSize(winx,winy);
glutInitWindowPosition(100,100);
planeWindow = glutCreateWindow("XY VIEW");
init();
glutDisplayFunc(TwoDdisplay); // 2D display
glutReshapeFunc(reshape);
} // if plane window

else if ( numslice > 1 )
{ // if volume

//plane window
glutInitWindowSize(winx,winy);
glutInitWindowPosition(100,100);
pw=glutCreateWindow("PLANE SLICES");
init();
glutDisplayFunc(display);
glutKeyboardFunc(keyboard);
glutReshapeFunc(reshape);

//sagittal window
glutInitWindowSize(winy,winz);
glutInitWindowPosition(200,200);
sw=glutCreateWindow("SAGITTAL SLICES");
init();
glutDisplayFunc(display);
glutKeyboardFunc(keyboard);
glutReshapeFunc(reshape);

//coronal window
glutInitWindowSize(winx,winz);
glutInitWindowPosition(300,300);
cw=glutCreateWindow("CORONAL SLICES");
init();
glutDisplayFunc(display);
glutKeyboardFunc(keyboard);
glutReshapeFunc(reshape);

} // if volume

glutMainLoop();

}
```

The method *void CImageToolDlg::init()* works much alike the ones seen so far with the purpose to initialize the OpenGL ® windows. Initially the method reads the text file named '*keyboard.txt*' in order to retrieve the resolution information. Subsequently the method reports the following set of instructions [1]:

✓ *if(glutGetWindow() == planeWindow) {*

✓ *glViewport(0, 0, (GLsizei)winx, (GLsizei)winy);*
✓ *glLoadIdentity();*
✓ *gluOrtho2D(0.0, (GLdouble)winx, 0.0, (GLdouble)winy);*

✓ *}*

Computer Science Applications

- ✓ *if(glutGetWindow() == pw) {*

- ✓ *glViewport(0, 0, (GLsizei)winx, (GLsizei)winy);*
- ✓ *glLoadIdentity();*
- ✓ *gluOrtho2D(0.0, (GLdouble)winx, 0.0, (GLdouble)winy);*

- ✓ *}*

- ✓ *if(glutGetWindow() == sw) {*

- ✓ *glViewport(0, 0, (GLsizei)winy, (GLsizei)winz);*
- ✓ *glLoadIdentity();*
- ✓ *gluOrtho2D(0.0, (GLdouble)winy, 0.0, (GLdouble)winz);*
- ✓ *}*

- ✓ *if(glutGetWindow() == cw) {*

- ✓ *glViewport(0, 0, (GLsizei)winx, (GLsizei)winz);*
- ✓ *glLoadIdentity();*
- ✓ *gluOrtho2D(0.0, (GLdouble)winx, 0.0, (GLdouble)winz);*

- ✓ *}*

For each of the windows the three functions '*glViewport()*', '*glLoadIdentity()*' and '*gluOrtho2D()*' set the viewport size, load the identity matrix and set the orthogonal 2D view size respectively.

void CImageToolDlg::init()

```
{

        int winx, winy, winz;
        // variables that are locally employed and are non static within
        // the scope of the method because of the OpenGL ® interactive graphics
        int rcxres;
        int rcyres;
        int numslice;
        float PSSZ;
        float PSPY;
        float PSPX;

        /// read the keyboard matrix resolution///
        FILE * pointToKeyboardFile;
        char keyboard[128]="keyboard.txt";

        if ((pointToKeyboardFile = fopen(keyboard,"r"))==NULL)
        {
        CString ExitMessage;
        ExitMessage.Format("%s\n" , "Cannot Open File: keyboard.txt: Exit" );
        AfxMessageBox(ExitMessage);
        exit(0);

        }else{

        fscanf(pointToKeyboardFile,"%d\n", &numslice);
        fscanf(pointToKeyboardFile,"%d\n", &rcxres);
        fscanf(pointToKeyboardFile,"%d\n", &rcyres);
```

```
fscanf(pointToKeyboardFile,"%f\n", &PSPX);
fscanf(pointToKeyboardFile,"%f\n", &PSPY);
fscanf(pointToKeyboardFile,"%f\n", &PSSZ);
fclose(pointToKeyboardFile);

}

winx=(int)rcxres*PSPX;
winy=(int)rcyres*PSPY;
winz=(int)numslice*PSSZ;

glClearColor(0.0, 0.0, 0.0, 0.0);
glShadeModel(GL_FLAT);
if(glutGetWindow() == planeWindow)
{
    glViewport(0, 0, (GLsizei)winx, (GLsizei)winy);
    glLoadIdentity();
    gluOrtho2D(0.0, (GLdouble)winx, 0.0, (GLdouble)winy);
}

if(glutGetWindow() == pw)
{
    glViewport(0, 0, (GLsizei)winx, (GLsizei)winy);
    glLoadIdentity();
    gluOrtho2D(0.0, (GLdouble)winx, 0.0, (GLdouble)winy);
}

if(glutGetWindow() == sw)
{
    glViewport(0, 0, (GLsizei)winy, (GLsizei)winz);
    glLoadIdentity();
    gluOrtho2D(0.0, (GLdouble)winy, 0.0, (GLdouble)winz);
}

if(glutGetWindow() == cw)
{
    glViewport(0, 0, (GLsizei)winx, (GLsizei)winz);
    glLoadIdentity();
    gluOrtho2D(0.0, (GLdouble)winx, 0.0, (GLdouble)winz);
}

}
```

There are lines of code in the methods *void CImageToolDlg::AllocateMemoryforOpenGLGraphics2D()* and *void CImage-ToolDlg::AllocateMemoryforOpenGLGraphics3D()* which are written to read the header portion of the file containing the data to visualize. The header portion of the file contains the resolution information, the information about the data type which can be 'CHAR' ('LabelData=='C'), 'INT' ('LabelData=='I'), 'SHORT' ('LabelData=='S'), 'FLOAT' ('La-belData=='F') or 'DOUBLE' ('LabelData=='D'), and also the information as to if the image data is stored in standard-ized ('StdLabel == Y') form or not ('StdLabel == N'). In the former case the routines are set to read average and stan-dard deviation of the data. The set of instructions is:

✓ *if ((pf = fopen(m_VolumeFileName,"rb+"))==NULL) {*

✓ *CString WarningMessage;*
✓ *WarningMessage.Format("%s%s\n%s\n%s\n" , "Cannot Open File: " , m_VolumeFileName,*
        "Please make sure the file is" , "located in the working directory");

- ✓ *MessageBox(WarningMessage);*
- ✓ *exit(0);*

- ✓ *}else{*

- ✓ *fread(&rcxres,sizeof(int),1,pf);*
- ✓ *fread(&rcyres,sizeof(int),1,pf);*
- ✓ *fread(&numslice,sizeof(int),1,pf);*
- ✓ *fread(&PSPX,sizeof(float),1,pf);*
- ✓ *fread(&PSPY,sizeof(float),1,pf);*
- ✓ *fread(&PSSZ,sizeof(float),1,pf);*
- ✓ *fread(&LabelData,sizeof(char),1,pf);*
- ✓ *fread(&StdLabel,sizeof(char),1,pf);*

- ✓ *if (StdLabel=='Y') {*

- ✓ *fread(&Average,sizeof(float),1,pf);*
- ✓ *fread(&Std,sizeof(float),1,pf);*

- ✓ *} else if (StdLabel=='N') { }*

For what pertains *Image Tool 2009*, the methods *void CImageToolDlg::AllocateMemoryforOpenGLGraphics2D()* and *void CImageToolDlg::AllocateMemoryforOpenGLGraphics3D()* present a main difference versus what was already seen in other OpenGL ®/Visual C++ ® projects of this manuscript. The difference is that the data to visualize is contained in a file which carries on a header, further, the image data is read in and discarded. For instance, in the case the format of the image data is '*CHAR*' (identified through the equality '*LabelData == C*'), the instructions are:

- ✓ *if (LabelData =='C') {*

- ✓ *unsigned char ReadNumber = 0;*
- ✓ *unsigned char valueToDiscard = 0;*

- ✓ *for(sl=1; sl<=numslice; sl++) {*
- ✓ *for(j=0; j<rcyres; j++){*
- ✓ *for(i=0; i<rcxres; i++){*

- ✓ *fread(&ReadNumber,sizeof(unsigned char),1,pf);*
- ✓ *valueToDiscard=(unsigned char)ReadNumber;*

- ✓ *}*
- ✓ *}*
- ✓ *}*

- ✓ *}*

Reading data into the program, storing it through dynamic memory allocation and releasing it through a pointer is instead an operation delegated to the method *float * CImageToolDlg::data(char filename[])*.

There are additional lines of code inside the methods *void CImageToolDlg::AllocateMemoryforOpenGLGraphics2D()* and *void CImageToolDlg::AllocateMemoryforOpenGLGraphics3D()* which are devoted to dynamic memory allocation for 2D and 3D visualization respectively. Specifically, the method *void CImageToolDlg::AllocateMemoryforOpenGLGraphics2D()* uses the instruction '*planeWindowImage = (float *) malloc(rcxres*rcyres*3*sizeof(float))*' to assign memory containing data to display to the pointer '**(planeWindowImage)*'. Whereas, to achieve the same purpose, the method *void CImageToolDlg::AllocateMemoryforOpenGLGraphics3D()* uses the instructions: '*pimage = (float *) malloc(rcyres*rcxres*3*sizeof(float))*', '*simage = (float *) malloc(rcyres*numslice*3*sizeof(float))*' and '*cimage = (float *) malloc(rcxres*numslice*3*sizeof(float))*', to assign memory containing data to display to the pointers '**(pimage)*', '**(simage)*' and '**(cimage)*' respectively.

Before memory allocation takes place, the method *void CImageToolDlg::AllocateMemoryforOpenGLGraphics2D()* performs the check as to if the number of slices is exaxtly equal to one. If otherwise, the user is warned and the program exits. The lines of code are:

✓ *if (numslice == 1) {*

✓ *planeWindowImage = (float *) malloc(rcxres*rcyres*3*sizeof(float));*
✓ *plEraseMemoryFlag = 0;*
✓ *CString ViewMessage;*
✓ *ViewMessage.Format("%s\n%s\n%s\n" , "Ready to Launch OpenGL Visualization to" ,*
                          "view the 2D Image. Please Remember to" ,
                          "close the Window before Exiting the Program.");

✓ *AfxMessageBox(ViewMessage);*

✓ *}else{*

✓ *CString ExitMessage;*
✓ *ExitMessage.Format("%s\n %s\n %s\n %s\n" , "Mismatch Between the" ,*
                       "Image Type and Diplay: " , "This is a Plane 3D Image." , "Now Exit");
✓ *AfxMessageBox(ExitMessage);*
✓ *exit(0);*

✓ *}*

Similarly, the method *void CImageToolDlg::AllocateMemoryforOpenGLGraphics3D()* performs the check as to if the number of slices is greater than one. If otherwise, the program exits after proper warning to the user. The lines of code are:

✓ *if (numslice > 1) {*

✓ *pimage = (float *) malloc(rcyres*rcxres*3*sizeof(float));*
✓ *simage = (float *) malloc(rcyres*numslice*3*sizeof(float));*
✓ *cimage = (float *) malloc(rcxres*numslice*3*sizeof(float));*
✓ *tEraseMemoryFlag = 0;*
✓ *CString ViewMessage;*

✓ *ViewMessage.Format("%s\n %s\n %s\n" , "Ready to Launch OpenGL Visualization" ,*
                    "to View Image, please remember to close" , "the Window(s) before exiting the program.");

✓ *AfxMessageBox(ViewMessage);*

✓ *}else{*

✓ *CString ExitMessage;*

✓ *ExitMessage.Format("%s\n %s\n %s\n %s\n" , "Mismatch Between the" ,*
                    "Image Type and Diplay: " , "This is a Plane 2D Image" , "Now Exit");
✓ *AfxMessageBox(ExitMessage);*
✓ *exit(0);*

✓ *}*

The instructions '*plEraseMemoryFlag = 0*' and '*tEraseMemoryFlag = 0*' are located in the methods *void CImage-ToolDlg::AllocateMemoryforOpenGLGraphics2D()* and *void CImageToolDlg::AllocateMemoryforOpenGLGraphics3D()* respectively. Such instructions are given to the global extent of the program and they can be captured by the methods *void CImage-ToolDlg::OnClearMemory2D()* and *void CImageToolDlg::OnClearMemory3D()* in order to release the memory cells allocated to

Computer Science Applications

image data display. Specifically, when '*plEraseMemoryFlag = 0*' and '*tEraseMemoryFlag = 0*', it is possible to execute the instruction '*free(planeWindowImage)*' located in the method *void CImageToolDlg::OnClearMemory2D()* and also the instruction '*free(Imagedata)*' located in the method *void CImageToolDlg::OnClearMemory3D()*.

void CImageToolDlg::AllocateMemoryforOpenGLGraphics2D()

```
{

        // variables that are locally employed
        int rcxres;
        int rcyres;
        int numslice;
        int sl, j, i;
        float PSPX, PSPY, PSSZ;
        char LabelData = ' ', StdLabel = ' ';
        float Average = 0, Std = 0;
        FILE *pf;
        /// Scan and read Header Info in Image File 'm_VolumeFileName'
        if ((pf = fopen(m_VolumeFileName,"rb+"))==NULL)
        {

            CString WarningMessage;
            WarningMessage.Format("%s%s\n%s\n%s\n" , "Cannot Open File: " , m_VolumeFileName,
                            "Please make sure the file is" , "located in the working directory" );
            MessageBox(WarningMessage);
            exit(0);

        }else{ // read header portion and data of the file

        fread(&rcxres,sizeof(int),1,pf);
        fread(&rcyres,sizeof(int),1,pf);
        fread(&numslice,sizeof(int),1,pf);
        fread(&PSPX,sizeof(float),1,pf);
        fread(&PSPY,sizeof(float),1,pf);
        fread(&PSSZ,sizeof(float),1,pf);
        fread(&LabelData,sizeof(char),1,pf);
        /// label from file header of image file made with this GUI
        /// or Matlab program

        fread(&StdLabel,sizeof(char),1,pf);

        if (StdLabel=='Y')
        {

        fread(&Average,sizeof(float),1,pf);
        fread(&Std,sizeof(float),1,pf);

        } else if (StdLabel=='N') { }

        if ( LabelData =='C' )
        {

            unsigned char ReadNumber = 0;
            unsigned char valueToDiscard = 0;

        // read data and discard
        for(sl=1 ;sl<=numslice; sl++) {
```

220

```
            for(j=0;j<rcyres;j++){
                for(i=0;i<rcxres;i++){

fread(&ReadNumber,sizeof(unsigned char),1,pf);
valueToDiscard=(unsigned char)ReadNumber;

                            }
                        }
                    }
// read data and discard
}
else if ( LabelData =='S' )
{
        short ReadNumber = 0;
        short valueToDiscard = 0;
// read data and discard
for(sl=1 ;sl<=numslice; sl++) {
        for(j=0;j<rcyres;j++){
            for(i=0;i<rcxres;i++){

fread(&ReadNumber,sizeof(short),1,pf);
valueToDiscard=(short)ReadNumber;

                            }
                        }
                    }
// read data and discard
}
else if ( LabelData =='I' )
{

        int ReadNumber = 0;
        int valueToDiscard = 0;

// read data and discard
for(sl=1 ;sl<=numslice; sl++) {
        for(j=0;j<rcyres;j++){
            for(i=0;i<rcxres;i++){

fread(&ReadNumber,sizeof(int),1,pf);
valueToDiscard=(int)ReadNumber;

                            }
                        }
                    }
// read data and discard
}
else if ( LabelData =='F' )
{

        float ReadNumber = 0;
        float valueToDiscard = 0;

// read data and discard
for(sl=1 ;sl<=numslice; sl++) {
        for(j=0;j<rcyres;j++){
```

```
                    for(i=0;i<rcxres;i++){

fread(&ReadNumber,sizeof(float),1,pf);
valueToDiscard=(float)ReadNumber;

                                    }
                            }
                    }
// read data and discard
}
else if ( LabelData=='D' )
{
        double ReadNumber = 0;
        double valueToDiscard = 0;
// read data and discard
for(sl=1 ;sl<=numslice; sl++) {
        for(j=0;j<rcyres;j++){
                for(i=0;i<rcxres;i++){

fread(&ReadNumber,sizeof(double),1,pf);
valueToDiscard=(double)ReadNumber;

                                    }
                            }
                    }
// read data and discard
}
fclose(pf);

}// read header portion and data of the file
// allocate to 2D display

if ( numslice == 1 )
{

/// memory allocation ///
planeWindowImage = (float *) malloc(rcxres*rcyres*3*sizeof(float));
plEraseMemoryFlag = 0;
CString ViewMessage;
ViewMessage.Format("%s\n%s\n%s\n" , "Ready to Launch OpenGL Visualization to" ,
                                    "view the 2D Image. Please Remember to" ,
                                    "close the Window before Exiting the Program.");
AfxMessageBox(ViewMessage);

}else{ /// mismatch message ///

CString ExitMessage;
ExitMessage.Format("%s\n %s\n %s\n %s\n" , "Mismatch Between the" ,
                    "Image Type and Diplay: " , "This is a Plane 3D Image." , "Now Exit");
AfxMessageBox(ExitMessage);
exit(0);

    }/// mismatch message ///
// end of allocate to 2D display

}
```

```
void CImageToolDlg::AllocateMemoryforOpenGLGraphics3D()
{
        // variables that are locally employed
        int rcxres;
        int rcyres;
        int numslice;
        int sl, j, i;
        float PSPX, PSPY, PSSZ;
        char LabelData = ' ', StdLabel = ' ';
        float Average = 0, Std = 0;
        FILE *pf;
        /// Scan and read Header Info in Image File 'm_VolumeFileName'
        if ((pf = fopen(m_VolumeFileName,"rb+"))==NULL)
        {

            CString WarningMessage;
            WarningMessage.Format("%s%s\n%s\n%s\n" ,
                                "Cannot Open File: " , m_VolumeFileName,
                                "Please make sure the file is" ,
                                "located in the working directory" );
            MessageBox(WarningMessage);
            exit(0);

        }else{ // read header portion and data of the file
        fread(&rcxres,sizeof(int),1,pf);
        fread(&rcyres,sizeof(int),1,pf);
        fread(&numslice,sizeof(int),1,pf);
        fread(&PSPX,sizeof(float),1,pf);
        fread(&PSPY,sizeof(float),1,pf);
        fread(&PSSZ,sizeof(float),1,pf);
        fread(&LabelData,sizeof(char),1,pf);
        /// label from file header of image file made with this GUI
        /// or Matlab program

        fread(&StdLabel,sizeof(char),1,pf);
        if (StdLabel=='Y')
        {
        fread(&Average,sizeof(float),1,pf);
        fread(&Std,sizeof(float),1,pf);

        } else if (StdLabel=='N') { }

        if ( LabelData =='C' )
        {

            unsigned char ReadNumber = 0;
            unsigned char valueToDiscard = 0;

        // read data and discard
        for(sl=1 ;sl<=numslice; sl++) {
            for(j=0;j<rcyres;j++){
                for(i=0;i<rcxres;i++){

        fread(&ReadNumber,sizeof(unsigned char),1,pf);
        valueToDiscard=(unsigned char)ReadNumber;
```

```
                                    }
                                }
                            }
    // read data and discard
    }

    else if ( LabelData =='S' )
    {
        short ReadNumber = 0;
        short valueToDiscard = 0;
    // read data and discard
    for(sl=1 ;sl<=numslice; sl++) {
        for(j=0;j<rcyres;j++){
            for(i=0;i<rcxres;i++){

    fread(&ReadNumber,sizeof(short),1,pf);
    valueToDiscard=(short)ReadNumber;

                                    }
                                }
                            }
    // read data and discard
    }
    else if ( LabelData =='I' )
    {
        int ReadNumber = 0;
        int valueToDiscard = 0;

    // read data and discard
    for(sl=1 ;sl<=numslice; sl++) {
        for(j=0;j<rcyres;j++){
            for(i=0;i<rcxres;i++){

    fread(&ReadNumber,sizeof(int),1,pf);
    valueToDiscard=(int)ReadNumber;

                                    }
                                }
                            }
    // read data and discard
    }
    else if ( LabelData =='F' )
    {
        float ReadNumber = 0;
        float valueToDiscard = 0;

    // read data and discard
    for(sl=1 ;sl<=numslice; sl++) {
        for(j=0;j<rcyres;j++){
            for(i=0;i<rcxres;i++){

    fread(&ReadNumber,sizeof(float),1,pf);
    valueToDiscard=(float)ReadNumber;

                                    }
                                }
```

```
                        }
// read data and discard
}

else if ( LabelData=='D' ) {

    double ReadNumber = 0;
    double valueToDiscard = 0;

// read data and discard
for(sl=1;sl<=numslice; sl++) {
    for(j=0;j<rcyres;j++){
        for(i=0;i<rcxres;i++){

fread(&ReadNumber,sizeof(double),1,pf);
valueToDiscard=(double)ReadNumber;

                        }
                    }
                }
// read data and discard
}

fclose(pf);

}// read header portion and data of the file

// allocate to 3D display
if ( numslice > 1 )
{/// memory allocation ///

pimage = (float *) malloc(rcyres*rcxres*3*sizeof(float));
simage = (float *) malloc(rcyres*numslice*3*sizeof(float));
cimage = (float *) malloc(rcxres*numslice*3*sizeof(float));

tEraseMemoryFlag = 0;

CString ViewMessage;
ViewMessage.Format("%s\n %s\n %s\n" , "Ready to Launch OpenGL Visualization" ,
                "to View Image, please remember to close" ,
                "the Window(s) before exiting the program.");
AfxMessageBox(ViewMessage);

}else{ // mismatch message //

CString ExitMessage;
ExitMessage.Format("%s\n %s\n %s\n %s\n" , "Mismatch Between the" ,
"Image Type and Diplay: " , "This is a Plane 2D Image" , "Now Exit");
AfxMessageBox(ExitMessage);
exit(0);

}/// mismatch message //
// end of allocate to 3D display

}
```

Computer Science Applications

The functions *void display(void)* and *void keyboard(unsigned char key, int x, int y)* are written similarly to those already seen in this manuscript for other OpenGL ®/Visual C++ ® projects. Specifically, the function *void keyboard(unsigned char key, int x, int y)* works with the pointers '*(pimage)*' (plane view), '*(simage)*' (sagittal view) and '*(cimage)*' (coronal view) to visualize 3D data with three composite 2D views. Like wise the pointers '*(simage)*' and '*(cimage)*', also in the case of the pointer '*(pimage)*', the following set of instructions [1] are employed in order (i) to draw the buffer, (ii) to set raster position, (iii) to zoom the pixel, (iv) to draw the pixel and (v) to flush the display:

- ✓ *glDrawBuffer(GL_FRONT)*
- ✓ *glRasterPos2i(0,0)*
- ✓ *glPixelZoom((GLfloat) PSPX, (GLfloat) PSPY)*
- ✓ *glDrawPixels((GLsizei)rcxres, (GLsizei)rcyres, GL_LUMINANCE, GL_FLOAT, pimage)*
- ✓ *glFlush()*

These instructions follow after the assignments '*(pimage + k3) = (GLfloat) *(Imagedata+k2)/255*', '*(pimage + k3*2) = (GLfloat) *(Imagedata+k2)/255*' and '*(pimage + k3*3) = (GLfloat) *(Imagedata+k2)/255*' given to set the pixel color in grey level scale. Worth mention that everytime the user hits one of the selected keys from the keyboard, either: 'U', 'D', 'L', 'R', 'F' or 'B', the structure comprising two *for* loops is updated along with the counter '*Slice*' ('*sagSlice*' for the sagittal view and '*corSlice*' for the coronal view) assigned to identify the slice number and so one slice is stored in the pointer such that it can be rendered to the image display. For instance, in the case 'U' is hit from the keyboard, the following lines of code will store one slice in '*(pimage)*'.

- ✓ *Slice++*

- ✓ *for(j=0; j<rcyres; j++){*

- ✓ *for(i=0; i<rcxres; i++){*

- ✓ *k2=(j*rcxres+i)+((Slice-1)*rcyres*rcxres);*

- ✓ *k3 = (j*rcxres+i);*

- ✓ **(pimage + k3) = (GLfloat) *(Imagedata+k2)/255;*

- ✓ **(pimage + k3*2) = (GLfloat) *(Imagedata+k2)/255;*

- ✓ **(pimage + k3*3) = (GLfloat) *(Imagedata+k2)/255;*

- ✓ *}*

- ✓ *}*

void display(void)

```
{
        glClear(GL_COLOR_BUFFER_BIT);
}
```

void keyboard(unsigned char key, int x, int y)

```
{

        int sl,j,i,k2,k3;
        // variables that are locally employed and are static within the scope of the method
        int rcxres;
        int rcyres;
        int numslice;
        // Above variables can be retrieved from file. The function
```

```
// keyboard(unsigned char key, int x, int y) is inside the scope
// of the user-application interaction and specifically
// this function runs within the glutMainLoop(). The value of
// the following variables can change because of the function:
// void reshape(int w, int h)

float PSCZ;
float PSSZ;

float PSSY;
float PSPY;

float PSPX;
float PSCX;

/// read the keyboard matrix resolution///
FILE * pointToKeyboardFile;
char keyboard[128]="keyboard.txt";

if ((pointToKeyboardFile = fopen(keyboard,"r"))==NULL)
{

CString ExitMessage;
ExitMessage.Format("%s\n" , "Cannot Open File: keyboard.txt: Exit" );
AfxMessageBox(ExitMessage);
exit(0);

}else{

fscanf(pointToKeyboardFile,"%d\n", &numslice);
fscanf(pointToKeyboardFile,"%d\n", &rcxres);
fscanf(pointToKeyboardFile,"%d\n", &rcyres);
fscanf(pointToKeyboardFile,"%f\n", &PSPX);
fscanf(pointToKeyboardFile,"%f\n", &PSPY);
fscanf(pointToKeyboardFile,"%f\n", &PSSZ);

//// initialize variables: PSCZ, PSSY, PSCX
PSCZ = (float)PSSZ;
PSSY = (float)PSPY;
PSCX = (float)PSPX;

fclose(pointToKeyboardFile);

}

key=toupper(key);
if(glutGetWindow() == pw)
{
switch(key){

case 'U':
if( (Slice>=0)&&(Slice<numslice) )
{
Slice++;
for(j=0;j<rcyres;j++){
    for(i=0;i<rcxres;i++){
```

```
k2=(j*rcxres+i)+((Slice-1)*rcyres*rcxres);
k3 = (j*rcxres+i);

*(pimage + k3)   = (GLfloat) *(Imagedata+k2)/255;
*(pimage + k3*2) = (GLfloat) *(Imagedata+k2)/255;
*(pimage + k3*3) = (GLfloat) *(Imagedata+k2)/255;

                            }
                        }

glDrawBuffer(GL_FRONT);
glRasterPos2i(0,0);
glPixelZoom((GLfloat) PSPX, (GLfloat) PSPY);
glDrawPixels((GLsizei)rcxres, (GLsizei)rcyres, GL_LUMINANCE, GL_FLOAT, pimage);
glFlush();

}
break;

case 'D':
if( (Slice>1)&&(Slice<=numslice) )
{
Slice--;

for(j=0;j<rcyres;j++){
    for(i=0;i<rcxres;i++){

    k2=(j*rcxres+i)+((Slice-1)*rcyres*rcxres);
    k3 = (j*rcxres+i);

*(pimage + k3)   = (GLfloat) *(Imagedata+k2)/255;
*(pimage + k3*2) = (GLfloat) *(Imagedata+k2)/255;
*(pimage + k3*3) = (GLfloat) *(Imagedata+k2)/255;

                            }
                        }

glDrawBuffer(GL_FRONT);
glRasterPos2i(0,0);
glPixelZoom((GLfloat) PSPX, (GLfloat) PSPY);
glDrawPixels((GLsizei)rcxres, (GLsizei)rcyres, GL_LUMINANCE, GL_FLOAT, pimage);
glFlush();

}
break;

default:
break;

}///switch
}///if

if(glutGetWindow() == sw)
{
```

228

```
switch(key){
case 'L':
if( (sagSlice>=-1)&&(sagSlice<rcxres-1) )
{
sagSlice++;

for(sl=1;sl<=numslice; sl++) {
    for(j=0;j<rcyres;j++){

    k2=(j*rcxres+sagSlice)+((sl-1)*rcyres*rcxres);
    k3 = ((sl-1)*rcyres+j);

*(simage + k3)   = (GLfloat) *(Imagedata+k2)/255;
*(simage + k3*2) = (GLfloat) *(Imagedata+k2)/255;
*(simage + k3*3) = (GLfloat) *(Imagedata+k2)/255;

                            }
                        }

glDrawBuffer(GL_FRONT);
glRasterPos2i(0,0);
glPixelZoom((GLfloat) PSSY, (GLfloat) PSSZ);
glDrawPixels((GLsizei)rcyres, (GLsizei)numslice, GL_LUMINANCE, GL_FLOAT, simage);
glFlush();

}
break;

case 'R':

if( (sagSlice>0)&&(sagSlice<=rcxres-1) )
{
sagSlice--;

for(sl=1;sl<=numslice; sl++) {
    for(j=0;j<rcyres;j++){

    k2=(j*rcxres+sagSlice)+((sl-1)*rcyres*rcxres);
    k3 = ((sl-1)*rcyres+j);

    *(simage + k3)   = (GLfloat) *(Imagedata+k2)/255;
    *(simage + k3*2) = (GLfloat) *(Imagedata+k2)/255;
    *(simage + k3*3) = (GLfloat) *(Imagedata+k2)/255;

                            }
                        }

glDrawBuffer(GL_FRONT);
glRasterPos2i(0,0);
glPixelZoom((GLfloat) PSSY, (GLfloat) PSSZ);
glDrawPixels((GLsizei)rcyres, (GLsizei)numslice, GL_LUMINANCE, GL_FLOAT, simage);
glFlush();

}
break;
```

```
default:
break;

}///switch

}///if

if(glutGetWindow() == cw)
{

switch(key){

case 'F':
if( (corSlice>=-1)&&(corSlice<rcyres-1) )
{
corSlice++;

for(sl=1;sl<=numslice; sl++) {
    for(i=0;i<rcxres;i++){

    k2=(corSlice*rcxres+i)+((sl-1)*rcyres*rcxres);
    k3 = ((sl-1)*rcxres+i);

    *(cimage + k3)   = (GLfloat) *(Imagedata+k2)/255;
    *(cimage + k3*2) = (GLfloat) *(Imagedata+k2)/255;
    *(cimage + k3*3) = (GLfloat) *(Imagedata+k2)/255;

                            }
                        }

glDrawBuffer(GL_FRONT);
glRasterPos2i(0,0);
glPixelZoom((GLfloat) PSCX, (GLfloat) PSCZ);
glDrawPixels((GLsizei)rcxres, (GLsizei)numslice, GL_LUMINANCE, GL_FLOAT, cimage);
glFlush();
}

break;
case 'B':
if( (corSlice>0)&&(corSlice<=rcyres-1) )
{
corSlice--;

for(sl=1;sl<=numslice; sl++) {
    for(i=0;i<rcxres;i++){

    k2=(corSlice*rcxres+i)+((sl-1)*rcyres*rcxres);
    k3 = ((sl-1)*rcxres+i);

    *(cimage + k3)   = (GLfloat) *(Imagedata+k2)/255;
    *(cimage + k3*2) = (GLfloat) *(Imagedata+k2)/255;
    *(cimage + k3*3) = (GLfloat) *(Imagedata+k2)/255;

                            }
                        }
```

```
glDrawBuffer(GL_FRONT);
glRasterPos2i(0,0);
glPixelZoom((GLfloat) PSCX, (GLfloat) PSCZ);
glDrawPixels((GLsizei)rcxres, (GLsizei)numslice, GL_LUMINANCE, GL_FLOAT, cimage);
glFlush();


    }
    break;

    default:
    break;
    }///switch
    }///if


}
```

The function *void reshape(int w, int h)* makes use of the I/O file *'keyboard.txt'* to read in the variables related to the image resolution at the beginning of its processing. The function's purpose is to size the pixel and accordingly to size the window. The pixel size is defined by the ratio between the current window size and the number of pixels. For instance, the instructions *'PSPX=((float)w/rcxres)'* and *'PSPY=((float)h/rcyres)'* define the pixel size *'PSPX'* (along X), *'PSPY'* (along Y) as the ratio between the window size *'w'* (along X), *'h'* (along Y), and the number of pixels *'rcxres'* (along X), *'rcyres'* (along Y). Everytime a window is re-sized, the following instructions [1] take place inside the function: (i) setting the viewport size (*'glViewport(0, 0, (GLsizei)w, (GLsizei)h)'*), (ii) loading the identity matrix (*'glLoadIdentity()'*), and (iii) setting the orthogonal 2D view size (*'gluOrtho2D(0.0, (GLdouble)w, 0.0, (GLdouble)h)'*). The function saves the values of the re-sized windows once the instructions: *'glutGetWindow() == planeWindow'* (plane window for 2D display), *'glutGetWindow() == pw'* (plane window for 3D display), *'glutGetWindow() == sw'* (sagittal window for 3D display) and *'glutGetWindow() == cw'* (coronal window for 3D display) identify the window which is being resized because of the user interaction during the OpenGL ® interactive graphics event. The instructions needed to identify the current interactive graphic event are:

- ✓ *if(glutGetWindow() == planeWindow) {*

- ✓ *PSPX=((float)w/rcxres);*
- ✓ *PSPY=((float)h/rcyres);*

- ✓ *}*

- ✓ *if(glutGetWindow() == pw) {*

- ✓ *PSPX=((float)w/rcxres);*
- ✓ *PSPY=((float)h/rcyres);*

- ✓ *}*

- ✓ *if(glutGetWindow() == sw) {*

- ✓ *PSSY=((float)w/rcyres);*
- ✓ *PSSZ=((float)h/numslice);*

- ✓ *}*
- ✓ *if(glutGetWindow() == cw) {*

- ✓ *PSCX=((float)w/rcxres);*
- ✓ *PSCZ=((float)h/numslice);*

- ✓ *}*

Computer Science Applications

Whereas, the instructions needed to save the values of the re-sized windows are:

- ✓ *if(glutGetWindow() == planeWindow) {*

- ✓ *fprintf(pointToKeyboardFile,"%f\n", PSPX);*
- ✓ *fprintf(pointToKeyboardFile,"%f\n", PSPY);*
- ✓ *fprintf(pointToKeyboardFile,"%f\n", valueZ);*

- ✓ *}*

- ✓ *if(glutGetWindow() == pw) {*

- ✓ *fprintf(pointToKeyboardFile,"%f\n", PSPX);*
- ✓ *fprintf(pointToKeyboardFile,"%f\n", PSPY);*
- ✓ *fprintf(pointToKeyboardFile,"%f\n", valueZ);*

- ✓ *}*

- ✓ *if(glutGetWindow() == sw) {*

- ✓ *fprintf(pointToKeyboardFile,"%f\n", valueX);*
- ✓ *fprintf(pointToKeyboardFile,"%f\n", PSSY);*
- ✓ *fprintf(pointToKeyboardFile,"%f\n", PSSZ);*

- ✓ *}*

- ✓ *if(glutGetWindow() == cw) {*

- ✓ *fprintf(pointToKeyboardFile,"%f\n", PSCX);*
- ✓ *fprintf(pointToKeyboardFile,"%f\n", valueY);*
- ✓ *fprintf(pointToKeyboardFile,"%f\n", PSCZ);*

- ✓ *}*

```
void reshape(int w, int h)
{

        static int rcxres;
        static int rcyres;
        static int numslice;

        float valueX = 0, valueY = 0, valueZ = 0;
        /// read the keyboard matrix resolution///
        FILE * pointToKeyboardFile;
        char keyboardFile[128]="keyboard.txt";
        if ((pointToKeyboardFile = fopen(keyboardFile,"r"))==NULL)
        {
        CString ExitMessage;
        ExitMessage.Format("%s\n" , "Cannot Open File: keyboard.txt: Exit" );
        AfxMessageBox(ExitMessage);
        exit(0);
        }else{

        fscanf(pointToKeyboardFile,"%d\n", &numslice);
        fscanf(pointToKeyboardFile,"%d\n", &rcxres);
```

```
fscanf(pointToKeyboardFile,"%d\n", &rcyres);
fscanf(pointToKeyboardFile,"%f\n", &valueX);
fscanf(pointToKeyboardFile,"%f\n", &valueY);
fscanf(pointToKeyboardFile,"%f\n", &valueZ);
fclose(pointToKeyboardFile);

}


//// initialize variables: PSPX, PSPY, PSSZ
float PSPX = (float)valueX;
float PSPY = (float)valueY;
float PSSZ = (float)valueZ;
////                              ////
float PSCX, PSCZ, PSSY;

glViewport(0, 0, (GLsizei)w, (GLsizei)h);
glLoadIdentity();
gluOrtho2D(0.0, (GLdouble)w, 0.0, (GLdouble)h);

if(glutGetWindow() == planeWindow)
{
    PSPX=((float)w/rcxres);
    PSPY=((float)h/rcyres);
}
if(glutGetWindow() == pw)
{
    PSPX=((float)w/rcxres);
    PSPY=((float)h/rcyres);
}
if(glutGetWindow() == sw)
{
    PSSY=((float)w/rcyres);
    PSSZ=((float)h/numslice);
}
if(glutGetWindow() == cw)
{
    PSCX=((float)w/rcxres);
    PSCZ=((float)h/numslice);
}
// Once the windows' size is changed:
// re-write keyboard.txt containing the modified values of
// the variables: float PSPX; float PSPY; float PSSZ;

if ((pointToKeyboardFile = fopen(keyboardFile,"w"))==NULL)
{
CString ExitMessage;
ExitMessage.Format("%s\n" , "Cannot Open File: keyboard.txt: Exit" );
AfxMessageBox(ExitMessage);
exit(0);

}else{

fprintf(pointToKeyboardFile,"%d\n", numslice);
fprintf(pointToKeyboardFile,"%d\n", rcxres);
fprintf(pointToKeyboardFile,"%d\n", rcyres);
```

```
    if(glutGetWindow() == planeWindow)
    {

        fprintf(pointToKeyboardFile,"%f\n", PSPX);
        fprintf(pointToKeyboardFile,"%f\n", PSPY);
        fprintf(pointToKeyboardFile,"%f\n", valueZ);
    }
    if(glutGetWindow() == pw)
    {

        fprintf(pointToKeyboardFile,"%f\n", PSPX);
        fprintf(pointToKeyboardFile,"%f\n", PSPY);
        fprintf(pointToKeyboardFile,"%f\n", valueZ);
    }
    if(glutGetWindow() == sw)
    {

        fprintf(pointToKeyboardFile,"%f\n", valueX);
        fprintf(pointToKeyboardFile,"%f\n", PSSY);
        fprintf(pointToKeyboardFile,"%f\n", PSSZ);
    }
    if(glutGetWindow() == cw)
    {

        fprintf(pointToKeyboardFile,"%f\n", PSCX);
        fprintf(pointToKeyboardFile,"%f\n", valueY);
        fprintf(pointToKeyboardFile,"%f\n", PSCZ);
    }
    fclose(pointToKeyboardFile);
    }


}
```

The method *float * CImageToolDlg::data(char filename[])* is used regardless as to if the data to visualize is a 2D image or a 3D volume. The method *float * CImageToolDlg::data(char filename[])* uses the constructor *'ImageToolVariables(0, 0)'* to set the variables related to the resolution of the image data, specifically the number of pixels and the pixels' size. Also, the method *float * CImageToolDlg::data(char filename[])* uses the object called *'access'* of type *'ImageToolVariables'* to assign the variables' values. The instructions are:

- ✓ *ImageToolVariables(0, 0);*

- ✓ *int rcxres = access.Applicrcxres;*
- ✓ *int rcyres = access.Applicrcyres;*
- ✓ *int numslice = access.Applicnumslice;*

- ✓ *float PSCZ = access.ApplicPSCZ;*
- ✓ *float PSSZ = access.ApplicPSSZ;*

- ✓ *float PSSY = access.ApplicPSSY;*
- ✓ *float PSPY = access.ApplicPSPY;*
- ✓ *float PSPX = access.ApplicPSPX;*
- ✓ *float PSCX = access.ApplicPSCX;*

The method reads in the resolution information from the header portion of the file along with the variables *'StdLabel'* and *'dataLabel'*. The method saves two text files named *'keyboard2D.txt'* (2D) and *'keyboard.txt'* (3D), each containing the resolution parameters, specifically the number of pixels in each of the three directions X, Y and Z, and the relevant pixel sizes. These variables are read from the header portion of the file containing the image data. Image data is read in in one of the formats specified in the header: *'CHAR'*, *'INT'*, *'SHORT'*, *'FLOAT'* or *'DOUBLE'*. The value of the variable *'datatype'* is determined on the basis of the value of the variable *'dataLabel'*:

✓ *if (dataLabel=='C') sprintf(datatype, "%s", "CHAR");*
✓ *else if (dataLabel=='S') sprintf(datatype, "%s", "SHORT");*
✓ *else if (dataLabel=='I') sprintf(datatype, "%s", "INT");*
✓ *else if (dataLabel=='F') sprintf(datatype, "%s", "FLOAT");*
✓ *else if (dataLabel=='D') sprintf(datatype, "%s", "DOUBLE");*

Before reading in image data, the instruction '*pointer = (float *) calloc((numslice*rcyres*rcxres), sizeof(float))*' sets available a block of memory cells dynamically allocated. The float pointer '**(pointer)*' will be returned at the end of the routine for use inside the project. Image data are to be read in standardized format or non-standardized format. To this purpose the value of the variable '*StdLabel*' can be either 'Y' or 'N' which determine as to if is necessary to read the values of average and standard deviation in the header portion of the file. When data are read in, for instance in the case they are '*CHAR*' format, the following set of instructions is employed:

✓ *if(strcmp(datatype,"CHAR")==0) {*

✓ *for(sl=1; sl<=numslice; sl++) {*
✓ *for(j=0; j<rcyres; j++){*
✓ *for(i=0; i<rcxres; i++){*

✓ *fread(&number,sizeof(unsigned char),1,pf);*
✓ *k2=(j*rcxres+i)+((sl-1)*rcyres*rcxres);*
✓ **(pointer+k2)=(float)number;*

✓ *}*
✓ *}*
✓ *}*

✓ *fclose (pf);*

✓ *}*

If '*StdLabel == Y*', it also means that image data is stored in the binary file in standardized format, therefore data needs to be converted back to non standardized format:

✓ *if (StdLabel=='Y') {*

✓ *if (numslice > 1) {*

✓ *for(sl=2; sl<=numslice-1; sl++) {*
✓ *for(j=1; j<rcyres-1; j++){*
✓ *for(i=1; i<rcxres-1; i++){*

✓ *k2=(j*rcxres+i)+((sl-1)*rcyres*rcxres);*
✓ **(pointer+k2)= (*(pointer+k2) * Std) + Average;*

✓ *}*
✓ *}*
✓ *}*

✓ *}else if (numslice == 1){*

✓ *for(j=1; j<rcyres-1; j++){*
✓ *for(i=1; i<rcxres-1; i++){*

✓ *k2=(j*rcxres+i);*

235

✓   *(pointer+k2)= (*(pointer+k2) * Std) + Average;

✓   }
✓   }
✓   }

✓   }

Finally, image data is scaled inside the range [0, 255] with the following instructions:

✓   max=-5000000000000000000;
✓   min=5000000000000000000;

✓   for(i=0; i<rcxres*rcyres*numslice; i++){

✓   if(*(pointer+i)>max) max = *(pointer+i);

✓   if(*(pointer+i)<min) min = *(pointer+i);

✓   }

✓   for(sl=1; sl<=numslice; sl++) {
✓   for(j=0; j<rcyres; j++) {
✓   for(i=0; i<rcxres; i++) {

✓   k2=(j*rcxres+i)+((sl-1)*rcyres*rcxres);
✓   if (max == min)
✓   *(pointer+k2) = (float) max;
✓   else *(pointer+k2) = (float) 255 * ((float)*(pointer+k2)-min) / ((float)max-min) ;

✓   }
✓   }
✓   }

float * CImageToolDlg::data(char filename[])
{

      UpdateData(true);

      // constructor call
      ImageToolVariables(0, 0);

      /// variables that belongs to Class ImageToolVariables
      /// and that are employed within the
      /// scope of the local method
      int rcxres = access.Applicrcxres;
      int rcyres = access.Applicrcyres;
      int numslice = access.Applicnumslice;

      float PSCZ = access.ApplicPSCZ;
      float PSSZ = access.ApplicPSSZ;

      float PSSY = access.ApplicPSSY;
      float PSPY = access.ApplicPSPY;

```
float PSPX = access.ApplicPSPX;
float PSCX = access.ApplicPSCX;

FILE *pf;
int sl,j,i,k2;
unsigned char number = 0;
short number1 = 0;
int number2 = 0;
float number3 = 0;
double number4 = 0.0;
float *pointer = 0;
double max, min;

char dataLabel = ' ';
char StdLabel = ' ';
/// this variable is read from and saved to
/// image files' header created with Matlab programs and
/// or this Visual C++ Application (such as for instance
/// the routine called OnCreatetheCube)
float Std = 0, Average = 0;
char logfilename[128];
sprintf(logfilename, "%s%s%s", "ImageTool", m_VolumeFileName, ".log");

if ((logfile = fopen(logfilename,"w"))==NULL)
{
exit(0);
}

if ((pf = fopen(filename,"rb+"))==NULL)
{
    fprintf(logfile,"%s%s\n", "Cannot open file: " , filename );
    exit(1);
}else{   // read header portion of the file
        // and display and save in file keadboard.txt what has been read

fread(&rcxres,sizeof(int),1,pf);
fread(&rcyres,sizeof(int),1,pf);
fread(&numslice,sizeof(int),1,pf);
fread(&PSPX,sizeof(float),1,pf);
fread(&PSPY,sizeof(float),1,pf);
fread(&PSSZ,sizeof(float),1,pf);
fread(&dataLabel,sizeof(char),1,pf);
fread(&StdLabel,sizeof(char),1,pf);
/// label from file header of image file made with this GUI
/// or Matlab program

//// initialize variables: PSCZ, PSSY, PSCX
PSCZ = (float)PSSZ;
PSSY = (float)PSPY;
PSCX = (float)PSPX;
if (StdLabel=='Y')
{

fread(&Average,sizeof(float),1,pf);
fread(&Std,sizeof(float),1,pf);
// data is assumed to be standardized
```

```
// and so converted back to non standardized numbers only if
// the numbers' format is either float or double
} else if (StdLabel=='N') { }

     if ( dataLabel=='C' ) sprintf(datatype, "%s", "CHAR");
else if ( dataLabel=='S' ) sprintf(datatype, "%s", "SHORT");
else if ( dataLabel=='I' ) sprintf(datatype, "%s", "INT");
else if ( dataLabel=='F' ) sprintf(datatype, "%s", "FLOAT");
else if ( dataLabel=='D' ) sprintf(datatype, "%s", "DOUBLE");

FILE * pointToKeyboardFile;

/// make the keyboard.txt file ///
char keyboard[128]="keyboard.txt";
if ((pointToKeyboardFile = fopen(keyboard,"w"))==NULL)
{
CString ExitMessage;
ExitMessage.Format("%s\n" , "Cannot Open File: keyboard.txt: Exit" );
MessageBox(ExitMessage);
exit(0);
}else{
fprintf(pointToKeyboardFile,"%d\n", numslice);
fprintf(pointToKeyboardFile,"%d\n", rcxres);
fprintf(pointToKeyboardFile,"%d\n", rcyres);
fprintf(pointToKeyboardFile,"%f\n", PSPX);
fprintf(pointToKeyboardFile,"%f\n", PSPY);
fprintf(pointToKeyboardFile,"%f\n", PSSZ);
fclose(pointToKeyboardFile);
}
/// make the keyboard.txt file ///

/// make the keyboard2D.txt file ///
char keyboard2D[128]="keyboard2D.txt";
if ((pointToKeyboardFile = fopen(keyboard2D,"w"))==NULL)
{
CString ExitMessage;
ExitMessage.Format("%s\n" , "Cannot Open File: keyboard2D.txt: Exit" );
MessageBox(ExitMessage);
exit(0);

}else{
int oneSlice = 1;
fprintf(pointToKeyboardFile,"%d\n", oneSlice);
fprintf(pointToKeyboardFile,"%d\n", rcxres);
fprintf(pointToKeyboardFile,"%d\n", rcyres);
fprintf(pointToKeyboardFile,"%f\n", PSPX);
fprintf(pointToKeyboardFile,"%f\n", PSPY);
fprintf(pointToKeyboardFile,"%f\n", PSSZ);
fclose(pointToKeyboardFile);
}

/// make the keyboard2D.txt file ///
fprintf(logfile,"%s\t %s\n", "Processing the Image: ", m_VolumeFileName);
fprintf(logfile,"%s\t %d\n", "Number of Slices: ", numslice);
fprintf(logfile,"%s\t %d\n", "X Matrix Resolution: ", rcxres);
fprintf(logfile,"%s\t %d\n", "Y Matrix Resolution: ", rcyres);
```

```
fprintf(logfile,"%s\t %f\n", "X Pixel Size: ", PSPX);
fprintf(logfile,"%s\t %f\n", "Y Pixel Size: ", PSPY);
fprintf(logfile,"%s\t %f\n", "Z Pixel Size: ", PSSZ);
fprintf(logfile,"%s\t %s\n", "Data Type: ", datatype);


}// read header portion of the file
// and display and save in file keadboard what has been read


/// allocate memory
if ((pointer = (float *) calloc( (numslice*rcyres*rcxres), sizeof(float)) ) == NULL)
{
fprintf(logfile,"%s\n", "Not enough memory to allocate Image data");
exit(0);
}
/// allocate memory
/// read data in
if(strcmp(datatype,"CHAR")==0)
{ // if
for(sl=1;sl<=numslice; sl++) {
     for(j=0;j<rcyres;j++){
          for(i=0;i<rcxres;i++){

fread(&number,sizeof(unsigned char),1,pf);
k2=(j*rcxres+i)+((sl-1)*rcyres*rcxres);
*(pointer+k2)=(float)number;


               }
          }
     }
fclose (pf);
}else if(strcmp(datatype,"SHORT")==0)
{
for(sl=1;sl<=numslice; sl++) {
     for(j=0;j<rcyres;j++){
          for(i=0;i<rcxres;i++){

fread(&number1,sizeof(short),1,pf);
k2=(j*rcxres+i)+((sl-1)*rcyres*rcxres);
*(pointer+k2)=(float)number1;
               }
          }
     }
fclose (pf);
}else if(strcmp(datatype,"INT")==0)
{
for(sl=1;sl<=numslice; sl++) {
     for(j=0;j<rcyres;j++){
          for(i=0;i<rcxres;i++){

fread(&number2,sizeof(int),1,pf);
k2=(j*rcxres+i)+((sl-1)*rcyres*rcxres);
*(pointer+k2)=(float)number2;


               }
          }
     }
```

Computer Science Applications

```
fclose (pf);
}else if(strcmp(datatype,"FLOAT")==0)
{
for(sl=1;sl<=numslice; sl++) {
    for(j=0;j<rcyres;j++){
        for(i=0;i<rcxres;i++){

fread(&number3,sizeof(float),1,pf);
k2=(j*rcxres+i)+((sl-1)*rcyres*rcxres);
*(pointer+k2)=(float)number3;

                    }
                }
            }
fclose (pf);
}else if(strcmp(datatype,"DOUBLE")==0)
{
for(sl=1;sl<=numslice; sl++) {
    for(j=0;j<rcyres;j++){
        for(i=0;i<rcxres;i++){

fread(&number4,sizeof(double),1,pf);
k2=(j*rcxres+i)+((sl-1)*rcyres*rcxres);
*(pointer+k2) = (float)number4;

                    }
                }
            }
fclose (pf);
} // else if
/// read data in

if (StdLabel=='Y')
{   // data is assumed to be standardized
    // and so convert back to non standardized numbers
if ( numslice > 1 )
{
    for(sl=2;sl<=numslice-1; sl++) {
        for(j=1;j<rcyres-1;j++){
            for(i=1;i<rcxres-1;i++){

        k2=(j*rcxres+i)+((sl-1)*rcyres*rcxres);
        *(pointer+k2)= (*(pointer+k2) * Std ) + Average;

                    }
                }
            }

}else if ( numslice == 1 ){
        for(j=1;j<rcyres-1;j++){
            for(i=1;i<rcxres-1;i++){

        k2=(j*rcxres+i);
        *(pointer+k2)= (*(pointer+k2) * Std ) + Average;

                    }
```

240

```
                              }
                         }

  }    // data is assumed to be standardized
// and so convert back to non standardized numbers
     /// compute max and min of data
     max=-5000000000000000000;
     min=5000000000000000000;

     for(i=0;i<rcxres*rcyres*numslice;i++){

     if( *(pointer+i)>max ) max = *(pointer+i);

     if( *(pointer+i)<min ) min = *(pointer+i);

                              }

/// convert data into scale [0, 255] ///
for(sl=1;sl<=numslice; sl++) {
     for(j=0;j<rcyres;j++){
          for(i=0;i<rcxres;i++){

     k2=(j*rcxres+i)+((sl-1)*rcyres*rcxres);
     if (max == min)
     *(pointer+k2) = (float) max;
     else
     *(pointer+k2) = (float) 255 * ((float)*(pointer+k2)-min) / ((float)max-min) ;

                    }
               }
          }

     fprintf(logfile,"%s\n", "IMAGE DATA LOADED AND CONVERTED");
     return(pointer);

}
```

The function *void TwoDdisplay(void)* is dedicated to the display of two dimensional data. The tasks performed through this function are mainly two. One task is that of reading the resolution information from the I/O file called *'keyboard.txt'*, and the other task is that of setting up the OpenGL ® display.

In order to do so, the function takes advantage of the pointer called *'*(planeWindowImage)'*, which is the recipient of the pointer *'*(TwoDdata)'*, which is dynamically allocated from the method *float * CImageToolDlg::data(char filename[])*. The pointer *'*(planeWindowImage)'* is set globally visible. The instructions employed to fill in the memory cells of the pointer *'*(TwoDdata)'* and to prepare the display with OpenGL ® are:

✓ *glClear(GL_COLOR_BUFFER_BIT);*

✓ *if(glutGetWindow() == planeWindow) {*

✓ *for(j=0; j<rcyres; j++) {*
✓ *for(i=0; i<rcxres; i++) {*

✓ *k3 = (j*rcxres+i);*

✓ **(planeWindowImage + k3) = (GLfloat) *(TwoDdata+k3)/255;*

Computer Science Applications

- ✓ *(planeWindowImage + k3*2) = (GLfloat) *(TwoDdata+k3)/255;*
- ✓ *(planeWindowImage + k3*3) = (GLfloat) *(TwoDdata+k3)/255;*

- ✓ }
- ✓ }

- ✓ *glDrawBuffer(GL_FRONT);*
- ✓ *glRasterPos2i(0,0);*
- ✓ *glPixelZoom((GLfloat) PSPX, (GLfloat) PSPY);*
- ✓ *glDrawPixels((GLsizei)rcxres, (GLsizei)rcyres, GL_LUMINANCE, GL_FLOAT, planeWindowImage);*
- ✓ *glFlush();*

- ✓ }

The pointer '**(planeWindowImage)*' was previously allocated as recipient of memory through the use of '*malloc*' from the method *void CImageToolDlg::AllocateMemoryforOpenGLGraphics2D()*. When employed in the function *void TwoDdisplay(void)*, the pointer '**(planeWindowImage)*' is set to be sent to display. This is possible because the function *void TwoDdisplay(void)* is used inside the OpenGL ® main loop in the method *void CImageToolDlg::LaunchOpenGL()*.

void TwoDdisplay(void)
```
{

        // variables that are locally employed and are static within
        // the scope of the method
        int i, j, k3;
        // Variables can be retrieved from file: "keyboard.txt".
        int rcxres;
        int rcyres;
        // The function: keyboard(unsigned char key, int x, int y) is not active
        // inside the scope of the user-application interaction
        // while displaying 2D images. Specifically: void TwoDdisplay(void) runs within the glutMainLoop().
        float PSPY;
        float PSPX;
        // these two variables are not relevant to the scope of the function however read from file "keyboard.txt"
        int numslice;
        float PSSZ;
        /// now read the keyboard matrix resolution///
        FILE * pointToKeyboardFile;
        char keyboard[128]="keyboard.txt";
        if ((pointToKeyboardFile = fopen(keyboard,"r"))==NULL)
        {
        CString ExitMessage;
        ExitMessage.Format("%s\n" , "Cannot Open File: keyboard.txt: Exit" );
        AfxMessageBox(ExitMessage);
        exit(0);
        }else{

        fscanf(pointToKeyboardFile,"%d\n", &numslice);
        fscanf(pointToKeyboardFile,"%d\n", &rcxres);
        fscanf(pointToKeyboardFile,"%d\n", &rcyres);
        fscanf(pointToKeyboardFile,"%f\n", &PSPX);
        fscanf(pointToKeyboardFile,"%f\n", &PSPY);
        fscanf(pointToKeyboardFile,"%f\n", &PSSZ);
        fclose(pointToKeyboardFile);
```

```
        }
        glClear(GL_COLOR_BUFFER_BIT);

        if(glutGetWindow() == planeWindow)
        {
            for(j=0;j<rcyres;j++){
                for(i=0;i<rcxres;i++){

                    k3 = (j*rcxres + i);
                    *(planeWindowImage + k3)   = (GLfloat) *(TwoDdata+k3)/255;
                    *(planeWindowImage + k3*2) = (GLfloat) *(TwoDdata+k3)/255;
                    *(planeWindowImage + k3*3) = (GLfloat) *(TwoDdata+k3)/255;


                                }
                    }

        glDrawBuffer(GL_FRONT);
        glRasterPos2i(0,0);
        glPixelZoom((GLfloat) PSPX, (GLfloat) PSPY);
        glDrawPixels((GLsizei)rcxres, (GLsizei)rcyres, GL_LUMINANCE, GL_FLOAT, planeWindowImage);
        glFlush();

        }


}
```

The method *void CImageToolDlg::OnCreatetheCube()* performs the main task of creating through randomization the 3D volume and the 2D slice of chaotic data. The method takes as input from the GUI the edge of the cube (*'m_VolumeSize'*), which is also the size of the edge of square 2D slice, and also the pixel's size in the three directions X (*'m_PSizeX'*), Y (*'m_PSizeY'*) and Z (*'m_PSizeZ'*). The instruction *'pointer = (float *) calloc((Cubenum-slice*Cubercyres*Cubercxres), sizeof(float))'* sets available a memory block to contain the image data. Data is initialized with zero values at the beginning of the routine and subsequently the randomization makes the image data:

- ✓ *for(sl=1; sl<=Cubenumslice; sl++) {*
- ✓ *for(j=0; j<Cubercyres; j++) {*
- ✓ *for(i=0; i<Cubercxres; i++) {*
- ✓ *k2=(j*Cubercxres+i)+((sl-1)*Cubercyres*Cubercxres);*
- ✓ **(pointer+k2)=(float)0;*
- ✓ *}*
- ✓ *}*
- ✓ *}*

- ✓ *float chaos = 0;*

- ✓ *for(sl=2; sl<=Cubenumslice-1; sl++) {*
- ✓ *for(j=1; j<Cubercyres-1; j++) {*
- ✓ *for(i=1; i<Cubercxres-1; i++) {*

- ✓ *k2=(j*Cubercxres+i)+((sl-1)*Cubercyres*Cubercxres);*
- ✓ *chaos = (float)rand();*
- ✓ **(pointer+k2)=(float)chaos;*

- ✓ *}*
- ✓ *}*
- ✓ *}*

Computer Science Applications

- ✓ *fprintf(logfile, "%os\n" ,"The cube and the slice are loaded in memory");*

The method *void CImageToolDlg::OnCreatetheCube()* is programmed to determine from the check box of the panel called *'Create Image Data'* as to if the image data has to be standardized or not. In the former case the variable *'m_StdLabel'* is assigned the value *'TRUE'*, in the latter case the variable *'m_StdLabel'* is assigned the value *'FALSE'*. The lines of code are written in such way that the first slice and last slice of the stack are left with null values, and so are the four edges of each slice. The instructions employed to standardize the image data are:

- ✓ *if (m_StdLabel==TRUE) {*

- ✓ *fprintf(logfile, "%os\n" ,"Now Calculating Average and Standard Deviation of Data");*

- ✓ *StdLabel = 'Y';*

- ✓ *Average = 0;*
- ✓ *Average2D = 0;*

- ✓ *for(sl=2; sl<=Cubenumslice-1; sl++) {*
- ✓ *for(j=1; j<Cubercyres-1; j++) {*
- ✓ *for(i=1; i<Cubercxres-1; i++) {*

- ✓ *k2=(j*Cubercxres+i)+((sl-1)*Cubercyres*Cubercxres);*
- ✓ *Average = ((float)Average) + ((float)*(pointer+k2));*

- ✓ *}*
- ✓ *}*

- ✓ *if (sl == 2) Average2D = (float)Average / ((float) (Cubercyres-2) * (Cubercxres-2));*

- ✓ *}*

- ✓ *Average = (float) Average / ((float) (Cubenumslice-2) * (Cubercyres-2) * (Cubercxres-2));*

- ✓ *Std = 0;*
- ✓ *Std2D = 0;*

- ✓ *for(sl=2; sl<=Cubenumslice-1; sl++) {*
- ✓ *for(j=1; j<Cubercyres-1; j++) {*
- ✓ *for(i=1; i<Cubercxres-1; i++) {*

- ✓ *k2=(j*Cubercxres+i)+((sl-1)*Cubercyres*Cubercxres);*

- ✓ *Std = (float)Std + ((float) (Average - *(pointer+k2)) * (Average - *(pointer+k2)));*

- ✓ *}*
- ✓ *}*
- ✓ *}*

- ✓ *for(j=1; j<Cubercyres-1; j++) {*
- ✓ *for(i=1; i<Cubercxres-1; i++) {*

- ✓ *sl = 2;*
- ✓ *k2=(j*Cubercxres+i)+((sl-1)*Cubercyres*Cubercxres);*

- ✓ *Std2D = (float)Std2D + ((float) (Average2D - *(pointer+k2)) * (Average2D - *(pointer+k2)));*

244

- ✓ }
- ✓ }

- ✓ *Std = (float) sqrt((double) Std / ((float) (Cubenumslice-2) * (Cubercyres-2) * (Cubercxres-2)));*

- ✓ *Std2D = (float) sqrt((double) Std2D / ((float) (Cubercyres-2) * (Cubercxres-2)));*

- ✓ *for(sl=2; sl<=Cubenumslice-1; sl++) {*
- ✓ *for(j=1; j<Cubercyres-1; j++) {*
- ✓ *for(i=1; i<Cubercxres-1; i++) {*

- ✓ *k2=(j*Cubercxres+i)+((sl-1)*Cubercyres*Cubercxres);*

- ✓ **(pointer+k2) = (((float)*(pointer+k2) - (float)Average) / (float)Std;*

- ✓ }
- ✓ }
- ✓ }

- ✓ *fprintf(logfile, "%s\n" ,"CUBE:");*
- ✓ *fprintf(logfile, "%s%f\n" ,"Average: ", Average);*
- ✓ *fprintf(logfile, "%s%f\n" ,"Standard Deviation: ", Std);*

- ✓ *fprintf(logfile, "%s\n" ,"SLICE:");*
- ✓ *fprintf(logfile, "%s%f\n" ,"Average: ", Average2D);*
- ✓ *fprintf(logfile, "%s%f\n" ,"Standard Deviation: ", Std2D);*

- ✓ }

The method *void CImageToolDlg::OnCreatetheCube()* is programmed to find the center of mass of the 3D data volume:

- ✓ *double max=-5000000000000000000;*
- ✓ *double min=5000000000000000000;*

- ✓ *for(i=0; i<Cubercxres*Cubercyres*Cubenumslice; i++) {*

- ✓ *if(*(pointer+i) > max) max = *(pointer+i);*
- ✓ *if(*(pointer+i) < min) min = *(pointer+i);*

- ✓ }

- ✓ *if (max != 0) {*

- ✓ *for(sl=1; sl<=Cubenumslice; sl++) {*
- ✓ *for(j=0; j<Cubercyres; j++) {*
- ✓ *for(i=0; i<Cubercxres; i++) {*

- ✓ *k2=(j*Cubercxres+i)+((sl-1)*Cubercyres*Cubercxres);*

- ✓ *count += ((double) fabs((double)*(pointer+k2)/ max));*

- ✓ *sumi = sumi + ((double)i * ((double) fabs((double)*(pointer+k2)) / max));*
- ✓ *sumj = sumj + ((double)j * ((double) fabs((double)*(pointer+k2)) / max));*
- ✓ *sumsl = sumsl + (((double)sl-1) * ((double) fabs((double)*(pointer+k2)) / max));*

- ✓ }
- ✓ }
- ✓ }

- ✓ $comx = ((double)sumi / count);$
- ✓ $comy = ((double)sumj / count);$
- ✓ $comz = ((double)sumsl / count);$
- ✓ }

In either case '$m\_StdLabel == TRUE$' or '$m\_StdLabel == FALSE$', the value of the variable '$m\_StdLabel$' is saved in the header portion of the file, and if the data has been standardized the header will also contain the average and standard deviation of the data. Also, regardless to the value of the variable $m\_StdLabel$ ('$TRUE$' or '$FALSE$'), the method is programmed to save 3D data and 2D data in two separate binary files along with the header information. The format of the output data is '$FLOAT$' given that the variable '$dataLabel$' is assigned the value 'F'. The instructions are:

- ✓ *float savedata;*
- ✓ *char dataLabel = 'F';*

- ✓ *fprintf(logfile, "%os%os\n", "Now Saving File: ", filename);*
- ✓ *if ((pf = fopen(filename,"wb+"))==NULL) {*

- ✓ *fprintf(logfile, "%os\n", "Cannot open file to save Cube Volume...Now Exit");*
- ✓ *exit(0);*

- ✓ *} else {*

- ✓ *fwrite(&Cubercxres,sizeof(int),1,pf);*
- ✓ *fwrite(&Cubercyres,sizeof(int),1,pf);*
- ✓ *fwrite(&Cubenumslice,sizeof(int),1,pf);*
- ✓ *fwrite(&m_PSizeX,sizeof(float),1,pf);*
- ✓ *fwrite(&m_PSizeY,sizeof(float),1,pf);*
- ✓ *fwrite(&m_PSizeZ,sizeof(float),1,pf);*
- ✓ *fwrite(&dataLabel,sizeof(char),1,pf);*
- ✓ *fwrite(&StdLabel,sizeof(char),1,pf);*

- ✓ *if (StdLabel=='Y') {*

- ✓ *fwrite(&Average,sizeof(float),1,pf);*
- ✓ *fwrite(&Std,sizeof(float),1,pf);*

- ✓ *} else if (StdLabel=='N')*
- ✓ *{*
- ✓ *// this is so if the CheckBox is FALSE*
- ✓ *}*

- ✓ *for(sl=1; sl<=Cubenumslice; sl++) {*
- ✓ *for(j=0; j<Cubercyres; j++) {*
- ✓ *for(i=0; i<Cubercxres; i++) {*

- ✓ $k2=(j*Cubercxres+i)+((sl-1)*Cubercyres*Cubercxres);$
- ✓ *savedata=(float)*(pointer+k2);*
- ✓ *fwrite(&savedata,sizeof(float),1,pf);*

- ✓ *}*

- ✓ }
- ✓ }
- ✓ *fclose(pf);*

- ✓ }

- ✓ *fprintf(logfile, "%s%s\n", "Now Saving File: ", filename2);*

- ✓ *if ((pf = fopen(filename2,"wb+"))==NULL) {*

- ✓ *fprintf(logfile, "%s\n", "Cannot open file to save Cube Plane Slice...Now Exit");*
- ✓ *exit(0);*

- ✓ *} else {*

- ✓ *static int onlyOneSlice = 1;*
- ✓ *float onlyOneSliceThickness = 1;*

- ✓ *fwrite(&Cubecxres,sizeof(int),1,pf);*
- ✓ *fwrite(&Cubecyres,sizeof(int),1,pf);*
- ✓ *fwrite(&onlyOneSlice,sizeof(int),1,pf);*
- ✓ *fwrite(&m_PSizeX,sizeof(float),1,pf);*
- ✓ *fwrite(&m_PSizeY,sizeof(float),1,pf);*
- ✓ *fwrite(&onlyOneSliceThickness,sizeof(float),1,pf);*
- ✓ *fwrite(&dataLabel,sizeof(char),1,pf);*
- ✓ *fwrite(&StdLabel,sizeof(char),1,pf);*

- ✓ *if (StdLabel=='Y') {*

- ✓ *fwrite(&Average2D,sizeof(float),1,pf);*
- ✓ *fwrite(&Std2D,sizeof(float),1,pf);*
- ✓ *} else if (StdLabel=='N')*
- ✓ *{*
- ✓ *// this is so if the CheckBox is FALSE*
- ✓ *}*

- ✓ *for(j=0; j<Cubecyres; j++){*
- ✓ *for(i=0; i<Cubecxres; i++){*

- ✓ *sl = 2;*
- ✓ *k2=(j*Cubecxres+i)+((sl-1)*Cubecyres*Cubecxres);*
- ✓ *savedata=(float)*(pointer+k2);*
- ✓ *fwrite(&savedata,sizeof(float),1,pf);*

- ✓ }
- ✓ }

- ✓ *fclose(pf);*

- ✓ }

Computer Science Applications

```
void CImageToolDlg::OnCreatetheCube()
{
        UpdateData(true);

        int sl, j, i, k2;

        float number = 0;
        float *pointer = 0;
        char filename[128], filename2[128];
        FILE *pf;
        int Cubercxres;
        int Cubercyres;
        int Cubenumslice;

        double comx = 0, comy = 0, comz = 0, sumi = 0, sumj = 0, sumsl = 0;
        FILE * logfile;
        char logfilename[128];

        char StdLabel = ' ';
        /// this variable is read from and saved to
        /// image files' header created with Matlab programs and
        /// or this Visual C++ Application (such as for instance
        /// the routine called OnCreatetheCube)

        float Std = 0, Average = 0;
        float Std2D = 0, Average2D = 0;

        CString Message;

        sprintf(logfilename, "%s%d%s", "CHAOS", m_VolumeSize, ".log");
        sprintf(filename, "%s%d", "CHAOS-", m_VolumeSize);
        sprintf(filename2, "%s%d%s", "CHAOS-", m_VolumeSize, "-Slice");
        if ((logfile = fopen(logfilename,"w+"))==NULL)
        {
            Message.Format("%s\n%s\n%s\n" , "Cannot open file: ", logfilename, "Now Exit");
            AfxMessageBox(Message);
            exit(0);

        } else { // else

            fprintf(logfile,"%s%s\n", "Making the Cube Data in File: " , filename );
            fprintf(logfile,"%s%d\n", "Number of X, Y, Z Volume Voxels: " , m_VolumeSize );
            fprintf(logfile,"%s\n" , "Now creating the cube with random values of pixel intensity");

        } // else

        Cubercxres = (int)m_VolumeSize;
        Cubercyres = (int)m_VolumeSize;
        Cubenumslice = (int)m_VolumeSize;

        if ((pointer = (float *) calloc( (Cubenumslice*Cubercyres*Cubercxres), sizeof(float)) ) == NULL)
        {
            fprintf(logfile, "%s\n" , "Not enough memory to allocate the Cube data");
            exit(0);
        }
```

```
// initialize the cube
    for(sl=1 ;sl<=Cubenumslice; sl++) {
        for(j=0;j<Cubercyres;j++){
            for(i=0;i<Cubercxres;i++){

                k2=(j*Cubercxres+i)+((sl-1)*Cubercyres*Cubercxres);
                *(pointer+k2)=(float)0;

                        }
                    }
                }

// fill the cube (except border edges)
// with random values to create chaos volume

float chaos = 0;
for(sl=2 ;sl<=Cubenumslice-1; sl++) {
    for(j=1;j<Cubercyres-1;j++){
        for(i=1;i<Cubercxres-1;i++){

            k2=(j*Cubercxres+i)+((sl-1)*Cubercyres*Cubercxres);
            chaos = (float)rand();
            *(pointer+k2)=(float)chaos;

                    }
                }
            }

    fprintf(logfile, "%s\n" ,"The cube and the slice are loaded in memory");

if (m_StdLabel==TRUE)
{// if signal is to be standardized

// this condition is left as choice to the
// user through the CheckBox variable:
// m_StdLabel TRUE is ON and FALSE is OFF

 ////Standardize Data
fprintf(logfile, "%s\n" ,"Now Calculating Average and Standard Deviation of Data");

StdLabel = 'Y'; // to go in image file header

Average = 0;
Average2D = 0;

for(sl=2 ;sl<=Cubenumslice-1; sl++) {
    for(j=1;j<Cubercyres-1;j++){
        for(i=1;i<Cubercxres-1;i++){

        k2=(j*Cubercxres+i)+((sl-1)*Cubercyres*Cubercxres);

        Average = ((float)Average) + ((float)*(pointer+k2));

    }
    }
```

```
        if (sl == 2) Average2D = (float)Average / ( (float) (Cubercyres-2) * (Cubercxres-2) );

}

/// calculate average
Average = (float) Average / ( (float) (Cubenumslice-2) * (Cubercyres-2) * (Cubercxres-2) );

Std = 0;
Std2D = 0;

for(sl=2 ;sl<=Cubenumslice-1; sl++) {
    for(j=1;j<Cubercyres-1;j++){
        for(i=1;i<Cubercxres-1;i++){

        k2=(j*Cubercxres+i)+((sl-1)*Cubercyres*Cubercxres);

        Std = (float)Std + ((float) (Average - *(pointer+k2)) * (Average - *(pointer+k2)) );

                                    }
                                }
                            }

for(j=1;j<Cubercyres-1;j++){
    for(i=1;i<Cubercxres-1;i++){

    sl = 2;
    k2=(j*Cubercxres+i)+((sl-1)*Cubercyres*Cubercxres);

    Std2D = (float)Std2D + ((float) (Average2D - *(pointer+k2)) * (Average2D - *(pointer+k2)) );

                                }
                            }
// calculate standard deviation
Std = (float) sqrt( (double) Std / ( (float) (Cubenumslice-2) * (Cubercyres-2) * (Cubercxres-2) ) );

Std2D = (float) sqrt( (double) Std2D / ( (float) (Cubercyres-2) * (Cubercxres-2) ) );

///Standardize
for(sl=2 ;sl<=Cubenumslice-1; sl++) {
    for(j=1;j<Cubercyres-1;j++){
        for(i=1;i<Cubercxres-1;i++){

        k2=(j*Cubercxres+i)+((sl-1)*Cubercyres*Cubercxres);

        *(pointer+k2) = ((float)*(pointer+k2) - (float)Average) / (float)Std;

                                    }
                                }
                            }

fprintf(logfile, "%s\n" ,"CUBE:");
fprintf(logfile, "%s%f\n" ,"Average: ", Average);
fprintf(logfile, "%s%f\n" ,"Standard Deviation: ", Std);
/// end of 3D
```

```
/// begin of 2D
fprintf(logfile, "%s\n" ,"SLICE:");
fprintf(logfile, "%s%f\n" ,"Average: ", Average2D);
fprintf(logfile, "%s%f\n" ,"Standard Deviation: ", Std2D);
/// end of 2D

}// if signal is to be standardized
else if (m_StdLabel==FALSE)
// this condition is left as choice to the
// user through the CheckBox variable:
// m_StdLabel TRUE is ON and FALSE is OFF
{
     StdLabel = 'N'; // to go in image file header
}

fprintf(logfile,"%s\n" , "The program will find the Center of Mass (COM) of the cube");

//compute max and min of cube data
double max=-5000000000000000000;
double min=5000000000000000000;

for(i=0;i<Cubercxres*Cubercyres*Cubenumslice;i++){

        if( *(pointer+i) > max ) max = *(pointer+i);
        if( *(pointer+i) < min ) min = *(pointer+i);

                                                }
if ( max != 0 )
{// calculate COM (begin)

double count = 0.0;

    for(sl=1;sl<=Cubenumslice; sl++) {
        for(j=0;j<Cubercyres;j++){
            for(i=0;i<Cubercxres;i++){


k2=(j*Cubercxres+i)+((sl-1)*Cubercyres*Cubercxres);

count += ((double) fabs((double)*(pointer+k2)/max) );

sumi = sumi + ( (double)i * ((double) fabs((double)*(pointer+k2)) / max ));
sumj = sumj + ( (double)j * ((double) fabs((double)*(pointer+k2)) / max));
sumsl = sumsl + ( ((double)sl-1) * ((double) fabs((double)*(pointer+k2)) / max ));

                                    }
                                }
                            }

    comx = ((double)sumi/count);
    comy = ((double)sumj/count);
    comz = ((double)sumsl/count);

}// calculate COM (end)

fprintf(logfile, "%s%f\n", "The x coordinate of the COM: ", comx);
```

```
        fprintf(logfile, "%s%f\n", "The y coordinate of the COM: ", comy);
        fprintf(logfile, "%s%f\n", "The z coordinate of the COM: ", comz);

        /// save cube
        float savedata;
        char dataLabel = 'F';
        fprintf(logfile, "%s%s\n", "Now Saving File: ", filename);
        if ((pf = fopen(filename,"wb+"))==NULL)
        {

        fprintf(logfile, "%s\n", "Cannot open file to save Cube Volume...Now Exit");
        exit(0);

        } else { // else

        /// save header
        fwrite(&Cubercxres,sizeof(int),1,pf);
        fwrite(&Cubercyres,sizeof(int),1,pf);
        fwrite(&Cubenumslice,sizeof(int),1,pf);
        fwrite(&m_PSizeX,sizeof(float),1,pf);
        fwrite(&m_PSizeY,sizeof(float),1,pf);
        fwrite(&m_PSizeZ,sizeof(float),1,pf);
        fwrite(&dataLabel,sizeof(char),1,pf);
        fwrite(&StdLabel,sizeof(char),1,pf);
        // the value of StdLabel is set above
        if (StdLabel=='Y') // this is so if the CheckBox is TRUE
        {
        fwrite(&Average,sizeof(float),1,pf);
        fwrite(&Std,sizeof(float),1,pf);

        // data is assumed to be standardized
        // and so converted back to non standardized numbers only if
        // the numbers' format is either float or double

        } else if (StdLabel=='N')
        {
        // this is so if the CheckBox is FALSE
        }
            /// save cube
            for(sl=1;sl<=Cubenumslice; sl++) {
                for(j=0;j<Cubercyres;j++){
                    for(i=0;i<Cubercxres;i++){

                    k2=(j*Cubercxres+i)+((sl-1)*Cubercyres*Cubercxres);
                    savedata=(float)*(pointer+k2);
                    fwrite(&savedata,sizeof(float),1,pf);

                                        }
                                }
                        }
        fclose(pf);
        } // else

        /// save Plane Slice of the cube
        fprintf(logfile, "%s%s\n", "Now Saving File: ", filename2);
        if ((pf = fopen(filename2,"wb+"))==NULL)
```

```
{
fprintf(logfile, "%s\n", "Cannot open file to save Cube Plane Slice...Now Exit");
exit(0);
} else { // else
    /// save header
    static int onlyOneSlice = 1;
    float onlyOneSliceThickness = 1;

    fwrite(&Cubercxres,sizeof(int),1,pf);
    fwrite(&Cubercyres,sizeof(int),1,pf);
    fwrite(&onlyOneSlice,sizeof(int),1,pf);
    fwrite(&m_PSizeX,sizeof(float),1,pf);
    fwrite(&m_PSizeY,sizeof(float),1,pf);
    fwrite(&onlyOneSliceThickness,sizeof(float),1,pf);
    fwrite(&dataLabel,sizeof(char),1,pf);
    fwrite(&StdLabel,sizeof(char),1,pf);
    // the value of StdLabel is set above

    if (StdLabel=='Y')
    { // this is so if the CheckBox is TRUE
        fwrite(&Average2D,sizeof(float),1,pf);
        fwrite(&Std2D,sizeof(float),1,pf);
    // data is assumed to be standardized
    // and so converted back to non standardized numbers only if
    // the numbers' format is either float or double

    } else if (StdLabel=='N')
    {
    // this is so if the CheckBox is FALSE
    }
    /// save Plane Slice
    for(j=0;j<Cubercyres;j++){
      for(i=0;i<Cubercxres;i++){

        sl = 2;
        k2=(j*Cubercxres+i)+((sl-1)*Cubercyres*Cubercxres);
        savedata=(float)*(pointer+k2);
        fwrite(&savedata,sizeof(float),1,pf);

      }
    }
fclose(pf);

} // else /// save Plane Slice of the cube

// remove data from memory
free(pointer);
fprintf(logfile, "%s%s%s\n", "Cube Saved in file: ", filename, " (3D Image)" );
fprintf(logfile, "%s%s%s\n", "Plane Slice of the Cube Saved in file: ", filename2, " (2D Image)" );
fprintf(logfile, "%s\n", "DataType: Float (32-bits Real)");
fclose(logfile);
system(logfilename);


}
```

Computer Science Applications

The method *void CImageToolDlg::OnHelpCube()* provides the user with a message box with relevant information to aid the comprehension of the processing and the ease of use of the program. The method *void CImageToolDlg::OnHelpDisplay()* instructs the user to clear the memory utilized by OpenGL ®. In order to clear the memory, two push buttons are available by the name of '*Clear Memory 2D*' and '*Clear Memory 3D*' (see Fig. 2).

void CImageToolDlg::OnHelpCube()
```
{

        CString HelpMessage;

        HelpMessage.Format("%s\n%s\n%s\n%s\n%s\n" ,
                        "Please chose X Y Z Number of Voxels as powers of 2.",
                        "To do this, enter the Number of Voxels in the Edit Box" ,
                        "located to the right of the push button named Cube and Slice." ,
                        "Please chose the Cube Pixel Sizes X, Y and Z in mm. Also, it" ,
                        "will be Generated 2D Data Consisting of one Slice of the Cube.");
        AfxMessageBox(HelpMessage);


}
```

void CImageToolDlg::OnHelpDisplay()
```
{

        CString HelpMessage;

        HelpMessage.Format("%s\n %s\n" , "This panel Diplays either 2D or 3D Image Data through",
                        "the buttons named Display Image (2D or 3D)" );
        MessageBox(HelpMessage);
        HelpMessage.Format("%s\n %s\n %s\n %s\n %s\n" ,
                        "Multiple sessions are allowed.",
                        "Please make sure that Memory", "is Cleared after Display: either 2D or 3D.",
                        "Specifically: Clear Memory 2D after 2D Display,",
                        "and Clear Memory 3D after 3D Display.");
        MessageBox(HelpMessage);
}
```

The method *void CImageToolDlg::OnDisplay2D()* is the one that retrieves 2D data from the binary file through the use of the method *float * CImageToolDlg::data(char filename[])* and also through the use of the pointer '*(TwoDdata)*'. Specifically, the pointer '*(TwoDdata)*' is the recipient of the image data released with the instruction '*TwoDdata = data(filename)*'. Data are sent to display through the method *void CImageToolDlg::LaunchOpenGL()* using the instruction '*LaunchOpenGL()*'.

void CImageToolDlg::OnDisplay2D()
```
{

        UpdateData(true);

        char filename[128];
        sprintf(filename, "%s", m_VolumeFileName);

        TwoDdata=data(filename);
        WhoIsONDisplay = 2;
        LaunchOpenGL();


}
```

The method *void CImageToolDlg::OnDisplay2D()* sets the variable '*WhoIsONDisplay*' equal to the value '*2*' to indicate that the memory to be allocated is that one relevant to 2D data. The memory allocation is done inside the method *void CImageToolDlg::LaunchOpenGL()* through *void CImageToolDlg::AllocateMemoryforOpenGLGraphics2D()*. The methods *void CImageToolDlg::OnClearMemory2D()* and *void CImageToolDlg::OnClearMemory3D()* were written in order to free the memory relevant to data display after closing the OpenGL ® window.

void CImageToolDlg::OnClearMemory2D()

```
{

        CString ViewMessage;
        ViewMessage.Format("%s\n %s\n" , "Press this button only Once", "per Visualization Session");
        AfxMessageBox(ViewMessage);

        if ( planeWindowImage != NULL )
        {
            if (plEraseMemoryFlag == 0)
            {
                free(planeWindowImage);
                plEraseMemoryFlag = 1;
            }
        }

}
```

void CImageToolDlg::OnClearMemory3D()

```
{

        CString ViewMessage;
        ViewMessage.Format("%s\n %s\n" , "Press this button only Once", "per Visualization Session");
        AfxMessageBox(ViewMessage);
        if (Imagedata != NULL)
        {
            if (tEraseMemoryFlag == 0)
            {
                free(Imagedata);
                tEraseMemoryFlag = 1;
            }

        }

}
```

Summary

This chapter relates to the presentation of the source code of *ImageViewer 2009* and *ImageTool 2009*. While the former is a program fully utilized for 2D and 3D data visualization thus placing specific focus on the inclusion of OpenGL ® routines inside the Visual C++ ® GUI, the latter takes advantage of such knowledge and presents additional methods that are relevant to the creation of randomized data in 2D and 3D.

Computer Science Applications

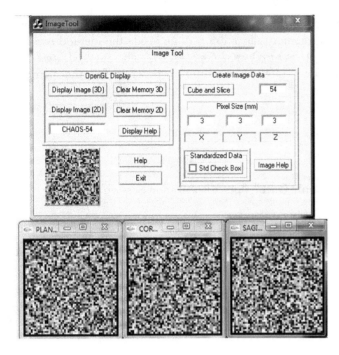

Figure 4: *ImageTool 2009* employed to visualize randomized 3D data with composite 2D window display [2-3] made of plane, coronal and sagittal windows visible in the lower row of the figure from left to right.

The OpenGL ® routines utilized in *ImageViewer 2009* and *ImageTool 2009* are relevant: (i) to data input from file in 2D or 3D through the use of pointers, (ii) dynamic allocation of the memory for the display of the data, (iii) formation of the OpenGL ® main loop [1] which sustains data visualization, (iv) programming of functions and methods to launch the OpenGL ® routines.

References

[1] Shreiner, D., Woo, M., Neider, J., Davis, T. (2007). *OpenGL Programming Guide: The Official Guide to Learning OpenGL.* Version 2.1 (6th Edition), Addison-Wesley Professional.

[2] Ciulla, C. (2000). *Development and Characterization of Techniques for Neuroimaging Alignment.* Master's Thesis, New Jersey Institute of Technology, Newark, NJ, USA.

[3] Ciulla, C. (2008). *AUTOALIGN: Methodology and Technology for the Alignment of Functional Magnetic Resonance Imaging Time Series. Image Registration: The case of Functional MRI.* VDM Verlag Dr. Müller.

CHAPTER 9

Discussion and Inspirational View

Summary of the Contents

Results presented in this manuscript are of qualitative nature and display a panorama of contribution to students' learning which is within the domain of computer science applications and more generally in computing and engineering.

Specifically, results of sampling theory, direct and inverse Fourier transformation were presented along with the GUI embedding the code reproducing theoretical concepts, which would be otherwise left to a higher level of abstraction for students. To make easier students' understanding, the teacher's implementation of the code along with the release of it makes a substantial contribution to learning. In view of the structured form of the teaching approach outlined here, well defined methods are set for teaching consistently with the guidelines of the scientific discipline. In other words teaching is confirmed a science because structured with well defined methods. Along this line of thought results relating to the other Computer Science (CS) applications presented in this manuscript are discussed.

Sub-pixel Efficacy region (SRE) results were published elsewhere [1]. In this manuscript is presented the GUI of the computer programs employed for validation along with some samples of novel re-sampling locations which introduce students as to what is the concept of non-uniform re-sampling in interpolation.

Educational slide sets on logic gates and binary arithmetic of the Booth algorithm for binary multiplication [2] combined with the software implementation of the Booth algorithm may become a semester project to assign in CS majors. The effort of the teacher here is two folded. On one hand the Booth algorithm is detailed in its software counterpart and on the other hand the Booth algorithm is detailed in its first layout of hardware implementation through basic principles of computer architecture.

ROTRA 2008, another CS project relating to biomedical imaging, was presented providing students with hands on approach to three dimensional image computing as well as to the implementation of concepts relating to computational geometry through routines performing rigid-body rotations.

Worth noting is the recurrent use of OpenGL ® in the projects to display the visual results in 2D and in 3D through three composite 2D views. The teacher in this case makes its own contribution to the students' curriculum through a structured explanation of basics in computer graphics employed for 2D image display and 3D image display (with three 2D composite views) and this is another branch of CS applications in computing.

Although the software code connected to *ANN98* and *SPACE 2010* is available to students, the two GUIs shown in Figs. 5 and 7 in chapter 1 are here presented as results of qualitative nature enriching the panorama of teaching samples and learning tools employed to show students how to create an interface and also how to connect it to executable files. In the specific case of *ANN98*, the teaching sample is an artificial neural network (*ObjNet*) and in the case of *SPACE 2010*, the teaching samples are more generally oriented computing applications in engineering. Worth noting that *ANN98* comprises of source code which make clarity to students on how effectively implement an artificial neural network, thus being of complement to theory in courses like pattern recognition in the CS curriculum.

ImageTool (shown in chapter 1 in Figs. 6 in its versions 2009) is another implementation more focused on the production of randomized data and on the display through OpenGL ® routines.

The Nature of the Book and its Approach

The purpose of the manuscript is that of presenting technological computer based tools for higher learning in academic environments like colleges and universities, with the intent to prompt the attention of the reader to the fact that technology development of higher education tools goes in parallel with students' learning process. *The nature of the book is educational.* The book may serve various purposes.

(i) To provide homework/semester project assignments that are customized to the students/instructors need which is that of clarity in the explanation. Clarity is provided in the book with lengthy source codes which set the basis for the implementation in ANSI C/Visual C++/OpenGL programming languages.

(ii) It is possible through the use of the book to devise syllabi which includes topics that can be deeply understood in their practical implications because of the level of details. This point works in favour to students because they can expect a favourable outcome in learning which then can be used in career oriented prospects. It also works in favor to the instructor because of the level of success of the students in the course.

(iii) To provide students and instructors with readily accessible implementation of course materials having theoretical nature. For instance the Fourier Transformations is a topic of great theoretical nature and impact.

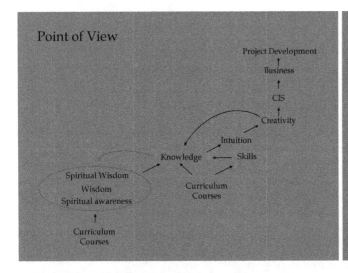

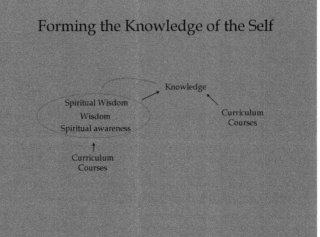

Forming the Knowledge of the Self

- Spiritual awareness can be seen as the conscious realization of the inner self of the individual.

- Wisdom can be achieved through recognizing the big thing into the right thing.

- Spiritual wisdom is more than spiritual awareness. It can be thought as the conscious capability to do well, what we can do well, and for the best interest of the collectivity.

Forming the Knowledge of the Self

- The knowledge provided through the combination of the courses chosen in the array of elective disciplines can increase the spiritual wisdom.

- Question. Who directs the choice?

- Answer: The awareness of the soul purpose.

Forming the Knowledge of the Self

- Philosophy
- History
- Trigonometry
- Probability and Statistics
- Physical Sciences
- Calculus
- Computer Organization and Architecture

Philosophy

- PHIL - The Meaning of Life
- PHIL - Introduction to Philosophy

Why?

A mind set that is educated to logical reasoning, is prone to derive the aptitude to conceptualize, question and therefore to elaborate well balanced propositions of thought.

Figure 1: From curriculum courses to project development passing through the formation of the spiritual wisdom in the individual involved in higher learning within the context of the computer science curriculum.
The implementation in source code of direct and inverse Fourier Transformations provide the students with the practical details which would be otherwise left unattended and with such details the level of understanding of the course materials is increased.

History

- HIST - Historical Methods

Why?

History may provide wise and complete answers to past and present questions.

Trigonometry

- MATH - Trigonometry

Why?

A readily accessible discipline that provides immediate access to see the intersections between the beautiful harmony of Mother Nature and Humanly Made Devices.

Probability and Statistics

- MATH - Probability and Statistics

Why?

To answer the question as to if the inner nature of the self descends from a deterministic process, and/or a probabilistic one which is featured with the one's choices. The question is relevant to spiritual awareness.

Physical Sciences

- PHYS - Introduction to Physics
- PHYS - General Physics I

Why?

A corridor to the understanding that the universe may evolve through stages of dynamic equilibrium, and each stage is associated with a resulting energy level.

Calculus

- MATH - Calculus

Why?

Mathematics is able to lay the foundation and structure to scientific disciplines. Also is a wonderful training to logical reasoning.

Computer Organization and Architecture

- Contribution:
  An exploration of the basic concepts at the root foundation of computer science corroborated with samples of algorithmic logic within the context of the computing device.

Why?

Seeing the logic of computing and achieving the transformation of a cognitive process into a computer program.

Figure 2: History, Trigonometry, Probability and Statistics, Physical Sciences, Calculus and Computer Organization and Architecture are justified in their inclusion in the students' curriculum each with a commentary as to the scope they serve in the formation of the students' knowledge.

(iv) To provide students with high level of specificity in programming thus increasing their skills in computing. The level of coding in the book is not for beginners and can be understood after the students have passed at least an introductory course in C/Visual C++ ®.

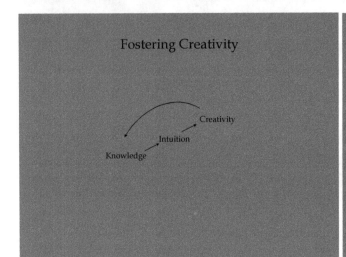

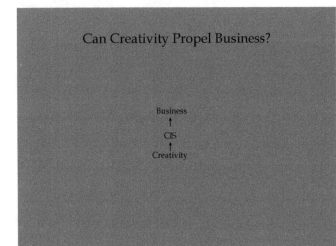

Figure 3: Forming the knowledge, fostering creativity and employing creativity to propel business is the outline in this picture, where business can be seen to the widest extent as the activity of the human being to serve society in the most beneficial form possible within the extent of the formed spiritual wisdom.

(v) To provide students with specialized topics that can be introductory to further research to be conducted after graduation or during the thesis in College/University. The scientific problems addressed in the book provide the students with the possibility to involve themselves in additional study to be conducted thereafter.

The approach of the book is research like. Within this context the instructor becomes the main researcher in class. The manuscript offers the possibility to explore scientific problems in computing which have been solved in the book along with the code reported to explain the practical involvement. The instructor as researcher in classroom can also take advantage of the book materials to devise homework/projects which are customized to his/her own background. Therefore, he/she can go beyond the book and set the basis for the actualization of personalized assignments.

The conclusion is that combining teaching with the teacher's software development increases success in students' outcome in higher learning. The code can be provided to the students as handout and explained to understand the practical implications of the theoretical concepts.

Inspirational View

Framing the teacher activity in the classroom into a well structured set of methods makes teaching a science. The science involves the conceptualization of a view point that the author expresses through the writings of this book. The view point is connected to the significance of the students' interaction with the didactical materials. The author thinks that instructing students to research-like settings may help develop students' spiritual wisdom as that awareness of the set of skills and capabilities which are of most interest to them. This is because such skills and capabilities allow students to perform at their best during the course and at the same time initiate them to the understanding of what is the intellectual activity which makes the best of their contribution to society. Specifically, it is anticipated that the meaning of spiritual wisdom is that of finding the true consciousness of the self at the purpose to serve society in the best possible manner, within the good, and in consistency with what the individual is best prone to do. The computer science curriculum can thus be corroborated with some additional courses which allow the students to find the path to reach such awareness called spiritual wisdom.

Starting from a positive experience through a course in computing it is possible to discover a specific interest which relates to students' career settings in the long term. This makes the course like an exploration of what is the best interest of the student in relationship to future prospects in life. To employ course materials to discover life interests which relate to career oriented prospects is auspicious as much as it is a good expectance from the course. This may be possible through the involvement of the students in one of the topics treated in the book.

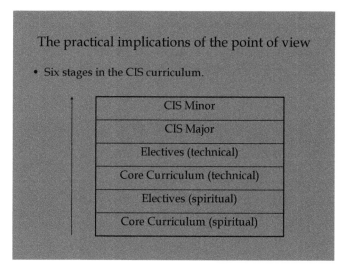

Figure 4: The practical implication of the point of view in the actualization of the Computer Information Science (CIS) curriculum in college and/or university.

The set of slides herein presented are, to the opinion of the writer, a presentation of a viable option to find the spiritual wisdom for students in undergraduate and graduate settings. Nowadays the world of technology or even hyper-technology fulfills in its premise to bring wellbeing. There are also other options to pursue in order to find the wellbeing of an individual though, and one of them is certainly instruction and higher learning. Starting the presentation from Fig. 1 a general overview of one possible path to follow in higher learning is outlined.

In Fig. 1 the spiritual awareness serve the purpose to build foundations for the understanding of the individual's spiritual wisdom and to set the foundations of the formation of the individual's knowledge. The core to emphasize is constituted of the spiritual awareness, the wisdom and the spiritual wisdom. Through the understanding of each of these components, the students can enter a stage which can be called the awareness of the soul purpose and the direction to choose in life to best serve society with the means provided in academic contexts through higher learning.

In Fig. 2 is a presentation of some courses that can be chosen by the students and more to it is the justification as to why they serve the purpose of laying the foundation of students' knowledge and students' spiritual wisdom. Such courses may depict a panorama for the students to search for the true knowledge of the self and a suitable environment where this can happen (to the view of the author) is the college or university.

In Fig. 3 is presented the pathway that from the formation of the knowledge, passing through intuition, arrives to creativity and sets a point which is that fostering creativity can, might, propel business. The aim of the knowledge is accomplished in view of the outlined pathway and in view of the fact that business can be seen as any activity which serves to the benefit of society. This happens because the individual can be set in the condition to serve society in the most beneficial way and consistently with his or her spiritual wisdom. Wellness of the individual is thus derived because the common interest is reached while pursuing the individuals' contribution to the whole community.

Fig. 4 draws a summary of the point of view of the author in showing that the CIS curriculum can be structured in six stages. In first instance (i) core curriculum and (ii) electives, lay down the foundations of the quest for spiritual wisdom. In second instance, once again core curriculum and electives lay down the technical part of the students' curriculum. In third instance the CIS major and CIS minor can be approached by the students with a good degree of spiritual wisdom and knowledge thus they are most prone to foster creativity.

Summary

This chapter makes a summary of the features offered by the computer programs described in the manuscript and also recalls that teaching is a science because built on solid and well structured methodologies. Within this context it is recalled to the reader that during students' learning the effort of the teacher in building learning tools customized to his or her own background can simply improve the outcome in the classroom settings. To conclude the book, is given a presentation in support to the hypothesis that learning in academic context, both at the undergraduate and the graduate levels, is one viable option for the students to build their spiritual wisdom.

References

[1] Ciulla, C. (2009). *Improved Signal and Image Interpolation in Biomedical Applications: The Case of Magnetic Resonance Imaging (MRI)* - Medical Information Science Reference - IGI Global Publisher, Hershey, PA, U.S.A.

[2] Booth, A.D. (1951). *A Signed Binary Multiplication Algorithm.* Quarterly Journal of Mechanics and Applied Mathematics. Clarendon Press; Oxford University Press. England.

CHAPTER 10

Teaching Complements

Synopsis

The programming languages of the teaching complements are suggested to be ANSI C, or Visual C++ or MATLAB. The choice of these programming languages is justified through the portability across various platforms, and the benefits to the students are relevant but not limited to further development in research which can be undertaken for instance at a later stage of the students' development in graduate schools.

The idea is to make the students' work useful, reusable and with the prospect of further study during a more advanced stage of their careers.

The teaching complements are three and they incorporate in the students' curriculum three typologies of Computing in Educational Sciences: (i) SRE-based interpolation functions & Graphical User Interface Programming, (ii) Artificial Intelligence in Pattern Recognition using artificial Neural Networks, and (iii) Image Rotations.

The teaching complements are intended to provide the students with research skills foundations through the exposure to computer implementations of signal processing techniques. The teaching complements are also intended to prepare the students to further their studies in academia or more generally to prepare the students to undertake their career.

Organization of the Teaching Complements

Each of the teaching complements can be organized on the basis of three main propaedeutics phases, and a compendium which the inner essence is the education to thinking.

(A) The first phase is the <u>explanation</u> of the theoretical background comprising of algorithms relevant to the signal processing techniques. The explanation of the theoretical background can be provided to the students with at the aid of the board and/or through Powerpoint handouts.

(B) The second phase is that of <u>teaching</u>. The teacher explains to the students how to implement the Graphical User Interface (GUI) which connects to the computer programs which reproduce the signal processing applications. The signal processing applications are written employing ANSI C, C++ or MATLAB coding. Also teaching can be provided to the students with at the aid of the board and/or through Powerpoint handouts.

(C) The third stage is that one of the <u>implementation</u>. At the third stage the teacher assigns homework tasks. The students will be asked to implement the code in computer programs, run the computer programs and obtain the results of the algorithms relevant to the signal processing techniques.

Within the context of the implementation, the role of the teacher is that one of the mediator of the intellectual content which consists of the students' understanding of both: (i) how the software coding relates to the concepts underlying the theory of which the algorithm is the implementation of (theory), and (ii) the software coding which implements the algorithm (practice).

The mediation of the teacher is exerted through the didactics which are defined within the domain of the interaction between the teacher and the students. Within the context of the didactics, the teacher role of mediator can be viewed within the following principle of teaching philosophy:

Since language is believed to be a vehicle of communication, necessary but not sufficient to achieve understanding, the principle of philosophy of teaching, that can be used while exerting the role of the teacher, is that of bringing in solution of practical examples. Solution of practical examples can yield students to a high level of understanding of both of the aforementioned theory and practice, and also set the grounds for the maturation of the theoretical concepts to a higher level of understanding.

For instance, while teaching, the instructor can provide the students with several practical examples of Visual C++ programs, binary operations (multiplication and division among others). The practical examples are later detailed and explained in classroom, at the board and/or through Powerpoint handouts. This approach makes easier the task of solving the homework (high level of understanding) and sets the basis for a higher level of understanding such to propel the students' career with increased spiritual wisdom.

Computer Science Applications

(D) As a compendium, which the inner essence is the <u>education to thinking</u>, and which is explicated at the end of the teaching complement, the student is welcome to present a published research paper on one of the topics treated by the teacher. The student is asked to show understanding of the research paper and to show analytical and critical thinking through the discussion of the topics presented in the research paper. The student can earn additional credit through the performance of the task in education to thinking.

Teaching complements Typology: Special Topics in Applied Signal Processing

(i) SRE-based interpolation functions & Graphical User Interface Programming

<u>Explanation:</u>

In this teaching complement, the algorithms relevant to the signal processing techniques, relate to the SRE-based interpolation functions. This teaching complement opens up with an introduction to the problem of signal interpolation as conceived by Isaac Newton, which provides the students with the theoretical background.

To appreciate diversity, instead of pointing to differences, the teaching complement learns from the basis of the theoretical background the capability to emphasize on the linear interpolation paradigm in two dimensions.

The capability to emphasize is offered through the viability of the mathematics and the immediate understanding of the math in relationship to practical applications such as two-dimensional images. The mathematics of the SRE-based bivariate linear interpolation function [1] provides the students with both viability and understanding which can be explored.

A sample PowerPoint set of slides is being shown hereto follow to show the first propaedeutics phase which is that of one of the explanation.

GUI Programming for SRE-based interpolation functions

Concepts and Applications

Acknowledgment

The Magnetic Resonance Imaging (MRI)
Images were provided through the Courtesy of:
Open Access Series of Imaging Studies (OASIS):

The original fMRI images are courtesy of:
The Wellcome Trust Centre
for Neuroimaging (University College London - UK),

Agenda

- The approximate nature of the interpolation functions.

- SRE-based interpolation functions Graphical User Interface Programming

The approximate nature of the interpolation functions

Sampling theory requires that:

$$\int_{-\infty}^{+\infty} |f(t)| \, dt = \text{a finite number}$$

Certain Topics in Telegraph Transmission Theory. H. Nyquist.
Proceedings of the IEEE, Vol. 90, No. 2, February (2002).

The approximate nature of the interpolation functions

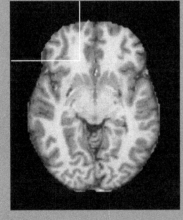 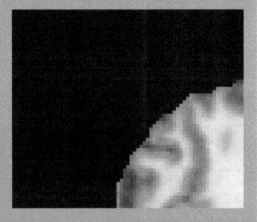

Concept: Resolution →
Derived Concept: The   is produced
through the interpolation function.

The approximate nature of the interpolation functions

Interpolation Functions and Neighborhoods: Bivariate Linear

$h(x, y) = f(0,0) + x\ (f(1,0) - f(0,0)) + y\ (f(0,1) - f(0,0)) + xy\ (f(1,1) + f(0,0) - f(0,1) - f(1,0))$

 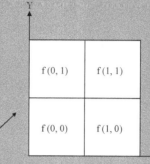

Concept: Neighborhoods are regions of the image, which pixels are employed to determine the   .

The approximate nature of the interpolation functions

What is the   in signal-image interpolation ?

It is an estimate of the true and unknown signal which is calculated on the basis of the sequel of discrete samples.

For instance, for the Bivariate Linear Interpolation function:

$h(x, y) = f(0,0) + x\ (f(1,0) - f(0,0)) + y\ (f(0,1) - f(0,0)) + xy\ (f(1,1) + f(0,0) - f(0,1) - f(1,0))$

the discrete samples are: f(0,0), f(1,0), f(0,1) and f(1,1). And, the convolution consists of the non-linear combination of pixel intensity values and misplacement (identified through the x and y coordinates of the location (x, y) where the signal ought to be estimated.

The approximate nature of the interpolation functions

The   is a direct consequence of
the discrete nature of the signal.

The signal is discrete because of the Resolution.

It follows the link between
Resolution and Convolution.

The approximate nature of the interpolation functions

What is the outcome of the relationship between the
Resolution and the Convolution ?

Answer: Smoothing.

What is Smoothing ?

The approximate nature of the interpolation functions

Original Image   Interpolated Image

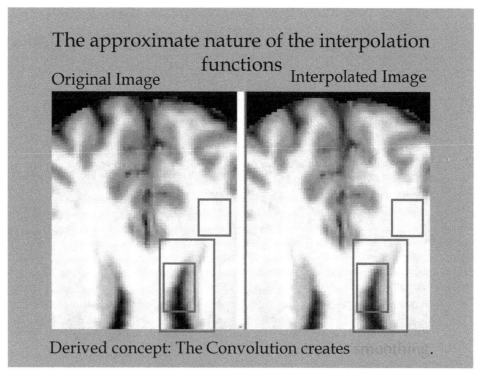

Derived concept: The Convolution creates smoothing.

The approximate nature of the interpolation functions

Why interpolation functions create smoothing

$\varepsilon = |\, \beta - \alpha\, |$

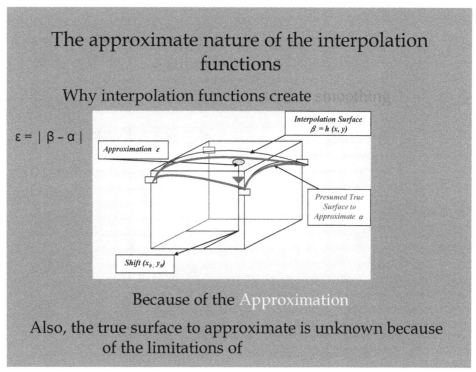

Because of the Approximation

Also, the true surface to approximate is unknown because of the limitations of

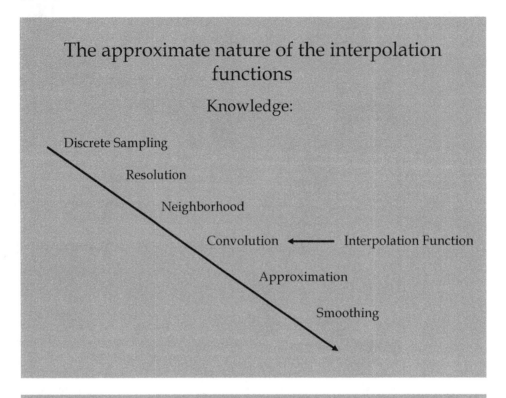

The approximate nature of the interpolation functions

Knowledge:

Discrete Sampling

Resolution

Neighborhood

Convolution ⟵ Interpolation Function

Approximation

Smoothing

The approximate nature of the interpolation functions

From the Knowledge it descends the Purpose:

To improve the approximation produced through the interpolation function, therefore to reduce the interpolation error.

How the re-organization of the independent variable is determined

Classic Bivariate Linear Interpolation Function

$h(x, y) = f(0,0) + x (f(1,0) - f(0,0)) + y (f(0,1) - f(0,0)) + xy (f(1,1) + f(0,0) - f(0,1) - f(1,0))$

For given pixel Ψ, the intensity-curvature term at the generic intra-pixel location (x, y) is:

$E_{IN} = E_{IN} (x, y) = E_{IN} (\Psi_{yy}) + E_{IN} (\Psi_{yx}) =$

$\int_0^x \int_0^y h (x, y) \left(\partial^2 (h(x, y))/\partial x \partial y + \partial^2 (h(x, y))/\partial y \partial x \right) dx\, dy =$

$\int_0^x \int_0^y h (x, y)\, 2\, \omega_f\, dx\, dy = 2\, \omega_f\, H_{xy} (x, y)$

The intensity-curvature term at the grid point $(x, y) = (0, 0)$ is:

$E_o = E_o (x, y) = E_o (\Psi_{xy}) + E_o (\Psi_{yx}) =$

$\int_0^x \int_0^y f (0, 0) \left(\partial^2 (h(x, y))/\partial x \partial y + \partial^2 (h(x, y))/\partial y \partial x \right) (0, 0)\, dx\, dy =$

$\int_0^x \int_0^y f (0, 0)\, 2\, \omega_f\, dx\, dy = f (0, 0)\, 2\, x\, y\, \omega_f$

> C. Ciulla and F.P. Deek. "On the Approximate Nature of the Bivariate Linear Interpolation Function: A Novel Scheme Based on Intensity-Curvature." ICGST International Journal on Graphics, Vision and Image Processing, 2005, 5(7): 9-19.

How the re-organization of the independent variable is determined

The Sub-pixel Efficacy Region is:

$\Phi = \{(x, y): \partial (\Delta E(x, y))/\partial x = 0 \text{ and } \partial (\Delta E(x, y)) /\partial y = 0\}$

$x_{sre} = -2 (f(0,1) - f(0,0)) / \omega_f$

$y_{sre} = -2 (f(1,0) - f(0,0)) / \omega_f$

The novel re-sampling location is:

$x^{r0} = (\eta_{xy} - \mu_x) / \lambda_x$

$y^{r0} = (\eta_{xy} - \mu_y) / \lambda_y$

Where:

$\eta_{xy} = [(f(0,0) + x_{sre}\, \theta_x + y_{sre}\, \theta_y + x_{sre}\, y_{sre}\, \omega_f)\, \Delta E^* - f(0,0)]$

$\mu_x = [(y_{sre} - y_0)\, \theta_y + x_{sre} (\theta_x + (y_{sre} - y_0)\omega_f)]$

$\mu_y = [(x_{sre} - x_0)\, \theta_x + y_{sre} (\theta_y + (x_{sre} - x_0)\omega_f)]$

$\lambda_x = [(y_{sre} - y_0)\, \omega_f - \theta_x]$

$\lambda_y = [(x_{sre} - x_0)\, \omega_f - \theta_y]$

ΔE is called Intensity-Curvature Functional and has been envisioned as the ratio between E_o and E_{IN}.

The calculation of the SRE is conceptually equivalent to a process that finds the intra-pixel locations where the change of image energy determined through the model interpolation function is either minimal or maximal.

$\Delta E^* = E_{IN} (x_{sre} - x_0,\, y_{sre} - y_0) / E_{IN} (x_{sre},\, y_{sre})$

Appendix

The approximate nature of the interpolation functions

The reason because there is not a one-to-one correspondence between the image space and the frequency domain seen in the FFT image can be explained through the Fourier Theorem in its discrete form:

$$I(t) = \frac{1}{2}\sum_{-\infty}^{+\infty} K(\omega) \cdot e^{i\omega t} \cdot \Delta\omega \qquad K(\omega) = \frac{1}{\pi}\int_{-\pi/\Delta\omega}^{+\pi/\Delta\omega} I(t) \cdot e^{-i\omega t} \cdot dt$$

T is period of the fundamental frequency component. And so, the FFT image shows as many pixels as many frequency components are seen in the image space.

Certain Topics in Telegraph Transmission Theory. H. Nyquist. Proceedings of the IEEE, Vol. 90, No. 2, February (2002).

Teaching:

The teacher explains how to implement the Graphical User Interface (GUI) which connects to the computer programs which reproduce the mathematics of the SRE-based interpolation functions [2].

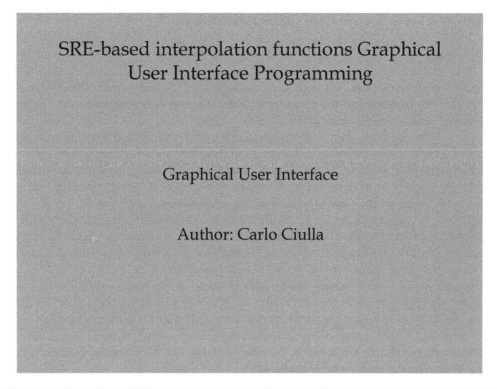

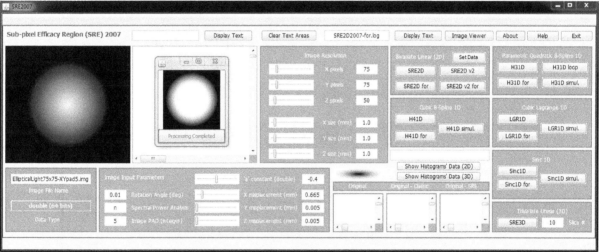

Figure 1: Image Interpolation: Graphical User Interface (author: Carlo Ciulla) developed with Java in NetBeans. The GUI is the 2011 Java based version of the Matlab ® GUI (author: Carlo Ciulla) which interfaces with the programs described elsewhere [2] and freely downloadable from www.sourcecodewebsiteCarloCiulla.com.

Implementation:

To raise the outcome of this teaching complement the student is required to implement software code. In this teaching complement the software code reproducing the computer programs to implement can either be released freely from the author: Carlo Ciulla. The implementation task may fulfill either the role of homework assignment or that one of the research project.

Compendium:

The compendium is released as the inner essence in the education to thinking in the form of a manuscript. In this teaching complement one viable option is the discussion of the manuscript [1].

Computer Science Applications

(ii) Artificial Intelligence in Pattern Recognition using artificial Neural Networks

Explanation:

This teaching complement opens up with an introduction to the mathematical background of Artificial Neural Networks for Pattern Recognition and the computational geometry concepts related to the significance of the creation of the artificial neural network architecture [3].

It will be clarified that the linear combinations of: inputs to the neurons and weights; correlates with the creation of hyperplanes (a geometrical shape in a space with more then three dimensions (hyperspace)) [3].

As far as the algorithms available in literature to study artificial neural network implementations, one excellent option offered to the students is to study the back-propagation algorithm [3] and the delta rule for the optimization of the cost function which embeds the error of training of the artificial neural network.

To emphasize on the theoretical background offered to the students, the teacher can mention the well recognized capability of the artificial neural networks for pattern recognition, to generalize on the basis of the knowledge provided through the training set. The training set consists of the patterns (ensemble of numerical values), which represent and reproduce the desired artificial neural network neurons' activation [3].

To emphasize further on the theoretical background, the teacher can also mention the well recognized capability of the artificial neural networks, which is explicable after the learning (training) process and consists of the evolution of training into the capability to classify patterns which are not included in the learning (training) set. The aforementioned capability [3] is a concept which descends from the system structure, which is made of the set of hyperplanes built by the artificial neural network during the learning (training) process, and such capability directly correlates with the data utilized in order to training the artificial neural network.

Teaching:

In this teaching complement the teacher can use both Graphical User Interface Programming concepts and Artificial Neural Networks (the signal processing application object of study) concepts.

(ii.1) Excerpt of Graphical User Interface Programming in relationship to teaching:

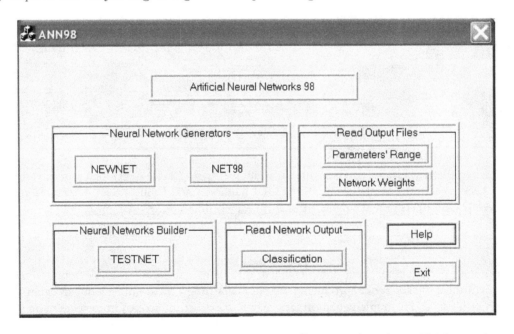

Figure 2: *ANN98* is the application GUI written in Visual C++ ® to interface the artificial neural network weights' calculators: *NEWNET* and *NET98*; and the neural network builder called *TESTNET*. The main feature of this GUI is that of being the interface to executables files running under Windows ® Systems. The GUI also allows reading the text files containing the parameters' range, the network weights and the classification performed through *TESTNET*. © Carlo Ciulla

(ii.2) Excerpt of system structure in relationship to teaching:

The function *float error_calculator(float * a1, float * a2, int q, int b)* is employed at each iteration of the learning process to calculate the error of fit between the current network output and the desired output. The function *float multiplier(float m)* correlates with the calculation of the correction term of the delta rule at the output layer. The correction term is the partial derivative of the error of fit and is given by: the current output (*'m'*), times one minus the current output, times the difference between the desired output and the current output. The function *float sigmoid(float input)* calculates the sigmoid of the current input, fed to either the hidden layer or the output layer, through the instruction *'(float)1/(1+exp((double)-input))'* such to determine the current output.

float error_calculator(float * a1, float * a2, int q, int b)
{

    int i,w;
    float fog;

    fog=0;

    for(i=1;i<q+1;i++){

    w=(q+i+(q*b));

    fog = fog + (((*(a1 + i)) - (*(a2 + w))) * ((*(a1 + i)) - (*(a2 + w))));

        }

    return fog;

}

float multiplier(float m)
{

    return (m * float(1-m));

}

float sigmoid(float input)
{

    float activate;

    activate=(float)1/(1+exp((double)-input));

    return activate;

}

Implementation:

In this teaching complement, the teacher can make use of the following handout in order to convey to the students one possible solution to the homework assignment. The homework assignment comprises of technological aspects relating to the computer system counterpart implementation in relationship to the connectivity of: one of the Graphical User Interface push buttons' output (the *Help.log* file) with the GUI, and also the users with the GUI.

(ii.3) Write the Help function which saves the Help.log file to be read by the users and connect the Help function to the GUI:

Computer Science Applications

```
void CANN98Dlg::OnHelp()
{

    char logfilename[128];

    CString HelpMessage;

    FILE * logfile;

    sprintf(logfilename,"%s","Help.log");

    if ((logfile = fopen(logfilename,"w"))==NULL)
    {

    HelpMessage.Format("%s\n%s\n" , "Cannot save the file Help.log" , "Now Click to Exit the
                        program" );
    MessageBox(HelpMessage);
    exit(0);

    } else {

        fprintf(logfile,"%s\n", "Welcome to Artificial Neural Networks 98");
        fprintf(logfile,"%s\n", "There are three programs that you can run:");
        fprintf(logfile,"\n");

        fprintf(logfile,"%s\n", "1. NET98:");
        fprintf(logfile,"%s\n", "Artificial Neural Network generator with added capability to adapt");
        fprintf(logfile,"%s\n", "the Hidden Layer Architecture to the given patter recognition
                        problem.");
        fprintf(logfile,"%s\n", "This program has been devised not to have restrictions on the maximum
                        number of output neurons.");
        fprintf(logfile,"%s\n", "However in order to be compatible with TESTNET please run NET98
                        with 2, 3 or 4 output neurons.");
        fprintf(logfile,"\n");

        fprintf(logfile,"%s\n", "2. NEWNET:");
        fprintf(logfile,"%s\n", "Artificial Neural Network generator with a fixed Architecture for the
                        Hidden Layer.");
        fprintf(logfile,"%s\n", "This program has been devised to have 2, 3 or 4 output neurons.");
        fprintf(logfile,"\n");

        fprintf(logfile,"%s\n", "NET98 and NEWNET might produce two completely different
                        architectures.");
        fprintf(logfile, "%s\n","This can be seen given that if the number of Hidden and Output
                        neurons are the same for both");
        fprintf(logfile,"%s\n", "programs, the weighting connections of NET98 and NEWNET");
        fprintf(logfile, "%s\n","(in both input and output layers) might be different.");
        fprintf(logfile,"%s\n","This happens because of the capability of NET98 to re-train neurons
                        during the learning process.");
        fprintf(logfile,"\n");
        fprintf(logfile,"%s\n", "NET98 and NEWNET produce 4 output files called:");
        fprintf(logfile,"%s\n", "'BIGGEST.A1', 'SMALLEST.A1' (which contain maximum and
                        minimum values for each parameter)");
        fprintf(logfile,"%s\n", "'WEIGHT.A1', 'WEIGHT.A2' (which contain hidden and output
                        network layers weighting connections)");
        fprintf(logfile,"%s\n", "These 4 output files are saved in the same folder where the programs
```

```
                                                   run.");
         fprintf(logfile,"\n");

         fprintf(logfile,"%s\n", "3. TESTNET:");
         fprintf(logfile,"%s\n", "Artificial Neural Network used to validate the non linear separation
                                  achieved through NEWNET or NET98.");
         fprintf(logfile,"\n");
         fprintf(logfile,"%s\n", "TESTNET produces the output file called 'RESPONSE.A1', which is
                                  placed in the same folder where the program runs.");
         fprintf(logfile,"\n");

         fprintf(logfile,"%s\n", "The three programs run on the system command window.");
         fprintf(logfile,"\n");
         fprintf(logfile,"%s\n", "Before running either of the three programs please do the following:");
         fprintf(logfile,"\n");
         fprintf(logfile,"%s\n", "Preferably, confirm that your computer has available a drive named C:");
         fprintf(logfile,"%s\n", "Create a directory under the C: drive and remember to input the
                                  directory");
         fprintf(logfile,"%s\n", "name to any of the three programs when prompted to enter it.");
         fprintf(logfile,"%s\n", "Each of the files under the directory identifies a given pattern");
         fprintf(logfile,"%s\n", "Each of the files' extension (e.g. .A1, .A2, etc...) identifies a different
                                  class of the pattern recognition problem.");
         fprintf(logfile,"\n");

         fprintf(logfile,"%s\n", "Other relevant information:");
         fprintf(logfile,"\n");
         fprintf(logfile,"%s\n", "When running NET98 please do interact with the Learning process to
                                  select");
         fprintf(logfile,"%s\n", "the desired Network internal architecture to achieve the desired
                                  minimum");
         fprintf(logfile,"%s\n", "at the end of the Learning Process.");
         fprintf(logfile,"\n");
         fprintf(logfile,"%s\n", "When running NEWNET the program suggests the number of neurons
                                  of the Hidden Layer");
         fprintf(logfile,"%s\n", "which may provide a suitable Network internal architecture to achieve
                                  the desired minimum");
         fprintf(logfile,"%s\n", "at the end of the Learning Process.");
         fprintf(logfile,"\n");
         fprintf(logfile,"%s\n", "When running TESTNET please set the number of Hidden neurons
                                  equal to that of NEWNET or NET98");
         fprintf(logfile,"%s\n", "so to match the Neural Network Architecture generated through
                                  NEWNET or NET98.");
         fprintf(logfile,"\n");
         fclose(logfile);
         HelpMessage.Format("%s\n%s\n" , "Please read the file Help.log just saved.",
              "Before using this Graphical Interface");
         MessageBox(HelpMessage);

      }//else

   }
```

Computer Science Applications

Compendium:

In this teaching complement, the discussion of the manuscript in reference [3] is recommended.

(iii) Image Rotations

Explanation:

This teaching complement introduces the students to Image Rotations with emphasis on techniques that employ the assumption of the rigid body motion. The student will be exposed to concepts of computational geometry that pertains to two and three dimensional rotations and translations in space [4]. The concepts in computational geometry can be explained to the students along with the issues involved in image rotations [4].

This teaching complement is related to Signal-Image Interpolation because it welcomes the student to apply the knowledge gained in the study of re-sampling algorithms [2]. An additional purpose of this teaching complement is to establish a relationship with Signal-Image Interpolation through the study and the implementation of re-sampling algorithms such as those presented in the teaching complement titled 'SRE-based interpolation functions & Graphical User Interface Programming'. Both of re-sampling algorithms [2] and signal-image interpolation algorithms [5-8] are an inherited intellectual effort which springs from the basic knowledge provided through the intellectual establishment in signal interpolation of Isaac Newton, and they are such to make possible the implementation of the image rotations.

Teaching:

The teaching phase of this teaching complement is focused on the implementation of the Graphical User Interface of the project called ROTRA 2008. The teacher can make use of the hereto follow figure.

(iii.1) Excerpt of Graphical User Interface Programming:

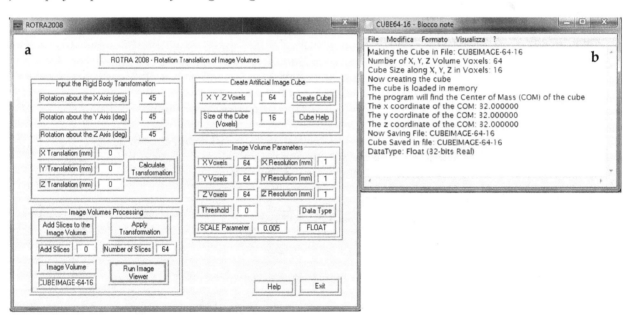

Figure 3: Rotra 2008 is designed to apply rigid body rotations to image volumes. The picture shows the Graphical User Interface in (a) and the result of the processing in (b) made in order to create an artificial volume of 64x64x64 pixels containing a cube of 16x16x16 pixels, which is shown in figure 4 along with the GUI of Image Viewer 2010. © Carlo Ciulla

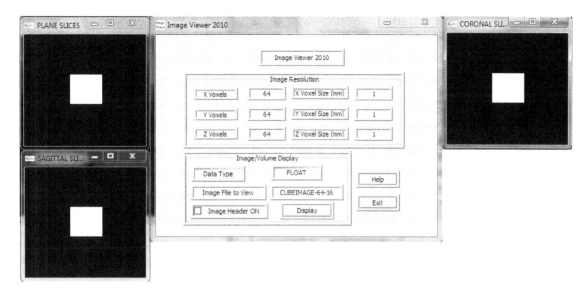

Figure 4: Image Viewer 2010 is designed to visualize 2D and 3D images (in three 2D composite views). The picture shows the three 2D composite views of the cube of 16x16x16 pixels made through Rotra 2008 (see result of processing in shown in figure 3(b)). © Carlo Ciulla

Implementation:

In this teaching complement the presentation of the theoretical background is accompanied with explanations on how to implement the image rotations application. Such presentation provides the students with the possibility to undertake homework assignments and/or a project during the semester.

(iii.2) Excerpt of implementation the image rotation application:

void CROTRA2008Dlg::OnApplyRT()

```
{

    UpdateData(true);
    char filename[254];
    char filename3[254];
    float number = 0;
    float *pointer = 0;
    int sl, j, i;
    FILE *pf;
    float XRES, YRES, ZRES;
    int TH;
    int rcxres;
    int rcyres;
    int numslice;
    CString Message;
    FILE * logfile;
    char logfilename[270];
    char DataType[30];
    float comx=0, comy=0, comz=0, sumi=0, sumj=0, sumsl=0;
    float aa, ba, ca, da, ea, fa, ga, ha, la;
    float xoa, yoa, zoa;
    float fi, theta, psi;
    float Xt, Yt, Zt, RAD;
    float cosfi, cospsi, costheta, senfi, senpsi, sentheta;
```

```
///////////////////// trivariate cubic Lagrange interpolation variables/////////
int k1, k2, k3, k4, k5, k6, k7, k8, k9, k10;
int k11, k12, k13, k14, k15, k16, k17, k18, k19, k20;
int k21, k22, k23, k24, k25, k26, k27;
float f000, fm101, f001, f101, fm100, f100, fm10m1, f00m1, f10m1, fm1m11, f0m11, f1m11, fm1m10,
f0m10;
float f1m10, fm1m1m1, f0m1m1, f1m1m1, fm111, f011, f111, fm110, f010, f110, fm11m1, f01m1,
f11m1;
float omega1, omega2, Mx, My, Mz, LGR1, LGR2;
float cubic_term, quadratic_term, power_one_term;
float SCALE;
int k0;
float tfLGR;
float convolution;
int xintegera, yintegera, zintegera;
///////////////////// trivariate cubic Lagrange interpolation variables/////////

        sprintf(filename3, "%s", m_VolumeName);
        sprintf(logfilename, "%s%s%s", "ROTRA", filename3, ".log");

        if ((logfile = fopen(logfilename,"w+"))==NULL)
{

                Message.Format("%s\n%s\n%s\n" , "Cannot open file: ", logfilename, "Now Exit");
                AfxMessageBox(Message);
                exit(0);
        } else { // load variables from user input and save to logfile

                rcxres = (int)m_rcxres;
                rcyres = (int)m_rcyres;
                numslice = (int)m_NofSlices;
                sprintf(DataType, "%s", m_DataType);

        if(strcmp(DataType,"FLOAT")!=0)
        { // if

        Message.Format("%s\n%s\n%s\n%s\n" , "The Image Volume DataType is: ",
        DataType, "Please Change to FLOAT", "Now Exit");
        AfxMessageBox(Message);
        fprintf(logfile, "%s\n%s\n%s\n%s\n" , "The Image Volume DataType is: ",
        DataType, "Please Change to FLOAT", "Now Exit");
        exit(0);

        } // if

        //// RotX * RotY * RotZ ///
        psi = (float)m_theta;
        fi = (float)m_fi;
        theta = (float)m_psi;
        Xt = (float)m_Xt;
        Yt = (float)m_Yt;
        Zt = (float)m_Zt;
        XRES = (float)m_XRES;
        YRES = (float)m_YRES;
        ZRES = (float)m_ZRES;
        TH = (int)m_TH;
```

280

```
    SCALE = (float)m_SCALE;

//// now save to logfile
fprintf(logfile, "%s\n", "Now Loading the Image Volume Data");
fprintf(logfile, "%s\n", "The program will find the Center of Mass (COM) of the Image
    Volume");
fprintf(logfile, "%s\n", "The program will apply the Rigid Body Tranformation to the Image
                        Data");
fprintf(logfile, "%s%s\n", "Image Volume being processed: ", filename3);
fprintf(logfile, "%s%d\n", "Number of Voxels Along X: ", rcxres);
fprintf(logfile, "%s%d\n", "Number of Voxels Along Y: ", rcyres);
fprintf(logfile, "%s%d\n", "Number of Voxels Along Z: ", numslice);
fprintf(logfile, "%s%f\n", "Voxels' Size Along the X axis: ", XRES);
fprintf(logfile, "%s%f\n", "Voxels' Size Along the Y axis: ", YRES);
fprintf(logfile, "%s%f\n", "Voxels' Size Along the Z axis: ", ZRES);

//// RotX * RotY * RotZ ///
fprintf(logfile, "%s%f\n", "Rotation about the X-axis: ", psi);
fprintf(logfile, "%s%f\n", "Rotation about the Y-axis: ", fi);
fprintf(logfile, "%s%f\n", "Rotation about the Z-axis: ", theta);
fprintf(logfile, "%s%f\n", "The Shift Along the X axis: ", Xt);
fprintf(logfile, "%s%f\n", "The Shift Along the Y axis: ", Yt);
fprintf(logfile, "%s%f\n", "The Shift Along the Z axis: ", Zt);
fprintf(logfile, "%s%d\n", "The Threshold: ", TH);
fprintf(logfile, "%s%f\n", "The SCALE parameter: ", SCALE);

} // load variables from user input and save to logfile

if ((pointer = (float *) calloc( ((numslice*rcyres*rcxres)+1), sizeof(float)) ) == NULL)
{

    fprintf(logfile, "%s\n", "Not enough memory to allocate Image Data... Now Exit");
    exit(0);

} else { // initialize and read data
    /// initialize pointer
    for(sl=1;sl<=numslice; sl++) {
        for(j=0;j<rcyres;j++){
            for(i=0;i<rcxres;i++){

                k2=(j*rcxres+i)+((sl-1)*rcyres*rcxres);
                *(pointer+k2)= (float)0;
                            }
                        }
                    }

    if ((pf = fopen(filename3,"rb+"))==NULL)
    {

    fprintf(logfile, "%s%s\n", "Cannot open file: ", filename3);
    free(pointer);
    exit(0);

    }
    /*these lines read the image data*/
    for(sl=1; sl<=numslice; sl++) {
```

```
            for(j=0;j<rcyres;j++){
                for(i=0;i<rcxres;i++){

                    fread(&number,sizeof(float),1,pf);
                    k2=(j*rcxres+i)+((sl-1)*rcyres*rcxres);
                    *(pointer+k2)= (float) number;

                                        }
                                }
                        }

        fclose (pf);
        fprintf(logfile, "%s%s%s\n", "The Image Data: ", filename3, " has been loaded");
} // initialize and read data

fprintf(logfile, "%s\n", "Now Calculating the Center of Mass (COM):");
long int count=0;
    for(sl=1;sl<=numslice; sl++) {
        for(j=0;j<rcyres;j++){
            for(i=0;i<rcxres;i++){

            k2=(j*rcxres+i)+((sl-1)*rcyres*rcxres);

            if ( *(pointer+k2) > TH )
            { // if

            count++;
            sumi = sumi + ((float)i);
            sumj = sumj + ((float)j);
            sumsl = sumsl + ((float)sl-1);

            }// if
                                }
                        }
                }

    comx = ((float)sumi/count);
    comy = ((float)sumj/count);
    comz = ((float)sumsl/count);

fprintf(logfile, "%s%f\n", "The x coordinate of the COM: ", comx);
fprintf(logfile, "%s%f\n", "The y coordinate of the COM: ", comy);
fprintf(logfile, "%s%f\n", "The z coordinate of the COM: ", comz);

///// calculate rotation translation transformation
fprintf(logfile, "%s\n", "Now Calculating the rigid body rotation translation transformation");
RAD=(float)360;

/*tranform in radiants*/
fprintf(logfile,"%s\n", "The Angles in Radians: ");
theta=((float)(2*3.14)/(RAD/theta));
psi=((float)(2*3.14)/(RAD/psi));
fi=((float)(2*3.14)/(RAD/fi));
//// RotX * RotY * RotZ ///
fprintf(logfile, "%s%f\n", "Pitch angle (Rotation about the X-axis): ", psi);
fprintf(logfile, "%s%f\n", "Roll angle (Rotation about the Y-axis): ", fi);
```

```
        fprintf(logfile, "%s%f\n", "Yaw angle (Rotation about the Z-axis): ", theta);

        costheta = (float)cos( (float)theta );
        cospsi = (float)cos( (float)psi );
        cosfi = (float)cos( (float)fi );

        //// RotX * RotY * RotZ ///
        fprintf(logfile, "%s%f\n", "Cosine Psi (Pitch angle): ", cospsi);
        fprintf(logfile, "%s%f\n", "Cosine Fi (Roll angle): ", cosfi);
        fprintf(logfile, "%s%f\n", "Cosine Theta (Yaw angle): ", costheta);

        sentheta = (float)sin( (float)theta );
        senpsi = (float)sin( (float)psi );
        senfi = (float)sin( (float)fi );

        //// RotX * RotY * RotZ ///
        fprintf(logfile, "%s%f\n", "Sine Psi (Pitch angle): ", senpsi);
        fprintf(logfile, "%s%f\n", "Sine Fi (Roll angle): ", senfi);
        fprintf(logfile, "%s%f\n", "Sine Theta (Yaw angle): ", sentheta);

            /*Computation of the rotation Matrix*/

            //// RotX * RotY * RotZ ///
            aa = ((float)costheta * cosfi);
            ba = -((float)cosfi * sentheta);
            ca = -((float)senfi);
            da = -((float)senpsi * senfi * costheta) + ((float)cospsi * sentheta);
            ea = ((float)senpsi * senfi * sentheta) + ((float)cospsi * costheta);
            fa = -((float)senpsi * cosfi);
            ga = ((float)cospsi * senfi * costheta) + ((float)senpsi * sentheta);
            ha = -((float)sentheta * cospsi * senfi) + ((float)senpsi * costheta);
            la = ((float)cosfi * cospsi);

            xoa = (float)Xt;
            yoa = (float)Yt;
            zoa = (float)Zt;

            fprintf(logfile, "%s\n", "The Rotation Matrix: ");
            fprintf(logfile, "%f\t%f\t%f\n", aa, ba, ca);
            fprintf(logfile, "%f\t%f\t%f\n", da, ea, fa);
            fprintf(logfile, "%f\t%f\t%f\n", ga, ha, la);
            fprintf(logfile, "%s\n", "The Shift Array: ");
            fprintf(logfile, "Xt = %f\t Yt = %f\t Zt = %f\n", xoa, yoa, zoa);
            float savedata = 0;
            sprintf(filename, "%s%s", filename3, "INT");

            float *interdata=0;
if ((interdata = (float *) calloc( ((numslice*rcyres*rcxres)+1), sizeof(float)) ) == NULL)
{
    fprintf(logfile, "%s\n", "Not enough memory to allocate fMRI data: Exit");
    free(pointer);
    exit(0);

} else { // else

        /// initialize interdata
```

```
            for(sl=1;sl<=numslice; sl++) {
                for(j=0;j<rcyres;j++){
                    for(i=0;i<rcxres;i++){

                        k2=(j*rcxres+i)+((sl-1)*rcyres*rcxres);
                        *(interdata+k2)= (float)0;
                                                    }
                                        }
                            }
        } // else
```

```
float *originalData=0;
if ((originalData = (float *) calloc( ((numslice*rcyres*rcxres)+1), sizeof(float)) ) == NULL)
{
    fprintf(logfile, "%s\n", "Not enough memory to allocate fMRI data: Exit");
    free(pointer);
    free(interdata);
    exit(0);

} else { // else

        /// initialize originalData
        for(sl=1;sl<=numslice; sl++) {
            for(j=0;j<rcyres;j++){
                for(i=0;i<rcxres;i++){

                    k2=(j*rcxres+i)+((sl-1)*rcyres*rcxres);
                    *(originalData+k2)= (float)0;


                                    }
                                }
                            }
    } // else
    /// the following lines calculate the fractionals of xcom, ycom and zcom that are the cause of the
    ///  misplacement of the center of mass.
    /// This misplacement happens because of rotations (rot x, rot y, or rot z) !=0

    xintegera = (int)(float)floor((float)comx);
    yintegera = (int)(float)floor((float)comy);
    zintegera = (int)(float)floor((float)comz);

    float fractionalx = ((float) comx - (float)floor((float)comx));
    float fractionaly = ((float) comy - (float)floor((float)comy));
    float fractionalz = ((float) comz - (float)floor((float)comz));

//////////////////////data re-sampling////////////////////////
            fprintf(logfile, "%s\n", "Now applying the 3D transformation (rotation-translation)");
            fprintf(logfile, "%s\n", "to the Image Volume, and interpolating data with the");
            fprintf(logfile, "%s\n", "Trivariate Cubic Lagrange Interpolation Function.");
            fprintf(logfile, "%s\n", "Now Resampling...");

            int ixnew = 0, iynew = 0, iznew = 0;
            int kk;
            float xnew = 0, ynew = 0, znew = 0;

            for(sl=1;sl<=numslice; sl++) {
```

```
                    for(j=0;j<rcyres;j++){
                        for(i=0;i<rcxres;i++){
                            k0=(j*rcxres+i)+((sl-1)*rcyres*rcxres);
```

// the shift along x y or z is determined here because of the coefficients of the
// rotation matrix that means that below lines in between are theoretically ill posed!
// also when this formula is used to correct for motion, another misplacement along
// x, y and z is introduced and that makes the motion correction paradigm theoretically ill posed!

```
/*
        xnew = ((float)aa * (i-comx)) +
               ((float)ba * (j-comy)) +
               ((float)ca * ((sl-1)-comz)) +
                (float)xoa + (float)comx;

        ynew = ((float)da * (i-comx)) +
               ((float)ea * (j-comy)) +
               ((float)fa * ((sl-1)-comz)) +
               (float)yoa + (float)comy;

        znew  = ((float)ga * (i-comx)) +
               ((float)ha * (j-comy)) +
               ((float)la * ((sl-1)-comz)) +
                (float)zoa + (float)comz;
*/
  if ( psi == 0 && fi == 0 && theta == 0 ) {
  // if RotX == 0 && RotY == 0 && RotZ == 0

     xnew =      ((float)aa * (float)(i-xintegera)) +
                 ((float)ba * (float)(j-yintegera)) +
                 ((float)ca * (float)((sl-1)-zintegera)) +
                  (float)xoa + (float)comx;

     ynew =      ((float)da * (float)(i-xintegera)) +
                 ((float)ea * (float)(j-yintegera)) +
                 ((float)fa * (float)((sl-1)-zintegera)) +
                 (float)yoa + (float)comy;
  } else if( psi == 0 && fi == 0 && theta != 0 ) {
  // if RotX == 0 && RotY == 0 && RotZ != 0

     xnew =      ((float)aa * (float)(i-xintegera)) +
                 ((float)ba * (float)(j-yintegera)) +
                 ((float)ca * (float)((sl-1)-zintegera)) +
                  (float)xoa + (float)comx + (float)fractionalx;

     ynew =      ((float)da * (float)(i-xintegera)) +
                 ((float)ea * (float)(j-yintegera)) +
                 ((float)fa * (float)((sl-1)-zintegera)) +
                 (float)yoa + (float)comy + (float)fractionaly;

  } else if ( psi != 0 && fi == 0 && theta == 0 ) {
  // if RotX != 0 && RotY == 0 && RotZ == 0
     xnew =      ((float)aa * (float)(i-xintegera)) +
                 ((float)ba * (float)(j-yintegera)) +
                 ((float)ca * (float)((sl-1)-zintegera)) +
                  (float)xoa + (float)comx;
```

```
ynew =      ((float)da * (float)(i-xintegera)) +
            ((float)ea * (float)(j-yintegera)) +
            ((float)fa * (float)((sl-1)-zintegera)) +
             (float)yoa + (float)comy + (float)fractionaly;


} else if ( psi != 0 && fi == 0 && theta != 0 ) {
// if RotX != 0 && RotY == 0 && RotZ != 0

xnew =      ((float)aa * (float)(i-xintegera)) +
            ((float)ba * (float)(j-yintegera)) +
            ((float)ca * (float)((sl-1)-zintegera)) +
             (float)xoa + (float)comx + (float)fractionalx;


ynew =      ((float)da * (float)(i-xintegera)) +
            ((float)ea * (float)(j-yintegera)) +
            ((float)fa * (float)((sl-1)-zintegera)) +
             (float)yoa + (float)comy + (float)fractionaly;


} else if ( psi == 0 && fi != 0 && theta == 0 ) {
// if RotX == 0 && RotY != 0 && RotZ == 0

xnew =      ((float)aa * (float)(i-xintegera)) +
            ((float)ba * (float)(j-yintegera)) +
            ((float)ca * (float)((sl-1)-zintegera)) +
             (float)xoa + (float)comx + (float)fractionalx;


ynew =      ((float)da * (float)(i-xintegera)) +
            ((float)ea * (float)(j-yintegera)) +
            ((float)fa * (float)((sl-1)-zintegera)) +
             (float)yoa + (float)comy;


} else if ( psi == 0 && fi != 0 && theta != 0 ) {
// if RotX == 0 && RotY != 0 && RotZ != 0

xnew =      ((float)aa * (float)(i-xintegera)) +
            ((float)ba * (float)(j-yintegera)) +
            ((float)ca * (float)((sl-1)-zintegera)) +
             (float)xoa + (float)comx + (float)fractionalx;


ynew =      ((float)da * (float)(i-xintegera)) +
            ((float)ea * (float)(j-yintegera)) +
            ((float)fa * (float)((sl-1)-zintegera)) +
             (float)yoa + (float)comy + (float)fractionaly;


} else if ( psi != 0 && fi != 0 && theta == 0 ) {
 // if RotX != 0 && RotY != 0 && RotZ == 0
   xnew = ((float)aa * (float)(i-xintegera)) +
            ((float)ba * (float)(j-yintegera)) +
            ((float)ca * (float)((sl-1)-zintegera)) +
             (float)xoa + (float)comx + (float)fractionalx;


   ynew =  (float)da * (float)(i-xintegera)) +
            ((float)ea * (float)(j-yintegera)) +
            ((float)fa * (float)((sl-1)-zintegera)) +
             (float)yoa + (float)comy + (float)fractionaly;
```

```
} else if ( psi != 0 && fi != 0 && theta != 0 ) {
// if RotX != 0 && RotY != 0 && RotZ != 0

xnew =       ((float)aa * (float)(i-xintegera)) +
             ((float)ba * (float)(j-yintegera)) +
             ((float)ca * (float)((sl-1)-zintegera)) +
              (float)xoa + (float)comx + (float)fractionalx;

ynew =       ((float)da * (float)(i-xintegera)) +
             ((float)ea * (float)(j-yintegera)) +
             ((float)fa * (float)((sl-1)-zintegera)) +
             (float)yoa + (float)comy + (float)fractionaly;
}

znew =       ((float)ga * (float)(i-xintegera)) +
             ((float)ha * (float)(j-yintegera)) +
             ((float)la * (float)((sl-1)-zintegera)) +
             (float)zoa + (float)comz;


ixnew = (int) (float)floor((float)xnew);
iynew = (int) (float)floor((float)ynew);
iznew = (int) (float)floor((float)znew);


if( (ixnew>=1)&&(ixnew<rcxres-2)&&
    (iynew>=1)&&(iynew<rcyres-2)&&
    (iznew>=2)&&(iznew<=numslice-2) // (1)
){

             //Central 3 x 3 Sub-neighborhood of f (0, 0, 0)

             k1=(iynew*rcxres+ixnew)+((iznew-1)*rcyres*rcxres); //f000

             f000 = (float)*(pointer+k1);

             k2=(iynew*rcxres+(ixnew-1))+((iznew-1)*rcyres*rcxres); //fm100

             fm100 = (float)*(pointer+k2);

             k3=(iynew*rcxres+(ixnew+1))+((iznew-1)*rcyres*rcxres); //f100

             f100 = (float)*(pointer+k3);

             k4=(iynew*rcxres+(ixnew-1))+( (iznew-2)*rcyres*rcxres ); //fm10m1

             fm10m1 = (float)*(pointer+k4);

             k5=(iynew*rcxres+ixnew)+( (iznew-2)*rcyres*rcxres); //f00m1

             f00m1 = (float)*(pointer+k5);

             k6=(iynew*rcxres+(ixnew+1))+( (iznew-2)*rcyres*rcxres); //f10m1

             f10m1 = (float)*(pointer+k6);

             k7=(iynew*rcxres+(ixnew-1))+( iznew*rcyres*rcxres); //fm101
```

```
fm101 = (float)*(pointer+k7);

k8=(iynew*rcxres+ixnew)+( iznew*rcyres*rcxres); //f001

f001 = (float)*(pointer+k8);

k9=(iynew*rcxres+(ixnew+1))+( iznew*rcyres*rcxres); //f101

f101 = (float)*(pointer+k9);

// Outer-Right 3 x 3 Sub-neighborhood of f (0, 0, 0)

k10=((iynew-1)*rcxres+ixnew)+((iznew-1)*rcyres*rcxres); //f0m10

f0m10 = (float)*(pointer+k10);

k11=((iynew-1)*rcxres+(ixnew-1))+((iznew-1)*rcyres*rcxres); //fm1m10

fm1m10 = (float)*(pointer+k11);

k12=((iynew-1)*rcxres+(ixnew+1))+((iznew-1)*rcyres*rcxres); //f1m10

f1m10 = (float)*(pointer+k12);

k13=((iynew-1)*rcxres+(ixnew-1))+( iznew-2)*rcyres*rcxres ); //fm1m1m1

fm1m1m1 = (float)*(pointer+k13);

k14=((iynew-1)*rcxres+ixnew)+( iznew-2)*rcyres*rcxres ); //f0m1m1

f0m1m1 = (float)*(pointer+k14);

k15=((iynew-1)*rcxres+(ixnew+1))+( iznew-2)*rcyres*rcxres ); //f1m1m1

f1m1m1 = (float)*(pointer+k15);

k16=((iynew-1)*rcxres+(ixnew-1))+( iznew*rcyres*rcxres ); //fm1m11

fm1m11 = (float)*(pointer+k16);

k17=((iynew-1)*rcxres+ixnew)+( iznew*rcyres*rcxres ); //f0m11

f0m11 = (float)*(pointer+k17);

k18=((iynew-1)*rcxres+(ixnew+1))+( iznew*rcyres*rcxres ); //f1m11

f1m11 = (float)*(pointer+k18);

// Outer-Left 3 x 3 Sub-neighborhood of f (0, 0, 0)

k19=((iynew+1)*rcxres+ixnew)+( iznew-1)*rcyres*rcxres ); //f010

f010 = (float)*(pointer+k19);

k20=((iynew+1)*rcxres+(ixnew-1))+( iznew-1)*rcyres*rcxres ); //fm110
```

```
        fm110 = (float)*(pointer+k20);

        k21=((iynew+1)*rcxres+(ixnew+1))+( iznew-1)*rcyres*rcxres ); //f110

        f110 = (float)*(pointer+k21);

        k22=((iynew+1)*rcxres+(ixnew-1))+( iznew-2)*rcyres*rcxres ); //fm11m1

        fm11m1 = (float)*(pointer+k22);

        k23=((iynew+1)*rcxres+ixnew)+( iznew-2)*rcyres*rcxres); //f01m1

        f01m1 = (float)*(pointer+k23);

        k24=((iynew+1)*rcxres+(ixnew+1))+( iznew-2)*rcyres*rcxres); //f11m1

        f11m1 = (float)*(pointer+k24);

        k25=((iynew+1)*rcxres+(ixnew-1))+( iznew*rcyres*rcxres); //fm111

        fm111 = (float)*(pointer+k25);

        k26=((iynew+1)*rcxres+ixnew)+( iznew*rcyres*rcxres); //f011

        f011 = (float)*(pointer+k26);

        k27=((iynew+1)*rcxres+(ixnew+1))+( iznew*rcyres*rcxres); //f111

        f111 = (float)*(pointer+k27);

        omega1 = ( (float) fm101 + fm100 + f100 + f10m1 + fm1m11 + fm1m10 + f1m10 + f1m1m1
                  + fm111 + fm110 + f110 + f11m1 );

        omega2 = ( (float) fm101 + f001 + f101 + fm100 + f100 + fm10m1 + f00m1 + f10m1 +
                  fm1m11 + f0m11 + f1m11 + fm1m10 + f0m10 + f1m10 + fm1m1m1 +
                  f0m1m1 + f1m1m1 + fm111 + f011 + f111 + fm110 + f010 + f110 +
                  fm11m1 + f01m1 + f11m1 );

        Mx = ((float)xnew) - (float)floor((float)xnew);
        My = ((float)ynew) - (float)floor((float)ynew);
        Mz = ((float)znew) - (float)floor((float)znew);

cubic_term = ( (float) ( Mx + My + Mz ) * ( Mx + My + Mz ) * ( Mx + My + Mz ) );
quadratic_term = ( (float) ( Mx + My + Mz ) * ( Mx + My + Mz ) );
power_one_term = ( (float) ( Mx + My + Mz ) );

LGR1 = ( (float) ( (1/2) * cubic_term ) - quadratic_term - ( (1/2) * power_one_term ) + 1 );
LGR2 = ( (float) ( -(1/6) * cubic_term ) + quadratic_term - ( (11/6) * power_one_term ) + 1 );

        convolution = ( (float) omega1 * LGR1 + omega2 * LGR2 );

    if ( convolution == 0 )
    tfLGR = (float)0;
    else
    tfLGR =  ( (float) SCALE / ( -convolution ) );
    tfLGR *= ( (float) 1 / (XRES * YRES * ZRES) );
```

```
        kk=(j*rcxres+i)+((sl-2)*rcyres*rcxres);

        if ( sl >= 2 )
        {

            *(interdata+kk) = ((float) f000 + tfLGR );
            *(originalData+kk) = ((float) f000);
            if ( *(interdata+kk) <= (TH + tfLGR) ) *(interdata+kk) = ((float)0);

        }
                        } // (1)

                    } // for loop
                    } // for loop
                } // for loop

    fprintf(logfile, "%s\n", "Resampling Completed.");
    /// save new image
    fprintf(logfile, "%s%s\n", "Now Saving New Interpolated Image Volume: ", filename);

    if ((pf = fopen(filename,"wb+"))==NULL)
    {

        fprintf(logfile, "%s", "Cannot open file to save 3D Transformed Image Volume");
        exit(0);

    }else{ // else save
            for(sl=1;sl<=numslice; sl++) {
                for(j=0;j<rcyres;j++){
                    for(i=0;i<rcxres;i++){

                    k2=(j*rcxres+i)+((sl-1)*rcyres*rcxres);

                    savedata=(float)*(interdata+k2);

                    fwrite(&savedata,sizeof(float),1,pf);

                        }
                    }
                }
    fclose(pf);
    }// else save

    fprintf(logfile, "%s%s\n", "Data has been Interpolated and Saved in file: ", filename);
    fprintf(logfile, "%s\n", "DataType: Float (32-bits Real)");
    fprintf(logfile, "%s\n", "Now Calculating the Center of Mass (COM after truncation)");
    fprintf(logfile, "%s\n", "of the 3D Transformed Image Volume (interpolated data)");

    count=0;
    sumi = (float)0;
    sumj = (float)0;
    sumsl = (float)0;

    float intcomx = 0, intcomy = 0, intcomz = 0;
        for(sl=1;sl<=numslice; sl++) {
            for(j=0;j<rcyres;j++){
```

```
                    for(i=0;i<rcxres;i++){

                    k2=(j*rcxres+i)+((sl-1)*rcyres*rcxres);

                    if ( *(interdata+k2) > TH )
                    //// shows the effect of the truncation of the new coordinates while re-slicing the grid
                    { // if
                        count++;
                        sumi = sumi + ((float)i);
                        sumj = sumj + ((float)j);
                        sumsl = sumsl + ((float)sl-1);
                    }// if
                                                        }
                                                    }
                                                }

intcomx = ((float)sumi/count);
intcomy = ((float)sumj/count);
intcomz = ((float)sumsl/count);

fprintf(logfile, "%s%f\n", "The x coordinate of the COM: ", intcomx);
fprintf(logfile, "%s%f\n", "The y coordinate of the COM: ", intcomy);
fprintf(logfile, "%s%f\n", "The z coordinate of the COM: ", intcomz);

fprintf(logfile, "%s\n%s\n", "Before and After the Application of the Rotation Translation to the
                             Grid", "The Variation of Center of Mass Position is: ");
fprintf(logfile, "%s%f\n", "xCOM - x_interpolated_COM: ", (comx - intcomx) );
fprintf(logfile, "%s%f\n", "yCOM - y_interpolated_COM: ", (comy - intcomy) );
fprintf(logfile, "%s%f\n", "zCOM - z_interpolated_COM: ", (comz - intcomz) );

/// save new image
    sprintf(filename, "%s%s", filename3, "RAW");
    fprintf(logfile, "%s%s\n", "Now Saving New Image Volume (Not Interpolated): ", filename);

    if ((pf = fopen(filename,"wb+"))==NULL)
    {

    fprintf(logfile, "%s\n", "Cannot open file to save 3D Transformed (Not Interpolated) Image
                             Volume");
    exit(0);

    } else { // else save

            for(sl=1;sl<=numslice; sl++) {
                for(j=0;j<rcyres;j++){
                    for(i=0;i<rcxres;i++){

                    k2=(j*rcxres+i)+((sl-1)*rcyres*rcxres);
                    savedata=(float)*(originalData+k2);
                    fwrite(&savedata,sizeof(float),1,pf);

                                                }
                                            }
                                        }
            fclose(pf);
```

```
        } // else save

   fprintf(logfile, "%s%s\n", "Not Interpolated Data Saved in: ", filename);
   fprintf(logfile, "%s\n", "DataType: Float (32-bits Real)");
   fprintf(logfile, "%s\n", "Now Calculating the Center of Mass (COM after truncation)");
   fprintf(logfile, "%s\n", "of the 3D Transformed Image Volume (NOT interpolated data)");

   count=0;
   sumi = (float)0;
   sumj = (float)0;
   sumsl = (float)0;

   float NOTintcomx = 0, NOTintcomy = 0, NOTintcomz = 0;

         for(sl=1;sl<=numslice; sl++) {
            for(j=0;j<rcyres;j++){
               for(i=0;i<rcxres;i++){

               k2=(j*rcxres+i)+((sl-1)*rcyres*rcxres);
               if ( *(originalData+k2) > TH )
```

//// shows the effect of the truncation of the new coordinates while re-slicing the grid

```
                  { // if

                     count++;
                     sumi = sumi + ((float)i);
                     sumj = sumj + ((float)j);
                     sumsl = sumsl + ((float)sl-1);

                  }// if
                                             }
                                          }
                                       }

   NOTintcomx = ((float)sumi/count);
   NOTintcomy = ((float)sumj/count);
   NOTintcomz = ((float)sumsl/count);

   fprintf(logfile, "%s%f\n", "The x coordinate of the COM: ", NOTintcomx);
   fprintf(logfile, "%s%f\n", "The y coordinate of the COM: ", NOTintcomy);
   fprintf(logfile, "%s%f\n", "The z coordinate of the COM: ", NOTintcomz);
   fprintf(logfile, "%s\n%s\n", "Before and After the Application of the Rotation Translation to the
            Grid", "The Variation of Center of Mass Position is: ");

   fprintf(logfile, "%s%f\n", "xCOM - x_NOTinterpolated_COM: ", (comx - NOTintcomx) );
   fprintf(logfile, "%s%f\n", "yCOM - y_NOTinterpolated_COM: ", (comy - NOTintcomy) );
   fprintf(logfile, "%s%f\n", "zCOM - z_NOTinterpolated_COM: ", (comz - NOTintcomz) );
   /////////////////////data re-sampling/////////////////////

   free(pointer);
   free(interdata);
   free(originalData);
   fclose(logfile);
   system(logfilename);

}
```

Compendium:

In this teaching complement it is advisable the discussion of the manuscript in reference [4].

References

[1] Ciulla, C. and Deek, F.P. (2005). *On the Approximate Nature of the Bivariate Linear Interpolation Function: A Novel Scheme Based on Intensity Curvature*, ICGST International Journal on Graphics, Vision and Image Processing, 5(7): 9-19.

[2] Ciulla, C. (2009). *Improved Signal and Image Interpolation in Biomedical Applications: The Case of Magnetic Resonance Imaging (MRI)* - Medical Information Science Reference - IGI Global Publisher, Hershey, PA, U.S.A.

[3] Werbos, P. J. (1990). *Backpropagation through time: what it does and how to do it.* Proceedings of the IEEE, 78(10), 1550-1560.

[4] Henri, C. J., Collins, D. L. and Peters, T. M. (1991). *Multimodality image integration for stereotaxic surgical planning.* Med. Phys., 18: 167-177.

[5] Unser, M., Aldroubi, A., & Eden, M. (1993a). *B-spline signal processing: Part I – theory.* IEEE Transactions on Signal Processing, 41(2), 821-833.

[6] Unser, M., Aldroubi, A., & Eden, M. (1993b). *B-spline signal processing: Part II – efficient design and applications.* IEEE Transactions on Signal Processing, 41(2), 834-848.

[7] Blu, T., Thevenaz, P. & Unser, M. (2004). *Linear interpolation revitalized.* IEEE Transaction on Image Processing, 13(5), 710-719.

[8] Lehmann, T. M., Gonner, C., & Spitzer, K. (1999). *Survey: Interpolation methods in medical image processing.* IEEE Transactions on Medical Imaging, 18(11), 1049-1075.

CARLO CIULLA had been undergraduate and graduate student at the University of Palermo, Italy, RUTGERS University, U.S.A. and the New Jersey Institute of Technology, U.S.A. from the year 1987 to the year 2002. He has earned the following graduate degrees: Laurea in Management Engineering (Italy); an M.S. in Information Systems and a Ph.D. in Computer and Information Science (U.S.A.). Carlo was pre-doctoral student at the National Institute of Bioscience and Human Technology (NIBH) in Tsukuba, Japan (1995-1997) and he worked with Magnetoencephalography (MEG) studying the spontaneous alpha rhythm of the human brain. Following the completion of the Doctoral degree, Carlo's former academic appointments were: Research Associate at Yale University (2002-2003); Postdoctoral Scholar at the University of Iowa (2004-2005); Postdoctoral Scholar at Wayne State University (2005-2007); Assistant Professor of Computer Science at Lane College (2007-2009). During the years 2009-2012 Carlo is a self employed scholar whom devoted his time to his research interest related to the development of innovative methods of signal interpolation and also to the development of educational software for students. During the course of his career the research interests remain in the domain of mathematics in computational engineering: Artificial Neural Networks, Image Registration in fMRI, Signal-Image Interpolation, and MEG Alpha Rhythm. He has authored and co-authored numerous papers in journals and conference proceedings, and is the author of the books: (i) *Improved Signal and Image Interpolation in Biomedical Applications: The Case of Magnetic Resonance Imaging (MRI); (ii) AUTOALIGN: Methodology and Technology for the Alignment of Functional Magnetic Resonance Imaging Time Series: Image Registration: The Case of Functional MRI; (iii) SIGNAL RESILIENT TO INTERPOLATION: An Exploration on the Approximation Properties of the Mathematical Functions; and (iv) Computer Science Signal Processing Applications in Higher Learning.*

www.ingramcontent.com/pod-product-compliance
Lightning Source LLC
Chambersburg PA
CBHW082109070326

40689CB00052B/4006